Neoconservatism

Neoconservatism

THE BIOGRAPHY OF A MOVEMENT

Justin Vaïsse

Translated by Arthur Goldhammer

The Belknap Press of Harvard University Press

Cambridge, Massachusetts

London, England

2010

Originally published as *Histoire du néoconservatisme aux États-Unis*
©Odile Jacob, 2008

Library of Congress Cataloging-in-Publication Data

Vaïsse, Justin.
[Histoire du néoconservatisme aux États-Unis. English]
Neoconservatism : the biography of a movement / Justin Vaïsse,
translated by Arthur Goldhammer.
p.   cm.
Includes bibliographical references and index.
ISBN 978-0-674-05051-8 (alk. paper)
1. Conservatism—United States—History.   I. Title.
JC573.2.U6V33 2010
320.52—dc22
2009040857

CONTENTS

ABBREVIATIONS

ABM	antiballistic missile
ACDA	Arms Control and Disarmament Agency
ADA	Americans for Democratic Action
AEI	American Enterprise Institute
AFL-CIO	American Federation of Labor–Congress of Industrial Organizations
CCNY	City College of New York
CDM	Coalition for a Democratic Majority
CIA	Central Intelligence Agency
CPD	Committee on the Present Danger
DLC	Democratic Leadership Council
JINSA	Jewish Institute for National Security Affairs
ICBM	intercontinental ballistic missile
NATO	North Atlantic Treaty Organization
NED	National Endowment for Democracy
NSC	National Security Council
NYRB	New York Review of Books
PNAC	Project for the New American Century
SALT	Strategic Arms Limitation Talks
UN	United Nations

Neoconservatism

INTRODUCTION:
THE THREE AGES OF NEOCONSERVATISM

"At the American Enterprise Institute, some of the finest minds in our nation are at work on some of the greatest challenges to our nation. You do such good work that my administration has borrowed 20 such minds."[1] Thus began President George W. Bush's speech of February 26, 2003, less than a month before the invasion of Iraq. He spoke to an audience of experts at the American Enterprise Institute, a neoconservative think tank in Washington, D.C., where at one time or another Irving Kristol, Richard Perle, Jeane Kirkpatrick, Paul Wolfowitz, and many other leading neoconservatives have worked. It was as if the president wanted personally to call attention to their influence upon his foreign policy.

"In Iraq," Bush went on, "a dictator is building and hiding weapons that could enable him to dominate the Middle East and intimidate the civilized world—and we will not allow it. (Applause.) This same tyrant has close ties to terrorist organizations, and could supply them with the terrible means to strike this country—and America will not permit it . . . retreat before a dictator guarantees even greater sacrifices in the future." Bush's speech, whose main purpose was to justify the imminent American intervention in Iraq, was filled with references to neoconservative themes. The exaggeration of both the urgency and gravity of the threat had been a neoconservative leitmotif since the 1970s. So was the implicit analogy with the policy of "appeasement" that democratic societies had adopted toward Adolf Hitler in the period between the two world wars—an analogy underscored by the mention of Winston Churchill later in the speech. For President Bush, as for the neoconservatives, the lesson of Vietnam had never replaced that of Munich; on the contrary: the sooner one took a stand against dictators, the greater the show of force, the more firmly one guaranteed the security of America—and the peace of the world. But security is not merely a matter of relative might.

"A liberated Iraq can show the power of freedom to transform that vital region, by bringing hope and progress into the lives of millions . . . A new regime in Iraq would serve as a dramatic and inspiring example of freedom for other nations in the region . . . The world has a clear interest in the spread of democratic values, because stable and free nations do not breed the ideologies of murder. They encourage the peaceful pursuit of a better life." Here, with this suggestion of a "democratic domino theory," President Bush's language echoed that of Woodrow Wilson and of American missionaries of the past. The goal was to make the world safe not only for but through democracy. Underlying this message was the idea that democracies never make war on one another.[2] Simply put, transforming all dictatorships into democracies would secure universal peace and put an end to "ideologies of murder" and terrorism. Palestine might be the best example: "Without this outside support for terrorism, Palestinians who are working for reform and long for democracy will be in a better position to choose new leaders," who would be able to negotiate seriously with Israel and work toward a "viable Palestinian state."

But is democracy possible everywhere? "There was a time when many said that the cultures of Japan and Germany were incapable of sustaining democratic values. Well, they were wrong. Some say the same of Iraq today." The universalism of democracy was yet another tenet of the neoconservative credo adopted by Bush. Unlike realists, who prefer to accommodate existing authoritarian regimes and often look upon culture as a factor with the potential to slow or even prevent a country from evolving toward democracy, neoconservatives are strict universalists. In this respect they can be compared to the Jacobins of the French Revolution. In both, one finds the same ambiguous mix of universalism and nationalism: progress, whether it takes the form of "reason" and *le Code civil* or of democracy and elections, turns out, as if by magic, to be spontaneously compatible with the strategic interests and dominance of the power that promises to achieve it, be it *la grande nation* (France) or "the benevolent empire" (the United States).

The rest is history. For all his brutality toward his own people, Saddam Hussein did not threaten the world either through his—nonexistent—ties to al-Qaeda or with his weapons of mass destruction, which had disappeared by the time Bush spoke. The stabilization and democratization of Iraq, which Bush compared to the stabilization and democratization of Japan and Germany, ran afoul of the country's ethnic and religious divisions. Despite a few green shoots, no democratic seedbed took root, and the region saw a reinforcement of authoritarian regimes instead. In January 2006, free elections in the Palestinian territories empowered Hamas, an organization fundamentally hostile to the existence of Israel, thus undermining naïve faith in the "magic wand" of democracy. And the United Nations—the bête noire of neoconservatives, which President Bush threatened to ignore—weathered the attack without serious damage.

In this respect, Bush's failure in Iraq was also the failure of the "finest minds" from the AEI, who advised him, as well as the failure of neoconservatism. Or, rather—and this distinction is fundamental—of a certain version of neoconservatism. Because it would be misleading to call Bush a neoconservative or, worse, a puppet in the hands of neoconservatives. By itself, neoconservatism cannot explain the war in Iraq—I will come back to this point. But neither should the story of neoconservatism be reduced to Iraq.

The original neoconservatism of the 1960s had nothing to do with the muscular assertion of American power or with the promotion of democracy. It even took no interest in questions of foreign policy. If it had a central message, it was on the contrary to stress the limits of state action, for example by highlighting the "law of unintended consequences," according to which the unanticipated and undesirable effects of social programs often outweigh the desired effects. For example, aid to poor unwed mothers became an instrument that allowed adolescent girls to emancipate themselves from their families, thus compounding the problem of poverty rather than solving it. What the neoconservatives recommended was above all prudence and attention to the human factors, and especially cultural factors, that can quickly derail grand schemes to change the world. Accordingly, the idea that the federal government should take it upon itself to administer and even democratize an unknown country of 25 million people 6,000 miles from Washington, D.C., would have seemed absurd to the original neoconservatives.

How, then, does one get from a movement born in left-wing circles in New York and focused on domestic politics to Bush's speech at the AEI and the invasion of Iraq? This is the challenge for the historian and the question to which this book will attempt to provide an answer.

Indeed, one might well argue that neoconservatism doesn't even exist, that it is a misleading shorthand, because there is after all no reason to apply the same label to individuals as different as Daniel Patrick Moynihan and Paul Wolfowitz or Nathan Glazer and Douglas Feith. Although it is true that numerous American thinkers and political actors have been described, or in some cases have described themselves, as neoconservatives, they are so diverse that one is hard put to deduce the existence of any well-defined school of thought, much less a political movement. Bear in mind these basic facts: neoconservatism has no electoral, economic, or religious base; it has never had an uncontested leader; and it has never been represented by any clearly defined organization. It is in no sense a political party. At most it is a school of thought, an intellectual outlook, or perhaps a "tendency" or "persuasion," as its godfathers Norman Podhoretz and Irving Kristol sometimes described it.[3] Yet even so modest a description as this does not really meet the main challenge posed by the neoconservative label: Is it coherent?

From the 1960s to the 2000s, neoconservatism transformed itself so thoroughly as to become unrecognizable. It moved from the left to the right side of the political chessboard. It shifted its focus from domestic issues to foreign affairs. In abandoning New York for Washington, it left the world of sociologists and intellectuals for that of influence and power. Born as a pure reaction to another intellectual and political movement—the protests of the 1960s, the counterculture, and the New Left—it survived that movement's demise. Yet this did not prevent Podhoretz, Kristol, and other neoconservatives as well as outside observers from prematurely writing the movement's obituary at various points in its history.[4]

But it would make no sense to attempt a survey of neoconservatism if the word were utterly empty of content, or if there were no connection at all between the original neoconservatives and those who championed the invasion of Iraq after 2001. But the connections are tenuous, and the filiation is complex and indirect. Hence the question arises of how best to tell the story of such a diverse intellectual movement. How does one describe such a thing?

The best way to respect the diversity of the movement would be to write a series of intellectual biographies, to talk about "neoconservatives" rather than "neoconservatism," and then to discuss the commonalities among these various thinkers. This is the course chosen by Gary Dorrien in his fundamental work on the subject.[5] At the other end of the spectrum, Mark Gerson's book begins by assuming that there is indeed a unified body of neoconservative thought over time, and he sets out to re-count its trials and tribulations.[6] But this approach erases the profound differences that exist among neoconservatives and ends up focusing on domestic issues. It is of almost no use for understanding the intellectual origins of the war in Iraq, for example.

More recently, Jacob Heilbrunn, himself a repentant neoconservative, proposed a linear narrative of the movement as a saga running continu-ously from the 1930s to the 2000s, as if the same group of men and women had shaped it throughout the period, and as if the experiences of some of them—the City College of New York, youthful involvement with Trotskyism, the influence of Leo Strauss, and so on—sufficed to ex-plain the others.[7] This approach, like Gerson's, attributes an artificial co-herence to the movement while neglecting its diverse sources as well as the deep divergences among members of the group, particularly in re-gard to foreign policy.

Consider just one example: Irving Kristol, celebrated as the "god-father of neoconservatism," who contributed more than anyone else to the theory of neoconservatism and to its promotion in the marketplace of ideas. Kristol always opposed Wilsonian idealism and even more strongly opposed efforts to promote democracy around the world. In the spring of 1991, not only did he support the realist policy of the first Pres-ident Bush, who chose not to overthrow Saddam Hussein after expelling his forces from Kuwait ("no civilized person in his right mind wants to govern Iraq"); he also mocked the "abstract moralism" and "senti-mentalism" of certain other observers. In his view, the definition of the American national interest "never implied a commitment to bring the blessings of democracy to the Arab world."[8] Twelve years later, when his son, William Kristol, as editor of the *Weekly Standard* and head of the neoconservative think tank Project for the New American Century (both located in the same building as the American Enterprise Institute), waged a vigorous and successful campaign in favor of the invasion of Iraq, the "godfather" remained strangely mute, silently disapproving. Must Irving Kristol therefore be read out of the neoconservative move-ment, even though he was in a sense its founder and original incarna-tion?

As this example clearly shows, the story of neoconservatism cannot be told in any simple, linear way, as one might write the history of a po-litical party—even a party with a number of "factions" or "wings." Discontinuity, heterogeneity, and contradiction are an integral part of neoconservatism, a word that is constantly in danger of losing any precise meaning. To reconcile the unity and diversity of the movement and to describe neoconservatism without stretching or diminishing it unduly, I adopt a more classical historical approach, similar to that of John Ehrman.[9] More concretely, I identify three main points of anchorage in American history, three formative impulses, three very different political and intellectual logics, loosely related to one another, which I term the three ages of neoconservatism.

The First Age of Neoconservatism

Neoconservatism was born in the realm of domestic rather than foreign policy, and more specifically in the realm of political ideology. Neoconservatism was first of all a reaction to the evolution of American liberalism, which took a left turn in the 1960s, moving away from the political center that it had occupied for nearly three decades and thereby opening up a space for "new conservatives."

To understand this evolution, we need to go back to Franklin D. Roosevelt's New Deal, which marked a turning point in American liberal doctrine. In response to the Great Depression, liberalism moved beyond championing individual liberties and laisser faire; liberals began asserting that state intervention was necessary to keep the economy and society running smoothly. New Deal liberalism, Roosevelt explained, was "plain English for a changed concept of the duty and responsibility of government toward economic life."[10] With Keynesian economic stimulus, redistributive social programs such as old-age pensions and medical insurance, and support for trade unions, liberalism now incorporated a doctrine of government action that aimed to make American democracy both more efficient and more just. This period marks the beginning of the opposition between "liberalism" in the American sense of the term—a left-wing policy of state intervention—and "liberalism" in the European sense—a right-wing doctrine referring primarily to laisser faire in the economic sphere.

But economic and social progress at home is worthwhile only if it is protected against threats from abroad, and the postwar liberals, who had previously been staunch antifascists, became just as staunch anticommunists. They approved Truman's dismissal in 1946 of Secretary of Commerce Henry Wallace, who advocated a policy of compromise with the Soviet Union, and backed Truman in launching the Cold War in

1947. Two years later the historian Arthur M. Schlesinger Jr., inspired by the theologian Reinhold Niebuhr among others, published *The Vital Center,* which summed up postwar liberal doctrine and offered itself as an ideological alternative to international communism. The book proposed an amalgam of anticommunism abroad and social progress at home. This "vital center" liberalism dominated the postwar years—the America of Truman, Eisenhower, and Kennedy.[11]

In the 1960s, however, everything seemed to go wrong. Overseas, the Vietnam War fostered growing doubts about the anticommunist crusade and the moral superiority of the United States. At home, the country was shaken by the struggle for civil rights, urban riots, and student protests with their accompanying counterculture. Lyndon B. Johnson's "Great Society" ventured onto new terrain: social engineering through increased transfer of wealth, very ambitious social programs, affirmative-action programs to help minorities, busing to alleviate racial segregation, and the like.

A group of Cold War intellectuals, many of them veterans of the anti-Stalinist struggles of previous decades, reacted negatively to this leftward trend in American liberalism. Many were sociologists or political scientists who criticized the failures and perverse effects of Johnson's "War on Poverty" as well as the excesses of the "adversary culture"—in their view individualistic, hedonistic, and relativistic—that had taken hold of the baby-boom generation on college campuses. Although the critics were not unconditional supporters of the free market or the night-watchman state, they did point out the limits of the welfare state, which in their view could never achieve the boundless egalitarian dreams of the New Left. Inspired more by Alexis de Tocqueville than by Edmund Burke or Friedrich Hayek, these intellectuals had almost nothing in common with the "real" conservative movement that had taken shape around William F. Buckley Jr. and the *National Review* from 1955 on. They also stressed the indispensable need for civic virtues and moderation in a democratic society, as well as the importance of ideas and political culture.

This first age of neoconservatism was built around two journals: *The Public Interest,* founded by Irving Kristol and Daniel Bell in 1965, and later *Commentary,* edited at that time by Norman Podhoretz, who began as an anticommunist liberal, underwent a "radical" phase, publishing articles from the far left in the mid-1960s, then in 1970 took an antiradical—in fact, neoconservative—turn. A number of prestigious intellectuals, mostly from New York, gravitated to these journals: Nathan Glazer, Seymour Martin Lipset, James Q. Wilson, Daniel Patrick Moynihan, and others. Legend has it that the socialist Michael Harrington dubbed these renegades "neoconservatives" so as to banish them beyond the boundaries of liberalism and brand them traitors (I shall return to this legend in Chapter 2). This split in the liberal camp was the founding moment of neoconservatism.

The Second Age of Neoconservatism

It did not take long for liberalism's leftward evolution to manifest itself in the realm of politics. The second age of neoconservatism was born in response to this development. In 1968, when Lyndon Johnson decided not to run for reelection, his vice-president, Hubert Humphrey, won the Democratic nomination: this event marked the last gasp of the "vital center" liberalism. Humphrey lost to Richard Nixon, and the Democratic party, relegated to the opposition, moved further to the left. In the 1972 presidential election, George McGovern, representing the "New Politics" that embodied the views of the party's left wing—supportive of minority preferences, massive social programs, and a penchant for a somewhat isolationist foreign policy—won the nomination and led the Democrats to a second defeat by Nixon—this time by a landslide. The turn to the left had riled the "silent majority" of the American population that had once voted for the Democrats, in particular blue-collar workers who felt that their party was abandoning "bread and butter issues" in order to devote all its attention to blacks, Hispanics, women, and homosexuals, and that it was officially embracing the counterculture rather than defending law and order and family values.

This view was shared by the second family of neoconservatives, which came to prominence in the 1970s. In contrast to the first generation, which consisted of New York intellectuals, many of whom had once been radicals, the second generation drew from the ranks of Democratic political activists in Washington who thought of themselves as guardians of the "vital center": in favor of social progress and civil liberties at home and anticommunism abroad, they took this to be the tradition of Roosevelt, Truman, Kennedy, Johnson, and Humphrey. Typical of this second family of neoconservatives was the Coalition for a Democratic Majority (CDM), an organization founded in 1972 in reaction to the leftward trend of the Democratic party under the influence of the McGovernites. The CDM enjoyed the support of the leadership of the AFL-CIO, the country's largest trade-union organization, which was also hostile to the New Politics, deeply anticommunist, and generally hawkish on foreign policy.

Although this second generation of neoconservatives led the fight to regain control of the Democratic party and reverse the turn toward more liberal social policies at home (including minority preference quotas, which it viewed as a perversion of the struggle for civil rights), its attention was increasingly focused on the liberal drift in foreign policy. For instance, the CDM adopted the slogan "Come Home, Democrats," an obvious play on one of McGovern's 1972 campaign slogans, "Come Home, America." While McGovern exhorted Americans to turn toward isolationism, curtail their commitments abroad, and reduce the defense budget, the neoconservatives invited the Democratic party to return to its traditional policy of robust containment of the Soviet Union and defense of democracies around the world, in keeping with the Truman doctrine and the legacy of Franklin D. Roosevelt. In their eyes, America's overreaction to the war in Vietnam was more dangerous than the war itself, even though the majority of them did not back that war.

Indeed, their target in the 1970s was increasingly the policy of "détente" with the Soviet Union advocated by Republicans Richard Nixon and Henry Kissinger—and later, to a certain extent, by Democrat Jimmy Carter. At this point they were usually referred to not as "neoconservatives" but rather as "Scoop Jackson Democrats," because of their support for Henry "Scoop" Jackson, the U.S. senator from Washington. Jackson, a Democratic hawk, embodied the persistence of "vital center" liberalism: in foreign policy he favored containment of the Soviet Union without concessions, while at home he advocated a Keynesian welfare state based on the model of the New Deal. He was an unrelenting critic of arms-control treaties (such as SALT I and II and the ABM treaty), and he attacked the government for compromising with the Soviets on moral issues such as the emigration of Soviet Jews (in 1974 he secured passage of the Jackson-Vanik amendment, which made liberalization of trade with Russia conditional upon relaxing the rules pertaining to Jewish emigration). His entourage included many who would later be celebrated as neoconservatives: Richard Perle, Paul Wolfowitz, Frank Gaffney, Charles Horner, Douglas Feith, and Elliott Abrams, among others.

Joined by the Coalition for a Democratic Majority, Jackson held meetings with Soviet and Cuban dissidents on whom the government had turned its back, while attacking liberals as moral relativists. For him, democracy was superior to all other systems, and America represented the best chance for the survival of democracy. The same note was sounded by Daniel Patrick Moynihan, who became the U.S. ambassador to the United Nations in 1975. Moynihan challenged Third World nations that denounced American imperialism (often with the backing of the Soviet Union) and voted in the General Assembly to approve a resolution labeling Zionism a form of racism. It is against this background that neoconservative support for Israel after 1967 was conceived: neoconservatives saw themselves as defending a democracy threatened by autocratic Arab nations armed by the Soviet Union. Not all neoconservatives are Jews, although a majority of them are (just as Jews were overrepresented among "vital center" liberals of the postwar period and among leftist radicals of the 1960s), but all, without exception, are strong defenders of Israel.

Paradoxically, then, the most ardent hawks in this period were to be found among Democrats. This paradox is confirmed by the composition of another group that was organized in 1976, a group that presented itself as bipartisan but in which Democrats outnumbered Republicans. The Committee on the Present Danger (CPD) would ultimately become a hotbed of neoconservatives. It led the fight against what it perceived as American military and strategic weakness in the confrontation with the Soviet Union, attempting to "sound the alarm" before it was too late. This penchant for strategic analysis was yet another facet of neoconservatism: democracy and freedom would be safe only if America was militarily strong, even dominant. If nuclear war broke out, it would do so because the United States was weak, not because it relied too much on force. The real danger was the Munich syndrome. Under the influence of strategic theorists such as Albert Wohlstetter and Paul Nitze (the gurus of Paul Wolfowitz and Richard Perle, among others), the CPD fought for increased military spending while adopting an extremely skeptical stance toward arms-control negotiations.

In fact it was the CPD that would serve the neoconservatives as a bridge to the Republican right of Ronald Reagan. The Scoop Jackson Democrats initially gave Jimmy Carter the benefit of the doubt, but in the end they deemed him too soft, and in 1980 most ended up supporting Reagan, who was himself a member of the CPD. In some respects they provided the ideological inspiration of Reagan's foreign policy. The neoconservatives had at last achieved power, but, much to their surprise, they had done so under a Republican president. Some of them, such as Jeane Kirkpatrick and Elliott Abrams, eventually became Republicans; but others, such as Richard Perle and Max Kampelman, remained Democrats, whether out of habit or for reasons of domestic policy.

The Third Age of Neoconservatism

In the late 1970s and early 1980s there was a degree of rapprochement between the two families of neoconservatives, the New York intellectuals and the Scoop Jackson Democrats, who shared a common enemy (the New Left), moved in the same circles, and worked in the same think tanks, such as the groups associated with *Commentary* and the American Enterprise Institute. With the end of the Reagan presidency, however, neoconservatives found themselves once again out in the cold, if only because the end of the Cold War had rendered some of their arguments obsolete. George H. W. Bush kept them at a distance (although Paul Wolfowitz, working under Dick Cheney, had some influence in the Pentagon, along with a network of like-minded officials such as I. Lewis "Scooter" Libby and Zalmay Khalilzad) while conducting a foreign policy based on Kissinger-style realpolitik rather than a crusade to defend democracy. His caution in the 1991 Gulf War, when he allowed Saddam Hussein to remain in power despite the consequences for Iraqi Kurds and Shi'ites, whose rebellions were crushed, was one sign of this distancing. After three consecutive defeats, in 1992 the Democratic party finally managed to stake out a position in the center behind Bill Clinton, whose moralistically tinged foreign policy brought some neoconservatives (among them James Woolsey, Joshua Muravchik, Ben Wattenberg, Penn Kemble, and Richard Schifter) back into major policy deliberations in the Clinton administration. Broadly speaking, however, the movement seemed dead and buried with the end of the Cold War.

In 1995, however, a new age of neoconservatism was born, that of the neocons, one that persists to this day. It was different from the two previous eras. Neoconservatism became a full-fledged element of the Republican party, now unambiguously on the right. The newcomers, such as William Kristol and Robert Kagan (the editors of the *Weekly Standard*), David Brooks, Gary Schmitt, Max Boot, and David Frum, were not former Trotskyites or even former Democrats. They were men of the right, even if their stance on domestic policy was somewhat different from that of other conservatives (they were not as hostile to the idea of an interventionist state, which they viewed as essential to "national greatness").

The most distinctive feature of the neocons was their stance on foreign policy. They attached great importance to military superiority and to the democratic principle: America must be strong and ready to act in order to shape the world according to its political and security interests, which sometimes include help in spreading democracy. In their view, multinational organizations such as the United Nations possess neither moral nor democratic legitimacy, nor do they have the strength necessary to ensure world order and defend freedom. Only America can and must meet these challenges. This "Wilsonianism with boots" was inspired partly by American exceptionalism and a patriotic and missionary spirit.[12] In this respect, there was nothing very "conservative" about the neoconservatives of the third age, who stood at a vast remove from both the pragmatic caution of Republican "realists" such as Henry Kissinger, George H. W. Bush, and Bush's advisers Brent Scowcroft and James Baker, and the skepticism of the original neoconservatives in regard to grand policy designs.

The most notable continuity was the one with the era of the Scoop Jackson Democrats, though with two important differences: first, progressive thinking about domestic policy had virtually disappeared; second, the relative power of the United States in the world had increased considerably with the fall of the Soviet Union and the modernization of the American military. Hence the cautious approach to foreign policy that had been necessary in a hostile world could now be set aside. Whereas the Scoop Jackson Democrats had urged Americans not to retreat, the neoconservatives of the third age exhorted them to advance and to act boldly—in other words, to use American power to shape a world safer for all.

Besides their adoption of an overconfident approach to foreign policy, the post-2000 neoconservatives were distinguished by another factor: they were mostly intellectuals. Most were thoroughly familiar with American history, and some were well-versed in international relations and strategic theory. With a few exceptions, however, none was an expert on the Middle East or indeed any other region. They attempted to compensate for this deficit in expertise with ideology, with a normative vision of the American role in the world, which at times resulted in simplistic arguments and a distorted and highly ethnocentric view of international affairs. Not that all the Scoop Jackson Democrats had been Soviet experts—far from it. But their stance had also been less interventionist, more cautious, and less arrogant than that of the third wave of neoconservatives.

At no time was the new neoconservatives' blind faith in America's appointed role in the world more apparent than in 2002 and 2003. Neoconservatives had been advocating the overthrow of Saddam Hussein, though not necessarily through direct American intervention, since 1997. They saw it as the prelude to a redrawing of the political map of the Middle East, and some even envisioned a democratic revolution in the region. The attacks of September 11, 2001, shifted the political climate in their favor. The presence of neoconservatives such as Wolfowitz, Feith, Libby, and Abrams and their allies Dick Cheney and Donald Rumsfeld in the administration of George W. Bush, coupled with the changed climate of public opinion, allowed their views to prevail. Had not the intervention in Afghanistan confounded somber forecasts and ended in resounding success? The neoconservative advocacy network girded for battle, turning out books and newspaper columns and exerting its influence through op-eds, conferences, the broadcast media, and sympathizers in the administration. Which brings us back to President Bush's speech at the American Enterprise Institute on February 26, 2003, praising the twenty "fine minds" whom he had recruited to work for his administration.

But although it is clear that neoconservatism played an important role in launching the war in Iraq, the history of the movement is more complex and far richer than an exclusive focus on the war can yield. Conversely, the decision to intervene militarily in Iraq cannot be ascribed solely to the influence of neoconservatives. This book seeks to put the intellectual history of the neoconservative movement in perspective so as to avoid errors of distortion.

The Role of Ideas in American Foreign Policy

This book is based on a conviction: in domestic and foreign policy, ideas matter. Although material forces are also crucial in the implementation of policy, the ideas, concepts, and representations that shape people's perceptions and interpretations of the world play an essential role in the formulation of policy. This principle applies not only to leaders (in this case, President George W. Bush) in a causal sense (such-and-such an idea leads to such-and-such an action) but also to the body politic and public opinion in establishing a permissive environment.

In order for the invasion of Iraq to become possible without provoking massive opposition, there had to be at least implicit agreement that the cost and danger of maintaining the status quo were exorbitant and that the cost and danger of overturning it were bearable. There had to be agreement about the ability of the United States to rearrange the political order in the Middle East (and elsewhere) to its own advantage. The neoconservatives played an important role in the diffusion of a vision of the world that made intervention possible and desirable. But they were not alone. For example, the book that had the greatest impact in justifying the invasion was written by a Democrat from the Brookings Institution, Kenneth Pollack.[13] Neoconservative ideas alone would not have led to war without the decisive help of objective material factors such as the September 11 attacks and the widespread suspicion that Saddam Hussein still possessed weapons of mass destruction at the beginning of 2003.

If one turns from the conditions that made the war possible to the decision to invade Iraq itself, one has to analyze the motives of President Bush and his entourage, without whom nothing would have happened. Once again, neoconservatism played a role—but certainly not an exclusive one. Bush himself was not a neoconservative, but he did incorporate numerous neoconservative ideas into "an astonishing ideological cocktail,"[14] whose other ingredients included his evangelical faith, his moralism, his profound conviction that he was right, and his stubborn insistence on adhering to a goal once set.

Among his top advisers, no neoconservative made it to the inner circle. Colin Powell, the secretary of state, directly opposed neoconservative recommendations (usually in vain). Condoleezza Rice, the national security adviser, remained neutral and did not propose an alternative vision. Rumsfeld, the secretary of defense, and Cheney, the vice-president, were closely allied with the neoconservatives, with whom they shared certain ideas. But as Ivo Daalder and James Lindsay have suggested, they were primarily "assertive nationalists" who favored a show of American force in the Middle East, a position that happened to coincide with an important part of the neoconservative agenda.[15] Rumsfeld had joined the Committee on the Present Danger in 1978 and later codirected the Committee for the Free World with Midge Decter. Cheney extensively consulted Bernard Lewis and Fouad Ajami, two neoconservative experts on the Muslim world, after September 11, and his chief of staff, I. Lewis "Scooter" Libby, was a neoconservative and disciple of Paul Wolfowitz. The number-two official at the Pentagon, Wolfowitz was the highest-ranking neoconservative in the administration, in which many other neoconservatives served in middle- and lower-level positions. It is therefore reasonable to conclude that neoconservative ideas exerted a strong though not exclusive influence on the worldview that underpinned the definition of the Bush administration's foreign policy.

Why did America invade Iraq? Although it is not my intention to suggest that ideas can explain everything, it seems clear that they played a more important role on this occasion than on others. For example, the Gulf War of 1991 was launched to prevent a dictator from seizing control of an oil-rich country as well as to assert, if not a "new world order," then at least the persistence of a world order safeguarded by the United States. The wars in Bosnia and Kosovo were waged to maintain the credibility of NATO and the United States and in reaction to ethnic cleansing in the Balkans. The war in Afghanistan was fought to destroy a terrorist base and avenge the attacks of September 11. The causes of the Iraq war of 2003 were more complex, however. More than the others, this was a war of choice. Some have argued that oil or the defense of Israel lay behind that choice. But oil was only a secondary consideration, not a genuine cause of war as in 1990–91. And Saddam Hussein did not threaten Israel's survival (even if he did pay indemnities to the families of suicide bombers, who continued their attacks after the invasion). For some years Jerusalem had been far more worried about Iran than about Iraq, and there was a risk that Iran would only be strengthened by the wars in Afghanistan and Iraq, as indeed turned out to be the case.

Paul Wolfowitz caused an uproar when he stated that the danger of weapons of mass destruction in Iraq was given prominence because it was the only issue around which it was possible to build a consensus in the American policymaking bureaucracy—and, one might add, in the international community, in view of the numerous Security Council resolutions on the subject since 1991.[16] He advanced three other reasons for the war: Saddam Hussein's support for terrorist groups, the danger that he might supply such groups with weapons of mass destruction, and his criminal oppression of the Iraqi people. In reality, these immediate grounds for war need to be set in a broader context, shaped by the implications of September 11 and the understanding of the Middle East.

September 11 fundamentally changed Americans' perception of their national security. Top officials became obsessed with doing everything possible to avoid a new wave of attacks, this time with weapons of mass destruction. They evolved a three-pronged strategy: attack the terrorists, prevent proliferation by going after those responsible, and deal with the underlying causes of terrorism. All three goals came together in what might be called the "greater Middle East" (stretching roughly from Mauritania to Pakistan). This convergence gave the neoconservatives of the third age the opening they needed to propose a coherent political vision, a critical part of which was the necessity of invading Iraq.

In their eyes, the regional status quo had become a dangerous source of instability. The Arab world, unlike Asia, had become bogged down on the road to modernity, stuck in a vicious circle of authoritarian rule and Islamic fundamentalism. Autocratic regimes diverted the frustrations of their people onto Israel and the West, fostering hatred. The United States could not challenge these dubious allies, however, because it needed them to supply the world with oil and to keep Saddam Hussein in check. In particular, it was obliged to maintain troops on the "holy soil" of Saudi Arabia—one of Osama bin Laden's chief grievances against the West. It had to conduct aerial operations to enforce the no-fly zones in northern and southern Iraq. And it had to maintain economic sanctions against Iraq, to the detriment of the Iraqi people and the American image abroad. Yet these sanctions were deemed to be ineffective. They did not prevent Saddam Hussein from stockpiling weapons of mass destruction (at a minimum, chemical and biological weapons) or from preparing to restart weapons programs that had been halted temporarily, including a nuclear weapons program. As early as 1997, neoconservatives denounced this stalemate and called for regime change as the only realistic solution, which they predicted would lead to overall improvement throughout the region. What changed after September 11 was America's tolerance for risk, which diminished because of fears that al-Qaeda might obtain weapons of mass destruction and launch a catastrophic attack on the United States.

Although neoconservatives did not in any sense anticipate September 11 (they showed little interest in terrorism or nonstate actors and worried more about ballistic missiles and possible threats from China), the new state of mind that prevailed after the attacks gave undeniable currency to some of their ideas, because those ideas provided a framework for a broader understanding of the crisis in the Middle East and answers to the questions that now obsessed the national security team: how to deal with the sources of the evil and how to prevent another attack on the United States—in other words, how to meet the new challenge rather than prepare to fight the last war.[17] For the neoconservatives, it was the entire status quo in the region that was rotten, and Iraq was a preeminent component. For them, the only solution was to overthrow Saddam Hussein (which seemed not only doable but easy as a result of his numerous violations of UN resolutions and his weakened grip on power). This move would resolve the problem of proliferation of weapons of mass destruction, put an end to any possible alliance with terrorists, permit the withdrawal of American troops from Saudi Arabia and thus decrease American dependence on Riyadh, improve the prospect of peace between Israel and Palestinians, and initiate a virtuous circle of stabilization and democratization in the region as the only conceivable long-term remedy for terrorism.

The neocons did not suggest invading Iraq in order to establish democracy there. The decision was driven by security considerations. Still, the absence of democracy figured in their vision of the region's security problems, with terrorism, proliferation, and instability as byproducts of a lack of democracy. In this sense, it would be wrong to reduce the question of democracy to an ex post facto rationalization or a propaganda point once no weapons of mass destruction were found. "America will take the side of the brave men and women who advocate these [democratic] values around the world, including the Islamic world, because we have a greater objective than eliminating threats and containing resentment," President Bush said in his "axis of evil" speech of 2002, more than a year before the war.[18] The Bush doctrine, which encompassed the need to preempt threats before they materialized and to oppose states that harbored terrorists, had democracy at its core. This was summed up in a speech that Bush delivered at the National Endowment for Democracy (an organization that Ronald Reagan created at the behest of neoconservatives, as we shall see in Chapter 6) in 2003, several months after the overthrow of Saddam Hussein:

> Sixty years of Western nations excusing and accommodating the lack of freedom in the Middle East did nothing to make us safe—because in the long run, stability cannot be purchased at the expense of liberty. As long as the Middle East remains a place where freedom does not flourish, it will remain a place of stagnation, resentment, and violence ready for export. And

with the spread of weapons that can bring catastrophic harm to our country and to our friends, it would be reckless to accept the status quo . . . The establishment of a free Iraq at the heart of the Middle East will be a watershed event in the global democratic revolution.[19]

The "democratic core" of the Bush doctrine drew its inspiration from neoconservatives. In a book published in 2007, Tony Smith showed that the theoretical underpinning of the Bush doctrine can be found in the work of liberal academics. In particular, three fundamental pillars of the doctrine were inspired by liberalism: the idea of democratic peace, the right to intervene redefined as the "responsibility to protect," and new ideas about the conditions for democratic transition.[20] And the need to defend and even help spread democracy had been developed by Scoop Jackson Democrats, the neoconservatives of the second age in the 1970s (as I will show in Chapter 3), and later by their successors of the third age. Without this attention to the nature of regimes, they would merely have been "assertive nationalists," to borrow the term used above to describe Cheney and Rumsfeld.

Neoconservatism as an American Phenomenon

Just as neoconservatism by itself cannot explain the war in Iraq, neither does the war exhaust the meaning of neoconservatism. It is therefore advisable not to interpret the movement in teleological terms. Indeed, as one explores the various facets of neoconservatism, including the most contradictory ones, one discovers issues of foreign policy that were not even present at the beginning or dominant, much less exclusive, until the late 1970s.

As soon as one steps away from the narrow path that leads straight to George Bush and the Iraq war, one discovers that the history of neoconservatism can shed a great deal of light on the political history of the United States. This is particularly true of the two organizations that will be studied in depth in the pages that follow, namely the Coalition for a Democratic Majority, established in 1972, and the Committee on the Present Danger, established in 1976.

For instance, the history of the CDM shows how intertwined neoconservatism was with the evolution of the Democratic party. Neoconservatives used the CDM to wage a fight to regain control of the party from

George McGovern and adepts of the New Politics. They sought to move the party back to the center by working through committees charged with reforming the way in which delegates were chosen in presidential primaries. Their failure, followed by their support for Reagan in the 1980 presidential campaign, symbolized and compounded the Democrats' inability to preserve their roots among white working-class voters (especially Catholics), who could no longer identify with a party that had allegedly sacrificed too much to minorities and shown itself to be insufficiently patriotic. The CDM continued to preach in the wilderness throughout the 1980s, exhausting itself in the process. Its message would later be successfully adopted by another group to which it was close on many issues and with which it came within a hair's breadth of merging: the Democratic Leadership Council, which gave Bill Clinton substantial assistance in his quest for the presidency in 1992 (see Chapter 6).

The history of neoconservatism was thus closely linked to that of the Democratic party. But it was also linked to that of the unions, and this is a largely neglected aspect of the Cold War. For example, the AFL-CIO, under the leadership first of George Meany and then of Lane Kirkland, became deeply involved in foreign policy issues that went well beyond straightforward trade-union concerns. The organization had a clear influence on public debate in favor of a tougher, more militaristic approach to containment of the Soviet Union and to defense of human rights and democracy. Kirkland, not content simply to fund both the CDM and CPD with AFL-CIO funds, served as co-president of the CPD from 1976 to 1982. In the struggle against McGovernite New Politics as well as in the campaign to "alert America" to the Soviet danger, trade unionists made common cause with neoconservatives.

Neoconservatism also offers a way into the very rich intellectual debate about politics that took place in the United States in the second half of the twentieth century. It can tell us a great deal about both liberalism (which neoconservatives angrily rejected in the end, but in a way that suggests that the narcissism of small differences may have played a role) and conservatism (which neoconservatives embraced but never fully identified with). Indeed, both the conservative movement and the Republican party benefited from the talents and ideas of neoconservative intellectuals of the first and second ages such as Irving Kristol (as early as 1972), Norman Podhoretz, Jeane Kirkpatrick, Michael Novak, and

Charles Krauthammer. It is not entirely false to say that by the 1980s the Grand Old Party had become "the party of ideas," largely thanks to the contribution of neoconservatives.

Finally, neoconservatism sheds a fascinating light on the way in which American political society works. Indeed, one of the aims of this book is to show concretely how ideas take hold and spread to the point where they influence political decisionmakers. Behind political ideas we find not only people but also networks linking intellectuals to journalists and decisionmakers, careers that take individuals back and forth between the academic and political worlds, and a variety of organizations from think tanks to citizen groups to political parties. The CDM and the CPD thus illustrate what Tocqueville said 150 years earlier about "the use that Americans make of association in civil life." "When Americans have a feeling or idea they wish to bring to the world's attention, they will immediately seek out others who share that feeling or idea and, if successful in finding them, join forces. From that point on, they cease to be isolated individuals and become a power to be reckoned with, whose actions serve as an example; a power that speaks, and to which people listen."[21]

1

INCUBATION:
FROM THE COLD WAR TO THE
COLLAPSE OF LIBERALISM

If you were the son of an immigrant Jew in New York City in the 1930s, if you lived in Brooklyn, the Bronx, or the Lower East Side, if your parents were lucky enough to be employed as textile workers or unlucky enough to be unemployed because of the Great Depression, and if in either case there wasn't much money in the family but you had the good fortune to go to college anyway, you didn't go to Columbia University. You went to the City College of New York (CCNY).[1] This public institution established by the city at the turn of the century for the children of immigrants was not nearly as prestigious as Columbia, but at least it was free. Most important, there was no quota limiting the number of Jewish students, as there was at Columbia, where the few Jews who were accepted were mainly of German origin, wealthy, and assimilated. There were also quotas at other Ivy League universities (these antisemitic quotas would not be eliminated until the 1950s). To be sure, the teaching at CCNY was far from the best available, but for many students, that was not the most important thing. Their real education took place not in the university's lecture halls but in its corridors, or, more precisely, its alcoves.

The alcoves were horseshoe-shaped open areas in the college dining hall, which, though not terribly clean, were always crowded with students. Different student groups used these alcoves as meeting places. The Communists, perhaps 400 or 500 in all and supported by a number of professors, met in alcove number 2, while all the anti-Stalinist Marxist groups (mainly Trotskyists but also anarchosyndicalists, social democrats, and others), which together had about a tenth as many members as the Communists, occupied alcove number 1. Catholics, Orthodox Jews, blacks, and athletes gathered in other alcoves, but these were of little interest to students like Irving Kristol, Daniel Bell, Nathan Glazer, Seymour Martin Lipset, Melvin Lasky, Irving Howe, and Philip Selznick, to mention only the most famous of those who gathered in alcove number 1. Many of these men would later play a role in the history of neoconservatism, whether as founder (Kristol), fellow travelers to one degree or another (Lipset, Glazer, and Bell), or opponents (Howe and Selznick).

It was in this world of student clubs that they acquired their real education. Daniel Bell describes it as a wonderful "political sandbox" that gave them the "opening to the world" that the university promised.[2] Nathan Glazer has described the illumination he experienced after a friend urged him to read an issue of the *Partisan Review,* the very modern Manhattan Marxist and literary journal, in the early 1940s.[3] These students were already politicized, if only because of their background: their immigrant Jewish parents had arrived from Europe with left-wing ideologies, which many retained after establishing themselves in the United States. In 1932, in the midst of the Great Depression, the Socialist Norman Thomas, who had inherited the party leadership from Eugene Debs, garnered nearly a million votes in the presidential election, many of them from the New York Jewish community. It was therefore only natural that CCNY came to be known as a "red" university. Hadn't students at the school rioted to protest the visit of a student delegation from Mussolini's Italy in 1934?

For many of these politicized CCNY students, the center of university life was endless and passionate political debate, coupled with reading of the works of Marx, Engels, and Rosa Luxemburg, as well as of Sidney Hook, the first American to offer a comprehensive interpretation of Marx's work. They also read the *New International* (a Trotskyist organ that published articles by Trotsky himself along with pieces by Max Shachtman, James Burnham, and others) and the *Partisan Review.*[4] They sparred verbally (and even physically when the atmosphere turned poisonous) with the Stalinists in alcove 2, who included Julius Rosenberg, the leader of the Young Communist League.[5] And they looked down on the denizens of alcove 2 as crude simpletons: in 1938, leaders of the YCL had forbidden their members to speak to the Trotskyists lest they become ideologically contaminated or, worse, defect to the enemy camp, as a growing number of the most brilliant young Communists had been doing. Of course the occupants of alcove 1 took a malign delight in provoking the Communists, who were no longer allowed to talk back to them.

The story of CCNY's student organizations and of the split between Stalinists and Trotskyists that defined the political context has become a staple of every history of neoconservatism, sometimes to the point of caricature. In point of fact, few neoconservatives were habitués of the CCNY dining hall, and few were Trotskyists. But this account of the origins of the movement serves several purposes. One is to call attention to the youthful intellectual and political fervor characteristic of many neoconservatives of all three ages, a fervor that none of them entirely got over. As Irving Kristol put it, "Joining a radical movement when one is young is very much like falling in love when one is young. The girl may turn out to be rotten, but the experience of love is so valuable it can never be entirely undone by the ultimate disenchantment."[6] Belief in the power of ideas and in the ability to argue and persuade, coupled with a taste for verbal jousting and polemic, is in one way or another part of the "genetic heritage" of neoconservatism and the neoconservative style.

The second reason to evoke the alcoves of CCNY is that this was the soil in which the virulent anticommunist seed took root, well before anticommunism became the trademark of the Cold War liberals who were the precursors of neoconservatism. But among those liberals, those who had once been Trotskyists were imbued with a far more rigid and ideological, and at times almost fanatical, brand of anticommunism than was the case with authentic New Deal or Truman-era Democrats. It was also an anticommunism that was better informed about the true nature of communism, of which the former Trotskyists had firsthand knowledge from having combatted it directly.

Echoes of the 1930s context can be detected in the 1960s, when neoconservatism was born. For one thing, the Cold War liberals vehemently rejected any suggestion that the anticommunist line ought to be softened. Such suggestions were sometimes heard from the New Left, which knew nothing of the ideological disputes of the 1930s and often found anticommunism stultifying—and irrelevant. For another, fledgling neoconservatives found themselves banished to the fringes of the broad liberal family, just as they had been expelled from the broad Marxist family by the Communists three decades earlier.

The third and final reason why the Trotskyist milieu of alcove number

1 matters is that it was symbolically important. In the 1940s and 1950s those who would become the first neoconservatives continued to move in intellectual circles composed for the most part of former Trotskyists. Three major figures stand out: Sidney Hook, Max Shachtman, and James Burnham. The intellectual legacy that they bequeathed to the three ages of the movement deserves closer examination.

Sidney Hook, James Burnham, and Max Shachtman

Hook, Burnham, and Shachtman were Communists who became Trotskyists in the 1930s and subsequently moved either toward social democracy or, in the case of Burnham, toward obsessive right-wing anticommunism. Gary Dorrien has already written an authoritative work on the evolution and thinking of these three men.[7]

In the 1930s Sidney Hook (1902–1989) and James Burnham (1905–1987) were friends and colleagues in the philosophy department at New York University.[8] Both were Marxists. Hook had traveled in Europe and been to Moscow. He described the Soviet Union in enthusiastic terms. In 1933 he published *Towards the Understanding of Karl Marx,* an ambitious interpretation of Marx inspired by the pragmatic philosophy of his teacher John Dewey.[9] Soon afterward he was summoned to a meeting with Earl Browder, the leader of the American Communist party, who asked him to organize a secret spy ring in the universities to keep the party informed about American military and industrial experiments.

The meeting shook Hook's political convictions, and he became increasingly disenchanted with the party's sterility and intellectual rigidity. For a short time he collaborated with Burnham, the very cultivated son of a wealthy Chicago manufacturer of railroad equipment, in founding the American Workers party, an independent and authentically American communist organization, before rejecting Leninist doctrine altogether. In 1939 he persuaded ten well-known intellectuals to publish a manifesto calling for a new organization, the Committee for Cultural Freedom. The manifesto warned against the rise of totalitarianism and placed Soviet communism in the same category as German and Japanese fascism.[10]

Hook denounced the principle of "moral equivalence." Dwight Mac-Donald, who was a Trotskyist intellectual in the late 1930s, conceded that Hitler was surely monstrous but that America was in no position to judge other countries, much less declare war on them, owing to its own failings in the realm of social justice. Hook, by contrast, favored going to war against the Nazis and refused to treat America's imperfections as in any way comparable to the enormities of Nazism.[11] Against moral equivalence Hook introduced an important neoconservative concept, "moral clarity," which would be frequently invoked six decades later in the wake of the September 11 attacks on the United States.[12] Following Hook's lead, subsequent generations of neoconservatives incessantly attacked the liberals of the New Left for their readiness to denounce America's faults while remaining blind to evils abroad. This was the theme of Jeane Kirkpatrick's famous speech to the 1984 Republican convention in Dallas, in which she attacked the "Blame America First Democrats" (see Chapter 6).

Hook eventually found his way to Norman Thomas's social democracy and in retrospect reconciled with the New Deal. He supported Truman's Fair Deal after 1947, as well as the civil rights struggle and Lyndon Johnson's Great Society. He argued that a "rollback" of the Soviet empire was unrealistic and favored an aggressive containment strategy instead. The worldwide struggle against communism should be waged on American terms, wherever possible as a crusade for democracy. Most neoconservatives of the second and third ages shared this position. The former Marxist ended his career at the Hoover Institution (a conservative think tank located on the campus of Stanford University), where he attacked even Ronald Reagan's anticommunism as "irresolute." Reagan bestowed the Medal of Freedom, the nation's highest civilian distinction, on him in 1985.[13]

James Burnham, too, abandoned Leninism for good in the late 1940s. Indeed, he turned his back on all forms of left-wing radicalism and in short order migrated from Trotskyism to an elitist antidemocratic politics of the right without passing through a liberal phase along the way. In 1955 he joined forces with William F. Buckley Jr. at the *National Review,* the house organ of the nascent conservative movement, where he remained until his death.

Between 1940 and 1955 Burnham published several important books, echoes of which can be found in the works of neoconservatives, who nevertheless rejected Burnham as antidemocratic. In *The Managerial Revolution* (1941), he argued that the hegemonic power of the capitalist class had been captured not by the working class but by a "new class" of managers and bureaucrats who controlled the means of production, even in the Soviet Union. Stalinism, Nazism, and the New Deal were merely variants of this new state of affairs, and the emergent world order would be determined by a clash among "superstates" ruled by bureaucratic collectivism. In this struggle, Burnham believed that European democracies were at a disadvantage: the appeasement of Hitler at Munich symbolized the waning faith of capitalist democracies. Neoconservatives would subsequently take up this refrain, expressing their disgust with bourgeois powerlessness and appeasement and embracing Burnham's warning against the inherent weakness of democracy in the battle against totalitarian regimes.

Toward the end of World War II, as the tide began to turn against Germany, Burnham was one of the first to warn of the need to prepare for a third world war with the Soviet Union. In 1947 he wrote *The Struggle for the World,* in which he argued that World War III had really begun in April 1944. He described the communist drive for world domination in terms very different from George F. Kennan's famous "long telegram," which *Foreign Affairs* would publish a few months later (Kennan's view was less paranoid, more subtle, and more accurate about the nature of the Soviet leadership).[14] Burnham deplored writers who were preoccupied with the guilt of the West and the immorality of power. He was critical of the influence of Jesus, Saint Francis, and even Buddha. For him, the first battle to be waged was at home, against the "culture of appeasement," which would become a favorite theme of neoconservatives of the second age, especially Norman Podhoretz.[15] In the struggle to the death against communism, neutrality was not an option. One finds echoes of this theme in neoconservative crusades during the Cold War and in the War on Terror: "Either you are with us, or you are with the terrorists," George W. Bush proclaimed on September 20, 2001, when he solemnly declared war on terrorism.[16]

In *Containment or Liberation?* (1953), Burnham suggested the need to truly roll back communism, a theme that also found a place in Republican campaign rhetoric in 1952. The problem was that his concrete proposals were unrealistic, especially his insistence that the United States must prepare to invade Eastern Europe. Although in 1983 he became the first intellectual to be awarded the Medal of Freedom, he never received explicit recognition from neoconservatives, although one can find clear echoes of his thought in some of their ideas. He had moved too quickly to the right and, worse yet, had gone too far. He also opposed democracy, unlike Max Shachtman and Sidney Hook, whom neoconservatives did cite as sources of inspiration.

Like Hook and Burnham, Shachtman had moved away from Trotskyism in the second half of the 1930s.[17] In the 1940s and the 1950s he called upon socialists to oppose communism as well as capitalism, but as the Cold War developed, he became convinced that communism was the greater danger. In his efforts to theorize a democratic form of Marxism, he, like Hook, moved toward right-wing social democracy. He defended the war in Vietnam and supported anticommunist Democrats such as Scoop Jackson and the AFL-CIO (backing armed containment, defense of democracies, and concrete action to help workers). He also enlisted numerous disciples, the so-called "Shachtmanites," loosely linked to the Social Democrats USA. Many of them became second-age neoconservatives in the early 1970s: Penn Kemble, Joshua Muravchik, Carl Gershman, Paul Seabury, and Bayard Rustin, to name a few.

The Cold War and the "Vital Center"

The intellectual contributions of Burnham, Hook, and Shachtman form part of the intellectual genealogy of neoconservatism, but other sources also contributed to the political origins of the movement. Most neoconservatives were not former Trotskyists, and many did not follow the theoretical debates that fascinated Irving Kristol, Daniel Bell, and Nathan Glazer. In order to understand the political context in which neoconservatism was born in the 1960s, and even more to understand the second age of neoconservatism in the 1970s, one needs to look carefully at the evolution of liberalism after World War II and the emergence of a distinctive—and historically specific—political doctrine. This doctrine might be called Cold War liberalism or anticommunist liberalism or, perhaps best of all, as suggested by John Ehrman, "the liberalism of the vital center," named for Arthur Schlesinger's 1949 book of that title.[18]

Despite the American Communist party's show of patriotism during World War II, many New Deal Democrats were wary both of the party and of Stalin's Soviet Union. This wariness led to the dumping of Henry Wallace, elected vice-president in 1940, from the 1944 Democratic presidential ticket. Wallace, who had served as secretary of agriculture from 1933 to 1940, was a charismatic idol of the party's left wing, but he was suspected of Communist sympathies and considered too conciliatory toward the Soviet Union. He was therefore pushed aside in favor of Harry Truman, an obscure senator from Missouri. Wallace had to settle for the post of secretary of commerce.

Even in that post, however, he continued to set himself apart from the administration line by criticizing American foreign policy vis-à-vis the Soviet Union as too aggressive, too militaristic, and too hard-line (Moscow, in his view, having adopted a defensive posture). After he made a speech at Madison Square Garden very critical of administration policy, Truman dismissed him on September 20, 1946. Wallace then founded an organization called the Progressive Citizens of America (PCA) so as to set himself apart from the main liberal organization, the Union for Democratic Action (UDA), which he judged to be excessively anticommunist. The following year he revived the Progressive party in a bid to win the presidency, and the Communists backed him. But the Progressives fared poorly (3 percent of the popular vote and no electors) and failed to bring down Truman, who, despite having to contend with the Dixiecrats in the South, won a slim victory in 1948.

Partly in reaction against Wallace's procommunist faction, many liberals became increasingly anticommunist. The UDA, which had been formed in 1941 by labor leaders and other well-known figures such as the theologian Reinhold Niebuhr (1892–1971) and A. Philip Randolph (1889–1975), the founder of the Brotherhood of Sleeping Car Porters, a black union engaged in the struggle for desegregation, transformed itself into the Americans for Democratic Action (ADA) in 1947.[19] The ADA garnered the support of such leading Democrats as Eleanor Roosevelt, the historian Arthur M. Schlesinger Jr., the journalist Stewart Alsop, and Walter White, president of the National Association for the Advancement of Colored People, as well as young anticommunist liberals such as Hubert Humphrey of Minnesota. The ADA lost no time in advertising its anticommunism, thereby setting itself apart from Wallace's PCA. The group adopted a platform advocating continuation of the New Deal and protection of individual liberties from an all-powerful state and intrusive big business, along with four principles to guide American foreign policy: support for free democratic peoples, opposition to communism and fascism, support for the United Nations, and support for the American plan for the control of atomic energy.[20] Over the next several weeks, the best-known members of the ADA crisscrossed the country to promote the creation of local chapters. Eleanor Roosevelt threw herself into the effort, as did Niebuhr, Schlesinger, and even a young actor named Ronald Reagan. They were opposed by various liberal groups that the Communists had infiltrated. Sociologically, the typical ADA member was male, urban, Jewish, in his forties, and college-educated.

In 1949 Arthur Schlesinger offered an articulate vision of the ADA's convictions in his book *The Vital Center*, which took much of its inspiration from the thought of Niebuhr, especially his book *The Children of Light and the Children of Darkness*.[21] Niebuhr, a Protestant minister with marked left-wing sympathies, had helped Norman Thomas reform the Socialist party in the 1930s and even served as the party's vice-chair.[22] Subsequently he moved to the center, supporting Roosevelt in 1940. He also backed the creation of the UDA and, later, the ADA. His view of the promise as well as the limitations of man—and of liberalism—was based on original sin. Schlesinger explained it as follows:

> Reinhold Niebuhr revived for my contemporaries the historic Christian insights into the mixed nature of human beings. Original sin came to seem a powerful explanation for the anomalies of the human condition. Democracy had to take account of the human propensity for self-pride and self-delusion. The children of light had to learn to live with darkness. Recognition of human frailty offered democracy a more solid foundation than a belief in human perfectibility. "Man's capacity for justice makes democracy possible," wrote Niebuhr; "but man's inclination to injustice makes democracy necessary."[23]

For Schlesinger, the concept of a free society—comprising at a minimum freedom of expression, freedom of conscience, and the right to political opposition—was the crowning achievement of Western history, and the primary mission of liberals was to defend it against totalitarian systems, which, as appealing as they might seem, had no better solution for the problems of the modern world than did free societies, and what solutions they did have made short shrift of individual liberties. This message was all the more pertinent in view of the assaults to which "bourgeois democracy" had been subjected in the 1930s. Still, as a faithful disciple of Niebuhr, Schlesinger also warned against the dangers of self-righteousness and self-certainty about the justice of one's cause, as if in anticipation of the excesses of the Vietnam and Iraq eras: "Despotism is never so much to be dreaded as when it pretends to do good: who would act the angel acts the brute . . . In our democratic tradition, the excessive self-love which transforms power into tyranny is the greatest of all dangers."[24]

On social issues, Schlesinger argued that the class struggle had always played a role in American history—a less important role than in Europe, to be sure, but not intrinsically harmful. What mattered, however, was the existence of upward social mobility, which ensured that elites were replenished and classes did not harden into castes. The state must intervene precisely when it was needed to guarantee healthy competition and ensure a minimum of social solidarity, but it must not go beyond that lest it impede the creation of wealth by fostering the growth of a stifling bureaucracy.

Analyzing the early days of the Cold War, Schlesinger showed that, even before the death of Roosevelt, the attitude of the Soviet Union had begun to harden for internal reasons and not in reaction to the American stance. In any case, the confrontation was ideological in nature, so that any naïve American initiative toward rapprochement was doomed in advance. At home, the Communist party had been able to infiltrate not only liberal organizations such as Henry Wallace's PCA and the trade unions but also black organizations, taking advantage of what Schlesinger called "the most appalling social injustice in this country."[25] Ultimately, the greatest challenge posed by the Communist party was not the risk to the nation itself, which Schlesinger deemed sufficiently serious to warrant defensive measures, but the risk to American liberalism, to a democratic left caught between the hammer of the right, which sought to undermine its credibility, and the sickle of communism.

Schlesinger's gospel of anticommunist liberalism served throughout the 1950s as the bible for many Democrats who supported democratic and social progress at home and anticommunism and forceful containment of the Soviet Union abroad. Some of them clung to this position even when the "vital center" seemed to buckle in the face of New Left protest on one side and resurgent Republican conservatism on the other: these were the neoconservatives of the second age, the Scoop Jackson Democrats.

The Passion of Anticommunism

Although the intellectuals who came out of the factional struggles of the extreme left of the 1930s and the Democratic reformers of the New Deal can be lumped together under the label "Cold War liberals," there were significant differences between them. While former Communists and Trotskyists such as Sidney Hook, Max Shachtman, and the writer Arthur Koestler made anticommunism the central issue, at times to the point of single-minded obsession, liberals of the "vital center" like Arthur Schlesinger took it as one tenet of their faith among others, refusing to allow that one part of their political vision to devour the rest.[26] In the 1950s, two episodes highlighted the similarities as well as the differences between the two positions. One was the creation of the Congress for Cultural Freedom, while the other was the advent of McCarthyism.

From 1947 to 1949, various Communist parties organized, at Moscow's behest, a series of "peace conferences" in Europe and the United States. The purpose of these conferences was to demonstrate Communist leadership in artistic and intellectual circles. In particular, a prestigious "Scientific and Cultural Conference for World Peace" was held at the Waldorf Astoria Hotel in New York in 1949. In reaction to this paean to the glory of the party, Sidney Hook mobilized veterans of his Committee for Cultural Freedom to infiltrate and disrupt the conference. Although he did not enlist as many "stars" as the Waldorf conference itself, he did succeed in enticing James Burnham, Norman Thomas, and the literary critic Lionel Trilling to participate, along with members of the younger generation, such as Schlesinger and Daniel Bell, and many other figures as well. He also enlisted the financial support of the International Ladies' Garment Workers' Union (ILGWU), a powerful noncommunist union representing workers in the New York–centered textile industry. The group attacked the persecution of Soviet intellectuals and artists and agreed on the need to take active measures to counter Communist propaganda and defend cultural freedom.

The following year a second conference was held in Berlin, organized by Melvin Lasky, who had been Irving Kristol's friend and partner in alcove 1 at CCNY. Lasky, who had served in the Office of Strategic Services during the war, had become the German correspondent for the *New Leader* and *Partisan Review,* and from his perch in Berlin he strongly denounced the purges of Soviet intellectuals. The Berlin conference led to the formation of the Congress for Cultural Freedom (CCF) in June 1950. This was a sort of anticommunist International with headquarters in Paris. The Paris branch of the organization was organized by Raymond Aron, Michael Josselson (another veteran of the Office of Strategic Services), and the novelist Arthur Koestler.[27]

In subsequent conferences the CCF took an interest in a variety of subjects ranging from the politics of science to the future of ideology to strategies of economic development and brought together anticommunists of all stripes from liberal to conservative, including social democrats. But the real strength of the CCF lay in the many anticommunist intellectual journals that it promoted and financed, such as Melvin Lasky's

Der Monat in Germany, Ignazio Silone and Nicola Chiaromonte's *Tempo Presente* in Italy, François Bondy's *Preuves* in France, Julian Gorkin's *Cuadernos* in Latin America (published in Paris), and of course *Encounter* in the United Kingdom. This British venture was entrusted to Irving Kristol, who had demonstrated his prowess at *Commentary,* and to the eminent British poet Stephen Spender. It soon became one of the premier English-language cultural and political magazines, with Spender taking charge of the literary section (where his most notable authors included Virginia Woolf and Albert Camus) and Kristol of the political section (he published Nathan Glazer, Vladimir Nabokov, and Denis de Rougemont, among others).

In 1966 the *New York Times* revealed that the Central Intelligence Agency had been secretly supporting the CCF and its magazines. The scandal was widely reported: the New Left (represented, for example, by the *New York Review of Books*) accused the anticommunist liberals of selling out to the establishment. The left-wing magazine *Ramparts* pursued the investigation and published further revelations, most notably a CIA contribution of $30,000 for the creation of *Encounter,* which it continued to support financially until 1964. The *Encounter* team defended itself, denied the charges, but ultimately was forced to beat a retreat and even offer its apologies to *Ramparts.*

Anticommunism had been an all-consuming obsession for many of these intellectuals. Following Sidney Hook, they made a distinction between communism as "heresy," which was acceptable, and communism as "conspiracy" to overthrow the state, which was not. Their attacks naturally focused on the latter: it was essential to deny Communists the right to act in the political sphere because they did not respect its rules.[28] The infiltration of the government by clandestine Communists made it necessary to take radical measures, including violation of their civil liberties. This issue took a dramatic form during the McCarthy era, exposing differences among anticommunist liberals.

The ADA, which had supported Truman's anticommunist policy, took a position against the "loyalty oaths" that federal officials were required to take after 1947. This requirement seemed unduly paranoid and posed a risk of abuse. After all, the ADA itself had been attacked by conservatives for its supposed Communist sympathies. In *The Vital Center,* Schlesinger was highly critical of the Alien and Sedition Act of 1798 and the Smith Act of 1940, both of which had been used to prosecute Communists.[29] He foresaw correctly that anticommunist hysteria could easily lead to the persecution of nonconformity of all kinds.

Persecution was precisely what ensued after Senator Joseph McCarthy launched his crusade in Wheeling, West Virginia, on February 9, 1950. McCarthy enjoyed the discreet support of Republicans, who were happy to have found at last a promising angle from which to attack New Deal Democrats, by accusing them of being Communists. In the Senate, Mc-Carthy subpoenaed hundreds of officials and representatives of groups suspected of having been infiltrated by Communists. Helped by the Korean War and the 1952 election, McCarthy's crusade gained strength and soon led to abuses of power: unjustified allegations were bandied about, careers were destroyed, books were burned, and so on, until in 1954 McCarthy was discredited by his own excesses (and by his accusations against the president and the U.S. Army).

How did the Cold War liberals react to all this? Some favored repudiating McCarthy completely. Most ADA members were in this camp, following the lead of Arthur Schlesinger and Diana Trilling, who went so far as to resign from the American branch of the Congress for Cultural Freedom. Cold War liberals who would subsequently become socialists rather than neoconservatives—Irving Howe and Michael Harrington—joined them. Daniel Bell and Irving Kristol were part of a centrist faction that tried to reconcile the two camps. They disliked McCarthy and agreed that he had gone too far and thereby discredited the anticommunist struggle, but they also believed that he was not a genuine threat to cultural freedom and that the real problem was Communist infiltration in the United States. This type of argument was summed up by Kristol in an article published in *Commentary* in March 1952, which remains famous to this day. The main idea was that while McCarthy was indeed "a vulgar demagogue," it was nevertheless absurd to protect the free speech of Communists, whose goal was to eliminate freedom of speech. In this respect, Kristol argued, liberals were naïve innocents. Ultimately, he was harder on them than on McCarthy: "For there is one thing that the American people know about Senator McCarthy: he, like them, is unequivocally anti-Communist. About the spokesmen for American liberalism, they feel they know no such thing. And with some justification."[30]

This article sparked a polemic with Schlesinger. Schlesinger felt that a wide gap had always separated the New Deal reformers from the New York intellectuals. During the 1930s, while the former worked to expand the concrete social and democratic gains of the New Deal, the latter had impatiently proclaimed that liberal democracy was on the verge of being overthrown by a great proletarian revolution. Now the New York intellectuals were again attacking the same reformers, but this time from the right, exhibiting consistency only in extremism, not to say hysteria.[31] In other words, Kristol, while ignoring the liberals' efforts to rid themselves of the Communists and fellow travelers who had infiltrated their ranks, neglected the real history of the ADA, in particular its determined opposition to Henry Wallace's Progressive Citizens of America.

This exchange shows clearly that Kristol's brand of anticommunist liberalism (which would culminate in the neoconservatism of the first age) was not the same as the anticommunist liberalism of Schlesinger and Niebuhr (which would culminate in the neoconservatism of the second age). Yet these differences with respect to communism did not precisely coincide with the gap between New York intellectuals and the ADA. For example, it was Hubert Humphrey, a founding member of the ADA and with a left-wing position on social issues, who in 1954, toward the end of the anticommunist wave, introduced in the Senate the Communist Control Act, which outlawed the Communist party, outraging Schlesinger and many other liberals. Three years later the act was struck down by the Supreme Court as unconstitutional. Humphrey's legislative adviser was none other than Max Kampelman, a second-age neoconservative and founding member of both the Coalition for a Democratic Majority and the Committee on the Present Danger.

The liberalism of the 1950s proved impossible to define. The concept was so vast and so vague that it could accommodate a wide range of very different, indeed almost opposing, sensibilities and tendencies, including precursors of both the New Left and neoconservatism. How could it fail eventually to implode?

The Perils of an Overly Broad Liberalism

To understand the struggles that would tear liberalism apart in the 1960s and 1970s, it is useful to establish a vantage point in the mid-1950s, when American society was reconciled with itself in a so-called "liberal consensus."[32] Among historians, Louis Hartz attempted to demonstrate that all of American history had been built around a liberal consensus.[33] Daniel Boorstin had taken a similar tack two years earlier, emphasizing the rejection of ideology as the hallmark of America's unique historical experience.[34] Richard Hofstadter explained that the engine of American history was not conflict but consensus: the appearance of strong political divisions was often deceptive, because the intellectual horizons of adversaries in both parties were always limited by notions of private property and free enterprise, and social mobility alleviated tensions.[35] In sociology, Daniel Bell wrote articles, often inspired by Raymond Aron, about "the end of ideology," which he collected in a book published in 1960.[36]

In short, this was a period in which a large segment of the political class, from the ADA to Dwight D. Eisenhower (who adopted a pragmatic policy of maintaining the achievements of the New Deal), described itself as partially or wholly "liberal." But what did liberalism mean, apart from the obviously fundamental principles of individual freedom, tolerance, and democracy? As we have seen, post–New Deal liberalism accepted the need for state intervention. Arthur Schlesinger explained this as follows: when laisser faire seemed the most appropriate way to achieve equal opportunity for all, as in the time of Jefferson, liberals adopted the Jeffersonian idea that the best government is that which governs least. But when the increasing complexity of the industrial world required more state intervention to ensure greater equality of opportunity, the liberal tradition gave priority to goals over dogma and altered its attitude toward the state.[37] Henceforth the government could and should compensate for the deficiencies of the American social and economic system by instituting New Deal–style social programs and adopting Keynesian policies of fiscal stimulus.

But how far should these new ideas be taken? A wide latitude for judgment remained, and different ways of "being liberal" began to emerge. In practice, the liberalism of the 1950s could accommodate a substantial dose of conservatism. Godfrey Hodgson recognized this in his account of that "strange hybrid, liberal conservatism, [which] blanketed the [political] scene," from the ADA, which marked the frontier of respectable liberalism, properly anticommunist and pro–free enterprise, to certain sectors of Wall Street and the manufacturing industries that accepted the existence of unions, a legitimate role for the state in economic life, and rights for minorities. Hodgson was thus led to introduce a useful distinction between liberals and the Left:

> To draw a distinction between the Left and the liberals may sound sectarian or obscure. It is not . . . What I mean by the "Left" is any broad, organized political force holding as a principle the need for far-reaching social and institutional change and consistently upholding the interests of the disadvantaged against the more powerful groups in the society. The liberals were never such a force . . .
>
> What I mean by the liberals is those who subscribed to the ideology I

have described: the ideology that held that American capitalism was a revolutionary force for social change, that economic growth was supremely good because it obviated the need for redistribution and social conflict, that class had no place in American politics. Not only are those not the ideas of the Left; at the theoretical level, they provide a sophisticated rationale for avoiding fundamental change. In practice, the liberals were almost always more concerned about distinguishing themselves from the Left than about distinguishing themselves from conservatives.[38]

In the 1950s, however, this semantic distinction was not commonly made, and there existed a "more leftist" form of liberalism that aimed to expand upon the promises of the New Deal and not simply to conserve and protect its achievements. For instance, in 1954 a group of intellectuals affiliated with Irving Howe, Lewis Coser, and the journal *Dissent* split off from mainstream anticommunist liberalism. As we have seen, Howe (1920–1993) had hung out with fellow Trotskyists Irving Kristol, Daniel Bell, and Nathan Glazer in alcove number 1 at CCNY. Indeed, it was he who had recruited Kristol, a decision that he would later describe as the greatest mistake of his life.[39] In 1940 he became a follower of Shachtman. As a leading democratic socialist, he founded *Dissent* in 1954. The intention was to create a more left-wing journal, less tolerant of American society and more critical of its injustices than such anticommunist publications as the *New Leader, Commentary,* and the *Partisan Review,* which had taken to celebrating America's virtues. *Dissent* challenged the anticommunist hysteria (in the very first issue, Howe went so far as to compare Eisenhower's refusal to confront McCarthy to Hindenburg's refusal to confront Hitler). It also charged that American foreign policy suffered from a failure to understand the problems of the Third World (especially national liberation movements).[40] Indeed, the word "neoconservative" apparently first came into common use in the late 1960s within the editorial team at *Dissent,* led by Michael Harrington, before finding its way into the public domain.

The ADA, the very incarnation of "vital center" liberalism, also experienced tensions in the 1950s. The left wing of the organization wanted to push more quickly toward desegregation and civil rights, while the right wing, though sympathetic to this goal, thought that the group's first priority should be to help Democratic candidates win elections.[41] The 1956 presidential election made this dilemma acute: in supporting the candidacy of Adlai Stevenson (in a necessarily discreet way after the

Republicans accused the ADA of being a Communist front), the group was obliged to moderate its position on the racial issue, and in the end it lost on both fronts. After the election the ADA turned its attention to economic issues and foreign policy. Leon Keyserling, who had been Truman's economic adviser, advocated an "economics of growth" sustained by federal spending and tax cuts. This agenda had foreign policy implications: in Keyserling's view, the United States could increase its defense budget, contrary to what Eisenhower claimed, without neglecting social programs. The ADA also recommended doubling U.S. aid to developing countries. The organization was able to support these "left-wing" ideas without reneging on its strong anticommunist stance (it also recommended support for the French in Indochina). Within less than twenty years, these same ideas would resurface among supporters of Scoop Jackson and the Coalition for a Democratic Majority, of which Keyserling was a founding member.

At the very end of the 1950s, however, economist John Kenneth Galbraith would argue that in an "age of affluence" and mass consumption, liberals were in need of new ideas.[42] Americans were on the whole well-housed and well-fed, so that it was necessary to take further steps in order to move from "quantitative liberalism" (to borrow the formulation of Schlesinger, who to some extent followed Galbraith) to a "qualitative liberalism" focused on dignity, identity, and self-realization in mass society. Galbraith also argued that the competition with the Soviet Union had become essentially economic and symbolic and that it was aimed at the Third World. A leading light of the ADA, Galbraith soon drew an angry response from Keyserling. The latter denied that America no longer suffered from poverty and hunger. Instead of chasing will-o'-the-wisps such as self-realization and identity, the organization should refocus its efforts on the struggle against poverty and on forging alliances with the trade unions rather than with intellectuals and students. He also ruled out any reconsideration of the policy of containment of communism as set forth in 1947. What we see in this debate is the first sign of what would become a split between the New Left (which would ultimately dominate the ADA) and neoconservatives loyal to the "vital center." This split, however, would not manifest itself clearly until the second half of the 1960s.

"Vital center" liberalism also came under attack from another quarter in the 1950s, this time from the cultural rather than the political sphere. The "beat generation" lambasted the conformism of the Eisenhower era, rejected the bourgeois ideology of success, and celebrated hedonism. Jack Kerouac published *On the Road* in 1955, the same year in which Herbert Marcuse published *Eros and Civilization,* a work that proposed a theory of hedonism and a critique of "Puritanism." It was also in 1955 that Bill Haley and Elvis Presley issued their first records (the birth of rock and roll). But the full significance of these cultural changes would not become apparent until later, after the protest movement began.

Liberalism had become an unwieldy edifice, too large for its own good, and all it would take to bring about its collapse was the rise of the civil rights movement, the proliferation of student protests, and above all opposition to the war in Vietnam. The "vital center" stood for only a few years after the onslaught began. Its last gasp was Hubert Humphrey's successful quest for the 1968 Democratic presidential nomination.

The Discreet Birth of Conservatism

The 1950s marked the birth of a true, modern, American conservative movement. Unlike neoconservatism, it did not emerge from liberalism, the left, or the extreme left. It derived from three distinct right-wing political and intellectual traditions: libertarianism and free-market conservatism in the mode of Ludwig von Mises, Friedrich Hayek, and Milton Friedman, who rejected Keynesianism and public spending; "traditionalist" conservatism, advocated by Russell Kirk, who in 1953 published *The Conservative Mind,*[43] as well as Erik Voegelin and Richard Weaver, who detested modern civilization and its technological progress to the detriment of man's spiritual well-being and who also deplored the decline of the West; and, finally, obsessive anticommunism, personified by men such as Whittaker Chambers (1901–1961) and, even more, Frank Meyer (1909–1972) and James Burnham (discussed above).

It was Frank Meyer who used the term "fusionism" to describe the combination or "fusion" of these three intellectual traditions in a single conservative intellectual current represented by the *National Review.* That journal was created in 1955 by William F. Buckley Jr. (1925–2008), a young intellectual who had attracted notice four years earlier with the publication of *God and Man at Yale.*[44] In that work he recounted his experience as a student at the prestigious university, which he saw as dominated by liberal thinking and by smug professors contemptuous of the religious beliefs of their students and eager to indoctrinate them with liberal ideas. Buckley added his own Catholic sensibility to the three types of conservatism "fused" in the *National Review*. Of course these three strands were not always compatible (how, for instance, could activist, not to say intrusive, anticommunism be reconciled with the minimal state advocated by the libertarians?), but the *National Review* was interesting precisely for its ability to bring these different tendencies together and to produce a body of conservative intellectual writing worthy of the name while developing a version of right-wing thought free of racism (in the style of the John Birch Society) and antisemitism.

All of those who would subsequently become neoconservatives were at this time still Cold War liberals, and Buckley gave them absolutely no credit for their visceral anticommunism. As he saw it, every form of liberalism was either a variant of communism or a first step in its direction, not least because of liberalism's intrinsic lack of backbone. Liberals were equally dismissive and disdainful of the *National Review*, as the following passage from Irving Kristol makes clear:

> When *National Review* was founded in 1955, I regarded it as an eccentricity on the ideological landscape—it seemed so completely out of phase. Essentially it continued the polemic against the New Deal that characterized American conservatism, as represented by the Republican party, throughout the 1930s and 1940s. As a child of the Depression who was outraged at the spectacle of idle factories, unused resources and vast unemployment all coexisting, I could not take seriously the seemingly blind faith in "free enterprise" that was the primal certainty of *National Review*. I simply found this point of view irrelevant. So did practically everyone else at the time—at least the "everyone else" I knew or read.[45]

The entire conservative stance toward history was incompatible with the worldview of the Cold War liberals—not just the idea of undoing the New Deal but the Burkean attitude of "[standing] athwart history, yelling Stop!" as the *National Review*'s first editorial put it in November 1955. The future neoconservatives exhibited no nostalgia or regret for any supposed golden age of the past (be it medieval Christianity, aristocratic England, the Old South, or the unbridled capitalism of the 1890s). They were at home in their time and did not regard their contemporaries or the innovations of the modern world as oddities.

Modern *National Review* conservatism did not succeed in wresting the Republican party from the centrists until Barry Goldwater won the

1964 presidential nomination. But Goldwater endured a sound thrashing in the general election, demonstrating that the country was not yet in a conservative mood. Goldwater's candidacy, however, sowed the seeds of future victory: Ronald Reagan, who had been a "Democrat for Nixon" in 1960, became a Republican in 1962 and before long was elected governor of California. In October 1964 he gave a memorable speech in support of Goldwater, and this catapulted him into the role of spokesman for the conservative wing of the party.[46] Nevertheless the conservatives continued to be dominated in the Republican party by centrists: Nixon in 1968 and 1972, Gerald Ford in 1976. Conservatives did not gain the upper hand until 1980, when Reagan captured the nomination and the presidency.

Meanwhile the conservative faction made gains in other areas: Christian fundamentalists mobilized politically in support of conservative Republicans; the Solid South, once a Democratic bastion, began to move toward the Republicans because of opposition to civil rights (and the growing white population of the Sun Belt); and conservatives scored numerous successes on the ideological front. After founding the *National Review*, Buckley helped to create the right-wing student group Young Americans for Freedom. Conservative think tanks proliferated in the 1970s. A conservative "counterestablishment" was created. Last but not least, a more highbrow intellectual current known as "neoconservatism" began to flow in a more rightward direction.

The Rise of the New Left

In the early 1960s, the focus of political debate shifted. As a protest movement got underway and then, after 1965, organized itself around the Vietnam War, a new split developed in the liberal camp. The old battles of the period 1930–1960 between Communists, "progressives," and fellow travelers on the one hand and anticommunist liberals on the other gave way to a clash between protesters, the counterculture, and the New Left on one side and "Old Left" liberals, mainly associated with the trade unions, on the other. It was out of this debate that the neoconservatives emerged in two waves, one primarily intellectual, the other primarily political. But in order to understand these first two ages of neoconservatism, we must first take a closer look at what they were reacting against.

From the 1940s on, the procommunist left suffered a series of setbacks: first, the failure of Henry Wallace's "progressives"; then, the anti-communist reaction of 1947–1954 (loyalty oaths, McCarthyism); and finally, the events of 1956 (de-Stalinization, the Khrushchev report, repression in Hungary). Nevertheless, an "authentically American" left did manage to constitute itself by reaching beyond the boundaries of the New Deal coalition, hence beyond the "vital center" of the 1950s and 1960s. It was inspired in part by cultural upheaval in the United States, including such phenomena as the emergence of rock and roll and of the Beat movement, which rejected the stifling conformity of 1950s America in favor of liberation of the individual, exaltation of creativity, the search for ecstasy, and rejection of the work ethic and the cult of success. The "counterculture" that came out of this cultural turmoil was an important element in the political upheavals of the 1960s and a force that converged in part—but only in part—with the New Left.

The New Left in the strict sense of the term emerged in the early 1960s as the confluence of various protest movements that found common ground in the struggle for civil rights and opposition to the war in Vietnam: anarchists, libertarians, pacifists, feminists, ecologists, some socialists, and some black nationalists joined in the new movement. Political activism was encouraged by two social developments: the drive for civil rights for blacks in the wake of the Supreme Court's 1954 decision in *Brown v. Board of Education* and, to a lesser extent, the women's liberation movement. Student protest also played an important role in the creation of the New Left, and a key group in this process was the Students for a Democratic Society (SDS), which was founded in 1959. Its Port Huron Statement, drafted mainly by Tom Hayden in 1962, combined standard left-wing critiques of large corporations, the military-industrial complex, nuclear testing, and so forth with ideas that were "in the air," such as alienation, the absurdity of modern life, and public apathy, along with individual aspirations to self-realization and brotherhood, including some overtones of Pope John XXIII's encyclical *Pacem in Terris*.[47] The Port Huron Statement was not Marxist in inspiration, but it made no mention, as Cold War liberals would have done, of the need to repudiate and fight communism. Nor did it mention the role of the working class—a revealing omission. The thinking of the New Left was in fact centered on the individual.

Like the Free Speech Movement, which began in Berkeley in 1964 (see below), the SDS called for "participatory democracy," an idea inspired by Tom Hayden's philosophy professor at the University of Michigan,

Arnold Kaufman, as an improvement on mere "representative democ-racy." Whereas the latter amounted to nothing more than casting a vote for some politician, the former was supposed to give individuals a far greater role in decisions affecting their lives. The institutions by which this goal was to be achieved were not clearly defined (although minority representation quotas would later be espoused as one of them).

The New Left never had a unified program and could never have agreed on one. The movement sought to realize all the promises (and more) that the traditional left had been unable to keep, in a new context of prosperity and security—a context very different from that of the Great Depression and wartime years; the new context had provided the background to the debate between Keyserling and Galbraith. One sign of the changing times was the rejection of the visceral anticommunism of the traditional liberals, who had come of age in the decades of intense ideological warfare. To the young activists of the New Left, the tradi-tional liberals seemed dogmatic, set in their ways, and dangerous: their blinkered anticommunism not only put a straitjacket on reform and free thinking but also led to provocations of the U.S.S.R. and warmongering in general. The New Leftists wanted to move beyond the prudence and pragmatism of Truman and Kennedy toward a transformation of society with the aid of the federal government.

In addition to the civil rights struggle and the whole ideology of multi-culturalism that went along with it (insisting on recognition of and re-spect for minority identities), the New Left brought other new political themes to the table: issues of individual liberty and values pertaining to the role of women, sexual freedom, homosexuality, conscientious objec-tion, drugs, ecology, and atheism. Enemies of the New Left mocked these "values issues" as "problems of the wealthy," of spoiled children raised according to the relaxed childrearing principles of Dr. Benjamin Spock.[48] The critics disapproved of what they saw as a turn away from the tradi-tional liberal emphasis on issues of social justice.

The Port Huron Statement reflected the New Left idea that the indoc-trinated and apathetic working class was no longer in the vanguard of social progress in the United States; that role had passed to the students and minorities. This "new class" of educated and therefore "enlight-ened" activists—many of whom had relatively little life experience—consisted mainly of middle-class individuals with time and money to spare. It saw as its enemy not so much the right, because conserva-tism was a negligible force in the 1960s, as the unnecessarily moderate liberalism of the "establishment," which remained closely tied to the unions and the less well-to-do, to the blue-collar workers and lower middle-class whites who constituted the bulk of the Democratic electorate. Jeane Kirkpatrick, a second-age neoconservative, attacked the New Left for running counter to the fundamentally mainstream liberal views of the American people:

> Against a belief in growth and abundance the new left advocates expansion of the wilderness and technological slowdown; against the allocation of role on the basis of individual achievement, the new left advocates role allocation on the basis of ascriptive group traits; against an active international role, the new left urges withdrawal; against resolute anticommunism, it recommends accommodation with communist expansion; against appreciation of American political, economic and social achievements, the new left asks that we meditate on our collective guilt.[49]

As the New Left and other protest movements evolved in the 1970s and 1980s, they changed in three somewhat paradoxical ways, as the columnist and political commentator E. J. Dionne has pointed out.[50] First, they became radicalized, in some cases engaging in factional quarrels, demonstrations of extreme anti-Americanism, and even armed struggle (on the part of such terrorist groups as the Weathermen and the Symbionese Liberation Army). This radicalization reduced their influence to nothing. Second, the movement discredited and by the 1970s helped destroy the "vital center" liberalism that had once sustained it. Finally, its emphasis on individual self-realization and its rejection of large unifying organizations laid the groundwork for antistatist Reaganism and even the excesses of unbridled capitalism in the 1980s (similar charges have been leveled against the legacy of May 1968 in France). Yet both first-age neoconservatism, which was an intellectual reaction to the New Left, and second-age neoconservatism, which was a political reaction to the same New Left, would survive the demise of the movement against which they were conceived.

Berkeley 1965: The First Birth of Neoconservatism

One place of particular interest for understanding the upheavals of the 1960s is the campus of the University of California at Berkeley, which served as a kind of laboratory of American political change. Indeed, neoconservatism appeared there quite early—or, more accurately, it was attacked there quite early, if only because New Left protest, against which neoconservatism was a reaction, was also early to emerge there.[51] One reason for this development was that Berkeley is a public, not a private, university: tuition there, while not free, as at CCNY, was lower than at many private universities. Like CCNY, moreover, Berkeley was politically very much to the left, and a veritable magnet for protesters of every stripe; it had survived the McCarthyist era relatively unscathed. The sequence of events by which Berkeley students were drawn into a new kind of politics is well known: protest began with the civil rights movement from 1960 to 1963, then turned against the university itself in 1964 and 1965, and finally against America's involvement in Vietnam after 1965.

Students initially mobilized in support of civil rights. Some went to the Deep South in the summer of 1963 to protest segregation, and even greater numbers went in 1964 to assist in the registration of black voters. Still more students participated in local demonstrations organized by activists from the Student Nonviolent Coordinating Committee (SNCC) and the Congress on Racial Equality (CORE). There were marches in California against supermarkets, fast-food restaurants, and hotels to protest racial discrimination in the workplace, which persisted despite already strict state laws prohibiting it.

Armed with protest tactics learned from the civil rights movement and more militant than ever, Berkeley students next launched protests against restrictions imposed in September 1964 on their freedom of political expression. At issue was not only freedom of speech but also the right to engage in political activity on university property: putting up posters, collecting contributions, holding meetings, and so forth. As the scope of the protest grew, its objectives became increasingly vague: the university was attacked as a "knowledge factory" that suffocated students and transformed them from free human beings into "products of the university." The spirit—and the excesses—of the student protest can be gauged from a speech given in late 1964 by Mario Savio, one of the leaders of the Free Speech Movement:

Last summer I went to Mississippi to join the struggle there for civil rights. This fall I am engaged in another phase of the same struggle, this time in Berkeley. The two battlefields may seem quite different to some observers, but this is not the case. The same rights are at stake in both places—the right to participate as citizens in democratic society and the right to due process of law. Further, it is a struggle against the same enemy. In Mississippi an autocratic and powerful minority rules, through organized violence, to suppress the vast, virtually powerless majority. In California, the privileged minority manipulates the university bureaucracy to suppress the students' political expression. That "respectable" bureaucracy masks the financial plutocrats; that impersonal bureaucracy is the efficient enemy in a "Brave New World." In our free-speech fight at the University of California, we have come up against what may emerge as the greatest problem of our nation—depersonalized, unresponsive bureaucracy. We have encountered the organized status quo in Mississippi, but it is the same in Berkeley.[52]

Yet some professors found it impossible to believe that freedom of speech was in serious jeopardy on the Berkeley campus. Nathan Glazer—a veteran of alcove number 1 and therefore someone who knew a thing or two about student militancy—observed that one could speak about anything at Berkeley and that political activity there was "vigorous beyond anything I had recently seen at any other American college." All shades of opinion could be found on the campus, from members of the American Nazi party to supporters of Fidel Castro, Mao Tse-tung, and Ho Chi Minh. At Berkeley, according to Glazer, students mocked the "backwardness" of East Coast universities, where sex among students was still a matter for debate. "Only homosexuality or perversion, it seemed, could make an issue at Berkeley."[53] Seymour Martin Lipset, another veteran of alcove number 1 who had also turned liberal, joined Paul Seabury, a future neoconservative, to produce an alarmist ideological analysis of what was going on:

> The Berkeley Revolt is not just another California curiosity. The new style of campus political action may affect other campuses, and eventually our national political life . . . The student leftist movements are growing and probably will continue to grow as they demand totally moral solutions to issues of racial discrimination, and foreign policy. The indifference to legality shown by serious students can threaten the foundations of democratic order if it becomes a model for student political action.[54]

Indeed, the student movement and the New Left quickly turned their attention to a more comprehensive critique of institutions and political power in the United States (a critique that also flourished in nonpolitical forms, such as experimentation with new lifestyles, new musical forms, sexual liberation, and drugs). Soon opposition to the Vietnam War served as a catalyst to further protest. And the enemy in this ideological struggle was not the right, and it was not conservatism: it was liberalism.

In an article published in February 1965, for example, Sol Stern, a student leader, soon to become a member of the editorial board of *Ramparts,* wrote that the students' principal "enemy" in the Berkeley protests was Clark Kerr, the president of the University of California, because in the eyes of the protesters he symbolized all the failures of liberalism. For Stern, liberalism had been drained of its passion and become a defender of the status quo. Having revealed its limitations, it had nothing more to offer the protesters. Liberalism lacked courage, and its penchant for seeking compromise often led to surrender. In both domestic politics and foreign policy, Stern concluded, liberalism had become synonymous with "*realpolitik* and opportunism."[55]

And that was not all. After Glazer, Lipset, Seabury, and Lewis Feuer (another CCNY veteran, somewhat older than the others) had all published articles criticizing the Free Speech Movement, its defenders responded in the *Partisan Review* in 1965 by branding these "sophisticated spokesmen for the liberal community" as "new conservatives."[56] Why new conservatives? Because these liberals valued stability and order more than their "pseudo-liberal rhetoric." To be sure, they did not oppose political conflict, but even conflict had to contribute to stability. It had to end in compromise or, at the very least, a balance of political forces within a stable institutional framework. The "new conservatives," for their part, rejected any form of social protest or social movement that attempted to go outside the established framework for resolving political conflicts through institutional channels or, worse, that threatened the very stability of established institutions.

Thus we see that in Berkeley in 1965, liberal New York Jewish intellectuals, some of them ex-Trotskyists, reacted negatively to the birth of the New Left and the counterculture by pointing out the threat that the movement posed, politically and ideologically, to American democracy. Their enemies responded by treating them as "new conservatives," thus attempting to banish them from the liberal camp and to associate them with the right. Even if there were as yet no "neoconservatives," neoconservatism had been born. The subsequent history of the movement was an extended variation on the themes sounded at Berkeley.

The Collapse of the Liberal Consensus

To understand the collapse of the liberal consensus, there is no better vantage point than the ADA, the organization that was the very embodiment of Cold War liberalism.[57] In 1960, despite the Galbraith-Keyserling debate, the ADA remained firmly attached to the "vital center." While it supported John F. Kennedy in 1960, its preferred candidate was Hubert Humphrey, a founding member of the organization. A split developed within the group between a more radical wing influenced by the New Left, mainly represented in the regional chapters, and a traditional wing, which dominated in Washington but seemed cut off from its base.

This split widened through controversy over the battle for civil rights. Some chapters wanted the organization to adopt civil disobedience as a principle of action, whereas moderates wanted to confine support to peaceful, legal demonstrations such as sit-ins. The moderates also wanted to support President Johnson in the 1964 election, even though this meant opposing the bid of a black Mississippi delegation to replace the segregationists in the regular delegation at the 1964 Democratic convention. To counter this threat from the more radical wing of the ADA, which might have threatened his nomination, Johnson chose Hubert Humphrey to be his vice-presidential running mate, thereby reinforcing ties with ADA moderates.

In other words, the ADA, the quintessential liberal organization in the United States, internalized the growing split in liberal ranks. It supported—and helped to pass—the 1964 Civil Rights Act as well as legislation promoting Johnson's War on Poverty, while chastising the president for not going far enough. But Vietnam soon undermined the group's resilience. U.S. involvement in the war exacerbated the divisions among three distinct factions, as Steven Gillon has convincingly argued.[58] The "traditionalists," such as ADA president John Roche (a professor of political science at Brandeis University and future neoconservative) and Paul Seabury, backed by the unions, rejected the idea of a new liberalism. They continued to believe in the New Deal and anticommunism and supported the containment of Communist expansion in Asia. They were opposed by "reformists," who were sympathetic to the students and for whom the war represented everything that was worst in American foreign policy. In between traditionalists and reformists were the "moderates," who sought to minimize the differences and to reconcile the other two wings of the organization. For instance, Arthur Schlesinger and John Kenneth Galbraith felt that the liberals' time for achieving their goals had come, and division in the ranks should not be allowed to spoil the moment. They were wary of the young protesters' simplistic critique of the war. From 1965 to 1967, the crisis intensified. Although Galbraith was elected president of the ADA at the beginning of 1967, his moderate wing found itself in an increasingly precarious position. Vietnam was a vortex that swallowed up all other issues and tended to radicalize the opposition. By the end of 1967, divisions in the country and among liberals had reached a point where compromise was impossible.

The impending presidential election accelerated the process. The traditionalists, led by Keyserling, lost out to an alliance of moderates and reformists, who chose to support Eugene McCarthy, a peace candidate whom the unions found unacceptable but who was the favorite of antiwar protesters. This vote marked a turning point for the organization: the oldest members of the ADA objected, and three union presidents resigned from the group. At Harvard, a student by the name of Elliott Abrams was ousted as president of the local chapter because he supported Humphrey. Together with another student, Daniel Pipes (son of the historian Richard Pipes), he soon organized a rival group to challenge campus protesters.[59]

In 1968 the balance of power within the ADA shifted definitively toward the New Left. The Cold War liberals and "vital center" Democrats had held out for several years, but in the end they lost. The sociological makeup of the ADA changed radically: students, professionals, and intellectuals—in other words, representatives of the "new class"—dominated, while blue-collar workers, represented by the unions, deserted the organization entirely. In terms of economic policy, the organization henceforth favored a massive redistribution of wealth and power in the United States, accompanied by a guaranteed minimum income and guaranteed employment. In foreign policy, the ADA favored total withdrawal from Vietnam, and its attention turned from the East-West conflict to relations between North and South (that is, rich nations and poor nations).

What did all these changes amount to in the end? Had the New Left really caused liberalism to deviate dramatically from the line it had followed since the 1930s, as neoconservatives would allege? Or did certain Cold War liberals themselves veer to the right and abandon the liberal cause, as left-wing groups would soon counter by labeling the deserters "neoconservatives"? The answer is of course a matter of political opinion, but there can be no doubt that the content of liberalism did indeed change in the 1960s, so that neoconservatives could legitimately criticize the liberals while continuing to invoke an earlier conception of liberalism. This was what Jeane Kirkpatrick did in 1980, when she summed up the neoconservative view as follows:

> The harshest political conflict of our times has taken place among persons who, as late as 1964, were all found within a broad liberal consensus. The shattering of that consensus occurred in conjunction with the rise of the counterculture and the emergence of neo-conservative re-evaluations. The traditional American liberal position had, and has, specific content which differentiates it from European left liberalism, from counterculture (New Left) romanticism, from the old right stinginess and isolationism, from new right stridence and tendency to bigotry, and from neo-conservative cautions.
>
> As compared to European liberal-left doctrines, traditional American liberalism is pragmatic rather than rationalist, optimistic rather than perfectibilist, religious rather than secular. As compared to counterculture romanticism, it emphasizes reason more than feeling; doing more than being; achieving more than enjoying; producing more than consuming. As compared to the old right traditional [*sic*], liberalism is internationalist rather than isolationist, generous rather than mean. As compared to the Wallaceite right it is inclusive rather than exclusive, tolerant rather than bigoted, flexible rather than rigid. As compared to neo-conservative perspectives it is more optimistic than pessimistic, more active than resigned, more daring than cautious. The differences between neo-conservatism and traditional liberalism are, I believe, more a matter of mood and degree than of values.[60]

2

THE FIRST AGE:
LIBERAL INTELLECTUALS IN DISSENT

In 1965, when two former comrades of alcove 1, Daniel Bell and Irving Kristol, founded a quarterly magazine named *The Public Interest,* they had already traveled quite a distance from where they began in politics. In the 1940s they had turned their backs on radicalism and abandoned revolutionary Trotskyist ideas. In the 1950s they reconciled with America and joined the liberal consensus, celebrating the country's virtues and applauding its firmness in the face of communism. In the 1960s, however, this centrist evolution placed them on a collision course with the rising power of the student protest movement and the New Left. What is more, the shift came at a time when President Lyndon Johnson was securing passage of some very ambitious social legislation whose goal was nothing less than to put an end to poverty in the United States and right the wrongs of segregation.

Founded in order to offer nonideological technical expertise on social policy, *The Public Interest* little by little evolved into a journal critical of the mischief done by the welfare state. It systematically explored numerous obstacles to the implementation of social programs. Doubt as to government's ability to achieve what it set out to achieve became a fundamental theme of the journal's editorial line and of first-age neoconservatism more generally. But what really shaped neoconservatism was its increasingly vehement reaction to the New Left, especially after 1967, as a result of the powerful impact of the Six-Day War on the American Jewish community, a breakdown in relations between Jews and blacks, and the rightward turn of the magazine *Commentary.*

"Knowing What One Is Talking About"

In the late 1950s, Daniel Bell became a professor of sociology at Columbia—a mark of success for this graduate of CCNY. He had worked for the Congress for Cultural Freedom (CCF) and *Fortune* magazine, where he covered union issues. *The End of Ideology,* published in 1960, made his name.[1] In 1965 he began to publish articles on postindustrial society and the technocratic class that went with it.[2]

Irving Kristol, meanwhile, had received military training near Chicago before going off to fight in France and Germany in 1944. When he encountered "real working-class Americans" in the army, he realized that "there was no way to build socialism with people like that," and concluded that he had been right to repudiate radicalism.[3] With his wife, the future historian Gertrude Himmelfarb, he spent some time in Britain as correspondent for the *New Leader* before returning to New York, where from 1945 to 1951 he served as assistant editor of *Commentary,* the magazine of the American Jewish Committee.[4] With Eliot Cohen, the editor-in-chief, he made *Commentary* a cultural and political journal of high intellectual quality, with a liberal anticommunist line. He next became executive secretary of the CCF at the behest of Sidney Hook and then, in 1953, coeditor of *Encounter* in the United Kingdom. We saw earlier how that magazine became engulfed in polemics because of its financing by the CIA. A year after returning to the United States in 1958 Kristol became executive vice-president of Basic Books and was later appointed "professor of urban values" at New York University.

To get *The Public Interest* off the ground, the two friends assembled some modest financial backing and many willing hands. The editorial aims of the journal, as stated in the introduction to the first issue, were simple and clear, at least at the beginning: the editors proposed to bring advances in sociology to bear on debates concerning American society and public policy, while avoiding preconceptions, cliché, sentimentality, and ideology.[5] The early 1960s had witnessed a sort of "rediscovery of poverty" with the publication of several books that focused attention on "the other America" (to borrow the title of a book by socialist Michael Harrington).[6] Major philanthropic foundations, especially the Ford Foundation, had plunged into a frenetic round of activity, much of it hastily conceived, shortsighted, naïvely optimistic, and interventionist. *The Public Interest* took the view that when it came to debating public policy and social intervention, it was best to "know what one is talking about." Ideology, Bell and Kristol wrote in their preface to the first issue, often stood in the way:

> "Knowing what one is talking about" is a deceptively simple phrase that is pregnant with larger implications. We do not wish to evade these implications, or pretend to be blind to them. Thus, we must admit—or, if you wish, assert—that such an emphasis is not easily reconcilable with a prior commitment to an ideology, whether it be liberal, conservative, or radical. For it is the nature of ideology to preconceive reality; and it is exactly such preconceptions that are the worst hindrances to knowing-what-one-is-talking-about . . . We shall doubtless publish ideological articles, if they seem particularly challenging and perceptive. But, we hope, not many; and not often. There is a danger in this, we must allow. The ideological essay, as a literary form, tends to be more "interesting"—it always seems to go deeper, point further, aspire higher. Its bland disregard of opposing fact, its very pretentiousness, sometimes even its very smug self-assurance, can give it a readability and literary attractiveness that a more matter-of-fact and more truthful essay does not often instantly achieve. While we shall certainly try to make *The Public Interest* as lively, as readable, and as controversial as possible, we nevertheless are determined to make room for the occasional "dull" article that merely reports the truth about a matter under public discussion.[7]

Clearly, then, the enemy was ideology—preconceived, unreflective thinking. Clearly, Bell's influence was at work here, with all the ambiguities inherent in his favorite theme. Implicit in the "end of ideology" was the notion that the intellectual and political ambition to radically transform society had been discredited both by the failure of fascism in its various forms and by the repudiation of the Soviet brand of Marxism-Leninism. The acute phase of class struggle and social upheaval in which these outmoded ideologies had taken root was now over. The social problems that remained were complex and not necessarily amenable to resolution by state action—or, for that matter, political action of any kind. Accordingly, the "end of ideology" evolved from a descriptive theme (no one was interested any longer in making the revolution or "changing life"—a finding that was ironically undermined at the same time by the emergence of the New Left and the protest movement) into a normative theme, in some sense a manifesto in favor of technocratic rule.

In the first issue of the new journal, Daniel Patrick Moynihan argued that reform had become the business of experts. The time of strikes, petitions, and demonstrations was over. Henceforth reform would come not from outside but from inside the state, from people with a background as academics, scientists, and engineers relying on arcane new sources of information. The growing complexity of economic science and "the exponential increase of knowledge" of society in the form of statistical and econometric data and new techniques of simulation militated in favor of a "new style" of reform through political and administrative action guided by consensus rather than conflict.[8]

In political terms, then, *The Public Interest* began with a technocratic, anti-ideological line. It advocated government by experts and scientists. For the first few years of its existence, the journal was seen as a reasonable and moderate liberal publication. In the summer of 1966, Irving Kristol himself wrote in the fourth issue that he generally approved of Lyndon Johnson's Great Society, although he was somewhat skeptical of the likelihood that such measures would lead to a better life in a better society.[9] Broadly speaking, the journal's contributors believed that the state did indeed have a role to play in the struggle against poverty— "a much larger role than conservatives thought appropriate," Kristol noted. "But we did not believe that political activism (a.k.a. 'the class struggle') could deliver people from poverty."[10]

"The Limits of Social Policy"

Slowly but surely, however, the technocratic faith that had marked the early days of *The Public Interest* evaporated. Looking back forty years later, Nathan Glazer recounted the change:

> What astonishes me in glancing over those early issues was how soon the simple notion that science and research could guide us in domestic social policy became complicated, how rapidly this theme was reduced to a much smaller place than originally expected, how early the themes that were shortly to be dubbed "neoconservative" emerged. Managing social problems was harder than we thought; people and society were more complicated than we thought . . . We began to realize that our successes in shaping a better and more harmonious society, if there were to be any, were more dependent on a fund of traditional orientations, "values," or, if you will, "virtue," than any social science or "social engineering" approach.[11]

The founders of *The Public Interest* had been driven by the idea of bringing new scientific and social knowledge to bear on the formulation and implementation of effective public policies. But after the first few issues their insistence on respect for the facts and common sense led them to diagnose and dissect the failure of government antipoverty programs, to explore the obstacles faced by social engineering, and to focus on the limits of all forms of state intervention. Their new goal was to douse the naïve enthusiasms of (other) liberals with buckets of cold water.

In 1967, for instance, Glazer examined the political impasses of Great Society housing policy.[12] Moynihan described the failures of the War on Poverty, and Aaron Wildavsky continued in the same vein in the next issue.[13] James Q. Wilson warned against the bureaucratization that interventionism inevitably bred.[14] John Bunzel attacked the basic premises of what would soon be called "multiculturalism" with a critique of the "Black Studies" curriculum at San Francisco State University.[15] One can of course ask whether this shift in the focus of *The Public Interest* was not implicit in the journal's initial plan. To stick scrupulously to the facts, to substitute realism and rigor for the noble sentiments of Great Society liberals, to banish ideology, not to say politics or even simply ambitious goals for the future—did not these aims ultimately imply setting extreme limits to any attempt to change society?

Indeed, in the eyes of *Public Interest* neoconservatives, the cultural sphere ranked high among the factors that set limits to social policy. The problem with bureaucrats and social planners was that they were privileged people who did not understand the poor. They assumed that the poor were people like themselves, only without money. The neoconservatives, most of whom had been poor in their youth and nursed fewer illusions, did not make that mistake. They knew that the bourgeois work ethic was not necessarily universally shared.[16] Over time, *The Public Interest* took an interest in every imaginable obstacle to the success of a social program. For example, in education, the family environment seems to be the primary determinant of success or failure, and this is a factor that all the federal money in the world is powerless to change.[17] Writers for the journal discovered, or rediscovered, the law of unintended consequences. For instance, rent control, though well-intentioned, leads to housing shortages (because landlords have no incentive to invest). As Mark Gerson has noted, the overall focus of *The Public Interest* became "the limits of social policy," to borrow the title of an article by Nathan Glazer that appeared in *Commentary* in September 1971.[18]

Little by little, *The Public Interest* developed a comprehensive critique of social intervention, which was based on three key ideas. First, the state cannot do much to remake society. The law of unintended consequences, which initially was seen as an unfortunate but infrequent phenomenon, became almost a rule in the eyes of the contributors to *The Public Interest*. Furthermore, if by chance one succeeded in obtaining the desired results, the cost was likely to be prohibitive: "An awful lot of money was invested without accomplishing very much," as Wildavsky put it in a critique of the Great Society, which in his view went too far compared with the New Deal.[19]

The second key idea was that the state itself creates expectations that it cannot satisfy, thereby endangering stability. Moynihan put it this way in 1973: "The modern welfare state was getting into activities no one understood very well. It had not reached the point of picking every man a wife, but it was getting close enough to other such imponderables to find itself increasingly held to account for failure in areas where no government could reasonably promise success."[20]

With hopeful rhetoric and promise, liberals were guilty of encouraging expectations far in excess of the ability of the federal government to deliver. There was slippage in two dimensions: from equality of opportunity to equality of outcome, and from equality between individuals to equality between groups.

The third key idea, analogous to the problem of inflated expectations, was that the fundamental obstacle to successful state intervention was not a social or economic but a cultural phenomenon, a matter of ideas and morals. After a few years *The Public Interest* began to devote more and more space to this theme, and Kristol published a book on the subject in 1972. In it he drew in part on Bell's ideas about the "cultural contradictions of capitalism."[21] For Kristol, capitalism failed to provide a moral ideal or foundation for society. All that one asks of a capitalist is to be enterprising: it scarcely matters whether he pursues gain out of virtue or vice, because private vices become public goods. But this moral foundation crumbles and leaves nothing in its place. Consumer society encourages individualism and hedonism. Artists and intellectuals attack the engine that makes society go and propose that it be governed in accordance with the loftiest ideals, thereby endangering capitalist democracy. In Kristol's view, therefore, the moral foundation of society needed to be reinforced. There was no need to tamper with capitalism itself, however: clearly, if Kristol's reasoning had an Achilles' heel, it was here.

Moynihan as a First-Age Paradigm

One of the leading figures of first-age neoconservatism was Daniel Patrick Moynihan.[22] Moynihan is especially interesting because he would also play a role in the second age of the movement (in particular as a participant in the activities of the Coalition for a Democratic Majority between 1975 and 1980), though not in the third. In 1979 Peter Steinfels, the first to publish a book about neoconservatism, described him as "the best known of the neoconservatives."[23]

Born in 1927 to a family of Irish descent, Moynihan grew up in a poor neighborhood of New York. He, too, went to CCNY in 1943 (the "great days" of Trotskyism in alcove number 1 were over by then) and then to the Fletcher School of Diplomacy at Tufts University and the London School of Economics. He served in the Navy for several years. A Cold War liberal and early member of the ADA, he was politically active in Democratic circles and in particular served as assistant to Averell Harriman, the governor of New York, in the 1950s. But he also made his mark as an intellectual, writing for *The Reporter* on Irving Kristol's recommendation. He was named professor of political science at Syracuse University and in 1963 collaborated with Nathan Glazer on an important book, *Beyond the Melting Pot,* which looked at identity issues in a number of New York ethnic groups. Moynihan and Glazer rejected the widespread view that ethnic identities were eroding. They predicted the persistence of distinct identities and, contradicting conventional wisdom, foresaw the identity revival of the 1960s and 1970s and the problems of multiculturalism.[24]

Moynihan joined the Kennedy administration as undersecretary of labor but quit soon after Johnson came to power. Nevertheless, he remained long enough to draft a controversial report that quickly made him famous, indeed notorious: *The Negro Family: The Case for National Action* (1965). The report, which relied on extensive statistical data, called attention to economic and social problems stemming from the breakdown of the black family unit, underscoring the prevalence of absent fathers. Only part of this problem could be blamed on the legacy of slavery and persistent unemployment.

Although the Moynihan report (many of whose insights were later confirmed) sparked a vast polemic and even scandal (Moynihan was accused of racism and of blaming victims for their situation), its author remained squarely within the framework of "vital center" liberalism: he still had faith in the state's ability to act if equipped with accurate information. That was the thrust of his article on the professionalization of reform in the first issue of *The Public Interest*. He was led to reconsider his optimistic stance, however, in the wake of attacks on his report by certain liberals, as well as spreading violence in the United States (which saw riots in various cities between 1965, when rioting broke out in the Watts section of Los Angeles, and 1968), growing antiwar protest on college campuses, and proliferating social unrest.

In a series of lectures delivered in 1967, Moynihan vehemently criticized the government's community action programs. Under the auspices of the Office of Economic Opportunity, headed by Sargent Shriver, the purpose of these programs was to involve the poor in the management of projects designed to assist them. Ultimately, however, they created a parasitic class of social workers and unrepresentative community leaders, who, Moynihan argued, hijacked the program and rendered it ineffective.[25] Speaking at the Willard Hotel in Washington, D.C., to the national council of the ADA on September 23, 1967, at a time when that organization was torn between traditionalists, moderates, and reformists, Moynihan delivered an astonishing speech:

1. Liberals must see more clearly that their essential interest is in the stability of the social order; and given the present threats to that stability, they must seek out and make much more effective alliances with political conservatives who share their interest and recognize that unyielding rigidity is just as great a threat to continuity of the social order as an anarchic desire for change . . .

2. Liberals must divest themselves of the notion that the nation—and especially the cities of the nation—can be run from agencies in Washington . . .

3. Liberals must somehow overcome the curious condescension that takes the form of defending and explaining away everything, however outrageous, which Negroes, individually or collectively, might do.[26]

This speech was a milestone in the history of neoconservatism. Moynihan himself would soon practice the stability-seeking "alliance with conservatives" that he preached: he joined the Nixon administration as adviser to the president in 1969. He did not go over to the right, however. His idea was to turn Nixon into an American Disraeli, an enlightened conservative who would carry out reforms on behalf of the people and in the interest of stability. Though highly critical of Great Society programs and bureaucracy, he did not reject the basic intention of the reforms and suggested an idea to Nixon that, while ultimately not adopted, gives an indication of his state of mind: this was the Family Assistance Program (FAP), which Nixon placed at the heart of his first-term domestic agenda.

The idea was to radically reorient the Great Society by flatly eliminating nearly all the programs it had begun and replacing them with a negative income tax, a guaranteed minimum annual income for everyone below a certain poverty line (plus various incentives to encourage recipients to accept work). The FAP was to kill two birds with one stone: it would eliminate the parasitic class of social workers and the welfare-state bureaucracy, thereby pleasing conservatives, and it would increase the amount of state aid to the poor, thereby pleasing liberals. But the Senate rejected the plan, and Moynihan became more of a "court intellectual" and symbol than a genuine adviser. He then turned his attention to international affairs, as we shall see.

One final aspect of Moynihan's turn from liberalism to neoconservatism between 1965 and 1972 is worth mentioning: his change in attitude toward experts and social scientists, which can be seen in his books *Maximum Feasible Misunderstanding* (1969) and *The Politics of a Guaranteed Income* (1973). The spirit of these books is a long way from the technocratic enthusiasm of "professionalized reform." Henceforth the role of social science lay "not in the elaboration of social policy but in measuring its results."[27] In other words, reform must continue, but "professional reformers" were no longer to serve as coaches or players but rather as referees, conservative sages, or even moralists.[28] This was precisely how first-age neoconservatives saw themselves.

American Jews Caught between Two Wars

In 1967–68 the American Jewish community experienced an identity crisis in the wake of the Six-Day War and growing tensions with the black community. The political fallout from this crisis was a factor in the birth of neoconservatism, which, as we have seen, drew on the contributions of many Jewish intellectuals.[29] In this respect, although Nathan Glazer was right to say that "foreign policy was no part of early neoconservatism," international developments did feed into it by exacerbating the reaction of part of the Jewish community to the New Left.[30]

In fact it was not until after the Israeli victory in the Six-Day War that the Jewish state found itself at the top of the American Jewish community's agenda. Support for Israel had initially been dutiful and repentant (owing to guilt among American Jews that they had not done more before, during, and immediately after the Holocaust, which loomed ever larger in American Jewish consciousness).[31] Now it came to seem natural and deliberate.[32] Last but not least, the growing Soviet involvement in the Middle East made Israel a valuable, albeit problematic, partner for Washington. The convergence of American and Israeli interests allowed American Jews to combine their two interests without internal conflict.

The historian Judith Klinghoffer has stressed the interaction between the Vietnam War and the Six-Day War in the birth of neoconservatism, especially among Jewish intellectuals, and her analysis is worth summarizing here.[33] Although American Jews preferred Democrats to Republicans (owing to their minority status, to Truman's recognition of Israel in 1948, and to Eisenhower's decision to call a sudden halt to the Suez expedition led by Israel, France, and Britain in 1956), and although they voted Democratic (82 percent in favor of Kennedy in 1960, 93 percent in favor of Johnson in 1964), they were vehement in their criticism of America's growing involvement in Vietnam, because most were on the left or even radical.

Nathan Glazer and the historian Arthur Liebman give similar statistical estimates: 30 to 50 percent of the students who made up the New Left were of Jewish descent.[34] Antoine Coppolani notes that the editorial boards of New Left magazines such as *Studies on the Left, New University Thought,* and *Ramparts* were largely made up of Jews. In 1966, half of the delegates to the national convention of the Students for a Democratic Society, the main New Left organization, were Jewish. Two years earlier, a third of the participants in the Free Speech Movement at Berkeley were Jewish as well.[35]

American Jews had also been in the forefront of the black civil rights movement. In the summer of 1961, two-thirds of the "freedom riders" (young whites who joined young blacks to ride segregated buses in protest against segregation) were Jewish, and a rabbi marched hand in hand with Martin Luther King Jr. in Washington in 1963 (many future neoconservatives also took part in this march). In a broader sense, it seemed that Jews were now fully integrated into American society, and their universalist commitment to the liberal cause and to civil rights apparently reflected their growing secularization and shedding of their ethnic particularity. The press discussed the phenomenon of the "vanishing Jew," meaning the total dissolution of Jewishness in the American melting pot.

During this period, relations between Washington and Tel Aviv were chilly and distant. In those days, France was Israel's primary ally. According to Klinghoffer, Lyndon Johnson tried to obtain Tel Aviv's symbolic support for his policy in Vietnam by asking Israel to establish diplomatic ties with Saigon and to send medical aid to South Vietnam. At the time, Israel's image in the non-Arab Third World was good: it was seen as a young social democracy struggling for survival. The Jewish state therefore hesitated to give Johnson what he wanted for fear of incurring accusations that it was an agent of American imperialism. Had not Yasser Arafat of the Palestine Liberation Organization (PLO) already gone in 1964 to Peking, which supported all "wars of national liberation"? But as a result of the indirect pressure of events in Vietnam and of increased competition between the Eastern and Western blocs for influence in the Third World, the forces in the Middle East moved inexorably toward alignment with outside forces, the Arabs allying themselves firmly with the Soviet camp and Israel with the American.

At home the logic of alignment would also prevail. As the Vietnam War became increasingly controversial and the situation in the Middle East deteriorated, President Johnson became more and more irritated by the position of American Jews, who were seen as "dawks" or "hoves"—that is, "doves" on Vietnam but "hawks" on Israel. He complained bitterly to Israeli foreign minister Abba Eban that "'a bunch of rabbis' told him 'to put the whole American fleet into the Gulf of Aqaba' but objected to his sending 'a [expletive deleted] screwdriver to Vietnam.'"[36]

Within the American Jewish community, the heightened tensions in the Middle East in the spring of 1967 and then the war itself tended to mute criticism of the Vietnam War and heighten concerns about the vulnerability of Israel and the need for support from the United States. More broadly, the events of that year had a powerful impact on American Jewish identity: after the Six-Day War, "Jews became more Jewish, more religious, and much more dedicated to Israel."[37] The contours of a new war emerged: Israel was the battlefield, the United States the supply base, and the Soviet Jews prisoners of war or even hostages. Indeed, the fate of Soviet Jewry pricked the consciences of Jews in both Israel and the Diaspora and became a focal point of growing concern.[38]

These effects were reinforced by the pro-Arab and antisemitic positions taken by black militants. For instance, the June–July 1967 issue of the Student Nonviolent Coordinating Committee newsletter included a purported analysis of Arab-Israeli relations that was in fact a PLO propaganda statement, complete with antisemitic caricatures. SNCC branded Israel an "illegal state" and condemned it for having seized "Arab homes and land through terror, force, and massacres."[39] The New Left increasingly embraced the equation of Zionism with imperialism. Jewish radicals who attended the "National Conference for the New Politics" (a New Left convention held in Chicago in early September 1967) assented to a motion by black militants that condemned "the Zionist imperialist war," called for "commissions to civilize Whites," and supported the Vietcong. Many young Jewish radicals were traumatized by this turn of events and quit the movement. Among them was Martin Peretz, who became the editor of the *New Republic* in 1974 and moved that magazine in a neoconservative direction.[40] The irony was that the Chicago convention had been funded mainly by Jewish Americans. In *Commentary,* Nathan Glazer launched ad-hominem attacks on Jewish intellectuals who agreed to support black radicals calling for war on Israel (the similarity to Tom Wolfe's satire of "radical chic" is striking).[41]

On the liberal side, confusion reigned. Arthur Schlesinger refused to sign a petition demanding that Johnson maintain freedom of navigation in the Gulf of Aqaba and that he intervene to save Israel. He explained that, since he opposed unilateral intervention in one part of the world (Vietnam), it was difficult for him to support unilateral intervention in another part of the world. Galbraith, another "moderate" ADA liberal, gave the same reason for not signing, adding that he also found the wording of the petition "too harsh."[42] But fifty-four intellectuals of various political persuasions did sign, and the document was published in the *New York Times* on June 7. Among the signers were many luminaries of the nascent neoconservative movement: Pat Moynihan, Daniel Bell, Nathan Glazer, Irving Kristol, Seymour Martin Lipset, Richard Pipes, Norman Podhoretz. Some who signed were not neoconservatives, such as Michael Harrington, Milton Friedman, Elia Kazan, and Hannah Arendt.[43]

Another petition, published a few days earlier, on June 4, was titled "Our Moral Responsibility in the Middle East" and signed by only three members of the group Clergy and Laymen, one of whom was Martin Luther King. It was also signed by Reinhold Niebuhr, but on the whole the response of the Christian clergy was weak.[44] By contrast, the Six-Day War marked the conservative right's first real embrace of Israel: the John Birch Society collected $300,000 for the United Jewish Appeal, while Hearst newspapers celebrated Israel's victory.[45] Fundamentalist Christians rejoiced in the return of the Jews to Jerusalem, which they took to be a fulfillment of biblical prophecy. This was the beginning of the convergence of the Christian right, still in gestation, and the neoconservatives, in the process of being born: it was Zionism that brought them together.

Judith Klinghoffer argues that because of America's ambivalent response to the appeals of American Jews when Israel's survival was at stake, many Jewish intellectuals concluded that they had blundered in opposing the Vietnam War. The real threat was not American imperialism but American isolationism. The threat stemmed from U.S. unwillingness to defend freedom from the machinations of the Soviet Union, which had revealed its true visage by supporting Nasser in Egypt and by increased persecution of Soviet Jews. Support American power so that it can in turn defend Israel: that was the lesson learned in 1967. To be sure, one also finds the reverse argument—defend Israel in order to consolidate American power in the region—in all three ages of neoconservatism, advanced in particular by Pat Moynihan, Scoop Jackson, Jeane Kirkpatrick, Penn Kemble, Michael Novak, and many other non-Jewish neoconservatives. The need for a strong America—morally as well as militarily strong—to defend democracy all over the world implied the need to defend not only Israel but also Taiwan and South Korea, as well as to intervene in Bosnia, Kosovo, Afghanistan, and elsewhere.

The Ocean Hill–Brownsville Affair

A second event, domestic rather than foreign, also helped to move certain Jewish intellectuals toward neoconservatism and away from the New Left and even, in some cases, away from liberalism: the breakdown of relations between the Jewish community and the black community.[46] Many Jews had participated in the "universalistic" struggle for civil rights and thought of themselves as one oppressed minority allied with another, but growing antisemitic sentiment in a part of the black community put an end to this alliance. The explanation of black antisemitism must be sought not only in opposition to Israel and imperialism but also in purely local conflicts. The most radical elements in the black community, such as the Black Panthers, denounced Jews as oppressors—at least in the cities of the Northeast. They were not allies but landlords to whom the rent had to be paid, merchants who sold products at exorbitant prices, and civil servants who took the place of blacks in jobs such as schoolteacher and welfare worker. "In other words, some blacks felt that Jews were prospering at their expense."[47]

Indeed, many of the whites with whom urban blacks came into contact happened to be Jews (welfare workers, teachers, officials, and the like). In New York City in particular, blacks wanted to control their own schools, in which most of the teachers were white. Such a change would entail a wholesale overhaul of the system of teacher assignment. The city's school board decided to allow "local control" of three schools, effectively handing power over to the black community. Between May and November 1968, the experiment degenerated into open conflict between blacks and Jews in the Ocean Hill–Brownsville section of Brooklyn. Tensions ran high, Jewish teachers went out on strike, demonstrations were held, insults flew, and antisemitic pamphlets circulated in the black community. There were even a few violent incidents. Relations between the two communities broke down entirely, and the effects of this breakdown spread far beyond the communities immediately involved. Because the New Left and many liberals supported the black community in the Ocean Hill–Brownsville affair, some Jewish observers came to the conclusion that the New Left was opposed to Jewish community interests across the board. Here was yet another reason to oppose the New Left.

Did American Jews move to the right, however? In 1972 Irving Kristol wrote an article titled "Why Jews Turn Conservative." He predicted that Jewish voters would vote in larger numbers than usual for the Republican candidate, Richard Nixon, in the November presidential election. (His prediction turned out to be correct: Humphrey had won 81 percent of the Jewish vote in 1968, but McGovern got only 64 percent in 1972. Subsequent history would prove Kristol wrong, however: apart from Reagan, no Republican won as much as 40 percent of the Jewish vote, and between 1992 and 2008 the Republican share of the Jewish vote varied from 10 to 25 percent.) The reason the Jews had distanced themselves from the left, Kristol explained, was to be sought not among the Jews but rather among the leftists. The New Left, inspired by Mao, Che Guevara, and Eldridge Cleaver (one of the founders of the Black Panthers), was neither liberal nor humanist. On the contrary, it tended toward totalitarianism, and in its utopia there was no place for Jews— witness the movement's growing sympathy for the Arab states despite episodes like the massacre of Israeli athletes at the Olympic Games in Munich a few weeks earlier. In short, it was the left that had rejected the Jews, not the other way around. Slowly but surely, Jews therefore moved toward a moderate conservatism that was "perfectly compatible with a care for social reform." Kristol saved his best shot for last, however, concluding his article with this prediction:

Jewish influence has never been primarily a matter of votes or money. Jews are important out of all relation to their population or wealth because they have such extraordinary talents in the intellectual and cultural spheres. It may be naive to think that Jews can offer political conservatism, both in the US and Israel and elsewhere, an intellectual vigor and cultural buoyancy it has so sadly lacked until now. It may be naive to think so—but it is now possible to think that, whereas only yesterday it was unimaginable.[48]

One may smile at the ingenuousness of Kristol's article: he was obviously describing not the political evolution of Jews but the political evolution of Irving Kristol. Moderate conservatism that was "perfectly compatible with a care for social reform" was neoconservatism. And the "intellectual vigor" to be imparted to ignorant conservatives would come from Kristol himself. Had he not dined with President Nixon only two years after serving as a campaign adviser to Hubert Humphrey? As he wrote this article, was he not in the process of taking a leave from his post as "professor of urban values" at New York University to take up residence as a scholar at the American Enterprise Institute, a think tank associated with right-wing businessmen?

Be that as it may, Kristol's account of the rejection of the New Left by certain liberal Jewish intellectuals was accurate. But most did not venture beyond neoconservatism on the model of the Coalition for a Democratic Majority. They were pleased to cling to "vital center" liberalism, to remain Democrats while adopting hawkish and anti–New Left positions. Within the CDM, as we shall see, they attempted to turn the Democratic party away from the New Left and back toward the old. The simple reason for all this was that Jews were fundamentally Democrats: to vote Republican was to feel torn within. For a Jew to vote Republican, as Kristol did as early as 1972, was, in his own terms, the equivalent of eating pork on Yom Kippur.[49]

Commentary Turns Neoconservative

Nowhere was the political impact of the events of 1967 and 1968 on the Jewish community more obvious than in the magazine *Commentary*, whose political position began to shift in June 1967, culminating in an embrace of neoconservatism in June 1970 (although the term "neoconservatism" was not yet in common use). Along with *The Public Interest*, *Commentary* was the publication in which first-age neoconservatism made its mark. Indeed, *Commentary* stood out because it did not hesitate to publish articles on foreign policy or culture (which was one of its specialties), nor did it turn its back on highly polemical political pieces. To understand how the magazine helped to define first-age neoconservatism, one has to look at the biography of the man who became its editor-in-chief in 1960, Norman Podhoretz, because from 1960 to 1995, or indeed to 2008, the magazine's intellectual and political fate was entirely bound up with its editor's (the American Jewish Committee, which owned *Commentary*, was and is in no way a neoconservative organization and did not interfere with its editorial content).[50]

In contrast to many first-age neoconservatives, Podhoretz had not been a Trotskyist or even a radical in his youth. He was a child prodigy who worked hard to succeed. It was not until the early 1960s that this liberal went through a radical phase (unrelated to the radicalism of the Trotskyists of alcove number 1) before gradually moving to the right.

Born in 1930, hence younger than the *Public Interest* generation (born between 1919 and 1924), Norman Podhoretz began his studies at Columbia University at the age of sixteen (despite the continued existence of a "Jewish quota" limiting the number of Jews to 17 percent of the student body).[51] He was encouraged to do so by his parents, modest immigrants (his father was a milkman) who lived in Brooklyn and were determined to see their son succeed. His exceptional intellectual talent won him a Pulitzer scholarship. Politically, he was a "1930s liberal" when he enrolled at Columbia, suspicious of America and rather sympathetic to the Soviet Union; but by the time he graduated he had become a true Cold War liberal, anticommunist and optimistic about America. He obtained bachelor's and master's degrees at Cambridge University, where he had to contend against European stereotypes of the United States, and this experience cured him of any residual anti-Americanism.

Meanwhile, at Columbia he had met the man he wished to emulate: Lionel Trilling, the first Jew to be appointed a professor of English literature at Columbia and a brilliant literary critic. Trilling and F. W. Dupee, another professor who was important to the young Podhoretz, quickly recognized his talent and lent him their goodwill and support. Podhoretz desired two things above all others: recognition from his fellow intellectuals and from literary New York, as well as the fame and material benefits that went along with it. His overwhelming drive to succeed, which was all too evident in his first autobiographical work, *Making It,* published in 1967, was also his Achilles' heel. Enemies such as Sidney Blumenthal would mock him for it mercilessly even long after publication.[52]

After finishing his studies at Cambridge, which had bored him, Podhoretz hastened back to New York. In 1952 a visit to the offices of *Commentary,* arranged by Lionel Trilling, changed his life. Eliot Cohen (the magazine's first editor), Kristol, and Glazer were all working there at the time. This was where he wanted to work, too: at the center of the New York intellectual world. He was unable really to settle down until 1960: he served in the military in Germany in 1953–1955; published book reviews, most notably of William Faulkner and Saul Bellow, which set off several literary storms and brought him notoriety; and worked at *Commentary* for two years before resigning because of difficult relations with Eliot Cohen. He was living in straitened circumstances when he married Midge Decter, a writer and the mother of two young children from a previous marriage. He eagerly accepted work offered by Kristol and an old friend from Columbia, Jason Epstein, who had acquired an influential position in the publishing world. Finally, in 1960, he took the reins at *Commentary,* with a promise of full editorial freedom. He would remain in charge at the magazine until 1995, after which he continued in the post of "editor-at-large." In 2009 his son, John, took over as editor.

It was upon assuming the editorship of *Commentary* that Podhoretz, the "celebrationist" anticommunist liberal, went through a brief—and superficial—radical utopian phase, taking the magazine in the same direction.[53] He attached great importance to de-Stalinization: although he remained an anticommunist, he felt that the Soviet danger had receded somewhat and that American intellectuals could allow themselves to explore ideas such as pacifism and nuclear arms control. With Nathan Glazer and David Riesman he even became active in the antinuclear organization SANE (National Committee for a Sane Nuclear Policy). He defended his utopianism against other intellectuals, including Trilling and Dupee (who disapproved), and proposed that America needed to undergo a revolution in the name of humanitarian idealism. As editor of *Commentary,* he experienced the adolescent rebellion that years of diligent study had repressed. In the early 1960s he mingled with a small group of East Coast radicals, from Marcus Raskin, who founded the Institute for Policy Studies (a markedly left-wing foreign policy think tank), to Norman Mailer and Noam Chomsky. He attacked certain liberal dogmas such as the need for a larger federal government, greater centralization, and economic growth, and instead called for more community and for humanization of industrial society (essentially advocating for "small is beautiful" before the slogan became fashionable).[54]

While continuing to publish sharply anticommunist pieces by Sidney Hook and other members of the Congress for Cultural Freedom, Podhoretz opened the pages of *Commentary* to anarchists, progressives, and democratic socialists, including Herbert Marcuse, Michael Harrington, David Riesman, and revisionist historians of the Cold War.[55] More than that, he published the best parts of Paul Goodman's *Growing Up Absurd,* one of the fundamental references of the counterculture, which he persuaded Jason Epstein to publish at Random House (it had been rejected by nineteen other publishers).[56] The book became a best-seller. In it, Goodman argued that students had become alienated from American society because not only was it incapable of inspiring them with an ideal worthy of enthusiasm or interest but, worse, it oppressed them. They ceased to belong to themselves and became slaves to the blandishments of the "affluent society." *Commentary* was the first magazine to take a serious interest in the New Left, even before Epstein and his wife Barbara created the *New York Review of Books* in 1963. Until 1968 or so, the two publications featured more or less the same writers. Everyone was talking about Podhoretz's "new *Commentary,*" and in six years the magazine's circulation increased from 20,000 to 60,000.[57]

Nevertheless, Podhoretz's radicalism never went very far. For one thing, the magazine maintained a balanced position on major domestic and foreign policy issues. For another, Podhoretz himself was not prepared to accept just any utopia: he remained attached to common sense and to the traditional virtues of self-fulfillment, middle America, and the common people and rejected state-centered utopian schemes (including liberal ones) as well as nihilistic dead ends. Was he not the author of "The Know-Nothing Bohemians," an attack on the Beat generation, especially Jack Kerouac and Allen Ginsberg, that appeared in the *Partisan Review* in 1958?[58] He was critical of the Beats for their nihilism and their inability to think coherently or to live coherent lives, which in his view accounted for their exaggerated contempt for the bourgeoisie and the ideal of success. Despite his interest in the New Left, he refused to publish an early version of the Port Huron Statement in *Commentary* in 1962 on the grounds that it was very badly written and watered down ideas that had already been brilliantly expressed by Goodman and

Riesman—in short, it was not only intellectually uninteresting but, even worse, used its self-professed humanism to hide an authoritarian penchant for telling Americans what was best for them.[59]

Transitions at *Commentary*

The years 1964–1970 were marked by two events that strongly affected the evolution of *Commentary:* the severe criticism, and in some cases mockery, that attended the publication of Podhoretz's autobiography *Making It,* and the bitter war of intellectuals that erupted between *Commentary* and the *New York Review of Books.*[60] The *NYRB* positioned itself to the left of *Commentary.* For instance, in late 1964 Podhoretz asked Nathan Glazer to write an article for *Commentary* on the Berkeley Free Speech Movement. Glazer refused because the *NYRB* had already commissioned an article. Later the *NYRB* changed its mind because two other Berkeley professors, John Schaar and Sheldon Wolin, had already written a piece in favor of the student movement, which came out soon thereafter.[61] Over the next two years the *NYRB* took a much more radical line than *Commentary,* especially in its opposition to the war in Vietnam.

In fact the two publications proceeded in opposite directions, as the *NYRB* turned more radical in 1964–65 (Jason Epstein becoming an enthusiastic supporter of the student movement), while Norman Podhoretz and *Commentary* moved back toward the center. Podhoretz had been shaken to see his radical ideas reduced to caricature in the Port Huron Statement. He was even more horrified to see them transformed (or deformed) into militant actions at Berkeley in 1964. Nevertheless, he was strongly opposed to the war and supported Eugene McCarthy, who challenged Johnson for the Democratic presidential nomination in 1968 (before Johnson decided not to run for reelection). But the campaign left a bitter taste in his mouth. It was then, he wrote, that he discovered "radical chic" (wealthy young people playing at radicalism) *avant la lettre*—Tom Wolfe would not coin the expression until two years later.[62]

In 1967–68 the Six-Day War and the Ocean Hill–Brownsville affair brought Podhoretz and *Commentary* to a pivotal moment. The time of "universalistic" struggles on behalf of other groups was over. The "ingratitude" of blacks led Podhoretz to focus on his own interests and the interests of Israel. The unforgivable sin would be to allow a second Holocaust to occur. The inward turn of the Jewish community in general was particularly striking in Podhoretz, who began to apply a new litmus test to all political judgments: "Is it good for the Jews?" It was not simply a question of worrying about Jewish interests but of considering all political issues in light of the consequences for Jews: "That is to say, I think that Jews must once again begin to look at proposals and policies from the point of view of the Jewish interest, and must once again begin to ask what the consequences, if any, of any proposal or policy are likely to be so far as the Jewish position is concerned."[63]

Podhoretz also established a link between antisemitism and anti-Americanism: the same radical intellectuals who criticized Israel also detested the United States. Leftist intellectuals who despised the values of middle America were also antisemites, because Jews embodied those values; they were the very incarnation of "Americanism," models of successful integration.[64] The quota issue also figured in the establishment of a link between foreign policy and domestic policy. Podhoretz told of being invited to Harvard to speak to the dean of admissions and his staff. He began by saying that he supported all efforts to help blacks attend Harvard but denounced the quota system as inherently racist, which made his audience uncomfortable:

> As a liberal I believed in the traditional principle of treating individuals as individuals and not as members of a group; as a Jew, I feared that a quota system designed to overcome discrimination against blacks would almost certainly result in discrimination against Jews—and I could not bring myself to believe that the only way to achieve social justice in the United States was to discriminate against my own children; and as an intellectual, I worried about the lowering and erosion of standards entailed by any system of reverse discrimination.[65]

But he also had another reason for taking his distance from radicalism. Too many Jews had participated in the protests of the 1960s, and a backlash against the protests had begun to develop among middle Americans. Podhoretz feared that this reaction might turn antisemitic. Walter Laqueur, a frequent contributor to *Commentary*, expressed this fear explicitly in February 1971.[66] Indeed, similar fears had long been harbored by the American Jewish community because of its strong involvement in politics, but nothing had ever come of them. Nevertheless, they recurred regularly, during World War II, in the 1970s when U.S. intervention on behalf of Israel provoked an oil embargo, at the time of the 1991 Gulf War, and in connection with the invasion of Iraq (2003).

To be sure, many Jews rejected the idea that Jewishness and left-wing politics were incompatible. For instance, Louis Harap, writing in the left-wing magazine *Jewish Currents,* was critical of Podhoretz's paranoid dramatization of the situation and challenged *Commentary*'s right to decide "what is good for the Jews." In conclusion he noted what had become obvious: "In effect, *Commentary*'s campaign against the left of necessity drives it toward the right."[67]

The "campaign" of which Harap spoke began in June 1970, after Podhoretz returned from a leave he had taken to write a book. By the time he emerged from his retreat, he had clarified his ideas and decided to launch "all-out war" on the New Left. To be sure, the magazine's politics had begun to turn as early as the mid-1960s. Attacks on "the Movement" (a catchall term for the New Left, the counterculture, radicals, and so on) became increasingly common in its pages. These included Glazer's critique of the Free Speech Movement, Bayard Rustin's attack on the Black Panthers, Diana Trilling's criticism of the Columbia student rebellion, and articles asserting that certain Great Society antipoverty programs were failures.[68] As Garry Dorrien has noted, however, these articles had previously been counterbalanced by attacks on the war in Vietnam or inequality in America by Robert Heilbroner, Noam Chomsky (who was still publishing in *Commentary* in 1969), and Norman Mailer.[69]

After June 1970, critiques of the latter type disappeared entirely from the pages of *Commentary.* Podhoretz himself took up his pen to lead his troops in the offensive against the New Left. One of their methods of attack was the portrait—which was usually a caricature. For instance, Dorothy Rabinowitz published portraits of the "radicalized professor" and the "activist cleric." Midge Decter portrayed "the liberated woman," whose principal demand was for the freedom of the spoiled child, the freedom that does not exist: freedom from all moral and material limitations.[70]

Yet by June 1970 radical leftist activism was on the wane. Hundreds of thousands of soldiers had been withdrawn from Vietnam since the beginning of Nixon's Vietnamization program in 1969. Peter Steinfels concluded that neoconservatism was striking out "at a force already on the decline."[71] What *Commentary* was fighting, he continued, was a less deadly but more diffuse and therefore more ambiguous enemy, a "spirit" from which all sorts of symptoms were supposed to have emanated: feminism, Ralph Nader's consumer activism, the American Civil Liberties Union, ecology, muckraking journalism, what have you.

Commentary bolstered its offensive against the New Left with careful, detailed critiques of welfare-state programs—a tried-and-true neoconservative approach. Articles of this sort were a less central, less systematic part of *Commentary*'s editorial line than of *The Public Interest*'s, but they were a regular feature, exemplified most notably by the contributions of Aaron Wildavsky.[72] Then, in 1972–73, *Commentary* moved seamlessly to issues associated with the second age of neoconservatism, doing battle on two fronts against isolationism in the Democratic party and détente in the Republican administration while simultaneously challenging procedural changes in the Democratic party's selection process. In fact it was Norman Podhoretz, with help from Midge Decter, who wrote the original draft of the founding manifesto of the Coalition for a Democratic Majority, "Come Home, Democrats."

"Neoconservatism": The Origins of a Political Label

> I am not sure at all that I did in fact "coin" the word. It was in common use among *Dissent* editors and others associates of mine, and I do not have the least idea who was the first to use it. It was occasioned, not by some tempest in a sectarian teapot, but by the fact that a sea change was taking place in the intellectual world—for instance, the *Commentary* magazine which published my first article on poverty in 1959 was in the process of a profound transformation—and in the Democratic Party.[73]

So said Michael Harrington in 1989, puncturing a widespread myth, since it was Harrington who was generally credited with, if not coining the word "neoconservative," at least giving it its contemporary meaning. Seymour Martin Lipset had contributed to the myth by asserting that the word had been coined for "tactical" purposes: Harrington supposedly brandished the epithet as a weapon with which to discredit right-wing socialists, to stigmatize them while at the same time burnishing his own "progressive" credentials with the young militants of the New Left in the course of a factional struggle inside the old Socialist party of Eugene Debs and Norman Thomas in 1972.[74] The split that divided the Socialists in that year was not very different from that which afflicted organizations such as the ADA and even the Democratic party from the mid-1960s onward: the conflict centered upon the issue of what attitude to adopt toward the New Left.

One faction of the Socialist party condemned the war in Vietnam. Led by Harrington and Irving Howe, it broke from the main party and established relations with younger New Left militants. Another faction, led by Max Shachtman (whose anticommunist fervor led him to support the Vietnam War) and the unions (which were influenced by close ties between the AFL-CIO and trade unions in South Vietnam), took over the party and renamed it Social Democrats USA (SDUSA).[75] Many neoconservatives would in fact derive their origins from this latter faction.

Among the elders who led or inspired the SDUSA were Sidney Hook, Shachtman, Emanuel Muravchik (a well-known Socialist and union leader and the father of Joshua Muravchik), Paul Seabury, John Roche, and Bayard Rustin. Among the young activists of the SDUSA were Carl Gershman (who for more than twenty-five years would direct the National Endowment for Democracy, created under Reagan), Rachelle Horowitz, Tom Kahn, Penn Kemble, his sister Eugenia, Joshua Muravchik, Arch Puddington, Linda Chavez, Norm and Valery Hill, David Jessup, Max Green, and Sandra Feldman. Young or old, Michael Harrington was right to observe that their opposition to the Vietnam War and contempt for the New Left and the "new class" in general (they preferred blue-collar workers, trade unionists, "real people") was combined with a fairly timid "socialist" politics that rarely went beyond the short-term demands of the AFL-CIO and eschewed grandiose ambitions to eliminate poverty and inequality.

As we have seen, Michael Harrington denied having coined the word "neoconservatism" as a weapon against the right wing of the Socialist party. In fact his first use of the term "neoconservative," in an article titled "The Welfare State and Its Neoconservative Critics" that appeared in *Dissent* in the fall of 1973, confirms his assertion.[76] The piece was a critique of first-age neoconservatives such as Nathan Glazer, Pat Moynihan, and Daniel Bell, who cast doubt on the usefulness of social policy. There was not a word about the Shachtmanites or the SDUSA. Harrington believed that the neoconservatives' unrelenting insistence on the complexities of social policy had itself turned into a form of simplistic reasoning. He was critical of their broad generalizations, their lack of respect for the facts when the facts didn't suit them (a criticism that stung contributors to *The Public Interest,* who prided themselves on accuracy and thoroughness), their hasty judgments, and their tendency to exaggerate their criticisms and create straw men (such as the ambitions of the federal government, which, as we saw earlier, Moynihan mocked as wanting to "choose a woman for every man"). He concluded:

> Insofar as the abstract and unhistorical view of the welfare state propounded by the neoconservatives persuades us to timidity and acquiescence, it is not preparing the way for the miraculous resurrection of *Gemeinschaft*. It is, for all the decency and intelligence of its proponents, unwittingly doing the work of the reactionaries who will have unchallenged dominance over the collectivism of the 21st century, once the people are persuaded that they are impotent.[77]

What, then, is the true date of the birth of neoconservatism? Everything depends on the kind of neoconservatism one has in mind. Some authors, such as Mark Gerson and Jacob Heilbrunn, argue that neoconservatism was born in the 1950s, with the anticommunist liberals of the Cold War.[78] This explanation is not convincing. The Cold War liberals were undeniably precursors of the neoconservatives, but they do not count as neoconservatives in the strict sense, because they remained within the basic contours of liberalism. Neoconservatism was a reaction. It was born in a battle over the legacy of liberalism, which had fragmented, with a majority of liberals moving to the left. Neoconservatism could not emerge until liberalism had entered its crisis phase. It took a rapid series of events (the civil rights movement, the student revolt, the war in Vietnam, and so forth) to launch the protest movements of the 1960s and the New Left. Interventionist liberalism also had to run its course, culminating in the vastly ambitious social programs of the Great Society.

The earliest date that can plausibly be proposed for the birth of neoconservatism is 1965. It was then that *The Public Interest* commenced publication. Nineteen sixty-five was also the year after the inception of the Berkeley Free Speech Movement, which saw certain former Trotskyist professors such as Nathan Glazer and Seymour Martin Lipset launch an ideological attack on the New Left and the counterculture—in return for which they were labeled "new conservatives." A second possible date is 1967, the year in which the first clearly neoconservative articles (emphasizing the counterproductive nature of certain social programs and denouncing the bureaucratization of social assistance and the like) appeared in *The Public Interest.* In June 1967 the Six-Day War broke out, imparting a shock to the Jewish community and swelling the ranks of liberal opponents of the radical anti-Zionist left. Finally, it was in September 1967 that Pat Moynihan delivered his celebrated speech to the ADA at the Willard Hotel in Washington.

A third possible birth date is 1970. Only one significant event took place in that year: the neoconservative turn of *Commentary,* which came in June. But 1970 may also be taken as a symbolic date marking the cumulative growth of neoconservatism, which had reached the threshold of existence as an autonomous movement at the culmination of a decade of protest, counterculture, and the New Left, against which it was reacting. Like Lipset, Podhoretz believes that the term "neoconservative" came into common use in the late 1960s.[79] He says that he himself used it in 1963, when he was still on the left, to attack Walter Lippmann and Clinton Rossiter on the grounds that they were too pessimistic about the potential of certain social programs because they were too aware of the complexity of human nature. My view is that the term did not come into widespread public use until the advent of the third age of neoconservatism, and that it did not begin to gain currency among a small intellectual elite until 1972 at the earliest.

Indeed, 1972 is the latest date that can be advanced for the birth of neoconservatism. It has the advantage of bringing together the first two ages of the movement: this was the year in which the Coalition for a Democratic Majority was launched in the wake of George McGovern's capture of the Democratic presidential nomination. The same year also marks the beginning of the struggle against both isolationism and détente, along with efforts to move the Democratic party back to the center. By this time, however, first-age neoconservatism had already achieved a certain maturity. It had produced a body of work, most of it published in *The Public Interest* and *Commentary.* It had identified friends and enemies. It had moved toward the right.

In any case, before the *Dissent* articles of 1972–73 (which did not use the term "neoconservative" until the fall of 1973; the editors of the journal preferred "new conservatives"), we find the hyphenated form "neo-conservative" in the *Wall Street Journal* in the spring of 1972, referring to "Irving Kristol and friends."[80] A year and a half before the oft-quoted Harrington article cited above, the columnist Robert Bartley, who would soon become editor of the *Journal*'s op-ed page, a place where neoconservatives would frequently express themselves, pointed to a "distinct group of thinkers that is distinctly identifiable but lacking a good label" in the course of a review of Kristol's *On the Democratic Idea in America*.[81] Casting about for a label, he considered several possibilities: "the *Public Interest* crowd" (too narrow), "the radical centrists" (too confusing), and "the neo-Whigs" (too imprecise). Despite the fact that certain members of the group discarded any label that incorporated the word "conservative," Bartley, who rejected Herman Kahn's suggestion "conservationists," opted for "neo-conservatives" as the most appropriate choice, in particular because it emphasized the difference from the conservative movement. In the same article, Bartley suggested that the "neoconservatives" offered the Republican party a chance to break the Democratic monopoly on intellectual talent and even to constitute an establishment of its own. Stressing the new group's astonishing influence, well beyond what the number of its members would suggest, he concluded: "This is why, when the intellectual history of the 1960's is ultimately written, we may find that the event of most lasting significance was not the advent of a new radicalism but the evolution of a new and newly relevant conservatism."[82]

Indeed, if liberals and radicals were prompt to denounce the neoconservatives' turn to the right, conservatives were no less attentive to what was going on. In November 1970 Bartley had already written an article in praise of Podhoretz's rightward turn at *Commentary*. Although he deplored the confusion of labels and categories (what was called "conservative" in Manhattan, he remarked, would seldom pass for conservative anywhere else), Bartley observed that "after years of demoralization, a pro-American type of intellectual is starting to speak up, to launch vigorous counterattacks on the chic radicalism, to debunk the debunkers."[83] Better yet—or worse yet from the standpoint of the newly labeled neoconservatives, most of whom still considered themselves liberals—the very right-wing *National Review* welcomed them in March 1971 with an editorial ironically titled "Come On In, the Water's Fine."[84] This appeal was meant to minimize the differences between the hard right and the intellectuals, most of whom, like Podhoretz, still choked at the mere mention of Richard Nixon's name.[85]

These accolades from people who had only recently been political enemies (and perhaps still were) were not always welcome, any more than the label "neoconservative," which really caught on in the second half of the 1970s. From 1972 to 1980 the term slowly worked its way into the public consciousness, in a process well described by Seymour Martin Lipset:

> Labels determine reactions to those labeled, whether they are described as psychotic, communist or conservative. In the case of the neo-conservatives, the label led many of our former friends and allies, for whom "conservative" is an invidious term, to reject us. Conversely, the label led many genuine traditional conservatives and business people, long unhappy about their limited support among intellectuals, to welcome as new allies this group of prominent intellectuals who, they were told, had come over to their side. We "neo-conservatives" found ourselves rejected by our old friends and welcomed by our opponents. Having lost substantial sources of income from the traditional supporters of left intellectuals, including universities and magazines, we found ourselves (often unwittingly) the beneficiaries of support from the right. This frequently included substantial lecture and writing fees and appreciative audiences—particularly when the neo-conservatives dealt with issues on which they and the conservatives agreed, including politics, foreign policy, affirmative-action quotas and the need for higher moral standards.[86]

In fact, although Irving Kristol would embrace and appropriate the term after 1975, most of his neoconservative colleagues still rejected it.[87] Pat Moynihan contended that he was the modern incarnation of a Wilsonian Progressive. Daniel Bell described himself as a right-wing social democrat, explaining that he was "a socialist in economics, a liberal in politics, and a conservative in culture" (Kristol suggested that he represented the "social-democratic wing" of neoconservatism).[88] As late as 1979, Podhoretz chose the label "centrist" or "liberal centrist."[89]

The Seven Pillars of Neoconservative Wisdom

But what were the precise contours of first-age neoconservatism? As we have seen, the sensibility of the early neoconservatives was based on reaction—to student protest, the counterculture, and the New Left. With this impetus they gradually built a coherent corpus of ideas, mainly published in *The Public Interest* and *Commentary*. We can sum up those ideas as follows.[90]

1. America was in crisis. Confidence in its institutions and elites had been undermined. The most urgent task was no longer to reform the

country. Reform, though not abandoned, was relegated to the background. The urgent task of the moment was rather to restore social stability and strengthen liberal civilization, which was threatened by New Left radicalism and the counterculture. Democracy itself was menaced with "overload," with a "democratic distemper" that threatened to make the country ungovernable, as Samuel Huntington argued in 1975.[91] Like the founding fathers, first-age neoconservatives were cautious in their approach to democracy. Its role was to safeguard liberty and allow elites to govern with the consent of the people.

2. The crisis was above all moral and cultural, a matter of ideas. America's socioeconomic framework was fairly decent, all things considered. The real issue was the decay of values, the decline of moral standards, and the corruption of manners as a result of the rise of an "adversary culture" (to borrow Lionel Trilling's expression), that is, the self-assertion of the individual in opposition to social constraints. This led to contempt for social conventions and for an "ordinary" life built around family, community, and work. These had been replaced by individualism and hedonism. The "moral capital" on which capitalist democracy depended had been eroded by the counterculture and the process of secularization. Capitalism by itself was incapable of engendering the civic virtues that democracy needed in order to survive.[92]

3. The breeding ground for these upheavals was "the new class." Here we find the revival of a concept that had figured in Trotskyist debates in the 1930s, updated by David Bazelon, a New York intellectual, in 1966.[93] As the economic structure evolved and power depended less on private property and more on the control of large organizations, a "new class" of managers had appeared—a new elite that encompassed the students of the baby-boom generation who filled American campuses in the 1960s (between 1920 and 1972, the number of university students rose from 48,000 to more than 600,000, with more than a quarter of that growth between 1965 and 1970). Interventionist liberalism could be interpreted as a rationalization of the interests of this class, a way of increasing their power by multiplying the institutions they dominated. This "new class" of intellectuals, academics, bureaucrats, social workers, managers, consultants, lawyers, and so forth therefore promoted an agenda very different from that of the Old Left. It abandoned the bread-and-butter trade-union issues of the working class (wages, hours, and the like) in favor of new issues (such as identity, morals, social values, minority rights, and the like). These new issues reflected the thinking of

"spoiled children" contemptuous of bourgeois family life and secular in their values and tastes.

4. The state had fallen victim to "inflated expectations." This was one reason for the crisis of authority. People expected the federal government to improve social and economic conditions in ways that the government could not meet. These inflated expectations could be traced back to the undue optimism of the liberals who came into power with the election of John F. Kennedy and, more generally, to the political strategy and egalitarian ideas of the "new class." The state was now supposed to ensure not only equality of opportunity but also equality of outcome, especially between groups. Here we see the influence of Tocqueville and his idea of envy, resentment, and egalitarian passion as threats to social stability.

5. The state's capacity for action was limited. One reason for this was the sheer complexity of life: because man knows so little about the world, his ability to change it is limited. Neoconservatives were suspicious of ambitious political programs. Centralized social engineering was unlikely to succeed. Its scope was limited by human nature itself and by culture. Hence it was best to be cautious and modest in developing any social policy and moderate in one's expectations, especially in view of the law of unintended consequences. Conversely, traditional social institutions must be respected and preserved. Even if they did not seem rational at first sight, they embodied the wisdom of longevity.

On the last two points, it is worth noting that although Kristol, Podhoretz, and Wildavsky were sharply critical of Johnson's Great Society, other neoconservatives were more cautious.[94] Some Great Society programs were ill-conceived and had indeed aroused inflated expectations (ultimately contributing to a general impression of failure) and in some cases had led to undesirable outcomes. But Michael Harrington was right to remind Pat Moynihan that 70 percent of the increase in social spending had gone to broadly accepted programs inspired by the New Deal and defended by neoconservatives: these included Social Security, Medicare, and Medicaid. Overall, poverty in America had been reduced by almost 50 percent, so that in all fairness the War on Poverty would have to be judged at least half successful.[95]

6. "Intellectuals" are not "experts." First-age neoconservatives took a very negative view of "intellectuals," a view that can be traced back not only to the British and Scottish Enlightenment and Edmund Burke, in opposition to the continental Enlightenment, but also to Tocqueville and his portrayal of "men of letters" in the French Revolution. This

was not anti-intellectualism but, in Peter Steinfels's phrase, "counter-intellectualism," that is, opposition to the role of intellectuals as systematic challengers of the status quo.[96] In contrast to the intellectual ("a man who speaks with general authority on a subject about which he has no particular competence" in Kristol's definition), who was invariably described as hypocritical, elitist, self-obsessed, secretly anxious about his social status, and the like, the neoconservatives favored experts or scholars, the famous "professionals of reform," technocrats who put their knowledge at the service of the government and who defended democratic institutions and social stability against the radicals.[97] Kristol evoked "the men who regularly commute to Washington, who help draw up programs for reorganizing the bureaucracy, who evaluate proposed weapons systems, who figure out ways to improve our cities and assist our poor, who analyze the course of economic growth, who reckon the cost and effectiveness of foreign aid programs, who dream up new approaches to such old social programs as the mental health of the aged, etc., etc."[98]

7. Freedom of thought was threatened in the universities. First-age neoconservatives were quick to diagnose the early signs of "political correctness" and were shocked by the uniformity of thought that reigned on college campuses and by the lack of intellectual courage displayed by liberals. Whether the issue was race, Vietnam, urban policy, the influence of heredity on intelligence, the condition of women, ecology, homosexuality, or Richard Nixon, New Left orthodoxy brooked no challenge, and anyone who proposed a "deviant" idea was branded a racist or fascist. James Q. Wilson, while telling of teaching at many different institutions over the course of his life—Catholic University, the University of Redlands, the Naval Academy, the University of Chicago, and Harvard—recalled that it was at Harvard in 1972 that he found it most difficult to engage in free and open debate.[99]

This neoconservative reaction against the perceived restriction of free debate crystallized around the stormy reception of Moynihan's policy suggestions (his 1965 report on the black family and his advice to Nixon in 1970 to adopt an attitude of "benign neglect" on racial issues and focus on class instead). Moynihan felt that the *National Review* had shown greater intellectual honesty in discussing these matters than had most liberals. There was also the case of Edward Banfield, a Harvard professor who analyzed the failures of the War on Poverty and came under such vehement attack by colleagues that he chose to leave Harvard for the University of Pennsylvania.[100] These affairs may stand as emblematic of first-age neoconservatism and, eventually, of second-age neoconservatism as well, as New Left ideas began to infiltrate the political sphere and exert their influence on the Democratic party.

3

THE SECOND AGE:
COLD WAR DEMOCRATS IN DISSENT

Nineteen sixty-eight was a crucial year for the Democratic party, an eventful and tragic year that began a long process of disintegration out of which would emerge, four years later, the Coalition for a Democratic Majority (CDM) and the second age of neoconservatism. During the 1960s, as we have seen, "vital center" liberalism experienced a crisis: it was blamed for the war in Vietnam and for excessively ambitious social programs and became the target of protests by the New Left and the counterculture. Yet it had provided the ideological underpinning for the Democratic party of Harry Truman, John Kennedy, Lyndon Johnson, and his vice-president, Hubert Humphrey. Hence it is not surprising that the Democratic party itself entered a time of crisis, along with other organizations that drew from the same ideological well, such as the Americans for Democratic Action (ADA) and even the tiny Socialist party.

If the conquest of the Democratic party by the forces of the New Left began in 1968, the nomination of George McGovern as the Democratic candidate in 1972 consummated their victory. The Cold War liberals, or Scoop Jackson Democrats, were quick to react: in December 1972 they created the CDM. In the years that followed, the CDM would counterattack on a number of fronts: party rules, ideological principles, domestic policy, and foreign policy. The goal was nothing more or less than to recapture the soul of the Democratic party, to prevent the ideological home of Roosevelt, Truman, Kennedy, and Johnson from being taken over by adepts of Jack Kerouac, Malcolm X, Tom Hayden, and Jane Fonda and losing all contact with the "real America" and the traditional Democratic electorate as a result. Had not McGovern lost to Nixon in a landslide because he had positioned himself too far to the left?

Upheaval in the Democratic Party

It will be useful to begin with a little political sociology. Among the less obvious ways in which the American political landscape evolved after 1945, James Q. Wilson, a political scientist and future neoconservative, has called attention to the proliferation of clubs of "amateur politicians" in large American cities. The members of these clubs were citizens who chose to participate in politics for ideological (and social) reasons rather than to run for office.[1] The clubs usually mobilized around the most liberal causes. There was a similar movement among conservatives: this was one of the reasons why Barry Goldwater defeated Nelson Rockefeller in the 1964 Republican primaries. The new party activists, more ideologically motivated than in the past, challenged the old party machines, which played an important social role but were also implicated in political corruption.

Slowly but surely, amateur politicians increasingly inspired by the New Left gained influence within the Democratic party. Their enemies included both southern conservatives and northern party bosses who controlled the selection of candidates and generally had little interest in promoting good government. "We plug the democratic process," the leader of one of New York's liberal clubs remarked. "I see reform politics as a life-or-death war with the regular organization" aimed at restoring power to the people, another activist explained.[2]

At the Democratic convention in Chicago in July 1968, a veritable confrontation erupted: antiwar protesters, liberal intellectuals, and representatives of the New Left voted against Hubert Humphrey, who was too closely identified with Lyndon Johnson.[3] Doves demonstrated in the streets in support of the antiwar candidate, Eugene McCarthy, and in protest against the war in Vietnam. These demonstrations ended in violent clashes with police dispatched by Chicago mayor and political boss Richard Daley. The police dealt harshly and even violently with the protesters, and all of it was caught by television cameras and viewed by millions.

Inside the convention hall itself, Daley insulted Connecticut senator Abraham Ribicoff and threatened him with his fists after Ribicoff denounced the "Gestapo tactics" of the Chicago police, while supporters of McCarthy and of the late Robert Kennedy (who had been assassinated a little more than a month earlier, on June 6) were convinced that Humphrey had "stolen" the nomination thanks to an unfair and opaque system for selecting delegates, which allowed party leaders to decide without consulting the rank and file. They demanded and obtained the formation of a commission to develop more transparent and democratic procedures.

There was a long history of similar demands in the American political tradition. At the turn of the twentieth century, one result of the Progressive movement was an increase in the number of party primaries, which made for a more democratic selection process and loosened the control of party leaders over the choice of candidate. Subsequently, however, the number of primaries had decreased, and party bosses and regulars continued to dominate the selection process. In short, it was political professionals who gathered in "smoke-filled rooms" to choose the party's presidential candidates.

At the 1968 convention, New Left and antiwar activists successfully pressed their demand for a commission to consider changes in candidate-selection and other party rules. Eventually this would lead to an upheaval in American politics. The reform commission's first chair was George McGovern, a senator from South Dakota, and he was succeeded by Donald Fraser, a congressman from Minnesota. Dominated by left-wing activists emboldened by Humphrey's defeat (by a small margin) in the November election, the commission went far beyond its initial mandate and insisted that each state delegation "faithfully represent" its state not only with regard to preferences among the various candidates for the presidential nomination but also in its "biological" makeup.[4] More specifically, for each of three groups subject to discrimination in the past—blacks, women, and youth—the proportion of delegates from each state must not differ appreciably from the proportion of that group in the state's population. This was tantamount to a quota system, although the commission refrained from using that word. Any state delegation that failed to respect the new rules could be denied the right to be seated at the national convention. The McGovern-Fraser commission, responding to the New Left's desire for "participatory democracy" and to "amateur politicians," considerably reduced the role of party professionals: no more than 10 percent of each delegation could be chosen by the state party organization, and all delegates were required to state their preference publicly before the vote in order to minimize "back-room deals" at the national convention.

As a result of the new rules, several state parties chose to hold primary elections to select delegates. In 1968, fifteen states had held primaries; by 1972 the number had risen to twenty-three and by 1976 to thirty. At that point nearly 75 percent of the delegates were chosen in primaries, compared with 30 to 40 percent in 1968. At the same time, the new rules promulgated by the McGovern-Fraser commission were so complex and opaque that there were many challenges to the seating of delegates at the Miami convention in 1972. For instance, Richard Daley's "politically incorrect" Illinois delegation (which included too few women and younger delegates) was replaced by a rival delegation led by Jesse Jackson among others.[5]

The problem was that the reforms did not benefit "ordinary citizens" so much as the "new class" of radicalized students and representatives of ethnic movements, who were demanding unprecedented—and indeed privileged—representation for themselves: this was the heart of the critique that the Coalition for a Democratic Majority began to develop in late 1972. The people who voted in primary elections and participated in caucuses were not "middle Americans" but activists with a higher educational level and social status than most voters and clearly more liberal, not to say more radical, than much of the electorate. Surveys of the political views of delegates to the 1972 convention revealed the breadth of this gap (which has not diminished much since then). On every issue, convention delegates stood well to the left of the voters whom they represented.

In other words, the Democratic party's effort to democratize itself actually had the effect of radicalizing the party and circumventing the principle of majority rule. If critics of the "new politics" are correct—and the CDM was foremost among those critics—it was party professionals and traditional elites (such as union leaders) who were in the best position to represent the desires of the typical voter, because they always tried to choose the candidate with the best chance of putting together a broad coalition in the general election, unlike the "new class," which favored the candidate with the most partisan—not to say the most revolutionary—program.

Blue-Collar Defection

As a result, many knowledgeable Democrats began to fear that, starting with the 1972 election, the party had lost contact with the real electorate, with the blue-collar workers who formed the silent majority of the Democratic party. They had already started worrying after reading Kevin Phillips's *The Emerging Republican Majority,* which came out in 1969, in the wake of Nixon's victory.[6] Phillips's book summed up the Republicans' hopes of achieving a "critical electoral realignment" by capturing white middle-class voters in the North anxious about urban unrest and all the attention being paid to minorities, as well as southern conservatives and ethnic voters in the cities (mainly descendants of East European immigrants).[7]

But the most important book was by Richard Scammon, a political scientist, and Ben Wattenberg, a former speechwriter for Lyndon Johnson, titled *The Real Majority* (1970). The two authors described the New Deal era as one in which economic issues dominated, giving Democrats the advantage and enabling them to put together a solid and durable coalition. The upheavals of the 1960s had brought "social values issues" to the fore, among which Scammon and Wattenberg included "crime, race, values, busing, drugs, disruption, quotas, welfare, pornography, patriotism, draft-dodging, dependency, permissiveness, capital punishment, [and] disparagement of America." If social values issues replaced economic issues as the fundamental line of cleavage in American politics, Democrats risked losing their dominant place—unless they managed somehow to move toward a "centrist" position on these issues. Scammon and Wattenberg created a fictional figure to represent this supposed median voter: the wife of a machinist in Dayton, Ohio, "unyoung, unpoor, unblack . . . middle-class, middle-aged, and middle-minded."[8]

The problem was that the McGovern commission reforms and the nomination of McGovern as the Democratic candidate in 1972 were moving the party in exactly the opposite direction. McGovern was the standard-bearer of minorities, of blacks, and of the young—the candidate most vulnerable to the slogan foisted on the "new" Democratic party by its adversaries: "Acid, Amnesty, and Abortion" (that is, liberalization of drug laws, amnesty for draft-dodgers and deserters, and legalization of abortion), in the famous phrase attributed to Republican senator Hugh Scott. Although McGovern had worked in the Kennedy administration and later with Bobby Kennedy, he was branded an extremist by more traditional candidates from Scoop Jackson to Hubert Humphrey. In particular, he proposed cutting the defense budget by $30 billion a year, eliminating funding for the F-14 and F-15 fighter jets, and ending the Safeguard antimissile program. Needless to say, he also favored immediate withdrawal from Vietnam, but he did not explain how he would obtain the return of prisoners of war held by the enemy.

On domestic issues McGovern took a very liberal stance, advocating policies that would have gone well beyond those of the Great Society: busing to hasten racial integration, the use of quotas, an increase in the size of the civil service, a broad expansion of Social Security, and, most significant of all, a guaranteed minimum annual income of $1,000 per American (a proposal that he would abandon during the campaign). Cold War liberals accused him of being soft on communism: had he not been a delegate to the 1948 convention of Henry Wallace's Progressive party?

At the Miami convention (July 10–13, 1972), supporters of Scoop Jackson and Hubert Humphrey formed a short-lived "anybody but McGovern" coalition, but to no avail: McGovern won the nomination, benefiting from the new rules that he himself had helped to write, rules that favored New Left activists at the expense of traditional Democrats. Some Democrats went public with their disappointment: for instance, John Connally, who had served as secretary of the Navy under Kennedy and been elected governor of Texas in 1963 (he was wounded in the assassination that cost President Kennedy his life), formed a group of anti-McGovern centrist Democrats called "Democrats for Nixon." In August 1972 this group paid for an ad in the *New York Times* calling on Democrats to reject the candidate of their party: "We're not leaving the party. But we cannot support Senator McGovern."[9] But most centrist Democrats who rejected McGovern and worked actively to oppose his candidacy were unwilling to betray their party and support Nixon.

The Launching of the CDM

After McGovern's crushing electoral defeat, the Coalition for a Democratic Majority was founded on December 7, 1972, in the words of Ben Wattenberg, "to counterbalance the other faction of the Democratic Party." It was "set up as a megaphone against the New Politics" and to defend a certain tradition, a certain vision of the Democratic party.[10] Penn Kemble, for his part, felt the need for an organized opposition to New Left groups that would take the fight to them and speak their language—in other words, an opposition that would be not just political but ideological. The idea of organizing such a group was born at the Miami convention, but it was kept secret in order to avoid any appearance of attempting to undermine McGovern's candidacy and thus betraying the Democratic camp, as "Democrats for Nixon" were doing.[11] A small organizing committee gathered around Ben Wattenberg, Penn Kemble, Max Kampelman, and Richard Schifter (the four most active promoters). Norman Podhoretz and his wife, Midge Decter, Nelson Polsby, Jeane Kirkpatrick, and her husband, Evron Kirkpatrick, joined them.[12]

In 1965 Ben Wattenberg (born in 1933), the product of a Democratic family and a graduate of Hobart College, published a book, *This USA*, that attracted the attention of Lyndon Johnson's White House, leading to a position for Wattenberg as speechwriter.[13] In 1969 he became a political consultant, and the next year he wrote *The Real Majority* with Richard Scammon. His work for Hubert Humphrey (in the 1970 senatorial campaign) and Scoop Jackson (in the 1972 presidential campaign) convinced him of the need to oppose the New Left.[14]

Penn Kemble (1941–2005) had an even more interesting career. His father, a great admirer of the Socialist leader Norman Thomas, worked for a newspaper in a Pennsylvania mining town with a rich history of trade-union activity. Penn entered the University of Colorado in 1959, at a time of considerable ideological ferment owing to the influence of left-wing activists from the nuclear laboratory at Los Alamos and young Ivy League professors attracted to this mountain state and its natural splendors. He became involved in debates about Cuba, civil rights, and nuclear disarmament and joined the Young People's Socialist League (YPSL), which took its inspiration not so much from Trotsky as from Max Shachtman. Kemble took an active part in the struggle for civil rights, participating in sit-ins and demonstrations across the country. To the delight of his father, who hoped he would become a journalist, he obtained a low-level position with the *New York Times*, but his participation in the newspaper strike of 1963 cost him his job. That same year he helped with preparations for the march on Washington led by Martin Luther King Jr. As a result of making numerous contacts while mailing out brochures in advance of the march, he was named national secretary of the YPSL. The group's principal enemy was the Students for a Democratic Society.[15]

Both Richard Schifter (born in 1923) and Max Kampelman (born in 1920) were lawyers with ties to the Democratic party, and both worked in Washington. Schifter was a member of the Maryland Board of Education. Kampelman was an adviser to Hubert Humphrey and worked in

Humphrey's campaigns. Indeed, he was under consideration to become secretary of state if Humphrey won in 1968.

Kampelman's career was unusual. Born to a modest Jewish family in the Bronx, he initially became interested in philosophical and theological questions.[16] After graduating from New York University in 1940, he fell under the influence of a reform rabbi and Quaker friends and became a conscientious objector to military service in World War II. After serving in various volunteer jobs for conscientious objectors, he volunteered in 1944 to become one of thirty-six guinea pigs in a study conducted by physicians at the University of Minnesota under contract to the U.S. Army to ascertain the effects of famine on the human body and to determine the best way to care for concentration-camp prisoners and civilians who had been subjected to prolonged periods of undernourishment. Placed on a severe diet, he lost a quarter of his weight but stuck with the protocol to the end, along with thirty-two of his comrades. The results of the study were used by American Army doctors in Europe in the winter of 1944–45, when the Nazi camps were liberated. In August 1945, toward the end of his civilian service, his pacifist convictions changed. After Hiroshima and Nagasaki, he concluded that nonviolence might prove to be a mistake in the face of destructive capacity of that magnitude. War might sometimes be necessary to root out evil. He became a Cold War liberal.

During his service as part of the Army study in Minnesota, Kampelman took courses with Hubert Humphrey's mentor, Evron Kirkpatrick, a leading American political scientist and the future husband of Jeane Kirkpatrick (whom he married in 1955). After befriending both Evron and Jeane, Kampelman persuaded them to join the organizing committee of the Coalition for a Democratic Majority, although Evron's participation would remain discreet, no doubt because of his official responsibilities with the American Political Science Association.[17] As we saw in the previous chapter, Norman Podhoretz and Midge Decter presided over the infancy of neoconservatism thanks to Norman's role as editor of *Commentary*. Decter, in addition to attacking the excesses of feminism in a pamphlet titled *The New Chastity*, wrote for *Harper's*, *Commentary*, and *World Magazine*.[18]

The first meeting of the CDM, and the only meeting to be held before the publication of the group's manifesto in the *New York Times* and the *Washington Post*, took place on November 8, 1972, a few days after McGovern's crushing defeat: he carried only one state out of fifty, winning just 17 electoral votes to Nixon's 521. The first order of business was to find additional names to append to the manifesto, which had been drafted by Podhoretz and Decter at Wattenberg's behest and then "toned down" by Jeane Kirkpatrick.[19] Among those present at the inception of the CDM on November 8 was Richard Perle, a member of Scoop Jackson's staff.[20]

But the real launch of the Coalition for a Democratic Majority came on December 7, 1972, the day on which the manifesto "Come Home, Democrats" appeared in the *Times* and *Post*.[21] Very well written, bristling with hard-hitting formulas, it called upon "common sense liberals" to reject "the blare of New Politics" and regain the road to success. "Coming home" meant rediscovering the true Democratic tradition as represented by candidates from Roosevelt to Humphrey. The manifesto was organized around four broad themes:

1. The New Politics had proven to be a failure. The "new class" of politicians had lost contact with voters by presuming to decide what was best for them. The basis of the New Politics was a contemptuous rejection of the "people and institutions on which the Democratic Party has built its electoral strength," starting with the unions. The party needed to "patch things up" with the Democratic voters who had deserted McGovern but not the Democratic party, a phenomenon signaled by the continuation of Democratic majorities in Congress and many state legislatures in the same elections of 1972. This was proof that the voters had rejected the idea that American society was "sick and guilty [and] morally corrupt" without going over to the Republicans, the "party of privilege."

2. The voters and their desire for order must be respected. The CDM manifesto took a populist turn in criticizing the New Left as contemptuous of and divorced from "ordinary people": "It is a 'New Politics' that has dismissed as morally unworthy the long-range values and daily concerns of tens of millions of ordinary people."

3. A society of ever-increasing fairness was a worthwhile goal; quotas were not. CDM members had fought, in some cases quite actively, for civil rights, yet all rejected the politics of quotas: "The principle of individual merit without regard to inherited status has been challenged by the idea of proportionalism in accordance with birth and group origin." For traditional liberals, the latter notion was a perversion of the progressive ideas of the Democratic party ("the great engine of reform for the past forty years").

4. In foreign policy, isolationism and defeatism were to be rejected. The manifesto's title, "Come Home, Democrats," stood on its head the leitmotif of George McGovern's July 14, 1972, acceptance speech at the Miami convention: "Come Home, America." The CDM manifesto called on Democrats to come home to the core principles of containing communism and shouldering America's international responsibilities.

In many respects, the CDM manifesto was reminiscent of the founding manifesto of the ADA a quarter of a century earlier, except that now the principal target was not Communists and their fellow travelers but the New Left—and thus, in a sense, the ADA itself as it had been transformed over the course of the 1960s.

The CDM on Domestic Policy

The bottom of the page on which the manifesto appeared was devoted to the list of signatories, comprising eighty names divided into two groups: organizing committee and sponsors.[22] Very few members of Congress appeared in the list: just four congressmen and no senators, not even Humphrey or Jackson. This absence of powerful political backing limited the CDM's visibility and potential impact from the start. The Democratic Leadership Council (DLC), which in many respects took up where the CDM left off in the 1980s, would adopt the opposite strategy: from the first it thought of itself as an organization of politicians. In electoral terms, the DLC was far more effective than the CDM; it played an important role in the election of Bill Clinton.

What united the Democrats who joined the CDM was their opposition to both the Republican party and the New Left. This political opposition coincided with a sociological difference: "blue collar vs. 'new class,'" to borrow Joshua Muravchik's formulation.[23] In the eyes of CDM liberals, who were allied with the unions, the "good class" was the working class, the true Democratic majority, and not the "new class" of college graduates who had been radicalized on campus without ever having had to confront life's realities. Still, it is possible to distinguish several groups among the signers of the manifesto and members of the CDM.

The first group consisted of advisers to traditional Democratic leaders, especially Scoop Jackson and Hubert Humphrey: Ben Wattenberg, Max Kampelman, Jeane Kirkpatrick, and Sonny Dogole (campaign treasurer). We even find people such as Peter Rosenblatt and Michael

Novak, who were close to Edmund Muskie (a presidential candidate who had moved some distance toward the New Politics, but not all the way).

The second group consisted of academics, mainly political scientists with ties to the Kirkpatricks, Austin Ranney, Nelson Polsby, and John Roche at Harvard. There were also lawyers such as Eugene Rostow and historians such as Richard Pipes, two names that we will encounter again later. These academics had been eyewitnesses to the campus up-heavals of the 1960s. Hence it will come as no surprise that the group in-cluded a number of first-age neoconservatives such as Seymour Martin Lipset, Daniel Bell, and Nathan Glazer, all three of whom signed "Come Home, Democrats." They were joined, of course, by Norman Podhoretz and Midge Decter (as well as their future son-in-law, the young Elliott Abrams, who became a member of the CDM in 1973), as well as Pat Moynihan, who would join in 1975, and Michael Novak, who repre-sented the Catholic point of view. In a sense these people embodied the link between the first age of neoconservatism, which rejected liberalism's change of direction, and the second age, which rejected the Democratic party's change of direction.

The third group consisted of "right-wing socialists" and Shacht-manites. The most prominent of these were Penn Kemble, Joshua Muravchik (who joined the organization in 1974), Paul Seabury, and Rachelle Horowitz—all former members of the Young People's Socialist League (of which Kemble and Muravchik had been leaders) and the So-cial Democrats USA (SDUSA). Bayard Rustin can also be included in this group. A former member of the SDUSA and a civil rights activist, he had always rejected what he regarded as excesses of the movement (such as black nationalism and the Black Panthers) and believed that the next step in the civil rights struggle should be advances toward economic progress led by the federal government and backed by the unions. What these "socialists" brought to the CDM was experience in ideological struggle, which was essential if the New Left was to be defeated on its own terrain. Neither the Republicans, including Nixon (whom Kemble remembers as "completely nonideological"),[24] nor the traditional Demo-crats and union leaders had much knowledge in this area.

Finally, a fourth group of CDM members—veritable pillars of the or-ganization—consisted of union leaders. Lane Kirkland, the number-two man in the AFL-CIO, offered direct encouragement to the organizers, and the unions supported the group financially. The unions shared the

CDM's attachment to bread-and-butter issues as opposed to the individ-
ualist concerns of the New Left. They also backed the group's anticommunism and believed in the need for a strong policy of containment. In
addition, they agreed on the need to combat the forces of the New Politics within the Democratic party. Along with Bayard Rustin and Norman Hill of the A. Philip Randolph Institute (a black union founded by a
celebrated union leader and advocate of civil rights), Albert Shanker,
president of the American Federation of Teachers, played an important
role in the CDM.[25]

Despite differences in the outlooks of these various groups within the
organization, the CDM remained united. To be sure, it never became
very large. It never took the path of the ADA, the Committee on the
Present Danger, or the Democratic Leadership Council. What is more,
there was no shortage of debate as to its exact nature and mission.
Should it become an electoral machine in support of candidates who
championed the causes it favored? The question was soon resolved by
the new campaign finance law of 1974, which placed the group in a tax
category that precluded endorsing any candidate. Should it become a
mass organization? Peter Rosenblatt responds: "At first we were talking
about enrolling thousands of people in CDM, but none of us had the
slightest idea about how to do that, or any interest in it."[26] Finally,
dreams of establishing regional chapters throughout the country on the
model of the ADA never materialized, beyond a few cities such as Boston
and New York. "We also must recognize that we, by and large, failed in
our efforts to build a significant membership," Richard Schifter conceded in a retrospective assessment of the CDM dated January 8, 1975.[27]
Should the CDM engage in active lobbying of Congress on behalf of the
"traditional liberal" ideas it advocated, as the Heritage Foundation had
begun doing in 1973 for the conservative cause with its "executive mem-
orandums"? Richard Schifter favored this course, but such lobbying
would have required resources that the CDM never possessed at any
point in its history. Finally, if not a lobby, should the group have transformed itself into a think tank, for instance by publishing an authentic
intellectual journal to spread centrist Democratic ideas? Once again, the
temptation arose often but never led anywhere.

Ultimately it was Jeane Kirkpatrick who best summed up the group's
long-term purpose, in a sense its ethos, at an executive committee meeting on October 22, 1975: "We were formed to demonstrate that there
are people in the Democratic Party who think as we do. We have done

this and can best proceed by continuing to uphold that position in party debate."[28] In fact the CDM remained a small organization, whose influence lay more in the quality of its membership and the force of their ideas than in mass mobilization. Indeed, its opponents were infuriated that it would get so much attention with so few logistical and grassroots efforts: "They don't have anything," railed Democratic representative Bella Abzug; "it's a fake."[29]

Within the CDM there were two "task forces" that published a number of texts on major political issues. One was led by Leon Keyserling, who had chaired the Council of Economic Advisors under Truman (and who was also active in the ADA, as we saw in Chapter 1). He advocated state intervention to stimulate the economy, in the tradition of the New Deal and John F. Kennedy.[30] The second task force was headed by Eugene Rostow and dealt with foreign policy, a subject to which I will return later. In 1973 the CDM published the first issue (March–April) of its bimonthly newsletter, *CDM Notes,* written essentially by members of the group. *CDM Notes* was sent to members, and several issues appeared in 1973 and 1974 at irregular intervals. In 1975 it was replaced by a more substantial newsletter, *Political Observer,* although there was no improvement in the regularity of publication. The CDM was chronically underfinanced. Wattenberg had initially dreamed of financing at a level of $300,00–400,000 per year, but in the first few years the annual budget was around $100,000, with a chronic deficit of $9,000–15,000 per fiscal year.[31]

To remain afloat, the CDM counted on private donors and organized fund-raisers, receptions, and conferences that also served to spread its message. Most of its funding, however (at least in the period 1973–1980), came from the unions. Lane Kirkland provided initial funding from the AFL-CIO in late 1972 to pay for publication of the "Come Home, Democrats" manifesto. Despite the convergence of views described above, the AFL-CIO could not participate directly in the Democratic party's internal struggles, because it was officially neutral. The CDM, joined by pro-union party leaders, was able to compensate for this structural disadvantage. Explains Joshua Muravchik:

> We saw our role to some extent—that was the most important political strategy—to achieve AFL-CIO dominance over the democratic party; that was our goal. And we saw our own role in the little group of being to help them in an intellectual or agitprop way, and being spokesman for prolabor

positions . . . One of my jobs was to develop a lot of expertise about some of the party rules issues—you may find some old memos. It was, in a sense, to try to serve the AFL–CIO, to help it with its operations to be more successful.[32]

The CDM Counteroffensive within the Democratic Party

During the first two years of its existence (1973–1975), the CDM devoted considerable energy to efforts to "reform the reforms" that had transformed the Democratic party from 1968 to 1972, especially in regard to delegate selection, so as to prevent a repeat of the 1972 landslide and to ensure the victory of a centrist candidate not beholden to the New Politics. The struggle, which involved political and legal issues of byzantine complexity, continued to play an important role in Democratic politics for the next forty years; the repercussions of what began in 1968 could be seen in the primary battle between Hillary Clinton and Barack Obama in 2008. The much-discussed "superdelegates," who enjoyed the right to vote at the party convention even though they were not elected in any primary, were a direct consequence of the stand taken by the CDM in the 1970s to ensure that officials of the regular party organization would be able to serve as a counterweight to the results of the primaries and thus increase the likelihood of choosing a competitive candidate (although these ex-officio delegates were not officially embraced until the Hunt Commission did so in 1982—and in the end they backed the candidate who had won in the primaries).

The CDM quickly identified two arenas in which it might press its cause, in addition to the regular party committees. These involved the delegate selection process (the province first of the Mikulski Commission in 1972–73 and then of the Wagner Commission in 1974–1976) and the drafting of a new charter for the party (a task entrusted to the Sanford Commission in 1972–1974). The group was also quick to identify its enemies: the party's left wing, represented most notably by the Democratic Planning Group under Alan Baron, a New Left activist close to McGovern, who favored quotas and "participatory democracy."

On January 10, 1973, at the very first meeting of the CDM's board of directors, a "task force on the structure of the party" was appointed under the chairmanship of Richard Schifter and Congressman James O'Hara. Its first product was a thirty-seven-page pamphlet titled *Toward Fairness and Unity for '76: A Review of the McGovern-Fraser Del-*

egate Selection Guidelines. In a press release, the task force put forward its suggestion that quotas be eliminated but that steps be taken to ensure that every interest group and minority was well-informed about the delegate selection process, the rules for which should be clear and open. The task force insisted on the need to restore power to regular party officials by making all governors, representatives, and senators ex-officio delegates (rather than excluding them) and by requiring that 20 (rather than 10) percent of the delegates from each state be named by the state party organization.[33]

That summer, members of the CDM, especially Kemble and Schifter, prepared to take part in the deliberations of the Mikulski Commission. They canvassed some forty union leaders, academics, and party leaders, whom they also supplied with resources and expert information in the hope of counterbalancing the activism of the New Politics.[34] The CDM's efforts were not wasted: the elimination of delegate quotas was an important victory. But many of the recommendations contained in *Toward Fairness and Unity for '76* were ignored. Kemble echoed the alarmed response of several state party organizations: the new rules were so ambiguous that the only concrete way of ensuring compliance would be to impose some form of quota.[35] Indeed, everything would depend on how the new rules were interpreted. From 1974 to 1976 the battleground therefore shifted to the Compliance Review Commission, also known as the Wagner Commission.

Another front in the war between the CDM and the New Politics was the Sanford Commission, whose mission was to pan the 1974 miniconvention and to draft a new charter for the Democratic party. Here the CDM enlisted a new recruit, Joshua Muravchik, who had initially been Penn Kemble's acolyte and later his successor as head of the Young People's Socialist League in the 1960s (when very young he had taken part in Martin Luther King's 1963 march on Washington). After joining the CDM, he managed with limited means to "orchestrate a scare" among party regulars and union leaders.[36] To do this, he enlisted CDM members and their networks to exaggerate the "menace" of the New Left, which, it was claimed, sought to "Europeanize," "ideologize," and centralize the Democratic party—changes that were neither in the party's traditions nor in its best interest. In the end, the threats fizzled, but although the CDM did not win a total victory over the New Left, it at least managed to neutralize it.

To deal with the Wagner Commission, charged with interpreting and then applying the new rules issued by the Mikulski Commission, the CDM in May 1975 launched a new "Task Force on Party Rules," chaired by Michigan congressman Jim O'Hara and including Jeane Kirkpatrick, Austin Ranney, Richard Schifter, and Congressman Jim Wright of Texas.[37] The task force scored a significant victory over the New Politics when its chairman, Jim O'Hara, who had been a member of the CDM from the beginning, proposed three criteria for evaluating state party "action plans" addressing the issue of minority representation without imposing any numerical proportionality, which would have been tantamount to reinstating quotas "through the back door." The new official standard was that a convention delegation could be challenged only on the basis of its failure to respect an approved state action plan, not on its numerical or "biological" makeup.[38] For Muravchik, this was the moment when the CDM defeated the quota system in the inner workings of the Democratic party once and for all.[39]

Ultimately, by the fall of 1975, the overall—and provisional—outcome of this institutional warfare was ambiguous. On the one hand, selection quotas for delegates were gone, the party had been neither centralized nor "Europeanized," and the New Politics had not carried the day—and the CDM could rightly claim to have had a hand in this outcome. On the other hand, the centrists, party regulars, and unions had not taken over either, nor had they succeeded in rejecting all the innovations inspired by the New Left and turning the clock back to 1968. The true test would come in the 1976 presidential election, as we shall see in the next chapter.

The CDM's Turn to Foreign Policy

What distinguished the second age of neoconservatism from the first was not only the involvement of neoconservatives in politics (particularly Democratic party politics) rather than intellectual debate but also their interest in foreign policy as well as domestic issues. Indeed, as the 1970s wore on, the interest in foreign policy increased until it became all but exclusive, foreshadowing the third age of neoconservatism. There is no better bellwether of this change than the evolution of the Coalition for a Democratic Majority.

Foreign policy did figure, albeit not in a central place, in the group's founding manifesto, "Come Home, Democrats" (1972). According to that document, among the principles that had guided Democratic presidents in recent decades had been "a sober but spirited assumption of America's share of responsibility for the establishment of a more secure international community" and "a knowledge that without democratic order there can be no justice and without justice there can be no democratic order."[40]

More precisely, what the founders of the CDM contested were the ideas of George McGovern. Although McGovern rejected the "isolationist" label, his 1972 platform did bear some of the hallmarks of isolationism. In Vietnam he advocated a cease-fire followed by a withdrawal of all American troops (without preconditions, and in particular without insisting that American prisoners of war be freed). He favored withdrawing 170,000 troops from Europe (after consultation with NATO allies but without waiting for comparable reductions by the Warsaw Pact). Finally, he proposed drastic cuts in the defense budget and a unilateral freeze on nuclear weapons development (on the grounds that mutual assured destruction already provided a reliable deterrent). Worse yet in the eyes of CDM members were McGovern's beliefs that the Soviet threat was "exaggerated," that Communist expansionism "existed more in our minds than in reality," and that it was better to promote mutual comprehension than to pursue a policy of containment.[41]

It does not follow, however, that all CDM members were hawks or proponents of the war in Vietnam. Among the signatories of the 1972 manifesto, several had for years favored withdrawal, including Zbigniew Brzezinski, Jim Woolsey, Nathan Glazer, and Norman Podhoretz, while others—among them Penn Kemble and Joshua Muravchik—advocated a sort of democratic third way with immediate negotiations. Still others—such as Ben Wattenberg, Peter Rosenblatt, and Max Kampelman—remained rather hawkish. This was also the position of the unions, or at any rate of George Meany, Lane Kirkland, and the rest of the AFL-CIO leadership. With few exceptions, however, no CDM member was a true dove. The slight differences among them were less important than their common opposition to the excesses of the dove spirit, to the mixture of isolationism, antimilitarism, and anti-American feelings of guilt that had grown out of the Vietnam quagmire. The "reaction to the reaction to Vietnam" extended well beyond foreign policy, as Norman Podhoretz explained:

> If at the beginning domestic criticism of our military intervention into Vietnam was restricted to tactical issues, and if toward the middle the political

wisdom of the intervention came into very serious question, by the end the moral character of the United States was being indicted and besmirched. Large numbers of Americans, including even many of the people who had led the intervention in the Kennedy years, were now joining the tiny minority on the Left who had at the time denounced them for stupidity and immorality, and were now saying that going into Vietnam had progressed from a folly to a crime.[42]

Jeane Kirkpatrick went even further in describing the importance of Vietnam in determining the neoconservatives' opposition to the New Left in areas well beyond foreign policy:

Originally, our disagreements focused on the Vietnam war—less on whether the U.S. should honor its commitments and remain involved than on whether that involvement was immoral, imperialistic, and genocidal— and on party leadership. It became progressively clear, however, that the disagreements extended to many questions of public policy, and most important, to the interpretation and evaluation of the American experience.

"We" affirmed the validity of the American dream and the morality of the American society. "They" adopted the characterizations of intellectuals like Charles Reich who described the U.S. as a sick society drunk on technology and materialism. "We" rejected the effort to revise American history, making it a dismal tale of dead Indians and double-dealing white settlers, imperialism, and war. "They" rejected facts and truths we hold dear. "Their" extravagant attack on American culture and institutions made "us" progressively aware of our attachment to both. "Their" urgent utopian schemes for the reform of almost everything made "us" more aware of our fundamental caution concerning radical reform.[43]

If the neoconservative reaction to the reaction to Vietnam is essential for understanding the mentality of neoconservatives, it is also important to examine the very distinctive foreign policy context of the early 1970s. Between 1965 and 1972, the foreign policy "establishment" divided between hawks and doves on Vietnam. Then, between 1972 and 1976, the intellectual outlook underwent a phase of transformation and renewal.[44]

On the extreme left of the political spectrum we find "radicals" associated with the New Left who embraced the work of revisionist historians such as William Appleman Williams and Walter LaFeber and who condemned U.S. action abroad, American imperialism, and even containment in all its forms: for them, "No more Munichs" gave way to "No more Vietnams," and isolationism was the only path to salvation.

Closer to the center but still on the left were many writers associated with *Foreign Policy,* a journal founded in 1970 by Samuel Huntington and Warren Demian Manshel (who had helped Kristol and Bell launch *The Public Interest*). *Foreign Policy* largely transformed the debate on international affairs. Articles dealt not only with the Cold War but also with the role of the economy and interdependence, technology, the oil crisis, environmental issues, immigration, and new nonstate actors such as multinational firms, the media, and nongovernmental organizations. Writers such as Stanley Hoffmann, C. Fred Bergsten, Leslie Gelb, Richard Holbrooke, Tony Lake, and Joseph Nye questioned the centrality of East-West conflict and emphasized the existence of a changing world order. Zbigniew Brzezinski insisted on the importance of technology, where America had the advantage over the Soviet Union, and of interdependence, although he still regarded the East-West conflict as fundamental.[45] He stressed the need for multilateral cooperation among the three main poles of the democratic industrial world: the United States, Europe, and Japan. This view of the world led to the formation of the Trilateral Commission in 1972, and through it Brzezinski became Georgia governor Jimmy Carter's tutor in international affairs.

In some respects, these views were not very far from those of Henry Kissinger, who embodied the view of the center right, the realist school among Republicans. Kissinger would put his ideas into practice as national security adviser and later secretary of state under Richard Nixon and Gerald Ford. But Kissinger's inspiration was different: a Spenglerian pessimist who came to office at a low ebb in American power, he looked upon détente as a way to limit the inevitable decline of the United States and to maintain an optimal foreign policy vis-à-vis the Soviet Union despite reduced means (as a result of cuts in the defense budget, isolationist feeling among American voters, and so on). In other respects, Kissinger's action was not unacceptable to the center left: he sought to "de-ideologize" relations with the Soviet Union; to negotiate all issues of concern to both superpowers at the same time ("linkage"), especially arms reduction and economic exchanges; and to establish a stable structure of peace that would end the bipolar confrontation by bringing China into the picture. On the principles and objectives of the policy of détente pursued by Nixon and Kissinger, the center left and the center right agreed.

In fact, the real break that developed in the 1970s was located to Kissinger's right. Paradoxically, it involved not nationalist Republican hawks, represented by Ronald Reagan, whose star was rapidly on the rise, but rather a group of Cold War liberals, the Scoop Jackson Democrats—in other words, neoconservatives. This group opposed not only the New Left, as we have seen, but also the center-left / center-right consensus on détente. Thus they challenged the vision of American foreign policy that was being set forth in the pages of *Foreign Policy,* which tended to downplay the importance of the bipolar superpower confrontation, its ideological tenor, and the military factor in international relations. Neoconservatives disagreed on all three points.

In their eyes, the Soviet Union was a totalitarian country whose internal structure dictated an expansionist international policy. Hence there was no point in seeking accommodation with it. Furthermore, it was a country in poor economic health to which no aid should be given (in the form of grain sales, technological assistance, and the like), not even to gain concessions on other issues (linkage). Finally, democracy mattered, and there was no alternative to American might to protect the democratic world from Communist efforts to destabilize it. Whereas Kissinger was wary of ideological crusades, which he regarded as a disruptive factor in international relations, the neoconservatives rejected this stance as amoral and not in keeping with American traditions. For them, the bipolar confrontation remained ideological.

Eugene Rostow as the Scourge of Détente

The Coalition for a Democratic Majority provides an early example of opposition to détente by traditional Cold War liberals. Their approach was quite similar to that which Walter Laqueur and others developed in the pages of *Commentary.* Although Laqueur did not become a member of the CDM, he did attend the organizational meeting on November 8, 1972. Another point of comparison is the approach taken in the Senate by Scoop Jackson and his legislative aide Richard Perle (also present at the November 8 meeting), which I will discuss in the next chapter.

The central figure in the CDM's growing opposition to détente was Eugene Rostow (1913–2002). A lawyer by training, Rostow worked as an attorney before becoming a professor of law at Yale (where he served as dean of the law school from 1955 to 1965). He was attracted to international affairs early on and worked as a State Department legal adviser in the Lend-Lease program during World War II. After the war, he worked with Dean Acheson in the implementation of the Marshall Plan. In 1966 he joined the Johnson administration as undersecretary of state for political affairs (number three in the State Department) and was assigned the task of defending the intervention in Vietnam. That intervention was in large part the brainchild of his brother, Walt Rostow, a celebrated economic historian and the author of a classic work on the stages of economic growth.[46] He served as director of the State Department's Policy Planning Staff from 1961 to 1966 and then as Johnson's national security adviser from 1966 to 1969. The Rostow brothers belonged to a highly cultivated family of Jewish socialists. Eugene owed his first name to Eugene Debs, while Walt owed his to the poet Walt Whitman. Eugene Rostow occupies a very important place in the second age of neoconservatism, because he was both an active member of the CDM and the founder of the Committee on the Present Danger. He would become head of the Arms Control and Disarmament Agency under Reagan from 1981 to 1983.

On November 3, 1973, almost exactly a year after the creation of the CDM and shortly after the end of the Yom Kippur War, a plenary meeting of the CDM's board of directors approved a statement on the Middle East that Rostow had drafted, titled "Implications of the War in the Middle East." It read: "The events of October in the Middle East should finally dispel the dangerous illusion that the President has, through personal diplomacy, achieved a detente with the Soviet Union, ended the Cold War, and initiated an era of negotiation instead of confrontation. There is no detente. *It takes two to détente.*"[47]

The resolution took the position that the Yom Kippur War implicated American-Soviet relations in general as well as relations between America and its allies (Europe and Japan). It backed Senator J. William Fulbright's call for a regular security treaty with Israel and strongly condemned the Hatfield-McGovern amendment to the administration's military aid bill for Israel, which insisted that prior congressional authority must be sought for any military action in the Middle East. This would have forced the United States to tie one hand behind its back and would have sent a very unfortunate signal to the Soviets.

But Gene Rostow's most important contribution was the creation of a foreign affairs and defense task force within the CDM, announced on

February 8, 1974.[48] Its members included various people whose names we have already encountered, such as Jeane Kirkpatrick, Norman Podhoretz, John Roche, Max Kampelman, Richard Pipes, Paul Seabury, and Albert Shanker.[49] The chief product of the task force was a July 1974 report titled *The Quest for Détente,* which was drafted in response to Kissinger's call for a broad public debate on U.S.-Soviet relations, especially on the issue of nuclear arms control, following the 1974 Moscow summit.[50] The Cold War historian Raymond Garthoff describes this document, which caused a considerable stir, as "the first major head-on assault on the entire Nixon-Kissinger policy of Détente."[51]

The Quest for Détente attacked the Nixon administration's contention that there had indeed been a relaxation of tensions between the United States and the Soviet Union. In reality, the report insisted, there was no serious evidence that the Soviets had changed. Nothing had come of the declaration of "Fundamental Principles of Soviet-American Relations," which Nixon had signed amid great pomp in Moscow on May 29, 1972 (just after the conclusion of the SALT accords, which included the ABM treaty). The Soviet Union "continues to repress and undermine democratic movements and governments. And it continues as well to provide military support for terrorism, guerrilla warfare and wars of aggression in direct violation of the Charter of the United Nations."[52]

The Rostow task force charged the Soviets with stirring up hatred of Israel in order to radicalize moderate Arab regimes, which would then be drawn into its orbit. Ultimately, this would allow Moscow to control "the broad arc from Morocco to Iran":

> This outcome would neutralize Europe, and bring it, too, under Soviet domination. As President [Georges] Pompidou has said, the Soviet presence in the Mediterranean basin threatens the soft underbelly of Europe, and constitutes a continuous Cuban missile crisis. Thus the Arab-Israeli conflict is not simply a regional quarrel, but a major weapon of Soviet imperial expansion. It is a thrust at the most vital interests of the United States, its NATO allies, and Japan.[53]

In the economic realm, Nixon's policy had proven even more disastrous, according to *The Quest for Détente:* Nixon had sold subsidized grain to Moscow, lent the Soviets money at below-market rates, and allowed them to buy advanced technologies while receiving nothing in return. *The Quest for Détente* attracted considerable attention.[54] Penn

Kemble explains that it "became a best-seller . . . It became *the* critique of Henry Kissinger, it was the only place where it was available. Then Gene realized that doing it as CDM was like a narrow intra-party issue, and he realized that in order to make that case more effectively, he had to go out to Republicans, business people, etc."[55] This account of course refers to Rostow's creation of the Committee on the Present Danger two years later.

Kissinger was among the first readers of the report. The secretary of state responded to the CDM pamphlet with a letter dated August 19, 1974, and addressed to Eugene Rostow as task force chair. The correspondence with the law professor would continue for several years, even after Kissinger had left the office of secretary of state; the letters can be found in the archives of the CPD. Kissinger defended himself against Rostow's charges. No, he explained, we were never under any illusions about Soviet intentions, but we sought to ensnare them in a network of intersecting interests, appealing "to the spirit of Pavlov rather than of Hegel." Furthermore, every commercial concession was dearly bought with tangible political benefits. Kissinger denied that the administration had been soft on the Soviets. Its policy had combined carrots and sticks. He also refuted the task force analysis of the Soviet attitude during the Yom Kippur War: "there is evidence that, were it not for the incentives the Soviets have to maintain relations with us on an even keel, their conduct during the crisis would undoubtedly have been less restrained and more unhelpful than it was."[56]

Rostow, writing on behalf of the task force, responded to Kissinger on September 4, 1974.[57] He began by pointing out that the belligerent nations in World War I had been involved in all sorts of close relationships, including commercial relationships, and that no Pavlovan reflex had prevented them from going to war. He then moved on to the heart of the disagreement, about the extent of détente, which Kissinger had tried to reduce to a matter of semantics. The period after the Moscow summit had been one of those brief times of cyclical enthusiasm that always follow important summits. This had been the case after Potsdam in 1945, Camp David in 1959, Geneva in 1961, and Glassboro in 1967. But, to cite just one example, Soviet conduct before and during the Yom Kippur War could not have been more inflammatory, in Rostow's estimation, because the Soviets had armed and lent political support to Arab states that had launched a war of aggression.

The Kissinger-Rostow exchange would continue, but in the meantime the CDM pursued its activist course and, at its board of directors meeting on November 22 and 23, 1974, adopted a quite alarmist resolution on national defense, with a tone that foreshadowed the communiqués of the CPD. It alluded to the group's "dismay over the drift toward military vulnerability and political diffidence in which our country is unquestionably caught up . . . Unless we set a new and responsible course, the next two years will see the military balance shift toward the Soviet Union and its allies, the irreversible deterioration of the network of our alliances, and the military destruction of small nations whose existence we have guaranteed—foremost among them the embattled state of Israel."[58]

The CDM called for an increase in the defense budget and modernization of American nuclear forces to increase their second-strike capacity. The statement ended by rejecting what it called the false choice between guns and butter. On the contrary, the CDM held, muscular foreign policy and rearmament could easily be combined with a progressive domestic program. In confirmation of this view, Penn Kemble a few months later sent Peter Rosenblatt a statement on national defense by the executive council of the AFL-CIO. It was virtually a copy of the November 1974 CDM resolution, at once staunchly anticommunist, alarmist, and hawkish, and it ended with a call for more defense spending: "No burden we must bear is too heavy to endure if the alternative is to live under dictatorship, or the constant prospect of war."[59]

Along the same lines, the CDM published another declaration in early 1975.[60] "Toward an Adequate Defense" formed the basis of Eugene Rostow's testimony before the House Armed Services Committee on April 17.[61] Rostow drew on the same source for an op-ed he published in the *Wall Street Journal* in May.[62] In subsequent years Rostow reduced his active involvement in the CDM, although he remained a member. The reason for the change was that from 1976 on he was mainly preoccupied with the Committee on the Present Danger, which he founded (see Chapter 5).

The Case of Elmo Zumwalt

When Ben Wattenberg opened the third meeting of the CDM board of directors in New York in February 1976, he explained to the audience what the CDM was and recalled that, back in 1972, the founders of the group had been impelled by a desire to react to the New Politics and its troubling "new dogmas," among which he listed—in this order—ideas about America's place in the world, quotas, unions, and growth. This re-ordering of priorities is revealing of the changes that had taken place in the interim: it was virtually the reverse of the order presented in "Come Home, Democrats."[63]

The CDM fought on several fronts in the 1976 presidential campaign, but foreign policy occupied a prominent place. For instance, Ben Wattenberg and Pat Moynihan (who had moved closer to the CDM) fought hard in debates over the party platform for a change in the Democratic position on issues such as criticizing Communist regimes (and not just right-wing dictatorships), rejection of moral equivalence, developing the B-1 bomber, reaffirming America's international commitments, and so on. During the campaign the CDM also set out to raise funds for the express purpose of combating the policy of détente. It attacked the Ford administration and Henry Kissinger in particular, expressing its displeasure with appeasement in the so-called "Sonnenfeldt doctrine," the immoral abandonment of "freedom-loving" Kurds in order to win the favors of Iraqi dictator Saddam Hussein, indifference to the fate of Lebanese Christians, the sale of sophisticated weapons systems to Saudi Arabia and Egypt, empty threats against Cuba, and so on. The CDM also called on the administration to develop a policy of energy independence and to fight the OPEC (Organization of Petroleum Exporting Countries) cartel.[64]

After remaining dormant from July 1976 to the spring of 1977, the CDM, in the wake of Carter's victory, turned its attention mainly to international issues and defense policy. In September 1977, for example, more than half of the items on the agenda of the CDM's executive council meeting concerned foreign policy: human rights as a central issue in American foreign policy; a series of notes on Carter's diplomacy; and studies of the PLO's role in Israeli-Arab negotiations, eventual withdrawal from South Korea, possible withdrawal from the International Labour Organization, the development of the neutron bomb, China policy, and energy policy.[65]

What were the factors that put foreign policy at the center of the CDM's concerns? Three stand out. First, foreign policy issues gained prominence in part because domestic issues and intraparty concerns receded in importance. The conflict between the CDM and the New Left settled into a predictable pattern, and the danger that the New Politics would dominate the party diminished. The war between the two sides had bogged down.

Joshua Muravchik offers a more materialist explanation. In his view, the CDM until 1975 was defined by its relation to the unions. It was both a tool that the AFL-CIO could use to influence the struggle over the identity of the Democratic party and a way for elements within the party to instrumentalize the AFL-CIO in their ideological combat with the New Left. After the 1974 miniconvention in Kansas City, however, George Meany became aware of the dangers of appearing too partisan and decided to withdraw from direct involvement in intraparty struggles. The CDM, according to Muravchik, then lost its Archimedean lever and its source of funding (a claim that is not entirely accurate). In 1976 it redirected all its efforts to the presidential campaign of Scoop Jackson, which ended in failure. As a result,

> CDM became a much more issue-oriented group; we got away from the fights about the party rules and we got away from any idea of trying to win the power in the party through positions on committees and things like that and instead we took to the idea of pushing our ideas on the Cold War, defense budget, human rights issues vis-à-vis the Soviet Union, and some of the domestic issues to some extent, quotas and all that; but in the period when I was the director, which was basically 1977–78, mostly CDM existed as a kind of agitational group about those issues.[66]

The second factor is obvious: the reality of Soviet expansionism (as well as Cuban expansionism, especially in Africa and Central America). Richard Schifter sums up the progressive, gradual shift of the CDM to foreign policy issues as follows: "Initially, it was mostly a rejection of the New Left; then we became increasingly concerned by Soviet expansion."[67] Ben Wattenberg confirms this view: "We thought the Soviet threat had become paramount."[68]

But a third factor also played a part in the "conversion" of many CDM (and CPD) members on the question of the Soviet menace: the influence of certain strong personalities. In particular, this was the case with Charls Walker and Richard Schifter, both of whom attribute to Admiral Elmo Zumwalt an important role in the evolution of their thinking.[69]

Admiral Zumwalt had a varied career, and one that is fascinating to follow in relation to the history of neoconservatism. Born in California in 1920, Zumwalt graduated from the Naval Academy and fought in the Pacific in 1944–45 (earning a Bronze Star for his service on a destroyer in the Gulf of Leyte). He also served on a cruiser during the Korean War. In the early 1960s he was tapped by the assistant secretary of defense, Paul Nitze, to serve as an adviser, a post he held during the Cuban missile crisis. When Nitze became secretary of the Navy, Zumwalt became his right-hand man. On Nitze's recommendation, Zumwalt was promoted to the rank of rear admiral in 1965 (at the age of forty-five, the youngest admiral in the history of the Navy), then to vice-admiral in 1968, when he became commander of all American naval forces in Vietnam, in a war of which he had personally disapproved from the beginning.

In that role, Zumwalt was in charge of the Brown Water Navy, that is, the boats (including the famous Swift boats) that patrolled the Mekong Delta to prevent the Vietcong from using the waterways. He ordered the use of a defoliant, Agent Orange, to clear the banks of rivers and canals in order to eliminate cover for snipers. This tactic noticeably decreased American casualties without posing any health risks to either the military or civilians—or so Zumwalt had been personally assured by the manufacturer of the chemical. In fact, Agent Orange ultimately killed thousands of Americans and Vietnamese who were exposed to it, including Zumwalt's own son (a Swift boat crew member, who died in 1988 after a lengthy bout with cancer).[70] Admiral Zumwalt devoted much of his time in the 1980s and 1990s to work on behalf of veterans suffering from illnesses contracted in the course of wartime service. In 2000 he himself died as a result of his exposure to asbestos while serving on American warships.

Admiral Zumwalt was recalled to Washington in April 1970 to serve as chief of naval operations. At fifty, he became the youngest four-star admiral in U.S. history. In that post, which he held until 1974, he was seen by some as "a bleeding-heart liberal" and by others as a dangerous militarist and Cold War hawk. On the one hand, he issued 121 directives (known as "Z-grams") that shook up the conservative Navy by requiring all base and unit commanders to appoint a special assistant for minorities (the first of these, "Equal Opportunity in the Navy," was especially significant in this regard). He also forced them to take action against housing discrimination, which affected many black sailors. Little by little, the number of African-American sailors in the U.S. Navy increased. The first black admiral was appointed during Zumwalt's tenure, and the number of women on ships also increased.

These actions aroused spirited protests and considerable discontent, however. Wives of sailors worried about their husbands' virtue and staged demonstrations. More insidiously, a silent resistance to the integration of blacks led to a whispering campaign against Zumwalt, who was accused of relaxing discipline and encouraging a permissive climate in the Navy. Had he not authorized sailors to wear beards and mustaches and even sideburns several inches in length? Racist incidents aboard the carriers *Constellation* and *Kitty Hawk* in 1972 were taken as evidence of the harm done by "liberal" measures. Curiously, Zumwalt's biography on the Navy website contains no mention of his efforts to combat discrimination against blacks in the Navy, although those efforts were the centerpiece of the speech that President Clinton gave when he awarded Zumwalt the Medal of Freedom in January 1998.[71] Zumwalt held on, however, and presided over a dramatic increase in Navy recruitment numbers, which had fallen sharply.[72]

As a member of the Joint Chiefs of Staff, Zumwalt devoted a good deal of time to the relative strength of the United States and the Soviet Union. His position was clear: Soviet armament efforts, especially in regard to naval forces, were giving the Soviets decisive advantages. In a global crisis, the Soviet Union could control major sea-lanes (or deny control to the United States). He sought to persuade Congress to allocate funds to modernize the American fleet. Within the Joint Chiefs, he was a powerful advocate for the defense of Israel, an ally that he viewed as a sort of stationary aircraft carrier in the heart of the Middle East.[73] Here was yet another example of a non-Jewish neoconservative.

Two years after stepping down as chief of naval operations, Zumwalt published a memoir, *On Watch*.[74] His vision of the world was not narrowly naval. In particular, he argued that the Russians had benefited far more than the United States from the strategic arms limitation treaties. He was severely critical of Henry Kissinger, whom he accused (rightly) of having delayed arms shipments to Israel during the Yom Kippur War, thereby preventing Israel from winning a decisive victory while shifting the blame to Defense Secretary James Schlesinger. Above all he criticized the secretary of state's negative and very pessimistic view of the United States.

One final biographical detail concerning Zumwalt is worth noting: from 1975 on, he increasingly participated in the work of the CDM (on whose behalf he delivered a lecture on February 4, 1975).[75] He was also a founding member of the Committee on the Present Danger (1976). In other words, Zumwalt is a perfect specimen of a second-age neoconservative: a Democrat (who ran for the Senate in 1976 but lost to the independent Harry F. Byrd Jr.), ardently in favor of civil rights, and by temperament a progressive, but also an anticommunist hawk, a proponent of a strong military, and staunchly pro-Israel.

As Dick Schifter tells it, it was in July 1973, when Scoop Jackson introduced CDM leaders to Zumwalt, then chief of naval operations, that CDM leaders first became aware of the scope of the geopolitical challenge posed by the Soviet Union.[76] At that point Zumwalt himself was interested in making contact with Washington political figures, and he even sent a car to bring Wattenberg, Kemble, and Schifter to the Pentagon. There he disclosed his worries about what he regarded as the unilateral disarmament of the United States. Under cover of détente, the Soviet Union was increasing its military capabilities and pursuing an expansionist policy. What he really feared was not war so much as an America weakened politically as a consequence of relative military weakness, leading to an ever more cautious foreign policy and ever-increasing unwillingness to confront Soviet regional challenges.[77]

This encounter began Schifter's conversion and persuaded him that the CDM ought to focus more of its effort on foreign policy. His experience was by no means unusual. Many others report similar influences. Among the "proselytizers" we find, in addition to Zumwalt, Eugene Rostow (mentioned by both Penn Kemble and Peter Rosenblatt),[78] the very charismatic Pat Moynihan, and Paul Nitze. Many who joined the CDM and CPD had been "converted" or at any rate alerted by one of these strong personalities.

On January 8, 1975, Schifter summed up this state of mind in striking terms: "To put it somewhat theatrically, I would suggest that Penn and the rest of us shift our attention from Alan Baron to Leonid Brezhnev."[79] (Alan Baron was a McGovern acolyte who took part in intraparty battles over rules and procedures.) That is what the CDM did, and in doing so it contributed to the development of an original body of thought about American foreign policy—neoconservative thought.

4

DIVERGENCE:
INVENTING A NEOCONSERVATIVE FOREIGN POLICY

The Democrats of the Coalition for a Democratic Majority were hardly alone in reacting to what they perceived as a wrong turn by their party in regard to both domestic policy and, increasingly, foreign policy in the 1970s. Their staunchest ally throughout the decade was Senator Henry M. "Scoop" Jackson, a Cold War Democrat who shared their vision of uncompromising anticommunism coupled with support for Israel and other threatened democracies abroad, and defense or even expansion of social programs at home. In addition, all these policies enjoyed the support of the major trade unions. The fact that second-age neoconservatives are often referred to as "Scoop Jackson Democrats" attests to the important leadership role played by the senator from Washington.

Alongside the CDM and the Scoop Jackson entourage, a third group formed around the magazine *Commentary*, its editor Norman Podhoretz, and regular contributors Walter Laqueur, Edward Luttwak, and Pat Moynihan. Numerous informal links connected these three "constellations" before 1976, when they joined forces to fight not so much the New Left as the Nixon-Kissinger policy of détente with the Soviet Union, which they believed Jimmy Carter was likely to continue without major changes. By the early 1980s this divergence on foreign policy had led neoconservatives to despair of the Democratic party and to turn, with hesitation though not without bitterness, to an old Cold War liberal, a former Democrat turned Republican: Ronald Reagan. In the meantime they had laid the foundations for a new vision of American foreign policy.

110

Scoop Jackson and Second-Age Neoconservatism

Henry M. "Scoop" Jackson (the nickname had been bestowed on him in childhood by his sister) was born on May 31, 1912, to a modest family of Norwegian immigrants in the state of Washington.[1] At the end of his freshman year at the University of Washington, he spent a summer at Stanford University, but the school proved to be too expensive for him and his family. After finishing law school at the University of Washington in the spring of 1935, he worked for the Federal Emergency Relief Administration, one of many New Deal agencies. While visiting his ancestral homeland in 1945, he fell seriously ill. He was impressed by the excellent medical care he received in Norway, where he was billed only fifteen dollars for a ten-day hospital stay. The experience turned him into a fervent proponent of socialized medicine in the United States. But what had already persuaded him of the need for state intervention was the Great Depression. Although in 1930 he had fought to allow Socialist leader Norman Thomas to speak at the University of Washington, his had not been a radical youth: while in college he never ventured beyond membership in the League for Industrial Democracy, a moderate organization that backed unions and democratic principles.[2] In short, he was a New Deal liberal and a "vital center" anticommunist liberal before the fact.

After taking his law degree, Jackson plunged into politics. As a state prosecutor in Washington he gained a reputation for incorruptibility that helped him win a seat in Congress in 1940. Still a bachelor, he thought of enlisting in the military, but Roosevelt ordered all representatives of military age to return to Congress instead. On April 22, 1945, he joined other congressmen on a visit to Buchenwald, which had just been liberated. This visit left an indelible impression on him, strengthened his antitotalitarian convictions, and constituted one of the main reasons for his staunch support of Israel throughout his career. Other reasons included friendships with Jews in his home state, his mother's philosemitism, and his insistence on defending democracies.

Jackson's positions were very close to Truman's. With support from Americans for Democratic Action, he was able to ward off both attacks from Wallaceites and Republican allegations that he was a Communist. In the House he became a member of the Joint Committee on Atomic Energy, partly for political reasons (his state was home to an important nuclear research laboratory), but also because he took a genuine interest in international affairs. In July 1949 the Soviets tested their first atomic bomb, two years earlier than the CIA had forecasted. That episode helped shape his opinions and made him wary of intelligence estimates and attentive to the danger of nuclear weapons. He was a vigorous proponent of hydrogen-bomb research and of NSC-68, the National Security Council document that laid out a strategy for armed containment of the Soviet Union. It had been drafted by one of the experts to whom he regularly turned for advice on such matters: Paul Nitze, the head of the Policy Planning Staff.

In 1952 Jackson won a Senate seat after a hard-fought campaign. Anti-Democratic sentiment was running high after twenty years of Democrats in the White House, and Jackson's opponent did not shrink from inviting Senator Joseph McCarthy to come to Washington and attack Jackson for being "soft on Communism." Jackson made a name for himself by standing up to McCarthy, especially in the televised Army-McCarthy hearings that led to the Wisconsin senator's downfall in 1954. Jackson's star had risen to the point that in January 1955 he was able to obtain nominations to the Senate committees he wanted: Armed Services, Atomic Energy, and Interior. Already in the 1950s he was defending the most advanced and costly weapons programs, including ICBMs, nuclear submarines, and submarine-launched ballistic missiles, on the grounds that America could afford to pay for both "guns and butter." He was quick to denounce the limitations of the doctrine of massive retaliation and very wary of the intentions of the Soviet Union, which he judged to be a totalitarian country that would one day implode under the weight of its contradictions.

A close friend of Senator John F. Kennedy, Jackson was sounded out about running as Kennedy's vice-president in 1960; but in the end it was felt that a southerner was needed to balance the ticket, and Lyndon Johnson was chosen. Jackson's relations with Kennedy slowly deteriorated after that. The senator from Washington took a more hawkish stance than the young president, whom he was unable to persuade to appoint Paul Nitze to the post of secretary of defense (although Kennedy did name Nitze secretary of the Navy). In two crises that pitted Kennedy against Soviet premier Nikita Khrushchev, the Berlin crisis of 1961 and the Cuban missile crisis of October 1962, Jackson felt that Kennedy had not been sufficiently firm. From the Cuban affair Jackson drew the lesson that it was essential for the United States to maintain nuclear superiority because of the danger of escalation from minor conflict to catastrophic confrontation. In March 1962 he gave a speech in which he argued that the security of the United States depended more on NATO than on the United Nations and that paying too much attention to the UN could undermine containment of the Soviets.

This hawkish stance and critical attitude toward the UN were traits that Jackson shared with second-age neoconservatives. There were two others: distrust of the arms-limitation treaties with the Soviets and support for antimissile defenses. Accordingly, he campaigned against ratification of the ban on atmospheric testing of nuclear weapons to which Moscow had agreed on August 5, 1963, and persuaded the Kennedy administration to adopt certain safeguards to ensure long-term technological improvements in American weaponry. He also defended the development of antimissile systems against Defense Secretary Robert McNamara, who deemed them useless on the grounds that "mutual assured destruction" (MAD) was enough to guarantee U.S. security.

After Johnson's accession to the presidency in November 1963, Jackson fully supported the president's position on civil rights as well as his Great Society program, and he also backed his foreign policy, invoking the "domino theory" as grounds defending the intervention in Vietnam to the bitter end. As a result, Jackson became a favorite target of New Left activists, who described him as a tool of the military-industrial lobby: he was "the senator from Boeing," the aircraft manufacturer whose corporate headquarters was located in Jackson's state. More than that, Nixon, after his election in 1968, strongly urged Jackson to become his secretary of defense in order to secure bipartisan support for his policies. But Jackson refused on the grounds that to accept would ruin his chances of becoming president and that in any case he could be more useful on defense issues by remaining in the Senate as a hawk inside the increasingly dovish majority party.

In 1970 his reelection to the Senate was challenged by left-wing liberals backed most notably by Eugene McCarthy. But although Jackson was the bête noire of the New Left, he retained the staunch backing of the unions and won the election hands down. On values issues he remained close to the median Democratic voter: opposed to abortion, in favor of civil rights but against quotas and wary of any effort to replace the "melting pot" with multiculturalism, and for active state intervention: he defended the expansion of the public sector, national health insurance, and even wage and price controls if necessary. Indeed, Tom

Foley, a congressman from Washington and future speaker of the House, remembered him as "the closest one in the Congress I can remember to a European Social Democrat . . . voting for all the social programs."[3] Clearly, he in no way shared the first-age neoconservatives' doubts and hesitations about social policy, and in the late 1970s his positions on economic issues could hardly have been further from those of, say, Irving Kristol.

Buoyed by the success of his senatorial reelection campaign, he set out to win the 1972 presidential nomination with the support of the AFL-CIO. His chief strategist was Ben Wattenberg, the future founder of the CDM. But Jackson was hampered by the visceral opposition of the New Left, his own lack of charisma (if he were to attempt a fireside chat in the manner of FDR, people joked, the fire would go out), and his failure to grasp the workings of the modern media (one day he refused to appear on NBC's *Today Show* because he didn't want to cancel a campaign event scheduled to take place in a bowling alley). But he also suffered from the new delegate-selection rules that the McGovern-Fraser commission had put in place and from the presence in the race of other candidates who were competing for the same segment of the Democratic electorate, most notably Hubert Humphrey. He lost the primary battle to McGovern and the forces of the New Politics. Then came the birth of the CDM in the fall of 1972.

The Jackson-Vanik Amendment

During Richard Nixon's first term as president (1969–1973), Jackson for the most part supported his foreign policy and helped to secure funding for a number of weapons programs, including the Trident submarine and the Safeguard antimissile system. He also approved of the overtures to open up dialogue with China. Throughout his life he retained a strangely nonideological and even romantic vision of China, which apparently came from reading Pearl Buck,[4] but also certainly from cold geopolitical calculations (Beijing as a nondangerous and useful counterweight to Moscow), a position that put him at odds with other anticommunists in the neoconservative camp, like George Meany at the AFL-CIO. In 1972 his position began to diverge from Nixon's. He rejected the policy of détente that Kissinger was pursuing vis-à-vis the Soviet Union and sought to obstruct or thwart it in any way he could. He even compared his efforts to Churchill's attempt to stop the appeasement of

Hitler in the late 1930s (this would become a favorite neoconservative theme). A key element in Jackson's battle against détente was the issue of Jewish emigration from the Soviet Union.

In the 1960s the American Jewish community became concerned about the plight of Soviet Jews, who suffered not only from widespread antisemitism but also from official hostility: although their Jewish identity was unacknowledged and repressed, they could neither assimilate nor emigrate. As Pauline Peretz has reported in her research, Israel encouraged the mobilization of American Jews around these issues. In 1953 the Jewish state established a secret bureau called Nativ, "with the mission of secretly promoting the emigration of Jews from the USSR to Israel in two ways: by direct action targeting Jews behind the Iron Curtain and by conducting campaigns in many Western countries to publicize the fate of Soviet Jewry."[5]

Tel Aviv's goal was the Zionist one of bringing the maximum possible number of Jews to Israel in order to strengthen the Jewish state. Until 1967, support for this objective among American Jews was moderate at best. American organizations emphasized instead the humanitarian objective: to improve the lot of Soviet Jews. After 1968 they attempted to influence the Nixon administration in this direction but obtained little in return for their efforts. As Nixon and Kissinger moved toward a policy of détente, they had little inclination to allow issues of this type to complicate negotiations with Moscow over major issues such as nuclear arms control. Jewish organizations therefore turned to Congress.

Scoop Jackson, already recognized as a friend of Israel because of his staunch support for the Jewish state following the 1967 war, took up the issue in late September 1972. A month earlier the U.S.S.R. had imposed a heavy tax on anyone who sought to emigrate permanently, including Jews who wished to move to Israel. The justification given for this tax was that emigrants needed to reimburse the state for the cost of their education. Jackson introduced an amendment based on the idea of "conditionality," the original version of which was drafted by his assistant Richard Perle.[6] What this meant was that "most favored nation" trading status, which allowed bilateral trade with minimum tariffs, could not be granted to the Soviet Union unless Moscow agreed to liberalize the rules governing emigration.

Following the May 1972 Moscow summit, Nixon and Kissinger had concluded a trade agreement with the Soviets that gave them access to Western technology and grain in exchange for repayment of Soviet debts stemming from the World War II Lend-Lease accords. Their real objective, however, was not the repayment, but an additional political instrument that could be used to extract concessions from the Soviets in other areas. This was the essential idea of "linkage": in any negotiation, the agenda included any number of items that could be traded off against one another, thus using common interests to moderate Cold War tensions.

In the Senate Jackson introduced an amendment, which Representative Charles Vanik quickly imitated in the House, the objectives of which were as complex as those of the Nixon-Kissinger diplomatic offensive. One of Jackson's goals was of course to come to the aid of Soviet Jews and to focus attention on repression in the Soviet Union. But the senator's refusal to compromise over the next two years hinted at other, less obvious aims. For one thing, he was preparing to run again for the presidency in 1976 and wanted to reinforce his standing as a "hero" in the eyes of the Jewish community, whose support in the campaign would be invaluable. Jackson also sought to improve his position with the unions, which did not approve of Nixon's trade policies for both political reasons (the Nixon policies offended their anticommunism) and economic reasons (Soviet exports competed with domestically produced goods). Finally, Jackson hoped to improve his position with certain segments of the electorate, such as voters of East European descent. Indeed, the battle over Soviet Jews, which dragged on for more than two years, helped to raise his national stature with all groups.

Even more significant were the foreign policy objectives of the Jackson-Vanik amendment. By forcing new demands on Moscow, Jackson reduced Kissinger's leeway in negotiations, if he did not eliminate it altogether. Indeed, the economic weapon was the linchpin of all détente policy, and the Jackson initiative aimed to render it inoperative. Ultimately, it was the principle of détente itself that was the primary target of the amendment. The goal was to put the ideological issues of values, democracy, and human rights back at the center of U.S.-Soviet relations. On these issues there could be no agreement: they laid bare the differences between East and West, unlike the pursuit of common interests that might lead to workable compromises, as Kissinger envisioned.

Nixon garnered support from business interests eager to trade with the Soviets and from groups that favored negotiations, such as the American Committee on U.S.-Soviet Relations, which was founded in 1974 and chaired by John Kenneth Galbraith. The committee mobilized in support of détente and closer ties with the Soviets. Its membership included businessmen, economists, diplomats, and distinguished academics. Samuel Pisar among others provided theoretical justification for the group's actions: increased trade would favor peace and lead to internal liberalization of Communist regimes through exposure to Western consumer goods.[7]

What mobilized Scoop Jackson and his supporters in their fight against détente and *Ostpolitik* was precisely the opposite theory. For them the goal was to deny the Soviets access to Western grain and technology, which they saw as life support for a moribund Soviet regime. Instead, they hoped to encourage internal dissidence and protest. The clash between, on the one hand, proponents of "engagement" (many of them Europeans), who hoped to transform hostile regimes by multiplying contacts with them, and, on the other hand, neoconservatives and hawks, who hoped to heighten internal contradictions in Communist countries and eventually bring down their regimes, first developed at this time. Over the next several decades it would flare up periodically: for instance, over the trans-Siberian gas pipeline in the early 1980s and in connection with Iraq, Iran, Cuba, and North Korea during the 1990s and 2000s.

After several rounds, the confrontation narrowed to a duel between Jackson and the Nixon administration, which had been steadily weakened by the Watergate crisis (and which ultimately forced Nixon to resign on August 9, 1974, bringing Gerald Ford to the presidency). The negotiations turned on the number of Jews to be authorized to leave the Soviet Union and on the type of assurances, public or private, to be given by the Soviets (public assurances would cause trouble between Moscow and its Arab allies, who took a dim view of any reinforcement of Israel). The two issues were linked: for example, in August 1974 the Soviets agreed to grant 50,000 exit visas per year if they were not required to provide written assurances of the number.

Jackson steadily increased his demands to 100,000 exit authorizations per year, going so far that he was abandoned for a time by his staunchest allies, Senators Jacob Javits and Abraham Ribicoff, and even by some Jewish organizations.[8] Kissinger played the role of intermediary and believed that he had an agreement, which was made official on October 18, 1974. The Jackson-Vanik amendment incorporating the agreed conditions was to be adopted but with a waiver procedure that the president could invoke if he guaranteed freedom of emigration in the country in question. But at the moment the agreement was announced at the White

House on October 18, Jackson trumpeted his victory, boasting of having forced the Soviets to back down and explicitly mentioning the figure of 60,000 exit visas annually even though no such figure appeared in any formal treaty.

As a result, the Soviets pulled back from the accord. Brezhnev, having lost face in the Politburo and with Arab countries, changed his mind, and the whole commercial treaty collapsed. The Jackson-Vanik amendment was approved by both houses of Congress on December 20, 1974, and signed by Gerald Ford on January 3, 1975, but Ford did not need to invoke the waiver because Moscow chose to give up "most favored nation" status so as not to be forced to alter its position on the emigration of Soviet Jews. Moscow had lost interest in the whole idea of the treaty.[9]

What came of all this turmoil? For the Soviet Jews, the bottom line was clearly negative: emigration fell considerably, from 35,000 in 1973 to around 13,000 in 1975, and it did not reach 35,000 again until 1979, after which it fell once more. There was no real increase until the late 1980s.[10] For Kissinger the bottom line was equally negative: he lost a key instrument of his linkage policy, namely, the ability to bargain over commercial interests. Détente was undermined. The whole affair revealed the underlying cynicism of realist foreign policy: whatever their differences over values, realists held, the two superpowers could nevertheless come to terms over trade. The issue of human rights was thus introduced into the foreign policy agenda. It would become central with the Helsinki accords and, later, in the foreign policy of Jimmy Carter. The real winner, along with the legislative branch, which reasserted its foreign policy prerogatives vis-à-vis the executive, was of course Scoop Jackson.

Jackson's Senate Staff: A Neoconservative Nursery

Senator Jackson's office on Capitol Hill was a veritable nursery for neoconservatives of the second and third ages. Two of his staffers, Dorothy Fosdick and Richard Perle, played a particularly important role. Fosdick, who had served as foreign policy adviser to Democratic presidential candidate Adlai Stevenson in 1952, met Jackson in 1954 and for the next twenty-nine years served as his chief adviser on international affairs. Hawkish in outlook and a genuine expert on strategic issues, "Dickie" became a well-known Washington personality. Her professionalism and rigorous approach to policy issues complemented the qualities of her colleague Richard Perle.

Perle did not begin working for Jackson until 1969, but his intellectual prowess and skill in political maneuvering soon gained him remarkable influence in the realm of international affairs. Born in New York in 1941, he grew up in California. While he was still in high school, one of his classmates, Joan Wohlstetter, invited him to her home to enjoy her parents' swimming pool. That is how young Richard became acquainted with Albert Wohlstetter, Joan's father, with whom he discussed a subject about which he knew very little at the time: nuclear strategy. At that point his views on the subject were close to the position of SANE (the National Committee for a Sane Nuclear Policy). Wohlstetter, yet another former Shachtmanite from CCNY, was at the time research director at RAND, a West Coast think tank specializing in military and strategic issues. He gave Perle an offprint of an important article he had written for *Foreign Affairs*, titled "The Delicate Balance of Terror." This was Perle's first exposure to strategic analysis, and it powerfully influenced his thinking.[11]

After studying English literature at the University of California, Perle did graduate work in political science. In 1963 he attended the London School of Economics (where one of his classmates was Edward Luttwak, another future neoconservative strategist), then got a master's degree at Princeton. During the 1960s he was a liberal Democrat, not a radical, and in any case not very politicized, although he claims to have been instinctively wary of Hollywood "radical chic" circles, with which he had some connection.[12] In the spring of 1969 Albert Wohlstetter offered him a job writing a report for a group that two Washington establishment figures, Paul Nitze and Truman's former secretary of state, Dean Acheson, had just created: the Committee to Maintain a Prudent Defense Policy.[13]

The job mainly involved interviewing experts and developing arguments in support of a proposed antimissile system that was under attack by Democratic senators such as William Fulbright and George McGovern but above all Stuart Symington from Missouri, who had somehow got his hands on a supposedly secret Pentagon report questioning the system's technical feasibility. Wohlstetter, Nitze, and Acheson wanted to help Jackson defeat Symington and were in need of research assistance. In addition to Perle, they hired one of Wohlstetter's students from the University of Chicago, a certain Paul Wolfowitz, the son of celebrated mathematician Jacob Wolfowitz, with whom Wohlstetter himself had studied. (Two other researchers would later be added to the staff: Peter Wilson and Edward Luttwak.)

Perle and Wolfowitz interviewed a number of experts, including Dorothy Fosdick, and then worked directly with Jackson himself in his Senate office, whose floor was littered with documents: the ones Symington had obtained from the Pentagon along with others that were to be used against the senator from Missouri in the confidential Senate hearing on ABMs.[14] (Congress approved funding for the Safeguard antimissile system by a razor-thin majority.) In the fall of 1969 Nitze invited Perle to come to work for him at the Pentagon (where he represented the secretary of defense at the SALT talks),[15] but it was too late: Jackson had offered him a job for a year, during which he could also finish work on his doctoral dissertation in his free time. Perle accepted and remained in Jackson's employ for the next eleven years. He never did finish his dissertation, because "there was never any spare time working for Scoop."[16] He became a sort of second son to the senator, who was an indulgent father, leaving it to "big sister" Dorothy Fosdick to scold him when he yet again showed up late at the office (where, to be sure, he had been working late the night before).

On the major foreign policy issues in which Jackson was involved, most notably Soviet Jews and the Middle East, Perle earned a reputation as a first-class "operator," skilled at using information in his possession to serve the interests of Jackson and his fellow hawks. He often obtained this information from officials at the Pentagon and State who had failed to persuade their superiors of the value of their ideas; at other times he got it from the Israeli embassy. When the neoconservatives opposed the nomination of Paul Warnke in 1976 to head the Arms Control and Disarmament Agency, Perle wrote speeches for no fewer than sixteen senators.[17] He knew how to manipulate the press by leaking sensitive information and how to woo important columnists such as Rowland Evans and Robert Novak of the *Washington Post* and Robert Bartley of the *Wall Street Journal*. Journalists repaid Perle by publishing countless flattering portraits of him, soon turning him into a legend: the "prince of darkness," the hawk who dared to contemplate nuclear apocalypse.[18]

Two years younger than Perle, Paul Wolfowitz studied at Cornell University, where his philosophy professor and faculty mentor at Telluride House, Allan Bloom, himself a student of the philosopher Leo Strauss, influenced his intellectual development (as he did that of other future intellectuals, whether neoconservatives or not, such as Francis Fukuyama, Abram Shulsky, Charles Fairbanks, Laurie Mylroie, and William Galston).[19] Wolfowitz chose to pursue political science rather than his father's specialty, mathematics. In 1963, at age twenty, he participated in Martin Luther King's march on Washington, as did other future neo-conservatives such as Penn Kemble, Joshua Muravchik, and Richard John Neuhaus, and went to the University of Chicago to take his doctorate and meet Leo Strauss. It was not Strauss, however, but Albert Wohlstetter who became his real mentor and dissertation adviser. It was also Wohlstetter who sent him to Washington to work with Perle for the Committee to Maintain a Prudent Defense Policy. Unlike Perle, in 1972 Wolfowitz did finish his dissertation, which dealt with desalinization plants that used nuclear power as a vehicle of nuclear proliferation in the Middle East.

In that same year Wolfowitz was hired, once again on Wohlstetter's recommendation, by Fred Iklé, the new director of the Arms Control and Disarmament Agency (ACDA). In 1976 he joined the famous Team B, which the new CIA director, George H. W. Bush, had just established to prepare an alternative assessment of the Soviet Union's strategic capabilities. In 1977 he was one of the rare neoconservatives to be hired by the Carter Pentagon. His position was quite modest (deputy undersecretary for regional programs), but it allowed him to follow developments in the Middle East. He helped to call attention to the vulnerability of the West's position in the region, especially the danger of an invasion of Saudi Arabia or Kuwait by Saddam Hussein, and began to think about possible responses.[20] He resigned from the Carter administration at the beginning of 1980, then in 1981 under the Reagan administration became head of the Policy Planning Staff at the Department of State, for which he hired a number of promising former students, including Francis Fukuyama, Dennis Ross, I. Lewis Libby, Alan Keyes, and Zalmay Khalilzad.

In addition to brilliant staffers such as Fosdick and Perle, Jackson's entourage included Charles Horner and others who worked for him or his campaign for only a few months or years, such as Elliott Abrams, Douglas Feith, Frank Gaffney, and even, for a time, William Kristol, Irving Kristol's son. As for James Woolsey (a future CDM member and CIA director under Clinton), it was Scoop Jackson who advised him to go work for another Democratic hawk, Senator John Stennis of Mississippi.[21]

Jackson also maintained a network of contacts in the strategic and intellectual community with people who supplied him with information and analyses.[22] In addition to Albert Wohlstetter, these included Harvard Soviet specialist Richard Pipes (a member of CDM, Team B, and the

Committee on the Present Danger), Fred Iklé (CPD member and director of the ACDA from 1973 to 1977), and Bernard Lewis, the well-known British historian of the Ottoman Empire and Muslim world, whose analysis of Islamism and of social paralysis in the Arab world would serve as inspiration to third-age neoconservatives.

Moynihan as a Second-Age Paradigm

In addition to Jackson's Senate staff and the CDM, there were other second-age neoconservatives associated with the unions and *Commentary*. Among these was Daniel Patrick Moynihan.

Both George Meany, who served as head of the AFL-CIO from 1955 to 1979, and his successor, Lane Kirkland, who served until 1995, were fierce anticommunists who lent considerable political support to the Scoop Jackson Democrats. They also gave substantial financial support to both the CDM and the CPD, of which Lane Kirkland would become cochair. Kirkland's passion for foreign affairs stemmed in part from his studies at Georgetown University's Foreign Service School, and he was much concerned with containing the Soviet Union. In 1977 he founded the Free Trade Union Institute, the international arm of the AFL-CIO, which supported the Solidarity movement in Poland and in 1983 became one of the four branches of Reagan's National Endowment for Democracy.

Another important constellation of second-age neoconservatives was linked to the magazine *Commentary*. By 1970 the magazine had been converted to first-age neoconservatism, and it joined the second age when it took up arms against both the influence of the New Left on the Democratic party and the Nixon-Kissinger policy of détente. The later fight was led mainly by Walter Laqueur, who wrote no fewer than forty articles on foreign policy between 1972 and the fall of the Berlin Wall in 1989. With considerable verve, Laqueur attacked "appeasement," the "Finlandization" of the West, the pusillanimity of Europe, and other such targets. Norman Podhoretz also wrote regularly about foreign policy issues, especially "liberal guilt" and the "culture of appeasement" that had taken hold of America and threatened to undermine the policy of containment. At times he echoed views that James Burnham had expressed in the 1940s and 1950s.[23] Between 1974 and 1981 *Commentary* also published six very important articles by Pat Moynihan, of which the first two, "Was Woodrow Wilson Right?" (May 1974) and "The United

States in Opposition" (March 1975), reportedly earned him his appointment as ambassador to the United Nations by Kissinger and Ford.[24]

Earlier we ended the biography of Moynihan "the political professor" in 1972, with the failure of his social policy recommendations to Nixon, of whom he had hoped, in true first-age neoconservative style, to make a new Disraeli. That failure led him to turn away from issues of race and class and toward international affairs. This decision was in some respects surprising: in 1949 he had failed the examination to become a Foreign Service officer.[25] But Moynihan was far from ignorant about international issues. With a doctorate from the Fletcher School of Law and Diplomacy, he continued his studies at the London School of Economics and later worked with the International Rescue Committee, an anti-communist organization that helped refugees who sought asylum in the United States. In the fall of 1971, his reformist hopes already dashed, he was appointed a delegate to the United Nations General Assembly, a very minor post that nevertheless made a great impression on him. There he acquired the conviction that American diplomats were ill equipped to counter ideological attacks from the Third World and the Soviet Union— attacks that were flourishing at the time. His insistence on the need for "moral clarity" in international affairs was strengthened as a result.

From February 1973 to the beginning of 1975 Moynihan served as ambassador to India. There he acquired international experience and firsthand knowledge of Third World nationalism. He also became convinced that empires built on force were destined to fail, foremost among them the Soviet Union. And he became an uncompromising critic of Third World "kleptocrats" and their American apologists.[26] In May 1974, writing from New Delhi, and again in March 1975, this time from New York, he published the important articles in *Commentary* mentioned above, in which he maintained that America's natural mission was to defend freedom and democracy throughout the world. He emphasized the need to wage ideological war at the United Nations, which he suggested ought to be regarded as a classic parliament in which it was essential to defend one's party interests unreservedly and without making excuses for America's imperfections, even when one's party happened to be in the minority.

Henry Kissinger admired these articles despite his differences with Moynihan, and President Ford offered him the post of ambassador to the United Nations. Moynihan served in that role for only a short time, from July 1975 to February 1976, yet he succeeded in the goal he had set for himself: to conduct a propaganda war against ambient anti-American sentiment and Communist and Third World influence. He also suffered a crushing defeat that he would once again turn into a personal triumph. On November 10, 1975, the General Assembly adopted resolution 3379, which stated that "Zionism is a form of racism and racial discrimination." Moynihan could not stop 72 countries from voting in favor of the resolution (35 voted against and 32 abstained). He did, however, deliver a brilliant attack on the proposal, which was widely publicized and gained him considerable popularity in the United States, where neoconservatives were galvanized by his remarks.[27]

The sudden increase in Moynihan's popularity contributed to the deterioration of his relations with Henry Kissinger, who was not pleased to see his UN ambassador surpass him in popularity. To be sure, there had been no shortage of disagreements between the two men. On July 2, 1975, Moynihan had joined Scoop Jackson and James Schlesinger (Ford's defense secretary) at an AFL-CIO dinner in honor of Alexander Solzhenitsyn—a dinner that the White House and State Department had studiously avoided so as not to offend the Soviet Union. By contrast, neoconservatives hailed such initiatives. Here, for example, is Ben Wattenberg, speaking in February 1976 at an event organized by the CDM:

> Somehow the dialogue has become very cold and abstract and dehumanized. People talk about the "balance of power" of "SALT treaties" of "cruise missiles" of "B-1 bombers" and, of course, about "détente." But it took a CDM member, Pat Moynihan, a dues-paying, paid-up CDM member, to remind Democrats and Americans what the struggle was really about beneath the discourse on hardware. What Pat said is that we Americans are the leaders of "The Liberty Party" on this planet—and it was high time that someone said it with gusto, with vigor, with style and with pride. And it took the American labor movement to bring Alexander Solzhenitsyn here to remind Americans that something strange was going on when heroes in the struggle for liberty can no longer be greeted in the White House.[28]

Kissinger attacked Moynihan repeatedly and leaked damaging information about him until in the end he decided to resign. He had been UN ambassador for only eight months, but that was long enough to win him sufficient popularity to run for the Senate from New York, after campaigning for Scoop Jackson in the Democratic presidential primaries.

Jackson failed to win the presidency, but Moynihan was elected to the Senate. For several years he became, along with Jackson, the political leader of the neoconservatives, the man on whom they pinned their hopes.

Neoconservative Doubts about Carter

As we have seen, by the end of 1975 the ambiguous outcome of internal Democratic party struggles had left CDM members dissatisfied. Left-wing proclivities remained strong within the party, and although the delegate-selection process had been reformed in 1972, it by no means assured that a moderate candidate would win. The CDM therefore used the resources at its disposal to promote its ideas, especially in foreign policy, during the 1976 presidential campaign.[29]

The group's favorite candidate was of course Senator Jackson, who enjoyed good name recognition and the support of the Jewish and Holly-wood communities, in addition to which he benefited from the decision of three party heavyweights (Ted Kennedy, Walter Mondale, and Hubert Humphrey) not to run. Ben Wattenberg became Jackson's chief strate-gist, with young Elliott Abrams for his assistant. The CDM did all it could to support him without crossing the legal line of open endorse-ment. As Peter Rosenblatt recalled, "We had a very close relationship with his staff—Fosdick, Perle; we were kind of seamless, kind of an ex-tension of his staff, for the presidential campaign."[30] In the end, how-ever, Jimmy Carter won the Democratic primary race despite having be-gun as a virtual unknown, with support of only 4 percent in the polls in January 1976.[31]

As a result, the CDM shifted its focus to the Democratic party plat-form, on which convention delegates would be asked to vote. The plat-form does not really determine the candidate's campaign commitments or, if elected, his future policy, but it is a good way of gauging the bal-ance of power within the party. Moynihan, who had just joined the CDM, worked with Wattenberg (representing the Jackson campaign) to achieve a moderate platform that would not yield on foreign policy is-sues to pro–Third World New Leftists. The final document devoted a great deal of attention to human rights issues. It offered implicit support to the Jackson-Vanik amendment and did not limit its criticism to U.S. allies such as South Korea and Chile but also challenged Communist countries such as North Korea, China, and the Soviet Union.[32] The platform contained no hint of American guilt or apology and no mention of moral equivalence.[33] Working in their subcommittee, moreover, Wattenberg and Moynihan managed to kill a proposed platform clause that would have condemned the B-1 bomber program, which was intended to provide a replacement for the aging B-52. No weapons program was singled out, and no withdrawal of troops from Europe or other places around the world was contemplated. Accordingly, the *Washington Post* was able to write on June 18, 1976, that although Scoop Jackson had lost the nomination, he had won the war over policy.[34]

But neither that victory nor the CDM's activism on other fronts ensured that Jimmy Carter would behave as a Cold War liberal. As Penn Kemble regretfully observed,

> Carter was not elected with any real ideological views, he was just somebody all people could coalesce around, and this was very uncomfortable for us, because we didn't have much confidence in Carter, we were against him, we were for Scoop. What happened to Nixon sort of spoiled the debate—we couldn't have a debate anymore about what our strategy should be, because the party didn't really need a strategy—it was enough to be just not Nixon.[35]

Who exactly was Jimmy Carter? A former naval officer and, more recently, governor of Georgia, Carter had not emerged from the ranks of the New Left, and for the CDM that fact alone marked a considerable advance over 1972. Accordingly, neoconservatives tended to grant him the benefit of the doubt. A year later, in the summer of 1977, the *Political Observer* (the CDM's newsletter) was still saying that the CDM had played a positive role in internal Democratic party debates because the party had chosen "a presidential candidate who stood clearly in its mainstream."[36]

Indeed, the benefit of the doubt was so great that in May 1976 the CDM began consulting certain of its members about their views on the future of the organization: should it not perhaps simply declare victory and disappear? Some, like Seymour Martin Lipset, favored complete dissolution: "I assume that there will be no further need for the CDM if Carter wins. I may be wrong, but he seems to be close to the CDM on most issues which have concerned us."[37] In early July the decision was made to place the CDM "on life support":[38] the organization was not dissolved, but its small full-time staff was let go, two-thirds of its office space was rented out to reduce costs, and its main organizers turned their attention elsewhere.[39]

Penn Kemble, Joshua Muravchik, Elliott Abrams, and Charles Horner all went to work for the Moynihan campaign in New York. Moynihan won election and would serve as senator from New York until 2000, when Hillary Clinton succeeded him. Richard Schifter quit the CDM in March to devote himself to the creation of JINSA, the Jewish Institute for National Security Affairs (to which we shall return). Max Kampelman and above all Eugene Rostow turned their attention to establishing the Committee on the Present Danger. In other words, the CDM demobilized and went into "sleep" mode.

The awakening after Jimmy Carter's victory in November 1976 therefore came as a rude shock. The first premonitory signs of a cooling of relations between the president and the right wing of the party was the break between Carter and Jackson. Their personal relations, never very good, did not recover from the intense primary battle.

The second sign came toward the end of 1976: Penn Kemble and Peter Rosenblatt submitted a list of personnel recommendations labeled "CDM" to Tony Lake, who was a close adviser of future Secretary of State Cyrus Vance and a friend of Rosenblatt's ever since both had worked together on Edmund Muskie's presidential campaign. The recommendations included the names of many people who were not CDM members, and the idea was to ensure that centrist Democratic views would be amply represented in the Carter administration.[40] Ultimately, however, only one or two of the people on the list were nominated. According to Rosenblatt, Lake claimed that he had mislaid the CDM list before he had a chance to speak to Vance about it. Rosenblatt was inclined to think that the list was not lost but rather pressed into service as a "black list" of those who were not to be appointed under any circumstances.[41] The president's national security adviser, Zbigniew Brzezinski, who represented Democratic hawks, has said that he had nothing to do with appointments at State and Pentagon, which far outnumbered National Security Council posts. He nevertheless concedes that certain political constraints did play a role: he had given some thought to hiring Richard Perle, for example, "but this was not feasible, because Carter and Jackson did not like each other."[42]

A few weeks later, Wattenberg, on Lake's recommendation, gave Vance a list of suggestions for nomination as ambassadors, which met with the same fate.[43] In the end, only three people with ties to the CDM obtained posts in the Carter administration. Early on, James Woolsey was named undersecretary of the Navy, only to resign in late 1979 in frustration over lack of funding and what he regarded as the administration's excessively dovish policy.[44] In 1980 Max Kampelman was named ambassador to the Conference on Security Cooperation in Europe (CSCE) negotiations in Madrid.[45] Peter Rosenblatt himself was named ambassador for negotiations on the status of Micronesia in the summer of 1977, which unleashed a round of sarcasm within the CDM: "They wouldn't give us Polynesia or Macronesia, only Micronesia."[46]

To be sure, there is a simple explanation for the marginalization of the neoconservatives: in the end Carter did not owe much to Scoop Jackson or the right wing of the Democratic party, and he owed nothing to the CDM, which supported him only after he had already won. In 1976 there was no revival of the "Democrats for Nixon" of 1972, and Carter knew that he was not sufficiently far to the left to drive away the centrists, especially in the post-Watergate environment. Hence there was nothing to force Carter to do any favors for the CDM. In foreign policy, it was the McGovernite camp that dominated and brought in a team hostile to the CDM's view of the world (with the exception of the National Security Council, headed by Brzezinski).

On February 10, 1977, Paul Seabury, speaking for the West Coast branch of the CDM, urged Moynihan to comment on Carter's recent nominations:

> What is now the case is that he [Carter] has simply (with exceptions such as Brzezinsky [sic]) collected a bunch of McGovernites coupled with a few singed repentant hawks. These in no way reflect the dominant views of the Democrats . . . In sum, they cast doubt upon Carter's own foreign policy views which he developed during the campaign . . .
>
> Somehow the President ought to be told that these people are not representative of mainstream democrats. Those who are (and I think that Brzezinski and [Samuel] Huntington are much closer), and who have positions of some influence need to know that there is political support in the Party for them. One way in which this could be signaled would be to pump some new life into CDM in Washington.[47]

Thus it was the Carter administration's foreign policy nominations that injected new life into the CDM: it became apparent that the new administration would bear watching by the centrist wing of the Democratic party.

The Warnke Nomination

Most of the State Department appointments came from what the neo-conservative Carl Gershman once labeled the "new foreign-policy establishment," that is, intellectuals associated with the journal *Foreign Policy* who proposed a liberal vision of American foreign policy for the post-Vietnam era (even though *Foreign Policy* was not exclusively liberal).[48] These included Tony Lake, Richard Holbrooke, Leslie Gelb, Morton Halperin, and Joseph Nye. But the straw that broke the camel's back and united the neoconservative opposition was the nomination of Paul Warnke to head the Arms Control and Disarmament Agency, which was responsible for the SALT negotiations.

This nomination was particularly sensitive for two reasons. First, the post was an especially important one at a time when negotiations with the Soviet Union seemed to be leading up to a second accord on strategic arms limitation, an accord whose basic principles neoconservatives disliked. Second, Warnke himself was an issue. A former McGovern adviser in the 1972 campaign and a staunch defender of arms control, he had published an article in *Foreign Policy* in 1975 titled "Apes on a Treadmill," in which he stressed the absurdity of the arms race and launched a direct attack on the idea of global American strategic superiority.[49] This was the heart of neoconservative strategic thinking, and Warnke denounced it as costly, unnecessary, and even dangerous. As he saw it, the arms race added nothing to American security. On the contrary, American initiatives were pushing the Soviets to go them one better, thus resulting in a self-fulfilling prophecy. Someone had to be first to climb down by demonstrating unilateral restraint and pushing toward mutual reductions of nuclear arsenals.

Ideas like these were clearly anathema to neoconservatives, who mobilized in February 1977 to prevent Senate confirmation of Warnke as head of the ACDA and chief SALT negotiator. Although neoconservatives lost this battle, it marked a crystallization of their movement. The CDM took part in the fight through Penn Kemble and Joshua Muravchik (who had become a member of Moynihan's Senate staff). They drafted a brief but devastating report on Warnke based on his own past statements, some of which were so radical that the embarrassed nominee was forced to say in the hearings that he had not really meant what he wrote. While testifying before both the Senate Foreign Relations Committee and the Armed Services Committee, Paul Nitze made use of the Kemble-Muravchik memo, which circulated widely inside the Beltway.

So did Scoop Jackson, who as one might expect led the charge against Warnke.

Although Warnke ultimately won easy confirmation to the ACDA post (the vote was 70 to 29), the vote on his appointment as SALT negotiator was much closer (58 to 40), and it came only after much political turmoil and media attention. This was a warning shot across the bow of the Carter administration, which was put on notice that 40 out of 100 senators opposed taking too soft a position in arms talks with the Soviets. Since ratification of any treaty would require the votes of at least 67 senators (a two-thirds majority), this warning had to be taken seriously.

The Neoconservative-Carter Gap Widens

The Warnke episode reinforced the Cold War Democrats' conviction that they needed to revive the CDM and use it to counter McGovernite tendencies in the Carter administration. In the spring of 1977 the CDM emerged from sleep mode and enjoyed a burst of activity that lasted until the 1980 campaign.[50] Penn Kemble left the day-to-day leadership of the organization to accept an offer from the American Enterprise Institute, where he did research in 1977–78 before going to work for Pat Moynihan in 1978–79, when Moynihan was pondering a Democratic presidential run in 1980. Kemble left Moynihan's team when the senator from New York finally abandoned that idea, to the great regret of centrist Democrats and neoconservatives, who saw him as their new champion, after Scoop Jackson. In 1977 Joshua Muravchik took over from Kemble as executive director of the CDM, just as he had taken over the reins of the Young People's Socialist League from Kemble ten years earlier. Muravchik would remain in his post until early 1979.

Whereas the goal of the CDM during its first four years of existence was to challenge the New Politics inside the Democratic party and to regain control of the party both institutionally and intellectually, from 1977 to 1980 it redirected its efforts toward oversight of the Carter administration and preparatory work for a new foreign policy, with a special focus on human rights. Both Jackson and Moynihan played an active role in the organization, presiding over its most important meetings and exerting influence on the composition of the executive committee and board of directors. Moynihan named one of his staffers, Elliott Abrams, as liaison to the CDM. On May 29, 1977, the *Washington Star* announced that the CDM was back in business after a year of hibernation. The headline read: "Jackson, Moynihan Revive Coalition."[51]

The CDM did not desert the battlefield of intraparty conflict, however. The group continued to take an interest in delegate-selection rules, quotas, trade union issues, and, increasingly, legislative activity. Nevertheless, foreign policy issues became predominant, and the CDM transformed itself into an organization dedicated primarily to the advancement of a muscular foreign and defense policy. Thanks to Jimmy Carter's shrewdness as a presidential candidate, both CDM centrists and McGovernites were persuaded that he shared their ideas and ultimately supported him. His four years in office, however, heightened tensions between the two groups and ended by disappointing both, and their dual defection contributed to Carter's defeat in 1980.[52]

The CDM's reactions to Carter's foreign policy can serve as an accurate indicator of the evolution of the Scoop Jackson Democrats, or second-age neoconservatives. The CDM moved from circumspection to overt criticism to a spectacular divorce in 1980 that took the Cold War Democrats straight into the orbit of Ronald Reagan.

At first, the group gave Carter the benefit of the doubt and sought to encourage him. Evidence for this can be seen in the publication of an open letter titled "Hang Tough, Mr. President" (the phrase was borrowed from Carter himself), in which the organization began by warmly congratulating Carter for his bold position on human rights and his quest for an arms-reduction treaty. For the CDM, this marked "the first necessary step in leading our nation away from the secretive strategies of pessimism and back to the kind of affirmative foreign policy that suits a great democracy."[53] Such a foreign policy not only protected U.S. national interests but also recognized that "primary among these interests [was] the defense and preservation of freedom in the world."

Still, the CDM was careful to draw some lines in the sand. Concerning the SALT negotiations, for instance, the letter stressed the group's worries in view of questions raised by "responsible American analysts" (probably an allusion to analysts from the Committee on the Present Danger, most notably Paul Nitze), who suggested that the initial American proposal was too favorable to the Soviets. The CDM's anti-Soviet rhetoric was far harsher than that employed by an administration eager to obtain an accord. The CDM assigned itself the role of watchdog: it aimed to be constructive but also demanding and suspicious. That stance was enough, however, to draw some favorable press commentary and even a positive response from the president.[54]

These exchanges of amenities did not last long. Carter's May 23, 1977, speech at Notre Dame on human rights, which Tony Lake wrote, shocked neoconservatives: in this first public statement of his foreign policy, Carter showed himself to be entirely under the influence of the McGovernites, embracing détente and relegating the Cold War and anti-communist ideology to the dustbin of history: "Being confident of our own future, we are now free of that inordinate fear of Communism which once led us to embrace any dictator who joined us in that fear. I'm glad that's being changed."[55]

By the fall of 1977, the CDM's tone turned critical. The first contentious issue involved the Middle East. The CDM reacted negatively to a joint U.S.-Soviet communiqué on October 1 on "Principles for a settlement of the conflict in the Middle East," which the group saw as an unwelcome legitimation of a Russian presence at the negotiating table and a first step toward imposing a solution on Israel.[56] Beyond this critique of regional policy, the CDM attacked the administration's overall approach to U.S.-Soviet relations, which it deemed too timid, and was worried that the administration was downplaying the initial American insistence on human rights in favor of a return to the linkage approach of previous administrations. In particular, it suspected Paul Warnke's negotiating team of having achieved a recent breakthrough in the SALT talks by simply caving in to Russian demands.

The spring of 1978 saw a deterioration of relations between the CDM and the administration, marking the beginning of the phase of overt criticism that would end two years later in divorce. On April 7 the CDM issued a press release imploring the administration not to cancel the neutron bomb project, a proposal that it said would signal a policy of "speak loudly and carry a twig."[57] In May, its public appeal to the administration to admit more Vietnamese Boat People to the United States was still fairly constructive and elicited a positive response from the White House and State Department.[58]

Less than a month later, however, the organization characterized the proposed sale of sixty F-15 fighter jets to Saudi Arabia as an act of "accommodation and retreat."[59] In the view of the CDM executive committee, the sale would contribute nothing essential to Saudi Arabia but would threaten the security of Israel by depriving the Israeli air force of air superiority. The CDM critique served to back up the positions taken by Senators Jackson and Moynihan, adding yet more heat to an already tense debate that saw pro-Israel forces such as the American Israel Public Affairs Committee (AIPAC) attempt to block the administration's proposal in Congress. This move drew considerable media attention, but the outcome was not what the CDM hoped for.[60]

In the following month the rift grew wider. On June 22 the CDM board of directors approved a thoroughgoing critique of Carter's foreign policy titled "Unilateral Restraint: The Experiment That Failed." The document argued that the moderation in the American position had been perceived by the Soviets as weakness rather than as a desire for reconciliation and had led them to press their advantage. "Arguing that 'only a change in our conduct will bring change in theirs,' the CDM statement calls on the president to take various steps, including: hiking defense spending; severing relations with Cuba; more boldly criticizing Soviet human rights violations; and imposing stricter political restraints on US–Soviet trade."[61]

From the end of 1978 to the beginning of the election year 1980, the CDM occupied itself chiefly with organizing demonstrations of support for Eastern Bloc dissidents, a subject to which I will return later. CDM hostility toward the administration continued to increase. Emblematic of this hostility was James Woolsey's resignation as undersecretary of the Navy at the end of 1979. Woolsey was frustrated by what he regarded as an inadequate budget.[62] Jimmy Carter's turn to a more hawkish stance following the Iranian revolution and the Soviet invasion of Afghanistan (Christmas 1979) was too little and too late for the CDM, which felt that these developments called for a far tougher response than the president's. The widening rift ended in a well-publicized divorce after President Carter met with representatives of the group in January 1980.

The Breakfast with Carter

It was apparently the president himself who initiated the meeting with the CDM and various people associated with it. Worried about what promised to be a difficult primary season and election campaign, Carter felt that he needed to seek the support of centrist Democrats, to whom he had moved closer when he adopted a more confrontational stance toward the Soviets in the wake of the invasion of Afghanistan. Max Kampelman recalls receiving telephone calls from two friends, Zbigniew Brzezinski (who had worked with him on the Humphrey campaign) and Vice-President Walter Mondale (whom he knew through his Minnesota connections). Now that Carter had changed his policy with respect to the Soviet Union, might not Kampelman play the role of go-between to reconcile the Democratic hawks with the administration?[63]

The breakfast meeting on January 31, 1980, went badly and achieved the opposite of the desired result: old quarrels were revived, and the president's attitude horrified his guests from the CDM and *Commentary*. Far from repudiating his past "errors," Carter insisted that he had been right all along and sought to persuade his visitors of this. The meeting was a momentous event in the history of the neoconservative movement: it can be seen as the last straw, putting an end to the sentimental loyalty that these Democrats still felt to their party and paving the way for the big move to the Republicans.[64]

On the morning of January 31, before the meeting, the leading figures in the CDM (including Ben Wattenberg, Jeane Kirkpatrick, Max Kampelman, Elmo Zumwalt, and Elliott Abrams) joined Norman Podhoretz and Midge Decter over coffee at the Hay-Adams Hotel to work out a strategy. They decided to have Austin Ranney, a political scientist, speak first. He was a respected moderate and somewhat to the left of the group as a whole. He was to stress the CDM's approval of Carter's hawkish turn post-Afghanistan and then attempt to determine whether the president's shift had brought him close to the position of the centrist Democrats. Then selected members of the group would explore the main issues in contention: Jeane Kirkpatrick on Central America, Admiral Zumwalt on shortcomings in American naval weaponry, and so on.

The meeting took place in the Roosevelt Room, in the West Wing. Jay Winik and John Ehrman, who wrote separate accounts of the event based on the testimony of some participants, both describe a very tense and defensive president.[65] Kirkpatrick confirms that the president interrupted Ranney's introductory presentation, despite its rather conciliatory tone, to deny a quote that all the media attributed to him, according to which he had learned more about the Soviets from the invasion of Afghanistan than he had in all the years up to that point.[66] Carter did not respond to criticisms or else interpreted them as praise, and his responses were incoherent. When, for instance, Norman Podhoretz urged him to orchestrate a vast campaign against the Soviet Union on the issue of human rights, he responded that he was aware of the issue's importance to the Cold War Democrats and asked for help from the CDM in dealing with human rights issues in Uruguay (where the army had seized power in 1973 and proceeded to commit numerous human rights violations). The neoconservatives were dumbfounded.

Max Kampelman, however, contests Winik's account of the meeting. For instance, whereas Winik maintains that Kampelman remained silent throughout the meeting, Kampelman recalls intervening in the middle of the debate to change its direction. Indeed, Kampelman suggests that it was his colleagues from the CDM and *Commentary* who struck the wrong note by challenging Carter on "yesterday's battle" and pointlessly wrangling over principles.

> And after this continued for a while I could see the president getting angry. So I interrupted the meeting and went on, saying, "Mr. President, would you excuse me for a moment, but I want to speak out loud in your presence to my colleagues." And I said to my colleagues, "This has got to stop. I want the president to hear this." I said, "You're talking about yesterday." I remember very vividly [saying], "The president of the United States has invited us to meet with him on this issue. I myself have no problems at all with the president's current position towards the Soviet Union. And neither do you. Why are we talking about yesterday? We should be talking about how we can help the president now, in connection with his current foreign policy." And that changed the tenor of the meeting, because in effect, because some of us took it over, and those who were still fighting yesterday's battle shut up.[67]

The meeting with the president lasted thirty minutes, at the end of which Carter had to move on to other matters. But Walter Mondale remained with the small group for another hour, laying out the administration's new policy and explaining Carter's new hawkishness. He insisted that old ambiguities in Carter's policies had been eliminated and spoke to the group in their own language, touching all strings. In short, he launched a charm offensive, carrying out the kind of public-relations operation that Carter had been unable to muster. "I think that most of us . . . had few differences with Mondale but thought that he was not speaking for Carter," Jeane Kirkpatrick recalled.[68] In other words, the vice-president failed to dispel the disastrous impression left by the president, who in the neoconservatives' estimation had forgotten nothing and learned nothing—and with whom nothing could be done. In any case, the CDM would not support him in the upcoming election.

In one respect, this meeting marked the failure of the CDM's eight-year battle for the soul of the Democratic party, four years of which had been devoted mainly to foreign policy. The moment of choice had come. Since conservative Democrats were no longer welcome in the party, should they persist against all odds in their utopian dream of going back to the good old days of Truman and Kennedy? Did they have any choice but to look elsewhere? And where might that be, if not in the opposing camp?

The CDM's Neoconservative Vision

The political and intellectual distance traveled between 1972 and the end of the decade was momentous. What took shape around the CDM, Scoop Jackson, *Commentary,* the CPD, Pat Moynihan at the UN, and George Meany and Lane Kirkland at the AFL-CIO was neither more nor less than a neoconservative foreign policy. That policy cannot be understood apart from the context in which it developed. Until now the specific contribution of the CDM has been underestimated. The Committee on the Present Danger (discussed in the next chapter) was more concerned with details of the strategic and military aspects of foreign policy—issues that were almost technical in nature. The CDM was more political and ideological and thus, in a sense, more comprehensive.

The CDM's neoconservative vision contained five main elements: defense of democracy; promotion of human rights; assertion of American military power; support for Israel; and decreased emphasis on the United Nations and multilateralism.

Defense of Democracy

In a fundamental work on George W. Bush's foreign policy team, *The Rise of the Vulcans,* James Mann quotes William Kristol to the effect that neoconservatism did not really embrace the democratic imperative as part of its core foreign policy until the 1980s: "I don't think that neoconservatives at that time were particularly strong supporters of democracy."[69]

This assessment is inaccurate, as any number of the CDM texts quoted above will show, starting with the manifesto "Come Home, Democrats." Indeed, the CDM provides the missing link between the Cold War liberal tradition in the Democratic party and more recent neoconservatism, which includes the promotion of democracy as part of its foreign policy vision and is politically situated on the Republican side of the spectrum. "The CDM," says Penn Kemble, "became the incubator and the transmission system for this idea about democracy as a key element of U.S. foreign policy. The Committee on the Present Danger was more concerned with the military balance . . . But the other thing, about the importance of democracy—not just rhetorically—this was something that the CDM really contributed and which proved to be very important."[70]

There is no need to rehearse here the importance of democracy in Woodrow Wilson's worldview. His Democratic successors also stressed democracy, starting with Franklin Roosevelt and the Atlantic Charter, which Roosevelt and Winston Churchill signed on August 14, 1941, and which was later adopted by all the Allies. Even more interesting is the Truman doctrine, enunciated by FDR's successor on March 12, 1947, at the beginning of the Cold War:

> I believe that it must be the policy of the United States to support free peoples who are resisting attempted subjugation by armed minorities or by outside pressures. I believe that we must assist free peoples to work out their own destinies in their own way . . . This is no more than a frank recognition that totalitarian regimes imposed on free peoples, by direct or indirect aggression, undermine the foundations of international peace and hence the security of the United States.[71]

On January 20, 1961, America's determination to defend democracy and human rights was reaffirmed in the Kennedy doctrine, enunciated in the young president's Inaugural Address:

> Let every nation know, whether it wishes us well or ill, that we shall pay any price, bear any burden, meet any hardship, support any friend, oppose any foe, in order to assure the survival and the success of liberty . . . and [that we are] unwilling to witness or permit the slow undoing of those human rights to which this Nation has always been committed, and to which we are committed today at home and around the world.[72]

The existence of this tradition—the tradition of Wilson, Roosevelt, Truman, and Kennedy—does not mean that American foreign policy has always been neoconservative, as Robert Kagan, seeking to confound his critics, has suggested.[73] It means that the defense of "freedom," or, in concrete terms, of democracy, has played an important role in the worldview and policy of twentieth-century Democratic presidents—far more than in the worldview of Eisenhower, Nixon, and Ford, the Republican presidents before Reagan. What happened in the 1960s and early 1970s as a result of the Vietnam War was that the New Left rejected this component of the liberal worldview, which it saw—to caricature the position somewhat—as an arrogant or insincere alibi for a culpable policy of imperialism. Meanwhile, on the Republican side, Henry Kissinger contributed to the "de-ideologization" of the Cold War by treating it abstractly in terms of balance of power. It was against both of these tendencies that the neoconservatives of the CDM, *Commentary,* the AFL-CIO, and the Jackson staff staked out their position. In this respect, they were not as innovative as is sometimes thought: they simply continued an aspect of the traditional liberal worldview that had always been important, namely, the defense of democracy.

And "defense" is indeed the operative word. In this respect, the 2003 war in Iraq blurred the lines, because it was widely asserted that neoconservatives sought to export democracy by force of arms. This attribution of motive is both true and false: democracy promotion was not a sufficient reason to intervene, nor was it the primary objective of the intervention. Still, regime change was by then an integral component of the neoconservative vision of the Middle East. The move from the defense to the active promotion of democracy reflected the fact that America's relative power in the world had increased considerably between the time of Nixon and Carter (and the second-age neoconservatives) and that of George W. Bush (and the third-age neoconservatives).

That distinction between defense and active promotion of democracy is the basis of my divergence from James Mann in *The Rise of the Vulcans.* To bolster his argument that democracy was not an issue for neoconservatives in the 1970s, he looks at the attitude of Paul Wolfowitz at the time Ferdinand Marcos was overthrown in the Philippines in 1986, when Wolfowitz was undersecretary of state for East Asia and the Pacific (and his assistant was Scooter Libby).[74] In order to give democracy a chance, Wolfowitz joined George Shultz in trying to persuade a more-than-reluctant President Reagan to make the bold decision of withdrawing all support from the dictator when Marcos attempted to tamper with election results after losing at the ballot box. (In the end, democracy won out.) Mann deduces that the neoconservative view had changed sometime between the late 1970s and the late 1980s.[75]

In fact, Wolfowitz embraced the second-age neoconservative consensus best expressed by Pat Moynihan.[76] In February 1974, while still serving as ambassador to India, Moynihan had published in *Commentary* an article titled "Was Woodrow Wilson Right?" The reference was to Wilson's battle for democracy and self-determination, and Moynihan answered in the affirmative. In his paean to Wilson, he took American multiculturalism and multiethnicity as his point of departure: "We are a nation of nations." He argued that any battle for freedom and democracy anywhere in the world necessarily resonated in the United States—

increasingly so. Hence it was natural "for the United States to bring its influence to bear on behalf of those regimes which promise the largest degree of personal and national liberty."[77] Yet it must do so in a restrained manner (no interference and no "going abroad," as President John Quincy Adams had put it, "in search of dragons to slay").

In August 1977, after he had won a Senate seat in New York, Moynihan attacked George Kennan, who in his book *The Cloud of Danger* had asserted that democracy was a strictly North Atlantic cultural phenomenon and by no means a natural form of government for nations outside a certain narrow perimeter.[78] In an article that George W. Bush could have signed, the neoconservative senator from New York replied that "this is an arguable point—does it not display a lofty disdain for what is after all a well-documented and universal human aspiration, namely, the desire to be free?"[79] Between 1974 and 1980 it was common to find, especially in the pages of *Commentary,* the idea of defending democracy described as an American mission, to be undertaken despite the trauma of Vietnam and the temptation of retreat into isolationism.[80] Nathan Glazer acknowledged the existence of doubts:

> Even if we agree, however, that an interventionist foreign policy in defense of democratic values can be justified, do we have the power for such a policy, do we have the wisdom for it? Especially after Vietnam these are serious questions . . . For at least it is not being accepted without argument that what is still the most powerful country in the world, in many ways the most democratic, and the one that still remains to a hundred nations the symbol of an open, free, and desirable social order in which every man may make his way without hindrance, should acknowledge that it is both unable and unwilling to engage in a balanced defense of democracy and freedom.

Quoting Moynihan, Glazer nevertheless concluded that the United States remained genuinely committed to the "balanced defense of democracy and freedom."[81]

One of the most important exhibits in this case is Jeane Kirkpatrick's famous article, "Dictatorships and Double Standards," which appeared in *Commentary* in November 1979.[82] This piece is sometimes read as a denigration of democracy promotion and an argument in favor of a kind of realpolitik. Would that not be proof of the neoconservatives' lack of faith in democracy, or even of their hypocrisy?[83]

In reality, Kirkpatrick was not critical of support for democracy in general as a goal of American foreign policy and still less as a moral objective. Her real target was the Carter administration's naïve and inept implementation of such a policy and what Kirkpatrick took to be skewed priorities. In her eyes, the administration had adopted a double standard, attacking right-wing authoritarian regimes and insisting that they democratize while doing nothing about totalitarian Communist regimes such as Cuba. While the latter, enemies of America, were thereby reinforced, the former were destabilized, so that they not only became worse from the standpoint of human rights and democracy but also turned increasingly anti-American (Kirkpatrick cited Iran and Nicaragua as cases in point).

Kirkpatrick's conclusion summed up her carefully nuanced argument and offered a ringing defense of democratic ambitions: "Liberal idealism need not be identical with masochism, and need not be incompatible with the defense of freedom and the national interest."[84] In other words, Kirkpatrick did not condemn the goal of supporting democracy altogether, but insisted that it must be subject to tests of efficacy and priority. A quotation from a 1985 *Commentary* article by Michael Ledeen may help to clarify Kirkpatrick's view:

> Indeed, our struggle with Communist totalitarianism—like our previous war with fascist totalitarianism, and like our struggle with dictatorships of all stripes—is unavoidable, a matter of political principle which is simultaneously a strategic national interest. It is not the other side of the coin, it is the same coin as our support for the democratic revolution. Needless to say, solid unflinching support for the democratic revolution does not mean the abandonment of good sense. American policymakers cannot be deprived of such essential tools as the choice of the lesser of two evils, the strategic pause, and the wait-and-see.[85]

During the 1980 campaign, after the disastrous breakfast meeting with Carter, the CDM put forward two noteworthy proposals that would become part of the neoconservative position for decades to come. The first concerned a new direction in Middle East policy. In an article commissioned by the CDM, David Bar-Ilan (also a member of the CPD) argued that the current U.S. policy tended to strengthen nondemocratic Arab states, with which there was no chance that Washington and Tel Aviv would ever achieve a durable understanding. Bar-Ilan did not go as far as George W. Bush would in 2003, when he called for abandoning "sixty years of . . . excusing and accommodating the lack of freedom in the Middle East," but he did challenge the wisdom of continued alliances with Arab states that had previously been considered essential.[86]

Another idea with a bright future was that of constituting an "alliance of democracies" to advance the cause of freedom. The CDM included this item among the recommendations it sent to Carter following the January 1980 White House meeting.

> The United States should take the lead in organizing an alliance of world's democracies, based on their common values and ideals, which will work at the United Nations and other world-forums to advance democratic principles and interests: freedom of the press, free elections, civil liberties, free trade unions, and other basic liberties.[87]

The idea of an "alliance of democracies," including that of a UN caucus, would be taken up in the 1990s and 2000s by neoconservatives—but also by liberal Democrats. For example, in June 2000 Madeleine Albright launched the "Community of Democracies" initiative at a ministerial conference in Warsaw, for which she drew, from among other sources, on the work of Penn Kemble—at that time acting director of the United States Information Agency. The Bush administration also gave some thought to developing a similar project, which it hoped might constitute a multilateral alternative to the UN.[88] In 2008 the Republican candidate for the presidential election, John McCain, who was very close to the neoconservatives, called for a "league of democracies."[89]

The CDM also took various concrete steps to advance the democratic cause. In April 1979, for instance, Bayard Rustin, the vice-chair of the CDM, went to Rhodesia (now Zimbabwe) as part of a Freedom House delegation to observe the electoral process there. He telephoned the CDM with positive impressions, which became the basis of a press release.[90] More generally, the CDM exchanged views and information with the AFL-CIO on the state of trade unions in various nondemocratic countries, and on the ways to support them.

Promotion of Human Rights

Even more impressive were the CDM's efforts on behalf of Communist dissidents from 1978 to 1980 and, more generally, its activism on human rights. During the second half of the 1970s, American democratic idealism crystallized around this issue, which, though not new, was suddenly invested with new political importance. As Peter Berger wrote in 1977, the issue of basic human rights extended beyond the contingencies of geography and history, reflecting the universal aspiration for freedom (of expression, movement, and so forth).[91] Among the main roots of this intellectual and political movement in the United States were the moral ambiguity and "end of innocence" that marked the war in Vietnam. This reaction was surely reinforced by the Watergate affair, which triggered a deep moral aspiration, a desire for the "purification" of American foreign policy, in a context of religious revival.

Other structural factors also played a part: the media had turned the world into a "global village" in which it was easy to keep track of events around the world. For many, the Holocaust had become an increasing preoccupation as awareness of the enormity of the crime slowly sank in. Left-wing intellectuals abandoned any illusions they might have harbored about communism as they discovered the extent to which the Eastern Bloc countries had been deprived of freedom; the publication of Solzhenitsyn's *Gulag Archipelago* in 1974 played a part in this revelation. In the United States, it would be impossible to overstate the role of Scoop Jackson and his work on behalf of Soviet Jews, which brought the human rights issue to front and center. The Jackson-Vanik amendment made intervention in Soviet domestic affairs not only thinkable but also desirable. The issue became part of public debate. Jackson redrew the contours of U.S. foreign policy by putting the internal issues of other countries (or at any rate of the U.S.S.R.) on the agenda. This innovation ultimately helped undermine the foundations of sovereignty as that concept had been understood since the treaties of Westphalia (1648).

The question that inevitably arises is whether a coherent foreign policy can be built around the issue of human rights alone. Or is such an issue merely a secondary ethical concern or even a propaganda ploy or public relations device? Pat Moynihan, following Walter Laqueur, answered the first question in the affirmative in his 1977 *Commentary* article "The Politics of Human Rights":

> Human rights is a political component of American foreign policy, not a humanitarian program. It is entirely correct to say (as was repeatedly said during all those "years of silence" in Washington) that quiet diplomacy is much the more effective way to obtain near-term concessions from totalitarian regimes with respect to particular individuals who seek our help. But

the large result of proceeding in this fashion is that the democracies accommodate to the dictators. Concepts of human rights should be as integral to
American foreign policy as is Marxist-Leninism to Soviet or Chinese or Yu-
goslav operations and planning.[92]

Laqueur and Moynihan quoted dissident Russian physicist Andrei
Sakharov, who recommended that all human rights violations be transformed into political problems for Communist leaders. Against the advice of liberals such as Professor Marshall Shulman, a Carter adviser, the
most celebrated of Soviet dissidents explained that détente had not led to
greater respect for human rights, and so there was no reason to go easy
on Moscow on the issue.[93]

This intransigence would lead the neoconservatives to make an ironic
about-face. All the hawks and champions of human rights—the CDM,
Norman Podhoretz, Scoop Jackson, Alexander Solzhenitsyn, and even
the *Wall Street Journal* (which taunted Gerald Ford prior to his departure with an editorial titled "Jerry, Don't Go")—were critical of the Helsinki accords.[94] To the critics, these agreements, which were signed on
August 1, 1975, seemed to reward twenty years of Soviet efforts to
win the approval of the international community for the borders of
its empire in Eastern Europe. Then something unexpected occurred—
unexpected, at any rate, by these outside observers: opponents of the
Communist regimes in Eastern Europe and in the Soviet Union itself welcomed the "third basket" of accords (dealing with human rights, freedom of expression and movement, and the like) and insisted that these
agreements be implemented in Warsaw Pact countries. The dissident
movement (especially the Charter 77 in Czechoslovakia) was catapulted
into the political arena and media limelight, creating growing internal
problems for Moscow. Initially, Brezhnev responded with repression,
but ten years later, under Gorbachev, the Soviets finally recognized the
need for reforms. In short, the widely denounced Helsinki process soon
emerged as a formidable ideological weapon, and in the end the neoconservatives made it their own.

On January 26, 1978, on the occasion of the CDM's fifth anniversary
and the award of prizes to those responsible for verifying Soviet compliance with the Helsinki accords, Sol Chaikin, the president of the International Ladies' Garment Workers' Union and the U.S. representative
to the Belgrade conference on human rights (an offshoot of the Helsinki process), forthrightly praised the monitors and dissidents who had

made such good use of the "third basket": "Their determination and their steadfastness, their belief in the promise of the Helsinki final act, breathed life into a document that I consider to have been, from the American point of view, a total loss."[95]

In fact, it was in this context of growing concern with human rights and continued opposition to the Soviet Union and détente that the CDM would offer direct support to the dissidents. From 1978 into the early 1980s, they launched a media campaign and continued to work inside the system to focus attention on human rights. In the weeks before the Helsinki summit, Scoop Jackson and AFL-CIO leader George Meany had invited Alexander Solzhenitsyn to speak to the Senate, while the president refused to invite him to the White House so as not to offend Moscow (Pat Moynihan and James Schlesinger also attended the Senate reception). This invitation became the model for further agitation on the issue. The CDM, with support from the AFL-CIO and Senators Jackson and Moynihan, invited numerous dissidents from Communist countries to come to Washington over the next few years, thereby maintaining pressure on the Carter administration and eliciting wide public support through a series of fundraising dinners.

The CDM organized a plethora of events in support of Eastern Bloc dissidents.[96] For example, on January 26, 1978, the CDM's Human Rights Award was bestowed by Bayard Rustin on Lyudmila Alekseeva, representing the Soviet monitors of the Helsinki process (the Yuri Orlov group). A special prize was also given to Valentin Turchin, the founder of the Soviet branch of Amnesty International. During the dinner for that occasion there was a public reading of messages from leading Soviet dissidents (including Sakharov and six members of the observers' group that had been dissolved by the Soviets). Sakharov's message read: "We greatly value your support for the human rights movement in the USSR and the countries of Eastern Europe. The honorary award to the groups for implementation of the Helsinki accords in the USSR is yet another manifestation of this support."[97] Two other messages were read, one from Alexander Solzhenitsyn (who noted that this was the first prize to honor prisoners of the "Gulag Archipelago") and the other from Jimmy Carter (who promised that human rights would always be at the heart of his foreign policy). Moynihan and Jackson, the "convening authorities," also spoke. The ceremony was recorded for broadcast on Radio Liberty, Radio Free Europe, and the Voice of America to offer moral support to dissidents in the East. More than 600 guests attended the dinner despite a snowstorm.

Among the Soviet monitors of the Helsinki accords whom the CDM honored was Anatoly Shcharansky, better known in the West as Natan Sharansky. Close to Sakharov, Sharansky had tried unsuccessfully to emigrate to Israel in 1973. Later he became a champion of human rights, a "refusenik" who was sentenced to a long term at hard labor in 1978 and was ultimately exchanged for Soviet spies in 1986. After settling in Israel, he became a writer and Likud politician and in 2004 published *The Case for Democracy: The Power of Freedom to Overcome Tyranny and Terror,* a book revered by neoconservatives, which deals with the "transformational power" of freedom. It had a great impact on President George W. Bush, and one can find echoes of it in Bush's Second Inaugural Address.[98] Sharansky proposed what he called "the town square test": if a citizen can express his political opinions in the town square without being harassed in any way, then he is living in a free society; if he can't, he is living in a "society of fear," a form of tyranny. Second-age neoconservatives saw things in exactly this way.

Military Might, Israel, and Suspicion of the UN

The other elements of the neoconservative foreign policy that came together in the 1970s are less surprising and can therefore be treated more briefly. Support for an American military strong enough to counter Soviet expansion was of course an essential pillar of the neoconservative vision. This was primarily the province of the Committee on the Present Danger, which began to publish its strategic analyses in 1977 (as we shall see in the next chapter). The CDM preceded the CPD in this domain, however. The task force that Eugene Rostow created in 1973 called for nuclear-weapons development and an increase in the defense budget, and the unions agreed.[99] At bottom, the CDM acted as a sort of proto-CPD, a fact that is unsurprising given that Eugene Rostow was a founder of both the CDM foreign policy task force and the CPD. Many other members of the CDM migrated to the CPD, including Richard Pipes, Max Kampelman, Elmo Zumwalt, John Roche, Paul Seabury, Richard Schifter, and Valerie Earle. All told, three-quarters of the members of the Rostow task force became members of the CPD, and the two groups collaborated periodically.

Support for Israel constituted the fourth element of the CDM's foreign policy vision. The many reasons for this include the moral imperative (defense of democracies); the geopolitical imperative (rampart against a regional push by the Soviets); traditional Democratic political alliances (a majority of Jewish Americans had voted Democratic since 1932); the ideological break with the liberal left, which had become Third-Worldist and pro-Palestinian (with support for the Palestine Liberation Organization, especially by certain black activists); and, finally, a growing sense of solidarity with Israel on the part of American Jews (especially after the 1967 and 1973 wars and heightened awareness of the Holocaust, and given the strong representation of Jews in the ranks of the CDM). As we have seen, the Coalition published numerous articles and press releases on the Middle East and fought to defend the security of Israel, for instance in the debate over the sale of F-15 fighters to Saudi Arabia.

In the late 1970s, attention focused on the issue of Middle Eastern terrorism. For example, in July 1979 several members of the CDM and CPD participated in an international conference in Jerusalem organized by the Jonathan Institute (named in honor of Jonathan Netanyahu, the brother of Benjamin, who died at Entebbe, Uganda, while leading a commando raid to free hostages taken in a hijacking). Scoop Jackson attended, as did Ben Wattenberg, Norman Podhoretz, Bayard Rustin, Midge Decter, and Richard Pipes, all of whom spoke at the event. The Netanyahu family suggested that the CDM organize a second conference in Washington. This became the conference on "Totalitarianism, Terrorism, and American Foreign Policy," which was held at the Sheraton Hotel and was followed by a dinner in honor of Andrei Sakharov. The issues of terrorism and the Cold War converged, since the Soviet Union was accused of being the principal source of support for international terrorism.

The CDM's support for Israel again raises the issue of the relation between neoconservatism and Judaism. Insofar as the religious preferences of CDM members are known, it is a fact that many of them were Jews. But some of the group's most important leaders—Scoop Jackson, Pat Moynihan, Jeane Kirkpatrick, and Penn Kemble—were not (nor were many other prominent members, such as Bayard Rustin, Michael Novak, and Elmo Zumwalt). In fact the most important factor in the CDM's support for Israel was the group's ideological opposition to the isolationist, anti-American, Third-Worldist wing of the Democratic party and its support for a strong, internationalist America capable of countering Soviet activism and defending all democracies, including Israel.

There is additional evidence that public support for the CDM was not a predominantly Jewish phenomenon. The original purpose of the CDM was to take the Democratic party back from the New Left, and the bipartisan CPD directed its message to all of America, not just the Jewish community or the Democratic party. But a third group was created in a similar spirit and aimed specifically at the Jewish community. Clearly, the assumption was that much of that community was insufficiently aware of the linkage between maintaining a strong American military, the progress of the Cold War, and the fate of Israel. Too many Jews supported the Carter administration and the antimilitaristic left, so there was a need to drum up support among Jews for a firmer stance toward the Soviet Union and a bigger defense budget. The group was called the Jewish Institute for National Security Affairs, or JINSA, and its organizers came from the American Jewish Committee. Two members of the CDM, Richard Schifter and Max Kampelman, joined them, and in 1976 they received help from Peter Rosenblatt, as well as from a young Harvard graduate by the name of Douglas Feith.[100] Initially JINSA leaned toward Israel's Labor party, but eventually it took a harder line, closer to that of the Likud party, and as a result lost the support of Schifter, Kampelman, and Rosenblatt.

The last pillar of the neoconservative foreign policy of the 1970s was suspicion of multilateralism and international institutions. Suspicion did not yet mean outright rejection, as it would in the third age of neoconservatism. Although Scoop Jackson had long since been wary of the United Nations, having given a controversial speech on March 20, 1962, warning that American might and the NATO alliance were the only ways to keep the peace,[101] Pat Moynihan and Eugene Rostow continued to support the organization, which they believed to be in the national interest of the United States. They felt that the UN was worth fighting for despite its various shortcomings, and despite recent adverse political developments, such as the increase in the number of anti-American Third World countries in the wake of decolonization. After all, this was a generation of Cold War Democrats that had witnessed the birth of the UN, and the Roosevelt and Truman administrations had helped make it happen.

Perhaps because Rostow was a professor of law, he attached considerable importance to the United Nations and to international law in general, for example in his analyses of the situation in the Middle East in 1973.[102] He continued to believe in the importance of the international legal order established by the United States and favored acting in accordance with the law at all times. His basic position was close to Pat Moynihan's. Moynihan deplored the anti-American maneuvers of the "new majority" at the UN but favored fighting back rather than deserting.[103] He found himself increasingly in the minority among neo-conservatives, whose position on the UN tended to harden over time. The evolution that would lead to "war on the UN" in the third age of neoconservatism had begun: the suspicion of the 1970s would eventually turn to outright hostility. We draw nearer to the time when it would become possible for Richard Perle to write, in the wake of the Iraqi crisis of the spring of 2003, an article titled "Thank God for the Death of the UN."[104]

5

NUCLEAR ALARM:
THE COMMITTEE ON THE PRESENT DANGER

All neoconservatives are hawks, but not all hawks are neoconservatives. That is why it is misleading to treat the Committee on the Present Danger as an essentially neoconservative organization in the same class as the Coalition for a Democratic Majority, which had less of an immediate impact on the American political process but is more typical of the course of neoconservatism.

Within the second and third ages of the movement, however, there existed a distinctive element, which might be called nuclear and strategic neoconservatism. Its main proponents were Scoop Jackson, Albert Wohlstetter, Paul Nitze, "Team B," Eugene Rostow and the Committee on the Present Danger, Paul Wolfowitz and the 1992 Pentagon document "Defense Planning Guidance" (which advocated maintaining American strategic superiority after the Cold War), and the military experts of the Project for the New American Century and the American Enterprise Institute in the late 1990s and 2000s (see Chapter 7). In other words, a porous border divided second- and third-age neoconservatives from nuclear strategists, and more precisely from the hawkish ones. The two realms did not precisely coincide. For example, in the George W. Bush administration at the time of the intervention in Iraq, Dick Cheney, Donald Rumsfeld, John Bolton, and other hawks were allies of the neoconservatives but not neoconservatives themselves. What cannot be found, however, is a neoconservative dove.

The Committee on the Present Danger embodied this "strategic" wing of second-age neoconservatism and played a key role in the shift of allegiance by certain Democrats—Scoop Jackson Democrats—to the administration of Ronald Reagan, who was himself a member of the CPD. Inside the Reagan administration they were at last able to implement policies that reflected their ideas and preferences. The CPD also served as an incubator for those ideas and a source of inspiration for the neo-conservatism of the third age.

Albert Wohlstetter, Prophet of Nuclear Neoconservatism

On November 7, 1985, in a ceremony at the White House, President Reagan awarded the Medal of Freedom, the nation's highest civilian distinction, to three individuals who were in various ways founders of nuclear neoconservatism: Paul Nitze (1907–2004), Albert Wohlstetter (1913–1997), and his wife, Roberta Wohlstetter (1912–2007), a historian who was an expert on Pearl Harbor and the analysis of strategic surprise.[1] I will have more to say about Paul Nitze below. A cofounder of the Committee on the Present Danger, he had a public career that extended over more than four decades, and throughout that time he never identified himself as a neoconservative. By contrast, Albert Wohlstetter was both an inspiration to neoconservatives and himself a man of neoconservative leanings—even if he never endorsed the label.[2]

Born to a family with Austrian roots, Wohlstetter studied at the City College of New York in the early days of the first generation of neoconservatives and the war of the alcoves. Although he was a follower of Trotskyite luminary Max Shachtman, he devoted the bulk of his time to the study of mathematics and quickly found his way to Columbia University, where he did work under the supervision of Jacob Wolfowitz, a celebrated mathematician and the father of Paul Wolfowitz. After a short stint in the private sector and wartime work with the War Production Board, he went to work for a brand-new think tank, the RAND Corporation, which did contract work for the U.S. Air Force. He was a full-time researcher at RAND from 1951 to 1963 and maintained ties to the institution even after becoming a professor at the University of Chicago, where he taught from 1964 to 1980, and later at the University of California in Los Angeles. He traveled widely, flying from conference to conference and meeting peers, disciples, and friends of many ages in many countries, from Robert Bartley (editor of the *Wall Street Journal*'s op-ed page) to Raymond Aron disciple and leading strategic thinker Pierre Hassner, from Paul Wolfowitz to Iraqi banker and political figure Ahmed Chalabi, from General Pierre Marie Gallois, one of the theorists of France's nuclear force, to Zalmay Khalilzad.

At RAND he was able to put his critical mind to work. It was a mind that emphasized analytical clarity, precision, and above all "discrimination," Wohlstetter's watchword.[3] Toward the end of his life, for instance, after he fell ill, he prided himself, as a passionate gourmet, on his ability to distinguish those parts of a lobster that contained good cholesterol from those parts that contained bad.[4] His obsessive concern with clarity is all the more important because the strategic issues that occupied him were issues of life and death. His meticulous study of nuclear holocaust made him one of the inspirations for the role of Dr. Strangelove in Stanley Kubrick's 1964 film of that title. Indeed, another possible title contemplated for the film was "The Delicate Balance of Terror," the title of one of Wohlstetter's most important articles on strategy, published in 1959 (this was the very article that Wohlstetter would give Richard Perle at poolside some years later).[5] In point of fact, however, Wohlstetter was not Dr. Strangelove. Deeply anticommunist and opposed to moral equivalence, he objected to the immorality implicit in "mutual assured destruction" and preferred giving American decisionmakers more options than the choice between "destruction or surrender." It was to technology that he looked to provide those options, in the form of antimissile systems, high-precision warheads, and so on.

In "The Delicate Balance of Terror" Wohlstetter began by attacking the consensus view that "a balance of terror" was enough to make nuclear war impossible:

> Would not a general thermonuclear war mean "extinction" for the aggressor as well as the defender? "Extinction" is a state that badly needs analysis. Russian fatalities in World War II were more than 20,000,000. Yet Russia recovered extremely well from this catastrophe. There are several quite plausible circumstances in the future when the Russians might be confident of being able to limit damage to considerably less than this number—if they make sensible strategic choices and we do not. On the other hand, the risks of not striking might at some juncture appear very great to the Soviets, involving, for example, disastrous defeat in peripheral war, loss of key satellites with danger of revolt spreading—possibly to Russia itself—or fear of an attack by ourselves. Then, striking first, by surprise, would be the sensible choice for them, and from their point of view the smaller risk.[6]

Consequently, it was important to pay special attention to the question of second-strike capability and to make sure that any potential aggressor knew that retaliation would be absolutely certain and automatic. Wohlstetter listed six conditions that would have to be met to ensure this outcome. His article set forth the ideas that would form the basis of the loose doctrinal body that could be called "nuclear neoconservatism." In essence, it contained the following points:

The balance of terror is an unstable equilibrium, which requires constant attention to the modernization of weapons systems. It is essential to give the president a range of responses so that he can deal with escalation without being forced into a choice between destruction and inaction. Hence technological innovation (including antimissile systems and precision warheads) contributes to stability rather than instability.

A nuclear exchange is not necessarily synonymous with "mutual assured destruction," as Paul Nitze found in Hiroshima in 1945 when he surveyed the extent, but more importantly the limits, of destruction inflicted by a nuclear weapon. He explained his thinking on this point in 1978: "In a nuclear war there will be a military victor and a military loser. Further, if you make the necessary effort, it is possible for most of your people and much of your industry to survive."[7]

Antimissile defenses are not incompatible with deterrence but complementary to it. They reinforce deterrence. And they are inherently more "moral" than the destruction of civilian populations.

Arms-control treaties are not useless, but their potential is quite limited, because the real cause of the arms race is the hostility between the United States and the Soviet Union, which is political and ideological in nature and a consequence of Soviet expansionism.

Any attempt to strike a "balance" between the United States and the Soviet Union by means of arms-control treaties will handicap the United States, depriving it of one of its essential advantages, technological superiority, by allowing the Soviets to spend less on defense. In the long run, this is their Achilles' heel, and the better course is to drive them into ruin by pursuing the arms race. Furthermore, arms control would allow the Russians to "deter America's deterrent" (as Nitze would put it in 1976).[8] If balance were achieved through nuclear arms control, the Russians would be free to wage peripheral wars without fear of serious American reprisals. "Nuclear balance" would give the advantage to the expansionist power. Hence it is essential for the United States to achieve nuclear superiority, as the Cuban crisis demonstrated.

Finally, one must be wary of information supplied by the intelligence agencies, as the surprise attack on Pearl Harbor and the first Soviet nuclear weapons test in 1949 proved. The Central Intelligence Agency did not believe that this test could occur very soon. But all too often, in its analyses the CIA simply projected American realities and arguments onto the adversary, producing "Western-preferred Soviet strategies."[9]

More generally, this school of thought argued that the American people and establishment consistently failed to take the measure of the danger they faced. Hence neoconservatives often felt the need to "sound the tocsin," as Sam Wells put it, to educate both the public and elites about the need for a larger defense budget.[10] In this strategy they saw themselves as reviving the tradition of Paul Revere.[11] They pursued this effort in two ways: by pressing for revisions of intelligence estimates that they regarded as too comforting, not to say naïve, and by attempting to alert the public to the real risks facing the United States. Under the first head we can place the National Security Council report NSC-68 of April 1950 (discussed below), the Gaither report of 1957 (following the Soviet launch of Sputnik), Team B (discussed below), the Rumsfeld commission on the ballistic missile threat in 1998, the Cox commission on Chinese espionage in 1998–99, and the Office of Special Plans (2002–03), a small unit inside the Pentagon charged with compiling and second-guessing CIA estimates of Iraqi weapons of mass destruction. In the second category we can place *three* Committees on the Present Danger: that of 1950–1953 (see below); that of 1976–1992, by far the most important; and that which came into being in 2004 in connection with the threat of Islamist radicalism (see Chapter 7). Alarmism and exaggeration of the threat have indeed been a constant feature of the neoconservative worldview.

The Team B Episode

During the 1960s Albert Wohlstetter cultivated a relationship with Scoop Jackson. Both the senator and the strategic analyst harbored doubts about the 1963 ban on atmospheric testing of nuclear weapons. In 1969, as we saw earlier, Jackson joined Paul Nitze and Dean Acheson in supporting the development of antimissile systems. As we have also seen, the Committee to Maintain a Prudent Defense Policy helped to launch the careers of both Paul Wolfowitz and Richard Perle. Perle, who was in frequent contact with Wohlstetter, supported Jackson's unsuccessful effort to block ratification of the SALT I agreement of May 1972 (as well as the ABM treaty, signed at the same time, limiting antimissile systems).

Increasingly worried by what he perceived as rapid Soviet advances, Wohlstetter organized a conference in Los Angeles in June 1974, at which time he accused the Pentagon of seriously underestimating Soviet weapons programs.[12] This meeting marked the opening of a new front in the war of the hawks and neoconservatives against Kissinger's détente. Wohlstetter's ideas received official sanction in the spring of 1976, when George H. W. Bush, the director of Central Intelligence, named a team of analysts to review CIA intelligence estimates that critics, who included Ronald Reagan, then pursuing the Republican nomination for the presidency, regarded as too rosy. This was the inception of the so-called Team B.

In fact, three "Team B's" were organized and given access to the same confidential information as three "Team A's" drawn from the ranks of the CIA. The various teams were put to work on three specific issues. To no one's great surprise, given the hawkish composition of the Team B's, all found that Soviet capabilities and threats had been substantially underestimated. The first Team B dealt with Soviet antiaircraft systems. Its estimates differed from those of the CIA concerning the quality of the Soviet equipment and especially their operational capability in detecting and thwarting a low-altitude attack by nuclear-armed B-52 bombers.[13] The second Team B looked at the accuracy of Soviet missiles, and its estimate was so different from Team A's that the confrontation between the two teams proved to be highly unpleasant.[14]

The third Team B dealt with "Soviet intentions." Directed by Richard Pipes, who had been recommended by Richard Perle, this was the best-known of the three Team B's. Pipes was a fiercely anti-Soviet Polish immigrant and professor of history at Harvard who consulted frequently with Senator Jackson. As we have seen, he was also an active member of the CDM. In fact the third Team B included other familiar figures: Paul Wolfowitz, Paul Nitze, and William Van Cleave (the latter two played a central role in the CPD). The team did most of its work from August to November 1976. On November 5, Team B met with Team A at CIA headquarters, and the exchange turned into a humiliating debacle for the young CIA analysts, who were mercilessly ridiculed by old hands at strategic debate such as Nitze and Daniel Graham and by imposing academics such as Pipes and Van Cleave.[15] The official report was submitted on December 21, 1976.

The Team B report sounded an alarm: the Soviets were engaged in a rapid increase of their military forces at a pace comparable with the re-militarization of Germany in the 1930s, "an intense military build-up in nuclear as well as conventional forces of all sorts, not moderated either by the West's self-imposed restraints or by SALT."[16] In a striking phrase, Team B predicted that a "window of vulnerability" would open for the United States in the 1980s:

> The size and the nature of the Soviet effort which involves considerable economic and political costs and risks, if long continued in the face of frustrated economic expectations within their own bloc and the possibility that the West may come to perceive the necessity of reversing current trends before they become irreversible, lead to the possibility of a relatively short-term threat cresting, say, in 1980 to 1983, as well as the more obvious long-range threat.[17]

The CIA's regular National Intelligence Estimates (NIEs) of the past several years had made no mention of this increasing threat. According to Team B, the reason for this omission was the failure to take account of Soviet intentions, of the "ideas, motives, and aspirations" behind Soviet capabilities, as well as the unabashed ethnocentrism of the CIA analysts, who proceeded by "mirror-imaging," that is, by attributing an American worldview to the Soviets. For Moscow, Team B argued, the goal was first and foremost to establish global superiority, with nuclear weapons as one element in a varied arsenal that included numerous nonmilitary methods of coercion in its "correlation of forces."[18] The CIA assumed that Moscow took mutual assured destruction seriously while completely ignoring the political uses that the Russians could make of nuclear parity: once America's deterrent power was blocked through the establishment of nuclear parity, the Soviets could strengthen their position in order to prevail in regional conflicts or resort to other means such as subversion. In other words, "*The NIEs tendency to view deterrence as an alternative to a war-fighting capability rather than as complementary to it,* is in the opinion of Team 'B,' a grave and dangerous flaw in their evaluations of Soviet strategic objectives."[19]

Was Team B (and the Committee on the Present Danger, which adopted its conclusions) right or wrong in sounding such an alarm about the Soviet threat? To answer this question, we need to take a longer view. The intelligence community had at first been unduly optimistic when it predicted in the years 1946–1949 that the Soviets would not test their first atomic bomb until mid-1950 (rather than 1949, as was the case).[20] Partly in order to avoid repeating this kind of error, it regularly overestimated Soviet capacities throughout the 1950s, leading to the famous error (publicized by the Gaither report in 1957) about the "missile gap," that is, the supposed Soviet lead in ballistic missiles.[21] After 1962 the CIA, chastened by the criticism it received for these exaggerations, failed to grasp the major change in Soviet thinking after the Cuban missile crisis, which led to a sharp increase in Soviet military power, especially in the realm of ICBMs. The agency regularly underestimated, and to an alarming degree, the arsenal that the Soviets were amassing.

After 1976, the Team B episode led the agency to correct its estimates, once again overreacting, this time in the direction of exaggerating Soviet strength. By 1983, Deputy Director Robert Gates acknowledged that the CIA had overestimated the Soviet military budget and production of offensive strategic arms such as ICBMs and surface-to-land ballistic missiles.[22] The agency also overestimated the performance of the Soviet economy in the late 1970s and throughout the 1980s.[23] Where Team B went wrong, in fact, was that, as the CIA revealed in 1983, the Soviet budget for purchasing new military equipment had achieved a plateau in 1976; thereafter the growth in overall military expenses had slowed considerably (to about 2 percent annually).[24]

As for Team B's more technical predictions, one observer, Raymond Garthoff, offered a harsh assessment:

> In retrospect, and with the Team B report and records now largely declassified, it is possible to see that virtually all of Team B's criticisms of the NIE proved to be wrong. On several important specific points it wrongly criticized and "corrected" the official estimates, always in the direction of enlarging the impression of danger and threat. For example, the range of the Backfire medium bomber was considerably overestimated, and the number of Backfires the Soviet Union would acquire by 1984 was overestimated by more than 100 percent (estimating 500 when the real figure was 235). Team B overestimated the accuracy of the SS-18 and SS-19 ICBMs, feeding the unwarranted fears of a "window of vulnerability" for the US ICBM deterrent. Team B estimated that the Soviet Union would field a mobile ABM system, which it did not.[25]

Despite this assessment, the Team B episode inaugurated a neoconservative tradition that has endured: a commission of experts warns decisionmakers about strategic dangers that have previously been underestimated, most notably by the CIA. These warnings are always accompanied by leaks to the press designed to launch a polemic and to reach a large public audience. In the case in point, the leaks began in October 1976 and intensified in December so as to exert pressure on the newly elected president, Jimmy Carter.[26] Carter was not impressed, however, and launched his own reevaluation of the relative strength of the United States and the Soviet Union. This was the so-called PD-18 process, led by Samuel Huntington, to which I return below.

The Origins of the CPD

"The intellectual basis for the Committee grew out of the work of the now-famous Team B, which presented its view that the CIA had consistently underestimated the massive Soviet military effort."[27] Although it is true that the CPD initially drew heavily on the work of Team B, the first impetus for the new organization came from Eugene Rostow, whose views reflected multiple influences. Among them were several other citizens' committees, in particular the William Allen White Committee (officially known as the Committee to Defend America by Aiding the Allies), which fought from 1940 to 1942 for aid to the European allies and then for American entry into the war, in opposition to the powerful America First Committee, led by the aviator Charles Lindbergh, which favored American neutrality and strict isolationism. A less important source of inspiration was the Comité d'Action pour les États-Unis d'Europe, created by Jean Monnet in 1955.

The third source of inspiration was an earlier Committee on the Present Danger (1950–1953), although the leading participants in the later CPD tend to minimize its role as a model. The two CPDs nevertheless have many points in common. Both trace their intellectual foundations to reports written by Paul Nitze: NSC-68 (see below) and the Team B report. Both sought to alert Americans to the danger represented by the Soviet Union so that they would support rearmament and renewed assertion of American power.[28]

In fact the most important precursor of the CPD was the CDM: it was because the CDM's foreign policy task force (1973–1976) was not sufficiently effective in combatting détente and alerting America to the growing Soviet threat that Gene Rostow decided to found the CPD, a larger and bipartisan organization that enlisted thirty-four members of the CDM along with Charls Walker and above all Paul Nitze.

A professor of law at Yale, where he served as dean of the law school from 1955 to 1966, Eugene ("Gene") Rostow had been involved in international affairs since World War II. He assisted Dean Acheson with the implementation of the Marshall Plan. Throughout his life he maintained close ties with Europe, as evidenced by his friendship with Jean Monnet. Indeed, neoconservatives of Rostow's generation, including Nitze, Zumwalt, and Kampelman, for whom World War II had been a formative experience, were likely to take European allies and NATO into consideration. By contrast, their younger counterparts, such as Perle, Wolfowitz, and Abrams, whose formative experiences dated from the 1970s and 1980s—the decades of *Ostpolitik,* the trans-Siberian oil pipeline crisis, and the Euromissile dispute—were often contemptuous of Europeans, and that contempt later turned into overt Europhobia among many third-age neoconservatives.[29]

Unlike Nitze, whose primary training was in economics and who remained a numbers man, Rostow, a lawyer, was a geopolitician, interested mainly in military history, the geography of great battles, and the reactions of various nations to the challenges they faced. After rejoining the State Department as undersecretary of state for political affairs (the number-three post) from 1966 to early 1969, he supported the war in Vietnam, as did his brother Walt, who was serving at the time as Lyndon Johnson's national security adviser.

In 1989 Rostow's wife, Edna, prepared a manuscript summarizing the next few years, which he revised.

> As the 1970's proceeded & the political scene in the US got more intense with anti-Vietnam activism & as the rush to left positions—to anti-war & pseudo-isolationist feeling grew, clouding a large part of the articulate population's vision and judgment especially as to the USSR & the danger it posed especially as it showed itself concretely on VN—& SE Asia (together, there, with China), EVR [Eugene V. Rostow] became more & more active in seeking to find ways to influence & move public opinion . . . He was a founding member of the Coalition for a Democratic Majority which was built around Scoop Jackson, and there found sympathetic hearers—Penn Kemble who was V. young—but able exec. Director; Max Kampelman; Joe Fowler and one or two others. In N.Y where he was on a Committee for

AT&T he found kindred spirits in Henry H. (Joe) Fowler, James Rowe, & Charls Walker. It became clear that the Coalition for a Democratic Majority could not influence the Democratic Party, and therefore could not reach the larger public. EVR therefore began to urge the formation of a bipartisan group that would act to educate public opinion about world affairs . . . It was not an easy job to get any of these individuals to become part of such a committee.[30]

In fact the person who was hardest to convince was Paul Nitze, whom Rostow had to beg to join the organization of which he ultimately became the leading figure and whose participation was for Rostow a sine qua non because of Nitze's prestige and expertise. Knowing this background makes it easier to understand why Nitze later tried to distance himself from the CPD, to which he devoted only two paragraphs of his own memoir.[31]

Paul Nitze was the scion of a wealthy German family that came to America just after the Civil War. After finishing Harvard, Nitze demonstrated his talent as an investor, despite the Depression. He married an heiress of the Standard Oil fortune, Phyllis Pratt (whose uncle donated a building he owned to the Council on Foreign Relations to use as its headquarters). Socially and culturally, Nitze was a quintessential representative of the establishment. He was brilliant, quick, and able but often too self-confident and stubborn and at times abrasive. During World War II he was called to Washington by James Forrestal, the president of the investment firm in which Nitze made his career (Dillon, Read & Co.). Working for the Roosevelt administration was not an inevitable choice for Paul Nitze: he had been a neutralist and isolationist and member of America First (perhaps because of his German roots).[32] But he supported the war effort and worked with the committee of experts assigned to evaluate the effects, and therefore the strategic value, of Allied aerial bombardment (the "U.S. Strategic Bombing Survey," produced at the end of World War II).

In that capacity he found himself on the ground in Hiroshima and Nagasaki in September 1945, just a few weeks after the only two nuclear bombings in the history of the world. This proved to be a crucial experience in Nitze's development. He of course witnessed the destructive power of nuclear weapons at first hand, but what struck him was that, even close to ground zero, people had survived if they had been protected from radiation (in shelters or, in some cases, simply behind windows). Important infrastructure was back in operation shortly after the blast (train service to Nagasaki was restored within forty-eight hours). Ultimately, the two nuclear bombs had resulted in roughly the same number of victims as the largest conventional raids in Europe, such as the attacks on Berlin and Dresden that Nitze had evaluated a few months earlier.[33] In other words, the atomic bomb was an awesome weapon but not, as it was sometimes made out to be, an apocalyptic device likely to put an end to life on Earth. It is important to appreciate this view in order to understand why Nitze and many other strategic hawks insisted that there was no reason to think of nuclear war as something entirely different from conventional war. They rejected the idea that nuclear war was "unthinkable" or "unimaginable" and that the use of nuclear weapons was something totally novel in the art of war, unrelated to the previous history of human conflict.

By chance, Nitze had met George Kennan on a train in 1944.[34] The diplomat, who at the time was number two in the Moscow embassy, was in Washington for consultations. He described Communist Russia to Nitze in somber terms and expressed his fear that the West remained blind to Stalin's machinations. Nitze was edified (Kennan would later quip that he had "edified him too much"). Two years later, in February 1946, Kennan dispatched his famous "long telegram" to Washington. In it he advocated "a long-term, patient but firm and vigilant containment of Russian expansive tendencies." A year after that, the text was reprinted anonymously in *Foreign Affairs* under the title "The Sources of Soviet Conduct."[35]

In Kennan's mind, however, systematic resistance to Moscow's expansion should not solely or even primarily take a military form: he saw it as above all economic and political. The United States should help free countries to rebuild their forces so as to ward off Communist subversion, to use propaganda to counter Soviet operations, and to reinforce American power while leaving the Soviets to deal with their own systemic weaknesses. "Such a policy," however, had "nothing to do with outward histrionics: with threats or blustering or superfluous gestures of outward 'toughness.' While the Kremlin is basically flexible in its reaction to political realities, it is by no means unamenable to considerations of prestige."[36] Soon after formulating the policy of containment, Kennan complained that it had been militarized and taken hostage by hard-core hawks.

A key figure in the militarization of containment was Nitze, who, as it happened, replaced Kennan after Acheson dismissed him from his post at State as director of policy planning. The new hard-line American position on the Soviet Union was set forth early in 1950 in a document known as NSC-68, which was drafted mainly by Nitze.[37] Truman had ordered this summary of the Soviet threat, which advocated a major effort of rearmament to counter Moscow's moves. Unless this was done, Nitze warned, America would find itself in a position of strategic inferiority and vulnerable to a surprise nuclear attack. According to Dean Acheson, the tone of the document was alarmist, "more vivid than the truth," with the avowed goal of "scaring" the president and other top officials.[38] Despite the urgent tone of alarm, however, NSC-68 would not have attained its goal had the Korean War not broken out a few months later, on June 25, 1950.[39] It was the war, and the war alone, that persuaded Truman to adopt the recommendations in the document, sharply increase defense spending, and turn to a more "muscular" version of containment.

Nitze was too close to Acheson to remain in his job under Eisenhower. After the Russians launched the first Sputnik in 1957, Nitze participated in drafting the Gaither Report, which warned that America was vulnerable to a Soviet ICBM strike and recommended rearmament. When Eisenhower did not react, Nitze and his allies leaked the Gaither Report to the press, and it was used by Democrats, including John F. Kennedy, who raised the issue of the (in fact nonexistent) "missile gap" in his campaign for the presidency against Richard Nixon. After his election, the young president made Nitze his assistant secretary of defense for international affairs, which put him in charge of the arms-control talks with Moscow that were just getting under way. In 1963 he was named secretary of the Navy, and in 1967 deputy secretary of defense (the number-two job at the Pentagon).[40] During the Cuban missile crisis, in October 1962, Nitze was a member of ExComm, the ad-hoc committee that Kennedy put together to come up with a response to the Soviet attempt to place missiles on the island. Unsurprisingly, Nitze was one of the hawks on the committee who advocated an air strike to take out the Soviet missile sites.

Immediately after leaving the government in January 1969, Nitze launched the Committee to Maintain a Prudent Defense Policy with Dean Acheson and Albert Wohlstetter. In an effort to persuade Congress to pay for antimissile defenses, the three men recruited Richard Perle, Paul Wolfowitz, Peter Wilson, and Edward Luttwak. In 1969, under Nixon, Nitze was named the Pentagon representative at the SALT talks.[41] After Senate ratification of the treaty (which Scoop Jackson tried unsuccessfully to block), the balance of power within the administration shifted. To counter Kissinger, who was working toward an agreement with the Soviets, the hawks formed a powerful axis opposed to conceding too much to the Russians. Among them were James Schlesinger, the new secretary of defense; Fred Iklé and Paul Wolfowitz at the Arms Control and Disarmament Agency (ACDA); Elmo Zumwalt, the chief of naval operations; and Paul Nitze, a member of the negotiating team in Geneva. It was no accident that nearly all of these men were included in the group that Eugene Rostow enlisted in 1974–75 when he took the first steps to found the Committee on the Present Danger.

Upset by Kissinger's concessions to the Soviets, Nitze resigned from the SALT delegation in 1974 and launched a campaign against the talks, which he had come to view as a threat to national security. After this came the episodes with which we are now familiar: Team B and the founding of the CPD at the behest of Gene Rostow.

The Founding of the CPD

In November 1974, while already working with the CDM against détente, Eugene Rostow discussed his plan to form a bipartisan "citizens' group" with Charls Walker and James Schlesinger. Walker, who had served as a pilot in World War II, was a conservative Democrat from Texas, close to Governor John Connally, and an expert on banking issues. He headed a very successful lobbying and consulting firm but maintained an interest in foreign policy. At a Pentagon lunch in 1972, Elmo Zumwalt had confirmed Rostow's worries about the deterioration of the United States' strategic posture vis-à-vis the Soviet Union.[42] Schlesinger, an expert on defense issues and a former RAND researcher, served briefly as director of the CIA before being appointed secretary of defense by Nixon. A hawk, he soon joined the opposition to Kissinger and his policy of détente.

Two more years would pass, however, before the CPD was finally launched. Rostow was very busy, and he needed to persuade others to join him, starting with Nitze. Events in 1975 strengthened the group's resolve: South Vietnam and Cambodia fell to the Communists in April, Cuba intervened in Angola, and the OPEC-driven energy crisis continued. Despite these developments, Ford and Kissinger maintained their policy of détente, refusing to receive Solzhenitsyn at the White House in July and signing the Helsinki accords in August.

As a result, the small group gathered strength. Republican Richard Allen wrote to Rostow in May 1975 to compliment him on his *Wall Street Journal* article on behalf of the CDM.[43] Rostow and Charls Walker soon enlisted him in the group.[44] As a member of the CPD, Allen would play a very important political role. A former aviator, Allen was a foreign policy specialist at Georgetown's Center for Strategic and International Studies (at that time a very conservative think tank). He had been Nixon's principal foreign policy adviser in the 1968 campaign, but Kissinger had supplanted him.[45] Allen was close to Ronald Reagan, who appointed him national security adviser in January 1981. It was Allen who recruited the future president for the CPD and, even more important, who helped organize the migration of the CPD's neoconservative Democrats into the Republican camp in 1980, thus laying the groundwork for Reagan's appointments of Jeane Kirkpatrick, Eugene Rostow, Paul Nitze, Max Kampelman, and others.

After multiple meetings, the group achieved a critical mass and found funding,[46] which allowed it to hire Charles Tyroler as executive director. Finally, on November 11, 1976, a few days after the election of Jimmy Carter, the CPD held its first press conference at the National Press Club in Washington. The entire executive committee participated, and a list of directors and members was distributed along with the group's manifesto, "Common Sense and the Common Danger."

The CPD consisted of two circles: an executive committee and a board of directors.[47] The group also hired staff: at its height there were four full-time employees and two part-time. As an elite organization, the CPD had no formal membership procedure: membership meant serving on the board of directors. When formal invitations were sent out the weekend before the press conference, no fewer than 141 "founding members" accepted—far more than was hoped. Max Kampelman, the CPD's legal adviser, was forced to amend the charter, which limited the board to 100 members. Each member drew on his or her network to recruit other members. For instance, it was Max Kampelman who invited Jeane Kirkpatrick to join.[48] Ultimately the board of directors consisted of roughly 60 percent Democrats and 40 percent Republicans. Allen even estimates that the board was 70 percent Democratic at the beginning in 1976. He also notes that not all the Republicans came from the same faction of the party: he was the only one who supported Reagan against Ford in 1976.[49]

The executive committee was composed of fifteen prominent figures, all recruited by Rostow. It was decided to name three cochairs: their role was mainly symbolic, but important to achieve political balance. The three chosen were Joe Fowler, a Democrat who had worked for the New Deal and served as secretary of the Treasury under Lyndon Johnson; David Packard, a Republican and founder of Hewlett-Packard; and Lane Kirkland, second-in-command of the AFL-CIO. The real power lay with the executive committee and its chair, Eugene Rostow, and Paul Nitze, who was named "research director" to set him apart from the other members of the committee without making him a cochair.

The press conference began with a reading of the group's manifesto; Nitze, Packard, and Kirkland each read a part of the document.[50] The text, titled "Common Sense and the Common Danger," had gone through a dozen revisions after Rostow sent the first draft to Walker and Nitze in December 1975.[51] Rostow had toned down the overly alarmist passages in the early drafts in order to ward off allegations that the CPD consisted solely of "unreconstructed Cold Warriors."[52] Nevertheless, the central message remained one of alarm: America faced a period of growing danger of which the public remained unaware. The main threat to the nation, world peace, and human freedom was the Soviet quest for hegemony, based on an unprecedented military buildup, far greater than that of the United States. American interests were threatened not only by direct attack but also by indirect aggression against American allies and gradual encirclement; in this respect, the Middle East was crucial to the defense of Europe and Japan. Although the CPD did not discuss ideological issues at length, it did underscore the essential moral difference between the two superpowers: the United States, for all its imperfections, remained indispensable to the defense of the free world. Soviet expansionism threatened to undermine the balance of power. An immediate response was called for, and public opinion would have to be mobilized in order to prevent the Soviets from surpassing the United States, lest America be faced one day with a choice between war and surrender.

There was no shortage of questions from the seventy journalists in attendance.[53] Was the group pro-Carter or anti-Carter? Was it anti-Kissinger? Did it represent the military-industrial complex? The CPD had taken the trouble to lay out its operating rules in a separate pamphlet.[54] Independent and nonpartisan, it consisted of private citizens. Any member elected or appointed to office would be "suspended" for the duration of his or her term. The CPD would not endorse any candidate for office. In the interest of avoiding undue influence, contributions from any single source could not exceed $10,000. Furthermore, to avoid charges of being manipulated by the military-industrial complex, the group would not accept any contribution from any person or corporation that derived "a substantial portion" of its income from the defense industry ("substantial portion" was defined as 15 percent or more, so as not to rule out contributions from Hewlett-Packard, part of whose business was defense related).

Lane Kirkland was reminded by a journalist that other unions had criticized the size of the defense budget. Did he not believe that public money would be better spent on urban renewal and housing than on building more missiles and nuclear warheads? Would the alternative use not create more jobs? Kirkland said that, although he did not challenge that analysis, "I don't think there's a tradeoff. I don't think that the choices are made by weighing one against the other. And to me it's a question of if you build a house, it's still prudent to take out fire insurance, particularly if you're living next door to a pyromaniac."[55]

The members of the executive committee were disappointed by the initial response to the launch of the CPD. Neither the *Washington Post* nor the *New York Times* published articles, and neither CBS nor NBC broadcast any report, although each of these news organizations had sent journalists to cover the event.[56] Slowly but surely, however, the opinion pages of many newspapers began to respond to the CPD's message, and on January 11, 1977, the *New York Times* published excerpts from the group's manifesto, albeit opposite a statement by the American Committee on U.S.-Soviet Relations, a group that supported détente and the SALT talks (and included George Kennan and John Kenneth Galbraith among its members).[57] Meanwhile a torrent of criticism poured forth from the Soviet press, which denounced the CPD as "a flight of hawks," an assemblage of "anti-Soviet has-beens," and "a committee of ex's." On November 13 *Pravda* proclaimed: "The more the beneficial process of the relaxation of international tension develops in the modern world, the greater the anxiety of those whose well-being depends on the arms race—people in the capitalist countries' military-industrial complex."[58]

Publications and Exaggerations of the CPD

Immediately after the November 11, 1976, press conference, the executive committee went to work. The CPD sought influence in a variety of ways, but it relied first and foremost on its publications, on which it lav-

ished a great deal of attention. Each of the forty-nine texts (sixty-six total, if one includes the seventeen updated versions of *Current Salt II Negotiating Posture,* by Paul Nitze) that the group published between 1976
and 1991 went through many drafts. Each was reviewed by all the members of the executive committee until no objections remained. For example, the group's first sixteen-page pamphlet, *What Is the Soviet Union
Up To?,* which was drafted by Richard Pipes and eventually printed
in 10,000 copies, went through seven drafts, each of which circulated
among executive committee members. It went through the major points
of Team B's final report, including the critique of the National Intelligence Estimate prepared by the CIA. Like the CIA, Pipes argued, American public opinion tended to view the Soviets as resembling Americans.
But the Soviet Union was a radically different nation, which lacked the
natural advantages of the United States and was therefore naturally inclined toward expansionism and, domestically, toward concentration
of power in the hands of an elite (first czarist and later Communist).
The current elite, which enjoyed a comfortable lifestyle, aimed for "the
worldwide triumph of Communism," and the Politburo wielded all the
power needed to advance toward that end. If present trends continued, Pipes warned, the Soviet Union would achieve strategic superiority
within a few years, and the United States would be forced first to limit its
commitment to defend the free world and ultimately to adopt an isolationist policy. America was urged to meet this threat while there was still
time.

On July 6, 1977, the CPD published its first critical study of the SALT
II talks, *Where We Stand on SALT,* marking the beginning of its offensive against the Carter administration's approach to arms control.[59] This
text, written by Paul Nitze and Richard Allen, sought to make the basics
of the SALT negotiations accessible to all, although the details remained
quite complex. The CPD argued that the talks had got off to a bad start:
while America hoped to limit a dangerous and costly competition in nuclear weapons, the Soviet Union was trying to block development of the
American arsenal by any means available while continuing to add to
its own arsenal. The Carter administration was not insisting on sufficient concessions from Moscow, which held an advantage in terms
of "MIRVed throw-weight" (that is, the total tonnage of nuclear warheads deliverable by multiple independently targeted reentry vehicles, or
MIRVs). The CPD recommended increasing both the quality and quan-
tity of American strategic forces, proceeding with the latest missile pro-

gram, the MX, and restoring the credibility of America's second-strike capability.

But the report to which the CPD attached the greatest importance, and which would become one of its trademark products, dealt with the strategic balance between the United States and the Soviet Union. The first version of this report, the fifty-two-page *Is America Becoming Number 2?: Current Trends in the U.S.-Soviet Military Balance,* appeared in October 1978 and attracted a great deal of attention. It owed its impact to a wealth of detail and precision, its critical apparatus, and its disturbing narrative, according to which the Soviets were on the way to surpassing the United States in nearly every aspect of military power. In June 1982 the CPD repeated the question: "Has America Become Number 2?" And its answer was yes: the Soviet Union had overtaken the United States to become the world's leading military power. Even the president of the United States, Ronald Reagan, accepted this conclusion, according to the pamphlet.[60] If we examine this claim a little more closely, however, we discover that Reagan was already asserting that the United States was "number 2" not only during his 1980 presidential campaign but also during his unsuccessful 1976 campaign, prompting Kissinger to launch a counterattack against what he called "fairy tales" (although Reagan's attack had borne fruit with the creation of Team B).[61]

Did the CPD exaggerate the threat—a natural tendency for hawks (and neoconservatives)? In fact, when one considers all the factors that form part of the military equation, it is extremely unlikely that at any point in the 1970s and 1980s America's generals would have wished to exchange their equipment and geographical situation with those of their Soviet counterparts. By contrast, Soviet generals would most likely have welcomed such an exchange.[62] The United States always retained the global edge, although the nuclear factor tended to reduce the gap between the two sides. One flaw in the CPD's reasoning was that it never looked at the American threat through Soviet eyes. Many Russian initiatives were reactions to American advantages rather than attempts to gain a decisive advantage over Washington or to lay the groundwork for an offensive war. This situation was what sustained the arms race.

To sort out truth from fiction here, two points should be kept in mind. First, Soviet expansionism was a reality in the 1970s, a decade in which America was suffering a crisis of confidence in the wake of Vietnam, and its leadership was diminishing. The Soviets supplied the Arab states with arms during the 1973 Yom Kippur War. The ensuing oil embargo showed that the West was dependent on its energy suppliers. Vietnam and Cambodia fell to the Communists in 1975. Cuban troops intervened in Angola in 1975 and in Ethiopia in 1977, with logistical support from the Soviet Union. Grenada and especially Nicaragua moved closer to communism. The shah of Iran was overthrown in 1979. And the Russians invaded Afghanistan at the end of 1979. In addition to these geopolitical developments, the CPD stressed Soviet gains in nuclear weaponry in the period from the Cuban missile crisis to roughly 1975.

Given this context, many Americans were genuinely worried, which brings us to the second point: the sincerity of American anxiety is attested by numerous spontaneous initiatives, traces of which can be found in the CPD archives. For instance, in 1976–77 John Connally and Edward Rowny, who eventually joined the CPD, proposed forming a similar organization. Rowny represented the Joint Chiefs of Staff at the SALT II talks in Geneva and would later serve in the Reagan administration. Still, it is possible to be both sincerely worried and sincerely mistaken. As we have seen, time seemed to have stopped for the neoconservatives at some point in the 1930s: they frequently drew analogies with that decade that obscured rather than clarified the issues of the moment.

Sincere worry is one thing, deliberate exaggeration another, and it is clear that the CPD exaggerated in its public statements and publications. The logic was simple: fear was the best ally of those who favored a stronger defense posture and a larger military budget. The CPD was able to move the debate in its direction precisely because it exaggerated the threat and painted a frightening picture. "I have no doubt we'll wake up if we're hit over the head, as we were at Pearl Harbor," Rostow explained. "Our problem is to arouse the sleeping giant before that kind of an event happens."[63] There was a risk of unintended consequences, however, as John Roche observed:

> Nothing undermined the British and French in 1939–1940 more than the ambience of defeatism and, unwittingly, our friends who quite honestly formulate worst-case scenarios contribute to "all is lost" mentality . . . The emphasis should be shifted from doomsday keening to the positive note . . . It's not that [the Russians] are ten feet tall; we are just suffering from self-induced anemia.[64]

The other problem is that the neoconservatives were clearly the last people to believe in the efficiency of Soviet-style Marxism-Leninism and to overlook the mediocre condition of the Russian military.

Two other factors having nothing to do with propaganda may help to account for the CPD's exaggerations. First, many members of the group felt that when it came to America's survival, it was unreasonable to run any risk, no matter how small. If in the end it turned out that too much was spent on defense, that outcome would be unfortunate, but it was better to err on the side of caution. The same logic could be seen at work after the attacks of September 11, 2001, for instance, in the "one-percent doctrine" advocated by Vice-President Dick Cheney.[65] If there was even as much as a one-percent chance that al-Qaeda might obtain an atomic bomb, the possibility should be treated as a certainty given the enormous danger that this would represent.

The other factor contributing to the CPD's exaggerations was ideological in nature. Although American public opinion generally favored the idea that the United States should be content to defend itself, many Americans believed they had a mission to defend the free world and that they must be capable of intervening to defend free countries everywhere in spite of Soviet dissuasion. And the capacity to intervene abroad in the face of Russian opposition required a much more significant military edge and a much larger arsenal than that needed simply to defend the homeland. In other words, "survival is not enough," as Richard Pipes put it in his 1984 book.[66] Third-age neoconservatives seem to have accepted the logic of this argument: what they fear is not that Iraq or Iran will launch a nuclear attack on New York but rather that they may be unable to dissuade America from intervening to defend its allies in the region. What their predecessors sought—on moral rather than purely strategic grounds—was ultimately not equivalence but superiority: not defense but victory. These considerations were thought to be justification enough for a few exaggerations.

The CPD and the Carter White House

In the summer of 1977 Gene Rostow had every reason to congratulate himself. The nascent CPD had published its first texts, its audience was growing, requests for pamphlets and lectures were pouring in, and the reception in the press had improved. The CPD was no longer referred to as "hawkish" but rather as "bipartisan," "prestigious," "influential," and at times without any adjective at all—a mark of institutional acceptance.[67] But the CPD did not really make its mark until it staked out a position in opposition to Carter's foreign policy, which it sought to reorient through a dual strategy of internal and external influence.

The internal influence consisted in trying to shape important political decisions before the administration made or announced them. Because of the group's ability to make trouble, Carter opened a channel of communication in the hope of persuading the CPD not to criticize his policy in public but rather to transmit its comments directly to top foreign policy officials. The CPD knew, however, that the administration paid attention to its critiques internally only because of the fear it inspired through its external influence on countervailing powers such as Congress, the media, and the general public. If it wanted to force the administration to modify its foreign and defense policy, for example by abandoning SALT II, it therefore had no interest in giving up its bird in the hand for two in the bush: without public attacks on the administration, there would be no invitations to the White House. It was also well aware of the inherent limits of internal influence: such a strategy might yield occasional results on specific issues but could not bring about a fundamental change in policy. It was a band-aid, not a heart transplant, and what the CPD wanted was nothing less than a sharp change in direction of the country's foreign and defense policy. Eventually it got what it wanted, but not until it had "become" the administration itself with the election of Ronald Reagan.

Relations between Carter and the CPD's founders were initially good but deteriorated rapidly. Paul Nitze, in particular, was one of the few foreign policy experts invited to the governor's mansion in Georgia in July 1976, but the meeting proved disastrous, and he was the only one who ended up with no job offer.[68] It was the nomination of Paul Warnke to head the ACDA (in charge of the SALT talks) early in 1977 that infuriated the CPD. An unofficial meeting between some CPD members and Senator Scoop Jackson was arranged on January 26, 1977, to coordinate the opposition.[69] Carter's foreign policy appointments generally caused as much consternation in the CPD as in the CDM.

Nevertheless, for the first six months of the Carter administration, the CPD, led by Rostow, adopted a strategy far more complex than systematic opposition. Rostow angrily attacked Carter's appointments, yet he maintained a regular correspondence with Secretary of State Cyrus

Vance from January to July 1977. In a letter dated April 7, 1977, he wrote: "it seemed to us that it . . . might well be useful if a few of us met occasionally with you and [Secretary of Defense] Harold Brown—separately or together, depending upon the issues, and your preference—to discuss problems before the policy of the administration was determined, and announced."[70] In other words, Rostow was demanding nothing less than privileged access to the secretary of state and secretary of defense before important decisions were made.

This mixture of pressure with a willingness to discuss issues privately bore fruit. On July 15, 1977, Cyrus Vance received Rostow and Nitze at the State Department. The two men presented their arguments and left Vance with some CPD position papers, but nothing concrete came of the meeting.[71] In fact it was an invitation to meet Carter in the White House that showed how effective the internal influence strategy was. Eight members of the CPD were invited to meet the president on two days' notice. The executive committee held an emergency evening meeting on Wednesday, August 3, 1977, to prepare for the session and to agree upon the statements that would be made by Rostow and Nitze.[72] The others invited were Lane Kirkland, David Packard, and Joe Fowler, the three cochairs, along with Elmo Zumwalt and Rita Hauser. (Melvin Laird, who was not a member of the CPD, was also invited.)

The meeting with the president lasted forty minutes, after which the discussion continued for another thirty minutes with Secretary of Defense Harold Brown and National Security Adviser Zbigniew Brzezinski. But the atmosphere was not cordial.[73] Rostow opened the discussion as planned. He thanked the president, described the CPD, emphasizing its bipartisan character, and laid out the concerns of the group—and, he claimed, of the general public—regarding the increase in Soviet military power.[74] Regarding the SALT talks, he repeated the arguments set forth in the pamphlet *Where We Stand on SALT*. Nitze also drew upon the pamphlet *What Is the Soviet Union Up To?* before turning to the relation between the overall strategic balance and the relative strength of the adversaries in different regional theaters of East-West conflict.[75] Carter cut him off before he had finished his presentation.[76]

The president challenged the Rostow-Nitze analysis of Soviet-American relations and in particular the pamphlet *Where We Stand on SALT*, which he said he had read. He defended the administration's position, at times vehemently, in a rambling monologue. In private, Rostow commented that "the Presidents [*sic*] personality and style came through as pathetic, almost pitiful." He reported that Carter's message was confused, a mixture of technical remarks and emotional comments: "This is a great country"; "I am not inclined to sell our country out to the Soviets."[77] He argued that the public would not support a sharp increase in the defense budget:

> "No, no, no," Paul Nitze was overheard murmuring . . .
> "Paul," the President complained to Nitze, "would you please let me finish?"[78]

Zbigniew Brzezinski confirms that the meeting did not go well. He attributes the president's sour mood to the prickly relationship between Carter and Scoop Jackson. In his personal diary for that day he noted:

> 8/4/77. Right after lunch, had a meeting with a group of right-wing critics of our policy toward the Soviet Union, led by Gene Rostow, Paul Nitze, Melvin Laird, David Packard, Zumwalt and others. While their statements were somewhat extreme, and irritating, the president's response was excessively defensive and showed real signs of anger. As a consequence, it wasn't very effective. In fact, it really wasn't very logical. I slipped him a note saying that he sounds too defensive and I suggested some points that he make in order to make a more effective case.[79]

How should we interpret this meeting? Several CPD members suspected the president's staff of having organized it in order to claim that the president had consulted with people of all shades of opinion, including hawks, before announcing his decisions concerning the SALT II talks. But the White House did not publicize the meeting, which did not even figure in the president's official calendar, and this fact argues in favor of a different hypothesis, namely, that Carter received the CPD at the White House in the hope of taming his critics. He wanted to encourage them to speak directly to the highest officials in his administration (and before leaving the room, he indicated that he wanted the dialogue to continue with Vance, Brown, and Brzezinski).[80] In short, he hoped to appease his critics by engaging them in a privileged secret dialogue, in exchange for which they would muffle their public attacks on his administration.

If so, he badly misjudged the members of the CPD, as well as the tactical situation. They were certainly not prepared to accept such a bargain. They knew that they had no reliable allies within the administration and that their only hope of prevailing was to rally public opinion in their favor. Hence abandoning outside pressure was out of the question. They at once leaked details of the August 4 meeting to Rowland Evans and Robert Novak, who obligingly painted a picture of a weak and confused president.

Over the next few months the Carter administration showed that it still believed that it might be possible to appease its critics on the CPD and expand its contacts with members of the group. The CPD accordingly pursued the strategy of internal influence, which achieved its high point in the fall of 1977.

On August 17 Nitze and Zumwalt met with Brown and Brzezinski to continue the discussion begun with the president two weeks earlier.[81] On September 2 Rostow was invited to the White House for the signing of the Panama Canal treaties (which provided for the return of the canal to Panama in 1999).[82] Rostow was not taken in. "Paul Nitze was the leader of the Warnke battle, & more than 1/3 of the Senate voted 'No.' It stands to reason, doesn't it, that we are to be won over if possible before a Treaty goes to the Senate?"[83] This was exactly the way the administration would approach SALT II. Meanwhile, as a result of lack of unanimity among the members of the executive committee, Rostow, Nitze, Zumwalt, and some others came out in favor of the Panama Canal treaties and supported their ratification by the Senate, which earned them points with the administration.

The administration now intensified its consultations with the CPD. Brzezinski accordingly asked Samuel Huntington, a former fellow student at Harvard whom he had named an adviser to his National Security Council, to come to Washington on September 16 in order to present the conclusions of a highly classified document, Presidential Directive 18 (PD-18).[84] After being appointed national security adviser, Brzezinski, disturbed by the debates surrounding détente and by the Team B episode, ordered his staff to begin a "net assessment" of the relative strength of the United States and the Soviet Union.[85] Huntington was in charge of this study, which looked at all aspects of East-West competition, including the economy as well as intelligence and propaganda capabilities of the two superpowers. "We concluded our report in May or June of 1977 with a summary report, which I wrote with the collaboration of three other people on the NSC staff," Huntington explained. "That summary report was 400 pages long."[86]

The National Security Council staff ultimately painted a mixed portrait with a great deal of variation from issue to issue and region to region, but on the whole its view was less somber than that of Team B and the CPD, and it stressed the American lead in nonmilitary areas such as the economy (which it suggested should be exploited more) and world public opinion (as a good political scientist, Huntington constructed a quantitative index to highlight the U.S. advantage in the diplomatic realm). PD-18, which President Carter signed on August 24, 1977, was the operational conclusion of this vast study. This was the top-secret document that Huntington presented to the CPD executive committee; "Brzezinski asked me to meet with them because he thought they might be more likely to believe me since I had a reputation of being rather conservative," Huntington explained with a smile.[87] In fact his portrait left no room for optimism: Huntington depicted an expansionist Soviet Union seeking unilateral advantage "unless deterred by an unacceptable risk."[88]

Conveying the sentiment of the executive committee, Rostow wrote to President Carter that PD-18 as set forth by Huntington seemed accurate and promising but added that its contents must be explained to the American people and the world in a major presidential speech and not leaked in haphazard fashion to the press. In other words, Carter must openly embrace the report.[89] Such a step was particularly necessary since the report seemed to be at odds with certain dovish initiatives of the administration. Translation: the neoconservatives were not convinced. Brzezinski answered for Carter in the vaguest of terms.[90] In the wake of this exchange, Secretary of Defense Brown attended the first annual conference of the CPD at the Sulgrave Club on November 11, 1977, and answered questions for an hour. His presence was a clear sign of the success of the organization and its strategy of internal influence.[91]

Yet this strategy had already begun to bog down. Contacts with the administration, instead of deepening and leading to tangible results, became ever more insubstantial. Huntington did not pursue the discussion of PD-18 with the executive committee. The pace of letter-writing slowed in the following months.

The CPD's Campaign against SALT II

In 1978 and early 1979 the CPD intensified its campaign to "alert America" and its strategy of external influence. The focus was put on the SALT II treaty negotiations between the Carter administration and the

Soviet Union, which the CPD saw as crucial to maintaining the strategic balance between the two superpowers. Soon afterward, the internal strategy was revisited and again began to produce results. Paul Nitze succeeded in modifying the administration's negotiating position on certain points, but when the final treaty was signed by Carter and Leonid Brezhnev in June 1979, the CPD deemed it a bad and even dangerous agreement and threw all its forces into the battle to prevent ratification by the Senate. Its efforts bore fruit, and the organization, working with allies such as Senator Scoop Jackson, certainly played a key role in the administration's decision to give up on ratification.

Recall that the Strategic Arms Limitation Talks, which began in 1969, resulted in two treaties that were signed in Moscow in May 1972: the SALT I agreement, limiting the number of ICBMs and submarine-launched missiles; and the ABM treaty, limiting the number of antiballistic missile sites to two for each country.[92] Although Scoop Jackson already felt that these treaties were unbalanced in Moscow's favor, he was unable to block their ratification. The SALT II negotiations resulted in a first provisional agreement signed in Vladivostok by Brezhnev and Ford in November 1974. The Carter administration then resumed the talks but with a different approach. We saw earlier that the CPD launched its first attack on SALT as early as July 1977 with the pamphlet *Where We Stand on SALT,* which was based on what was publicly known about the negotiations at that point.

This pamphlet drew the ire of the Carter administration and led to the August 4, 1977, "minisummit" at the White House. During that discussion, Nitze warned Carter that a clause in SALT II banning mobile missiles would endanger the MX missile program, which was necessary to ensure an American second-strike capability.[93] The administration ignored his warning, however, and did not change its negotiating stance.[94] The CPD therefore turned to trying to mobilize public opinion. On November 1, in a press conference held at CPD headquarters, Nitze discussed in detail the positions of the two parties to the Geneva talks. A new pamphlet, *Current SALT II Negotiating Posture,* was published; it would be updated no fewer than seventeen times between 1977 and 1979.

The White House was furious that the CPD was again on the front pages; it had hoped to keep the criticisms private by offering the group privileged access. Philip Habib, number three at the State Department, told Rostow that Nitze's conduct was tantamount to "a declaration of war" on the administration.[95] The press conference put the administration on alert: Brzezinski warned Carter that in view of this development, the White House needed to counterattack at once with a public-relations campaign to "sell" SALT II.[96] But the administration also decided to pay attention to the CPD and if necessary to modify its negotiating position in the hope of achieving a treaty acceptable to both Moscow and Paul Nitze. Forced to negotiate both domestically and internationally at the same time, the administration wasted time and lost credibility without ultimately convincing both of its negotiating partners.[97] With hindsight, it is fair to say that the unsuccessful effort to win the consent of the CPD delayed the conclusion of negotiations and made ratification more difficult (because the political context was less favorable than it had been earlier).[98]

What is more, a polemic erupted around the detailed information that Nitze supplied in his press conference, information that had in fact been leaked by the negotiating team. Neoconservatives are in the habit of using leaks. It was no accident that Richard Perle and Scoop Jackson were subsequently attacked by Senator John Culver from Iowa, who demanded that the Senate Armed Services Committee be relieved of responsibility for monitoring the SALT II talks because of "a torrent of leaks."[99] The selective use of leaks continued in the 1980s and 1990s (in connection with the Cox Committee investigation of Chinese espionage in 1998–99, for example).

The CPD held additional press conferences in 1978 and 1979 to publicize Nitze's updates of his pamphlet *Current SALT II Negotiating Posture*. This external pressure again led the administration to offer the CPD a role in the formulation of policy in the hope of winning its support for ratification. The CPD therefore turned once more to its internal strategy. On June 13, 1978, Nitze was received at the White House by Landon Butler, who was in charge of the political aspects of the SALT II negotiations. Butler sounded out Nitze on what it would take for him to approve the treaty.[100] He knew that Nitze's principal concern was whether American Minuteman missiles could survive a Soviet first strike. If the SALT II agreement authorized the MAPS (Multiple Aims Points System) tactics (a sort of shell game that involved moving nuclear missiles from silo to silo in order to fool the Russians), as Nitze wished, would Nitze then support the treaty?[101] Nitze said that he would be more inclined to do so, provided that a massive defense program was also adopted to reverse the decline in U.S. strength relative to the Soviet

Union and provided that certain "personnel changes" were made. In short, Nitze wanted Paul Warnke removed from his post.

Nitze and Butler ended their discussion by agreeing to continue the dialogue. Two weeks later, Harold Brown called Nitze and told him that the administration had decided to inform the Soviet Union that it interpreted the SALT II agreement as allowing the use of the MAPS tactics. In other words, the CPD had in fact succeeded in modifying the official American negotiating position. The ACDA fought fiercely against this decision.[102] Less than a month later, however, Butler again received Nitze, who was this time accompanied by Elmo Zumwalt.[103] Butler said that he was surprised by the CPD's lack of support for Carter, given the overtures that had been made to them, and he accused Nitze of failing to keep his promises. Nitze pointedly repeated his two conditions.

From the administration's standpoint, the failure was threefold. A new issue had been introduced into the negotiations, at the cost of time and credibility for the American team. The Soviets had expressed reservations about the shell game, so that no one knew exactly if the MAPS system was truly in compliance with the treaty. And the White House had not obtained any firm commitment or even encouragement from Nitze or the CPD.[104] The administration probably felt that it had no choice and that it would do no good to negotiate a treaty that the CPD would reject, for the latter might then persuade more than a third of the Senate to follow its lead and reject ratification. Another sign of the CPD's influence was Paul Warnke's resignation a few months later, in October 1978. Officially, he made the move for family reasons, but this excuse fooled no one. Would his departure be enough to win over the hawks?

On June 18, 1979, the SALT II agreement was signed by Carter and Brezhnev at the Vienna summit. To appease the hawks, Carter had announced a week earlier that he would authorize development of the MX missile. Shortly after the signing, he announced that the Rapid Deployment Force envisioned in PD-18 two years earlier was now operational: 100,000 men could be deployed to the Persian Gulf region on short notice. Finally, Carter asked NATO to allow the deployment of Pershing missiles to respond to the challenge of Soviet "Euromissiles" (the SS-20 intermediate-range missiles deployed by the U.S.S.R.). Would these assertions of American power be enough to co-opt the neoconservatives?

Although it seemed obvious that the CPD would eventually reject SALT II and campaign against its ratification, the executive committee did not issue a definitive judgment until it had read the final text, in order to preserve the appearance that it was conducting an objective analysis of the treaty on its "intrinsic merits." On June 20, 1979, after executive committee members had read the final text, Nitze and Rostow led a vigorous discussion at CPD headquarters.

The committee unanimously reaffirmed that its role was to contribute to public debate and comprehension of the treaty. "It was the Committee's conviction that the debate should not be confined to SALT II but should include the emerging overall military balance between the two superpowers and its implications for US foreign policy."[105] Indeed, many members of the CPD did not want the SALT II treaty because it had come to symbolize the decline of American power relative to the Soviet Union. Whatever the "intrinsic merits" of the treaty, they believed that a new departure was essential and that it ought to begin with a jolt, such as the rejection of SALT II.

Once the ratification debate got under way in the Senate, CPD members testified at least seventeen times before the competent committees, "more than all other opposition witnesses put together," Rostow boasted at the annual CPD conference in November.[106] In all, more than 100,000 copies of the eight CPD documents on SALT II were published.[107] By all accounts, the CPD was the most effective civil-society organization in the fight against SALT II.[108] The CPD joined forces with other groups (such as the American Security Council and the Coalition for Peace through Strength) and coordinated its efforts with Scoop Jackson, the leading Senate opponent of the treaty.[109] Witnesses of this Homeric battle attest to the efficacy of the CPD's memos:

> "[Nitze has] done quite a job of getting anti-SALT facts into the hands of editorial writers and commentators," says Thomas Halsted, a public-affairs adviser at the State Department. "Every place I go to speak or meet with an editorial board, somebody has got Nitze's documents and starts asking me questions. He's perceived to have a high reputation for accuracy and patriotism, and he's generated a lot of skepticism."[110]

If witnesses agreed about the CPD's remarkable efficacy, they were also unanimous in condemning the Carter administration's poor performance in attempting to win ratification.[111] The administration delayed its effort too long, not really getting under way until the end of April 1979.[112] What really did the treaty in, however, was the political context.

Not only had Jimmy Carter's popularity dropped to about 30 percent, but the international situation had also deteriorated, and it was becoming more and more worrisome. In 1978 a contingent of Cuban troops was sent to Ethiopia, with Soviet support. According to Brzezinski, this move heightened tensions and led to a deterioration of U.S.-Soviet relations: "SALT lies buried in the sands of the Ogaden," as he put it.[113] In July 1979 came the alleged discovery of a "Soviet brigade in Cuba" (it had actually been there since 1962).[114] Four months later, Moscow was suspected of having a covert hand in the seizure of hostages at the American embassy in Teheran on November 4, 1979. The final blow was clearly the Soviet invasion of Afghanistan in December 1979. On January 3, 1980, Carter gave up on ratification and withdrew the treaty from the Senate docket.

Would the treaty have been ratified if the Senate had voted before the invasion of Afghanistan? All observers agree that the answer is no. In mid-December 1979, 21 senators opposed ratification, 40 were in favor, and 39 remained undecided. It would therefore have been necessary to persuade 27 of the undecideds to win ratification. In other words, the CPD and its allies, aided by the international context, had won the battle. But was the SALT II treaty really so bad? In fact, despite the nonratification and despite having strongly opposed the treaty before coming to power, Ronald Reagan respected its terms even after it expired in 1985, apparently at the behest of the Joint Chiefs of Staff (who had recommended ratification).[115] Indeed, for budgetary reasons, the Reagan administration reduced the overall size of America's strategic forces (by taking older equipment such as the Titan II missile system and B-52 bombers out of service, for instance), and it did so without insisting on Soviet reciprocity.

The invasion of Afghanistan came as a shock and created a new geopolitical context that was suddenly much more favorable to the neoconservatives and the hawks of the CDM and CPD. They felt they had been prematurely correct. But now they were on the same wavelength as the American public, which they had been warning of the danger for the previous four years. Had Jimmy Carter finally learned his lesson? Was the Democratic party ready to adopt a more resolute defense policy and take a firmer stand against the Soviet empire? Or would a turn to the Republican party be necessary to restore America's might?

6

MIGRATION TO POWER:
JOINING THE REAGAN CAMP

It is often said that neoconservatives are people of the left who have turned to the right. In many cases, this description is accurate, although it is clearly does not suffice to define neoconservatism. The conversion took place quite differently in each of the movement's three ages, however. In the first age, former Cold War liberals, many of whom were ex-Trotskyists, reacted to what they saw as a dangerous deviation of liberalism. As a result, many moved to the center, and some, such as Irving Kristol, continued their rightward shift in the 1970s and 1980s, becoming early contributors to the growing American conservative movement. By contrast, the neoconservatives of the third age, which began in 1995, had never been on the left.

In fact the most interesting "migration" to the right took place among neoconservatives of the second age, precisely between January and November 1980, when some Democrats decided on foreign policy grounds that they could not support their party's candidate, Jimmy Carter, and that only Ronald Reagan was up to the challenge of restoring American might. Some of them, such as Jeane Kirkpatrick and Elliott Abrams, though deeply Democratic, never looked back and soon became members of the Republican party. Others, such as James Woolsey and Joshua Muravchik, maintained ties with the Democratic party, returning to the fold under Clinton, while others, such as Richard Perle, retained only a nominal affiliation with the party for sentimental reasons.

Neoconservatism benefited twice from a favorable alignment of public opinion with presidential power: in the early Reagan years (1981–1985) and in the early Bush years (2001–2005). Both presidents adopted many neoconservative foreign policy ideas, though neither limited himself to just those ideas or fully satisfied neoconservatives.

This chapter is concerned with the migration of second-age neoconservatives to the Reagan camp. It seeks to measure their impact on American foreign policy in the last decade of the Cold War—the years of the "Reagan doctrine," which aimed to make trouble for the Soviet empire by supporting "freedom fighters," an exhaustive arms race, "Star Wars," and all the rest. Meanwhile the neoconservative movement continued on course, independent of these developments, both on the Democratic side (not all Scoop Jackson Democrats gave up hope in the Democratic party) and among first-age neoconservative intellectuals, who joined other elements of the right in the "conservative revolution."

The Great Political Migration of 1980

The Coalition for a Democratic Majority and the Committee on the Present Danger were not merely observation posts from which one could witness this major transformation of the American political landscape. They were the place where it happened. Jump ahead twelve years. In a 1992 confidential letter to President George H. W. Bush, then in the midst of a tough primary campaign, Richard Allen, a veteran of the CPD and first national security adviser to Ronald Reagan, offered this strategic advice:

> 7. The neoconservatives, mostly Democrats, can be yours, too.
> They can't stand Pat Buchanan's isolationist agenda and, since they're domestically liberal, his domestic agenda either. In 1980 we converted the entire Committee on the Present Danger into a force supporting Reagan, and it was overwhelmingly Democrat in composition. Of its 125 members, nearly seventy served in the Reagan-Bush administration. An outstanding example: Jeane Kirkpatrick, whom I personally brought over the line into our camp. Nitze, Rostow, Kampelman—they all came from the CPD roster.
> Consult with these neoconservatives before they drift back to their natural home among the Democrats. We can get you names.[1]

In the end, Allen's advice fell on deaf ears, and many second-age neoconservatives who had once worked with him at the CPD (such as Max Kampelman and Richard Schifter) chose to support Bill Clinton after twelve years with the Republicans. Their migration in 1980 did not just happen by itself. As Richard Allen later explained, "It was not immediately that I thought of taking them to Reagan, but I wanted to take them slowly towards Reagan, because knowing Reagan's thoughts and his views which were identical with theirs, but without the detail and enormous experience that they had, people who were basically embracing the same goals . . . they ought to be talking."[2]

In the early spring of 1980, CPD Democrats had not yet entirely abandoned hope in their party. In several of his letters to Scoop Jackson, Eugene Rostow discussed the idea—the hope—of a "revolt against Carter" at the Democratic convention.[3] Had not Ted Kennedy entered the race for the nomination, throwing down the gauntlet to the unpopular incumbent? Yes, but the problem was that Kennedy was attacking Carter from the left, not from a centrist position, thereby forcing the president to protect his left flank by diverging even further from the neoconservative line. It will come as no surprise that Ted Kennedy's discussions with the CPD led nowhere.[4] Richard Allen saw an opening. As early as 1979 he had asked Max Kampelman to arrange a meeting between Ronald Reagan and certain Jewish groups.[5] In 1980 Allen relied mainly on Eugene Rostow, to whom he was close and who was obviously at the heart of the CPD network.

By the spring, Allen had already recruited twenty-six CPD members to serve among candidate Reagan's sixty-eight official foreign- and defense-policy advisers. Nearly a third were Democrats, including Jeane Kirkpatrick, Richard Pipes, and Nathan Glazer.[6] On July 8, 1980, Allen arranged for two Democratic members of the CPD executive committee to appear before the Republican platform committee in Detroit. Richard Pipes and Paul Nitze insisted on the need to restore a bipartisan consensus to counter Soviet expansionism.[7] Three weeks later, Reagan received a four-hour briefing at his campaign headquarters from various advisers, including some from the CPD. The briefers included both Republicans such as William Van Cleave and Fred Iklé and Democrats such as Gene Rostow, Paul Nitze, and Charles Tyroler.[8] In the fall, Nitze and Rostow made the jump and became official Reagan supporters, but only as individuals, not as representatives of the CPD.[9]

It took much longer for CDM Scoop Jackson Democrats to make up their minds to support Reagan. Whereas the CPD was bipartisan, the CDM was a Democratic group whose mission was to reform the party, so to support the Republican candidate would signify not just a betrayal but also an admission of failure. But the breakfast meeting with Carter on January 31, 1980, during which the president, in the view of CDM members, dug in his heels and seemed "to have forgotten nothing and learned nothing," shook their convictions. In the months that followed, Carter's much-publicized "conversion" to the idea that the Soviet threat was real failed to persuade them: it was too little, too late. Did he really believe that a boycott of the Olympic Games in Moscow or an embargo on grain sales to the U.S.S.R. in protest of the invasion of Afghanistan added up to a serious response to Soviet expansionism? Norman Podhoretz asked the question in a celebrated pamphlet that became a best-seller, *The Present Danger*: was Carter's new, more aggressive tone aimed at the Soviets or at the American voter?[10]

Hence when the CDM met to plan its approach to the 1980 campaign, the organization was in a state of disarray. Scoop Jackson and Pat Moynihan had decided not to challenge Jimmy Carter, so that the Democratic centrist line had no champion, and the CDM really had only one card to play: the threat to abandon the party if its views were not taken into account. As we have seen, by playing that card it was ultimately able to win a hearing before the Democratic platform committee, where it defended its own position statement, "A Platform for a Strong America," which drew clear lines in the sand.[11] There were three priorities: to restore America's position as the world's leading military power; to renew the fight against communism and promote democratic values throughout the world; and, finally, to forge ahead with an expansionist economic program whose primary objective was to diversify America's sources of energy.

As the campaign proceeded through the spring and summer, however, it became increasingly clear that Carter could not be made to fit the profile of the ideal candidate set forth in the CDM's "Platform for a Strong America." Conversely, Ronald Reagan seemed more and more to fill the bill. What had initially been simply speculation about "going over to the enemy" therefore became a live issue, even an existential dilemma. This dilemma was best encapsulated by Jeane Kirkpatrick's article "Why We Don't Become Republicans," which appeared in the right-wing magazine *Common Sense* in the fall of 1979, one year before Reagan's nomination of Kirkpatrick as ambassador to the United Nations. The article is important not only as a gauge of sentiment at the time but also for its intellectual quality. Kirkpatrick reported having questioned a dozen of her "associates" in the CDM, who, she wrote, "have been called neo-conservatives so often that they have stopped fighting the name":

> Eventually the question occurs: why, since our estrangement from the na-
> tional Democratic Party has lasted for a decade, since it embraces a range
> of important issues which are not likely to disappear, since we have tried
> participating, cooperating, compromising, and waiting, in the effort to
> win back some influence within the Party for our point of view—which is,
> after all, widely shared by the Party's rank and file—and all without effect,
> and since we often find Republican policies preferable to Democratic pro-
> grams, why don't we simply break with the Democratic Party and become
> Republicans?[12]

Things weren't that simple, however. Partisan commitment is not just an ornament; it is part of a person's self-definition. "Party identification is a real identification . . . To change party is therefore to deny a part of oneself and one's heritage."[13] One day one of Kirkpatrick's sons, Doug, seven years old at the time, came home from school with the story that the teacher had discussed differences of identity among the students:

> "Today, we talked about what we are. Jimmy said he was a Catholic.
> Then Annie said she was a Jew. My friend Timmy said he's Episcopalian."
> "Well, what did you say?" Jeane asked.
> Her son, all of seven years old, beamed. "I said we're Democrats."[14]

There were also sociological and ideological obstacles to overcome. The Democrats found it hard to accept the "Republican style" of "coun-try club WASPs." This was especially difficult for neoconservatives who emphasized their Jewish identity. Elliott Abrams alluded to the feeling that "Republicans aren't 'our kind of people.' The GOP, with its flavor of small-town midwestern business America, holds no comfort for Jews." Gertrude Himmelfarb, the wife of Irving Kristol, remarked that liberalism was no longer the natural home of Jewish Americans: "We are, for the moment, homeless . . ."[15] It was not, however, simply a social allergy, Kirkpatrick explained. Democrats continued to doubt that Re-publicans were sufficiently concerned about society in general, including those who for one reason or another were incapable of meeting their own needs. "The problem is that the Republican Party has not articu-lated any inclusive vision of the public good that reflects concern for the well-being of the whole community."[16] For instance, it never really accepted the welfare state as a necessary instrument of social relations in a modern industrial society. Consequently, not even the most incensed Democrats, including Kirkpatrick, were yet ready to make the jump.

As we know, however, Kirkpatrick, a member of both the CDM and the CPD, did become the emblematic figure of the neoconservative shift to Reagan only a few months later. Her *Commentary* article "Dictatorships and Double Standards" drew the attention of Reagan, who wrote her a long, flattering letter at the end of February 1980 in which he expressed the hope that they could soon meet for a longer conversation.[17] Richard Allen arranged at least two meetings between the candidate and his new adviser, who provided foreign policy advice during the campaign and then worked on the transition team before being nominated ambassador to the UN, with cabinet rank, on December 22.

Two factors facilitated the neoconservatives' shift of loyalties. First, CDM Democrats were discouraged, not to say vexed, by their own party. Penn Kemble puts it this way:

> I wished we could have done that with Democrats, but they lost! They wrote themselves out of the game. We tried to support them. We supported Jimmy Carter. Scoop Jackson campaigned all over the country for Jimmy Carter, and then what did he get? We didn't elect to become Republicans. The Democrats elected to blackball us.[18]

A second factor, social in nature, certainly facilitated the migration. Having been lambasted by liberals and come to know Republicans, who welcomed them and listened to them, not only in the CPD but also at the American Enterprise Institute, where Penn Kemble, Ben Wattenberg, and Jeane Kirkpatrick all spent time, neoconservative Democrats discovered that many Republicans were not as socially alien as they had feared. Not all Republicans were "country club WASPs" with narrow, intellectually limited outlooks. Furthermore, one did not need to adopt all their political ideas to collaborate with them on specific issues.

In the end, it seems that many members of the CDM voted for Reagan. Some even announced their support publicly and campaigned for him. Some were offered posts in the Republican administration and accepted. And some actually became Republicans.[19] How much did the conversion of the CDM—a symbol of the conversion of the Scoop Jackson Democrats—actually contribute to the Reagan victory? It is dif-

ficult to say. After all, neoconservatives were neither a political party nor
a mass movement. Still, Norman Podhoretz makes the case for a significant impact:

> The second point on which there is little disagreement is that the influence
> of the neo-conservatives contributed to the election of Ronald Reagan.
> This was not a matter of numbers. As a movement of dissident intellectu-
> als, the neo-conservatives were (and are) a minority within a minority.
> Nevertheless, if the grip of the conventional liberal wisdom and the leftist
> orthodoxies in the world of ideas had not been loosened by the criticisms
> of the neo-conservatives; if a correlative willingness to entertain new ideas
> had not thereby been created; and if these new ideas had not been plausibly
> articulated and skillfully defended in the trials by intellectual combats that
> do so much to shape public opinion in the United States—if not for all this,
> Ronald Reagan would in all probability have been unable to win over the
> traditionally Democratic constituencies (blue collar workers, white-ethnic
> groups like the Irish and the Italians and a surprisingly high percentage of
> Jews) whose support swept him into the White House.[20]

Reagan, the Neoconservatives, and the Cold War

There is no denying the fact that the Republican who was elected president in 1980 bore a striking resemblance to neoconservatives himself.
Was he not a former Democrat who had later moved to the right, becoming a Republican at the age of fifty-one? Was he not a former "vital center" liberal and active member of the Americans for Democratic Action?
Had he not been an anticommunist trade unionist? And he was also a
member of the Committee on the Present Danger. Legend to the contrary
notwithstanding, he was not a "founding member" of the CPD, much
less a member of the executive committee.[21] In fact Reagan joined the
board of directors in March 1977, four months after the list of 141
"founding members" was drawn up in preparation for the press conference of November 11, 1976.[22]

The people responsible for bringing Reagan into the CPD were Richard Allen, his foreign policy adviser in the 1976 campaign, and David
Packard, the founder of Hewlett-Packard and cochair of the CPD.[23] In
any event, the former governor of California was not a very diligent participant in the group: he never attended the annual convention and never
donated money. On the other hand, he did occasionally help the CPD
raise funds,[24] and he spread its message through his radio broadcasts.[25]

He drew heavily on Rostow's July 1978 briefing on the SALT talks, which the CPD published in August. Six Reagan broadcasts bore the title "Rostow Speeches," and he sent an enthusiastic letter of gratitude to the man who had inspired them.[26] Other important figures who belonged to the CPD include Donald Rumsfeld, who joined in 1978; George Shultz, who joined in 1979, and Richard Perle, who joined in 1981. Neither Scoop Jackson nor Paul Wolfowitz nor Albert Wohlstetter was a CPD member.[27]

As one might imagine, the atmosphere at the fourth annual CPD convention, held on November 6 and 7, 1980, was truly triumphal: a CPD member had just been elected president and had sent the group a friendly message, which was read aloud at the meeting.[28] Over Reagan's two terms, 65 of the group's directors received more than 100 appointments of one kind or another.[29] If we subtract appointments to purely advisory posts, we find that 27 CPD members, including numerous Democrats, were named to important posts in the executive branch, including, in addition to the president himself, a secretary of state (George Shultz), a national security adviser (Richard Allen), a UN ambassador (Jeane Kirkpatrick), a director of the Central Intelligence Agency (William Casey), a director of the Arms Control and Disarmament Agency (Eugene Rostow), and a special adviser to the president on arms control (Paul Nitze). Several CDM members also joined the administration. Some, such as Kirkpatrick, Pipes, Rostow, Kampelman, and Richard Schifter, belonged to both groups, while others, such as Elliott Abrams, Ben Wattenberg, and Arch Puddington, did not.

But the question remains: Was Reagan's foreign policy from 1981 to 1989 truly neoconservative? Behind this question lies another: What brought about the end of the Cold War? Did Reagan play a decisive role, and, if so, was it because he pursued a neoconservative line? In what follows I will merely summarize briefly the positions of two schools of thought on these questions.

The first holds that Reagan won the Cold War thanks to policy initiatives that brought the Soviet Union to its knees: he revived the arms race, in particular by introducing the Strategic Defense Initiative (SDI, popularly known as "Star Wars") antimissile shield, which drained Moscow's resources and forced the Kremlin to recognize the need for reforms (which led to an implosion of the system); he harassed the Communist bloc on its periphery by supporting "freedom fighters"; and he denounced the "evil empire," shifting the focus of the Cold War back to the ideological and moral terrain of democracy and human rights, where it should have remained all along. Neoconservatives claim to have been the inspirers of this winning strategy of confrontation, which they defended against other factions within the administration that were prepared to compromise on a whole series of issues. Indeed, in Jay Winik's book, which is representative of this school of thought, Reagan scarcely figures at all. The fall of the Berlin Wall is attributed to the formidable efforts of four neoconservatives: Jeane Kirkpatrick, Richard Perle, Elliott Abrams, and Max Kampelman.[30]

The second school of thought tends to minimize the role of external forces, including Reagan, compared with the many internal factors that helped to bring down the house of Lenin, many of them originating well before the 1980s. In this view, if any individual can be said to have mattered, it was Mikhail Gorbachev, not Ronald Reagan. The collapse of the U.S.S.R. did not come about because the Republican president took a hard line; it was in fact facilitated by the easing of tensions that he sought during his second term (actually from 1984 on), to the consternation of his neoconservative advisers. Reagan concluded several agreements with Gorbachev, which allowed the Soviet leader to pursue his reforms without having to make concessions to hard-liners in the Politburo. Contrary to the view of neoconservatives, the 1970s were not "lost years" that only delayed the eventual fall of the Soviet Union. Rather, détente, trade with the West, and the Helsinki accords opened the Communist bloc to the corrosive influences of the West and hastened its collapse. In this respect, even the counterculture that neoconservatives often combatted at home—from rock and roll to hedonistic individualism—contributed to the Soviets' defeat.

The relevance of this debate to our own time can scarcely be overemphasized. If Reagan won the Cold War—the greatest political and military confrontation of all time—by following a neoconservative line of American military assertiveness and insistence on "moral clarity," then that line gains historical validity, taking its place alongside the heroic stance of Churchill and offering a model of "regime change" applicable to other countries (such as Iraq, Iran, North Korea, Syria, and Libya). If, on the other hand, the Berlin Wall fell because of Reagan's willingness to compromise and his ability to negotiate with Gorbachev, then it would be better to avoid neoconservative bluster in favor of openness, engagement, and dialogue with hostile regimes. Neoconservatives were quick to recognize the importance of this "lesson of history" as validation or refutation of their view of the world and moved rapidly to claim credit for the fall of communism through their influence on Ronald Reagan.[31]

The Reagan Doctrine and the "Evil Empire"

The historical verdict on this question should be based on various pieces of evidence. We should certainly start by describing the neoconservative influence on certain key elements of Reagan's foreign policy. But we also need to delve beneath the myth to reveal the dissension that existed within the administration, not only between neoconservatives and realists, but even among neoconservatives. This exercise leads to a clear conclusion: over the years Reagan moved steadily away from the neoconservatives, in the end adopting policies in defiance of their wishes that probably contributed just as much to "winning the Cold War" as anything they proposed.

At no time did neoconservatives occupy the key foreign policy posts in the Reagan administration. In July 1982 George Shultz succeeded Alexander Haig as secretary of state and pursued a prudent, pragmatic foreign policy. He was inclined to explore any possibility of an arms-control agreement with the Soviets, as a result of which neoconservatives and the right tended to view him as a dove; in 1985 they even sought his resignation. Reagan's steadfast support clearly shows that Shultz's position was close to the president's and that the secretary of state had more influence on American policy than did any other official in the period 1982–1988.

Secretary of Defense Caspar Weinberger was much closer to the neoconservatives. It was he who presided over the sharp increase in the defense budget, staunchly defended the SDI program, and to some extent offset Shultz's influence, in particular by supporting Richard Perle in opposing various arms-control proposals, planning the invasion of Grenada (1983), bombing Libya (1986), and supporting the mujahideen of Afghanistan and the Contra rebels in Nicaragua. Hard-line "nuclear neoconservatism" was most influential at the Pentagon, which often allied itself with the National Security Council against the State Department, despite the presence there of a few neoconservatives, most notably Paul Wolfowitz on the Policy Planning Staff.

Finally, the National Security Council, initially headed by Richard Allen, often favored a neoconservative line, though its role was relatively minor. It was nevertheless the place where the plan of aiding the Contras was hatched, including the decision to resort to secret and illegal means, which led to the Iran-Contra scandal in which Elliott Abrams was involved. Mention should also be made of the role of Jeane Kirkpatrick as UN ambassador with cabinet rank (1981–1985). She, too, had a voice in the making of foreign policy. From these positions of influence neoconservatives were indeed able to inspire and implement the Reagan doctrine, as theorized in particular by Charles Krauthammer (about whom we shall hear more later). As Christopher Layne explained in 1987,

> The Reagan Doctrine has never been authoritatively defined, but its content can be inferred from various statements made by President Reagan and Secretary of State Shultz and the writings of such neoconservative foreign-policy theorists as Charles Krauthammer, Irving Kristol and Norman Podhoretz. Although usually thought of as a policy of aiding anticommunist insurgencies and building Western-style democracies in the Third World, the doctrine is much more than that. It aims to cause the Soviet empire's breakup and, ultimately, the collapse of the Soviet state itself by resisting Soviet and Soviet-supported aggression everywhere; engaging the Kremlin in a high-tech arms race; and pressuring Moscow economically.[32]

The Republican administration did launch multiple secret operations that continued and greatly expanded efforts to destabilize the Soviet Union begun under Carter.[33] NSDD-32, a National Security Decision Directive issued on May 20, 1982, unambiguously stated Reagan's foreign-policy objectives:

> —To contain and reverse the expansion of Soviet control and military presence throughout the world, and to increase the costs of Soviet support and use of proxy, terrorist and subversive forces.
> —To foster, if possible in concert with our allies, restraint in Soviet military spending, discourage Soviet adventurism, and weaken the Soviet alliance system by forcing the USSR to bear the brunt of its economic shortcomings, and to encourage long-term liberalizing and nationalist tendencies within the Soviet Union and allied countries.
> Despite increasing pressures on its economy and the growing vulnerabilities of its empire, the Soviet military will continue to expand and modernize . . . the decade of the eighties will likely pose the greatest challenge to our survival and well-being since World War II.[34]

The applications of this strategy are well known: support and arms for "freedom fighters" in Afghanistan (building on a policy initiated by

Zbigniew Brzezinski), Nicaragua, Cambodia, and Angola (Jonas Savimbi); support for the government of El Salvador, under threat from Communists; support for the Polish union Solidarity, which resisted the Communist government; support for Soviet dissidents; attempts to block all technology transfers to the Communist bloc (leading to tension with the Europeans over the construction of a gas pipeline to deliver Siberian gas to the West); manipulation of oil prices with Saudi Arabia to deprive Moscow of oil revenue; and so on.[35] In short, the Reagan administration took the steps advocated by neoconservatives to increase pressure on the Soviet empire. It also substantially increased spending on defense. Carter had raised the Pentagon's budget from $116 to $157.5 billion (in constant dollars) between 1979 and 1981; the "Reagan buildup" accelerated the trend and increased spending to $227 billion by 1984 and $303 billion by 1989, the year in which Reagan passed the baton to George H. W. Bush.

To be sure, all these measures might have been approved by any hawk, but another aspect of Reagan's foreign policy was without a doubt due to specific neoconservative influence, namely, his support for democratic forces around the world. Of course there were many exceptions to the emphasis on democracy throughout the Reagan years, from the indulgence of apartheid in South Arica to Suharto in Indonesia to the rather dubious democratic credentials of many of the so-called freedom fighters, such as the Nicaraguan Contras, the Afghan mujahideen, and the Angolan UNITA. Nevertheless, within the limits set forth in Jeane Kirkpatrick's article "Dictatorships and Double Standards," which cast the Soviet Union as the greatest obstacle to democracy in the world and made challenging it a priority,[36] the Reagan administration made the defense of democratic values a central tenet of its foreign policy. The neoconservative aspect of Reagan's foreign policy is especially evident in his famous speech to the British House of Commons on June 8, 1982, which was directly inspired by the neoconservative literature of the period 1974–1980.

> We must be staunch in our conviction that freedom is not the sole prerogative of a lucky few but the inalienable and universal right of all human beings . . . The objective I propose is quite simple to state: to foster the infrastructure of democracy, the system of a free press, unions, political parties, universities, which allows a people to choose their own way to develop their own culture, to reconcile their own differences through peaceful means . . .

> What I am describing now is a plan and a hope for the long term—the march of freedom and democracy which will leave Marxism-Leninism on the ash heap of history as it has left other tyrannies which stifle the freedom and muzzle the self-expression of the people . . .
>
> Let us now begin a major effort to secure the best—a crusade for freedom that will engage the faith and fortitude of the next generation.[37]

Following up on this speech, support for "the infrastructure of democracy" was provided by a new institution, the National Endowment for Democracy, for which Congress appropriated tens of millions of dollars. The NED came into being in 1983, and neoconservative Carl Gershman, a veteran of the Social Democrats USA who was close to Penn Kemble and Joshua Muravchik, was named its first president (a post he still occupied in 2010). It enjoyed broad support and was divided into four distinct branches: the International Republican Institute, under the aegis of the Republican party; the National Democratic Institute, under the Democratic party; the Center for International Private Enterprise, under the U.S. Chamber of Commerce, representing the business sector; and the Free Trade Union Institute, which dated back to 1977, and which later became the American Center for International Labor Solidarity (or simply Solidarity Center), under the AFL-CIO. It was this last branch, which was filled with neoconservatives, that was the most active, especially in Eastern Europe (where it actively supported Solidarity in Poland) and Central America (Nicaragua). The mission of the NED was not to overthrow foreign governments but to encourage, in a typically American vision of democracy, civil-society institutions that could exist independently of the state (and eventually resist the state should it become oppressive), such as trade unions, the press, political parties, and human rights groups.

Dissension among Hawks

Looking back on the Reagan administration, we tend to remember certain Homeric clashes between neoconservatives and proponents of a more "realist" line, often in the State Department, over Central America, Lebanon, and nuclear negotiations with the Soviet Union. What is often forgotten is that neoconservatives also clashed with one another, even in the area of arms control. For instance, Eugene Rostow accepted the post of director of the ACDA but obliged Richard Allen to accept the condition that he be allowed to bring Paul Nitze on board as negotiator. He had a hard time persuading Nitze to accept, even though Nitze would go on to add a major achievement to his personal history.[38]

At first the fault lines that developed were as expected: CPD members (Allen, Rostow, and Nitze, backed by their Pentagon colleagues Fred Iklé and Richard Perle as well as by Jeane Kirkpatrick) opposed anything that looked like a concession to the Soviets in the Strategic Arms Reduction Talks (START, the successor to the SALT process).[39] But in regard to negotiations concerning intermediate nuclear forces, or INF (the so-called Euromissiles), things took an unexpected turn. Rostow and Nitze did not want to concede any advantage to the Soviets, but they were quite worried about public opinion in Europe, where pacifist views were influential (there were massive demonstrations at the time against the deployment of U.S. Pershing missiles). In their view, it would be better to achieve an accord that would reassure Europeans than to remain inflexible and drive the Europeans toward neutralism.

The Pentagon saw things differently. Richard Perle pressed for and obtained the "double zero" negotiating strategy, which Reagan appreciated for its simplicity: America would give up its planned 1983 deployment of Pershings if the Russians would withdraw the already deployed SS-20 missiles that were aimed at Western Europe. But Nitze considered the double-zero option to be a basis for negotiation, not a definitive offer. Worried about the European reaction in case of failure and backed by his boss Eugene Rostow, Nitze entered into unauthorized secret negotiations with his counterpart Yuli Kvitsinsky: this was the famous "walk in the woods" episode of July 1982 (the two negotiators went hiking in the hills of the Jura Mountains to avoid listening devices).

When Perle found out about this, he fiercely attacked Nitze inside the administration, denouncing "an act of intellectual and political cowardice."[40] Through various bureaucratic maneuvers he managed to kill the compromise proposal. It was at this time that he outmaneuvered his superior Fred Iklé to become the leading Pentagon voice on arms control.[41] In the end, Reagan did not validate the "walk in the woods" proposal, and the episode led to the dismissal of Eugene Rostow—but not of Nitze—at the beginning of 1983.[42] He was succeeded by Kenneth Adelman, another CPD member and a protégé of Jeane Kirkpatrick, with whom he had worked at the UN since 1981.

This episode highlighted a clash that was at once generational and ideological. Nitze and Rostow were men formed by World War II, "present at the creation" of the American world, concerned about alliances, and with close ties to NATO. Writing about Nitze, Strobe Talbott said that "he was too closely associated with the old regime—the post–World War II political, diplomatic and military order—to be entirely comfortable in the new regime that proclaimed the Reagan Revolution."[43] Younger newcomers, such as Richard Perle, Kenneth Adelman, and Frank Gaffney, entered the fray in the era of *Ostpolitik* and détente. Their outlook was shaped by rejection of the protest against the war in Vietnam—in short, by the refusal of shabby compromise. The only kind of arms-control agreement acceptable to a Richard Perle was one that would have been tantamount to unilateral demilitarization by the Soviet Union. Early in 1983, when Rostow was sacked, Perle congratulated Richard Starr, the negotiator for conventional weapons, in these terms: "Congratulations! You obviously did a good job because nothing happened."[44]

In 1984 George Shultz took Nitze on as his "special adviser" on arms control in advance of the resumption of negotiations in January 1985, which followed Reagan's reelection in 1984. Nitze and Shultz became very close at this time. During the second Reagan administration, the clash between the Pentagon (Caspar Weinberger and Richard Perle) and their allies, most notably Kenneth Adelman at the ACDA, and the State Department (Shultz and Nitze) intensified, this time around the SDI antimissile shield.[45] The "superhawks" sought to make use of the president's dream to make an arms-control agreement difficult if not impossible, while at the same time killing off the 1972 ABM treaty. By contrast, Shultz and Nitze, together with Max Kampelman, who was placed in overall charge of negotiations in Geneva in 1985, sought to use the same dream as a bargaining chip to wrap up a "major deal" with the Soviets.[46] In the end, the superhawks lost out, and Perle and Adelman resigned in 1987; the INF accord, based on the double-zero option, was signed in Washington in December 1987. It opened the way to more serious START talks, but these did not come about before the end of Reagan's term, despite Nitze's efforts.[47]

Ronald Reagan: A Part-Time Neoconservative

Beyond the disagreement among hawks, it is clear that Reagan's CPD-style intransigence toward the "empire of evil" gave way to much greater foreign policy flexibility after 1983 or 1984, widening the gulf between hard-core neoconservatives, who were increasingly worried, and the president, who was joined by other, more pragmatic hawks such as Nitze and Kampelman. This growing divergence of views quickly became apparent in neoconservative criticism of Reagan. Less than nine months after being appointed, Robert C. Tucker accused Reagan of practicing "Carterism without Carter" in the Middle East.[48] Norman Podhoretz went so far as to evoke the "neo-conservative anguish over Reagan's foreign policy" as early as May 1982.[49]

The 1980 presidential campaign had led Podhoretz to expect much more resolute action in the Persian Gulf and the Caribbean, much like that in Poland. He accused Reagan (to some extent wrongly, but he had no way of knowing that) of not adhering to what would later be called the Reagan doctrine and of not putting enough pressure on the Soviet empire: "What President Reagan's response to the Polish crisis reveals is that he has in practice been following a strategy of helping the Soviet Union stabilize its empire, rather than a strategy aimed at encouraging the breakup of that empire from within."[50]

Nevertheless, Podhoretz still hoped that Reagan (who called him after the article appeared to reassure him) would somehow come to his senses: was he not the hawks' last best hope?[51] In 1983, while criticizing the administration's soft policies, which he considered tantamount to appeasement, he acknowledged the importance of internal political factors: the "consensus of 1980" had broken down, and the public, succumbing to pacifist influences, was no longer as steadfast as it had been.[52] In 1984–85, however, Podhoretz finally lost all hope in his champion: he described "the Reagan road to détente" and lamented the president's desire to do whatever it took to present himself to Europeans and above all to American voters as a "man of peace," ready to negotiate with the Soviets.[53]

Which was the real Reagan? There is no doubt that the president shared the neoconservative sensibility, but there is also no doubt that he had an antinuclear sensibility, and an evangelical sensibility, and a pragmatic sensibility, and, above all, a politician's sensibility. In short, his "moral clarity" and steadfastness in defending democracy in the face of the "evil empire" predominated only as long as these traits were compatible with other imperatives, mainly political, and other personal ambitions, such as his second-term wish to become a "peacemaker." Among those closest to him, several people with direct influence (including his wife Nancy and his adviser Michael Deaver) are said to have been wary that an overly militaristic and frightening anticommunism would be bad for his image.

In fact Reagan's foreign policy had clearly evolved, even though there remained a permanent rhetorical slippage from implacable hostility to the "evil empire," destined for "the ash heap of history," to a more conciliatory line based on the assumption that people everywhere aspired to live in peace. Although the early years were marked by a dramatic cooling of relations with the Soviets and a line that did indeed appear to be neoconservative, a counterweight soon emerged, most notably after George Shultz became secretary of state in mid-1982. Though he never became a dove (after all, he was a member of the CPD), he did resume the dialogue with Moscow in 1984–85, especially on arms control.

Reagan stuck to this more conciliatory line throughout the 1984 campaign, sensing the danger that voters might consider him too aggressive, although he also maintained his commitment to deploy Pershing missiles in Europe and the SDI antimissile shield at home. But his overtures to Moscow had no effect until Mikhail Gorbachev acceded to power in March 1985. After the Geneva summit in November (the first Soviet-American summit since 1979), the pace of negotiations picked up, and things began to move as quickly as they had in the 1970s. Although the Reykjavik summit of October 11, 1986, ended in failure, the two sides had come close to a sweeping agreement that would have cut their strategic arsenals by 50 percent and implemented the double-zero option on Euromissiles. The sticking point was the antimissile shield, yet the near-agreement shows how far Reagan's position had evolved. His last two years in office saw the conclusion of several arms-control agreements, most notably the INF treaty on Euromissiles (which finally did implement the double-zero option).

In other words, there was indeed a neoconservative Reagan, but he increasingly coexisted with "other Reagans" who took a more critical stance toward the hawks and ultimately adopted a more realist position as to the possibility of reducing tensions with Moscow in order to allow Gorbachev more room to maneuver. In December 1987 he dissociated himself from the anti-Soviet diehards: "Now, I think that some of the people who are objecting the most and just refusing even to accede to the idea of ever getting any understanding, whether they realize it or not, those people, basically, down in their deepest thoughts, have accepted that war is inevitable and that there must come to be a war between the two superpowers."[54] To sum up, Reagan in his second term was forced to "rebel," as James Mann has it[55]—to challenge his most hawkish advisers, who recommended a policy that, had he followed it, would have forced Gorbachev to take a harder line and therefore might have impeded or even undermined the reforms of Perestroika. In the end, it was probably the fact that Reagan switched from a bellicose policy to a policy of peace that enabled him to "win the Cold War."

"Cold Geniuses" Frozen in Time

The growing divergence between the president and the neoconservatives reminds us that the movement continued to evolve independently in the 1980s. But what is striking when one looks at the activities of *Commentary,* the CPD, and the Committee for the Free World (a new organization created by Midge Decter in 1981 to defend democracy against Communist totalitarianism) is the absence of conceptual innovation. The main ideas were refined in the 1970s, and neoconservatives who were not working for the administration were content to repeat them in ever more alarmist tones. This stance prevented them from recognizing the historic changes that began when Mikhail Gorbachev came to power in 1985.

For instance, *Commentary,* which published articles by old hands Norman Podhoretz, Richard Pipes, Edward Luttwak, and Walter Laqueur,[56] as well as newcomers such as Patrick Glynn and Angelo Codevilla,[57] gradually froze its representation of the West as a declining force and of the Soviet Union as formidable and invincible, demonstrating a faith in communism that existed nowhere else.[58] Except perhaps in France, where Jean-François Revel, who was in regular correspondence with American neoconservatives, explained that the world's democracies were inexorably losing the Cold War. Right up to the end (in the January 1989 issue of *Commentary*), Revel remained convinced that communism was irreversible.[59] In 1985, as John Ehrman has noted, *The National Interest* replaced *Commentary* as the most innovative journal of debate on foreign policy issues.[60] Founded by Irving Kristol with support from the conservative John Olin and Smith Richardson foundations, *The National Interest* was devoted to foreign policy, but it was not exclusively neoconservative and published less dogmatic and more creative pieces. The publication of Francis Fukuyama's article on the "end of history" in the summer of 1989 put the journal on the map.[61] In short, in the period 1989–1992, neoconservative thought was under duress and due for renewal.

Earlier in the decade, however, the question the CPD faced was whether or not its ideas would achieve real influence. To be sure, after Reagan's election, all signals were positive. Nevertheless, members were unanimously in favor of keeping the organization intact in order to "keep an eye" on the administration. In the event, the CPD would attack administration policies for predictable reasons: the group was critical of the timidity of Reagan's efforts to restore American military predominance.[62] But how far should the CPD go in criticizing a "friendly" administration? This question had to be faced as early as 1982, when the CPD published its first substantial assessment of Reagan's defense program, comparing Reagan's policy with the rearmament plan it had proposed in May 1980.[63] As impressive as Reagan's budgets may have seemed, they fell short of the maximalist goals that the CPD had set two years earlier. Although some members, such as William Van Cleave, wanted to make an explicit critique, others preferred to concentrate the group's fire on the administration's enemies, both in Congress and in the media.[64]

The years 1982 and 1983 witnessed the emergence in the United States of a vast movement in favor of nuclear disarmament, like the one that already existed in Europe. The CPD sought to counter the international campaign for a "nuclear freeze" with a barrage of polls, analyses, articles in the press, and appearances in the media. Its pamphlet *Is the Reagan Defense Program Adequate?* did criticize the administration but never mentioned Reagan by name.[65] The criticism did not pass unnoticed, however, and the *Washington Post* had a field day with it.[66] This neoconservative disillusionment with Reagan manifested itself two months before Podhoretz revealed the "neo-conservative anguish over Reagan's foreign policy." But Reagan, as he had done with Podhoretz, contacted the CPD to offer reassurance, and he would repeat the gesture in years to come.[67]

Having broken the taboo, the CPD pressed on, all the more so since the group found it difficult to understand the attitude of its former leaders Rostow and Nitze on the Euromissile question, especially the "walk in the woods" episode.[68] On November 30, 1984, a few weeks after Reagan's reelection, the CPD published *Can America Catch Up?: The US–Soviet Military Balance.*[69] But this pamphlet, which painted a very depressing and negative picture of the balance of power between the United States and the Soviet Union, had for months been a source of tension within the group as well as between it and its former members. Paul Nitze limited himself to a few technical corrections,[70] but Richard Perle protested the whole tone of the document:

> It does seem to me that the draft gives the administration too little credit for some of the strategic force improvements we have inaugurated, even granting the fact that some of those forces will not enter the inventory for another few years. Similarly, while I would not paint a comforting picture of the strategic balance, I believe that the discussion on pages 71 and 72— by focusing on some assumptions in the JCS [Joint Chiefs of Staff] analysis but overlooking other potential occurrences—somewhat overstates the situation we face today.[71]

To warrant criticism by Richard Perle for taking too dark a view of the Soviet Union takes some doing. This incident reveals the contrast between the maximalist, normative approach of the "citizens' group" and the attitude of CPD members working inside the administration and in touch with reality.

In fact, the issue that really sowed discord inside the CPD was the dispute over "guns and butter." If the CPD did not wish to cut itself off entirely from the concerns of ordinary Americans, it had in one way or another to answer the objections of those who felt that America could not long afford both the massive increase in military spending and the major decrease in taxes that the Reagan administration had initiated. While all CPD members agreed about the need for a strong defensive posture, they came from different ideological and political backgrounds. The Democrats and trade unionists among them were not prepared to reduce other public spending (which Reagan had already cut drastically), while the Republicans wanted no backpedaling on tax cuts. This debate, which flared up numerous times from 1984 into 1986, was never resolved. As a result, the climate within the CPD deteriorated, leading to the resignation of Charls Walker, one of the group's founders, early in 1987.

During Reagan's second term, the CPD seemed less energetic, more rigid, and more divided. The group never staked out a unified position on the two leading strategic issues of the day, the SDI antimissile shield and the arms-control talks with the Soviets. In the case of the treaty on Euromissiles, the group supported ratification by default, because it did not raise the red flag of national security as it had done for SALT II. Nevertheless, the majority of the group probably remained irremediably opposed to arms control, so the treaty took a toll. Indeed, Richard Perle and his assistant Frank Gaffney quit the administration and did what they could to oppose ratification, but they did so under the auspices of the American Enterprise Institute, in the way that Nitze, Rostow, and Zumwalt had made the CPD their instrument in combatting SALT II in 1979.[72]

In 1987 the British writer Martin Amis came to Washington and in a portrait of one arms expert employed by the CPD mocked the organization as a group of professional alarmists, threat-mongering bureaucrats:

His name is David . . . On his desk are scale models of intercontinental ballistic missiles (look at the size of those Soviet SS-18s!). On the wall behind his chair is a customized poster, jokingly accusing David of being a wanted man, "convicted of supporting the SDI program." Next to the poster is a cartoonish watercolor of an unreservedly grinning David, straddling the globe while missiles squirt this way and that; to his right is Uncle Sam, to his left the Russian Bear. David's pals or loved ones evidently felt relaxed enough to present David with this picture, and David evidently felt relaxed enough to hang it on his office wall. David works for the Committee on the Present Danger ("Present Danger?" sings the lady on the phone), the Recruiter think-tank that has supervised Reagan's nuclear policies . . . Otherwise, talking to David is like talking to your accountant. But I will certainly never forget the expression on David's face, one of saintly forbearance, as he told me the U.S. had decreased its overall megatonnage in recent years.[73]

The question that naturally arose in these times of change was whether the CPD could adapt itself to the new situation. In the spring of 1989, after several years of Glasnost and Perestroika (Gorbachev's programs of "transparency" and "reform") and even as Soviet troops were withdrawing from Afghanistan in defeat, the CPD published another analysis suggesting that the Russians were more powerful than ever.[74] Shortly thereafter, Eugene Rostow, who had resumed his position as chair of the executive committee at the beginning of 1987, suggested drafting a "second manifesto" to take account of the "Gorbachev phenomenon," although he remained cautious as to its significance.[75] In the text that he proposed in early 1990, he conceded that the Soviet Union "is losing an important round of the Cold War in Eastern Europe," but he also pointed out that Russia's (intact) nuclear capabilities needed to be taken into account, and he also emphasized the dangers inherent in an uncertain future: as payback for German reunification, Gorbachev might smash NATO, Finlandize Europe, and, with help from Japan and Western Europe, rebuild Russian power: "A helot Western Europe would be the inevitable agent of Soviet economic recovery. Gorbachev's hopeful spring would fade into autumn and winter. And a new Gorbachev would emerge as master of the Eurasian land mass from Brest and Cornwall to Vladivostok, a Gorbachev who had finally succeeded where Napoleon, the Kaiser, Hitler, and Stalin had failed."[76]

Despite the continued suspicion of the Soviet Union evident in this report, it was still too optimistic for the rest of the executive committee, which rejected it: there would be no "second manifesto."[77] Conceived to alert America to the lurking peril, the CPD did not want to be caught short if the situation reverted to a full-fledged cold war. As a result, the organization met a rather sad end, marked by increasing defections. The two cochairs, Douglas Dillon and Joe Fowler, resigned at the end of 1988.[78] Paul Nitze informally withdrew in 1989, while Elmo Zumwalt made his feelings clear: "Dear Charles: I am of the view of [sic] the Committee on the present danger has lost his momentum and is floundering. Please consider this letter as my resignation."[79] Eventually the philanthropic foundations abandoned the Committee, most notably the Sarah Scaife Foundation, its largest donor over time.[80] This irreversible decline did not prevent the CPD from publishing two alarmist pamphlets in 1991, two years after the fall of the Berlin Wall, one year after acceptance of reunified Germany's membership in NATO, and the year in which the Warsaw Pact, Yugoslavia, and, finally, the Soviet Union fell apart.

The first of these pamphlets, *Russian Military Expenditures* (April 24, 1991), argued that military spending for 1990 was equal in real terms to that of 1988 and would not decrease significantly. The second, *Has America Caught Up?: The US–Soviet Military Balance* (November 1991), prepared by William Van Cleave, insisted on the danger of the Soviet nuclear arsenal. The danger that worried him was not the threat of a rogue state or terrorist organization's obtaining weapons from that arsenal but rather the threat of an attack on the United States by the masters of the Kremlin: "there is little sign that the US-Soviet strategic balance will shift toward a favorable US posture before the end of the century."[81] Without a substantial and sustained increase in American defense spending and capabilities, the United States would enter the twenty-first century at a distinct disadvantage relative to the Soviet Union.

If further evidence of the CPD's astonishing divorce from reality were needed, it could be found in the fact that this pamphlet was published in November 1991, the very month in which Congress passed the Nunn-Lugar Act, which committed the United States to joining with Moscow to secure the nuclear arsenal of what would officially become, one month later, the "ex–Soviet Union." The world had changed, but the CPD seemed not to have noticed. The group met for the last time on March 12, 1992, congratulated itself on its contribution to ending the Cold War, and disbanded.

To be sure, the CPD was far from alone in its inability to perceive the changes that had taken place between 1985 and 1991. Neoconservatives and hawks fell into two groups: "cold geniuses," trapped in the ideological ice; and "pragmatics," more attentive to internal developments in the Communist bloc and to the continuing thaw. For instance, it was not until June 1989, when Norman Podhoretz traveled to Moscow, that he acknowledged the change that had taken place: "Glasnost, as we are proving right this minute, is a reality," he said to a crowd at the Kinocenter in Moscow. But he was quick to add, "I feel uncertain about this. Perhaps I too am being seduced by Gorbachev's smile." And he confessed his anxiety at the ease with which the Soviet leader, who still seemed to believe in the possibility of spreading the Socialist revolution around the world, had persuaded NATO to "disarm."[82] Of all the "cold geniuses" the prize for being the most frozen surely must go to Frank Gaffney, who in 1988 created the Center for Security Policy because he believed that the CPD had lost its resolve. For him, the nuclear-arsenal reductions to which Bush and Gorbachev agreed at the Washington–Camp David summit in June 1990 were "the worst strategic miscalculation on the part of a president of the United States since the Yalta Conference of 1945." A short while earlier, at the April 1990 meeting of the Committee for the Free World, he said: "Never since 1945 has the Soviet Union been so close to military preeminence in Europe as it is today."[83]

Irving Kristol, who belonged to the pragmatic camp, quipped that Gaffney sounded like someone who had fallen into a time warp.[84] As early as December 8, 1987, he had published an editorial in the *Wall Street Journal* titled "Taking Glasnost Seriously."[85] He explained that nothing lasts forever in this world and that totalitarian societies are not exempt from change, thereby contradicting the dominant line in *Com-*

mentary and to some extent the view expressed by Jeane Kirkpatrick in 1979 in "Dictatorships and Double Standards." He did not quite foresee what would happen two years later, but he did note the extent of the change that had taken place within Soviet society. This was important, he observed in 1988, as were the centripetal tendencies of the satellite states, which were like "an albatross around the neck of the Soviet Union" that would eventually necessitate a renegotiation of the status quo in Eastern Europe.[86]

The Persistence of First-Age Neoconservatism

Which brings us to the question of what became of Irving Kristol in the 1980s. More generally, what became of the first-age neoconservatives, who made their mark between 1965 and 1970 and whose interests were focused mainly on domestic affairs? We have seen earlier that a gap existed between Kristol and the Scoop Jackson Democrats on both foreign policy (where he opposed their idealism) and domestic policy (where he differed with Jackson himself on economic issues). If Kristol can nevertheless claim the title of "godfather of neoconservatism," it is because he played a key role in building a neoconservative network, a separate "establishment" that contributed significantly to the growing power of a broader conservative "counterestablishment" that competed with liberal elites and their traditional institutions in the 1970s, 1980s, and 1990s.[87] And the network that Irving Kristol built was composite: it included neoconservatives of both the first and second ages.

The Public Interest embodied the continuity of first-age neoconservatism in the era of Scoop Jackson and Ronald Reagan. Still concentrating on domestic issues, the journal continued to examine a range of sociological problems and to criticize liberal missteps, particularly in the realm of social programs, affirmative action, and the culture wars. On crime, for example, *The Public Interest* published numerous pathbreaking studies, including work by James Q. Wilson (whose most famous piece, coauthored with George Kelling, put forward the "theory of broken windows" to argue that police should protect communities and not just individuals—but it appeared in the *Atlantic Monthly*).[88] In 1966 *The Public Interest* also published an article by Christopher Jencks that helped to popularize the use of "school vouchers," an idea first proposed by Milton Friedman.[89] Its special issues on New York, universities, and public architecture became standard references.[90]

Vintage neoconservatism also ventured onto economic terrain. In 1975 *The Public Interest* published the original article on the Laffer curve (according to which high taxes lead to lower tax revenues);[91] and in 1978 Irving Kristol supported Jude Wanniski, the first writer to popularize the idea of supply-side economics.[92] Kristol, who became a regular contributor to the *Wall Street Journal* in the mid-1970s (thereby gaining contact with the world of business), accepted a position as visiting scholar at the American Enterprise Institute in 1976–77. He deepened his knowledge of economics and wrote a book whose title summed up the position of many first-age neoconservatives: *Two Cheers for Capitalism*.[93]

For it was the cultural side of capitalism that continued to interest—and worry—neoconservatives. Businessmen could not be trusted to combat the ideas of the New Left: captains of industry were unable to persuade their own protesting children of the benefits of capitalism. Neoconservatives therefore assigned themselves the (lucrative) mission of educating the business world in the methods of ideological warfare and the defense of a free society. In the late 1970s, Michael Novak, Irving Kristol, and Ben Wattenberg led seminars at the AEI in which they discussed the relation between ideas and economics with senior managers.[94] Their objective was to explain that capitalism was a precarious economic system that could collapse if not defended against ideological attack. In addition, they sought to dissuade business leaders from funding foundations and think tanks that attacked the underpinnings of capitalism. They also aimed to prevent conservative foundations from taking unduly extremist positions and thereby isolating themselves. As Kristol put it:

> In one of my essays in the *Wall Street Journal,* I had urged such foundations to stop moaning about the welfare state, the "road to serfdom," the death of free enterprise by "statism," and the iniquities of the income tax, and address the realities of the conservative situation. I wrote this not as a "movement conservative" but as someone who thought it would be best for the American democracy if conservatives would engage in a serious way the world as it existed—a world that in some respects was prospering, despite those fatal injuries the New Deal had presumably inflicted on it.[95]

Another neoconservative, Michael Novak, tried to show in *The Spirit of Democratic Capitalism* (1982) that capitalism was compatible with

Christianity, and specifically with Catholicism.[96] Novak was critical of both dependency theory and liberation theology and stressed the link between the free market and democracy. In the mid-1980s he opposed the National Conference of Catholic Bishops, which had criticized nuclear deterrence as immoral and attacked the Strategic Defense Initiative antimissile program.[97] Novak exemplifies the convergence of the first and second ages of neoconservatism.

We see the same convergence in Richard John Neuhaus, a Lutheran pastor who had initially been close to the New Left (as had Novak) but who, along with his colleague Peter Berger, the sociologist, had turned to the right in the 1970s. Along with Novak and Penn Kemble, he founded a small ecumenical think tank, the Institute on Religion and Democracy, which contested the influence of leftist Protestant groups (and of liberation theology). He then founded the Center for Religion and Society (later the Institute on Religion and Public Life), which campaigned against secularism in America and favored an interventionist foreign policy. The center also published the ecumenical monthly *First Things*. Neuhaus, who converted to Catholicism in 1990 and became a priest, also defended democratic capitalism and the role of religion as the moral foundation of society.[98] This small group of neoconservative theologians—joined later by George Weigel—carried the neoconservative banner in the culture and foreign policy wars. These "theocons," as Damon Linker describes them, should not be confused with the Christian right.[99] They remained active during the third age of the movement and sought in particular to apply the Christian idea of just war to the war on terror and the intervention in Iraq, the legitimacy of which Novak would defend at the Vatican.

The fundamental work done by neoconservatives in the period 1960–1990 undoubtedly helped to lay the intellectual foundation of the conservative revolution, which came to dominate the Republican party. "Without *The Public Interest*, no Newt Gingrich," as columnist George Will summed things up.[100] In other words, if the neoconservatives had not done their part by mounting an intellectual and ideological critique of liberalism—an informed, sophisticated critique from within the ranks of liberalism itself—Republicans would not have been able to implement the conservative reforms they pursued under Reagan, Newt Gingrich (who served as Speaker of the House from 1994 to 1998), and George W. Bush.

To some extent, the neoconservative network also insinuated itself into the conservative counterestablishment that developed in the 1970s and 1980s around certain foundations (Olin, Coors, Mellon-Scaife, and so on) and think tanks (mainly the Hoover Institution and the Heritage Foundation), magazines *(National Review),* and new networks (such as Richard Viguerie's), along with evangelicals in the "moral majority" led by the Reverend Jerry Falwell. On the neoconservative side, it was Irving Kristol, and to a lesser extent Norman Podhoretz, who stood at the center of the network that slowly grew over a period of many years.

A noteworthy achievement of the growing neoconservative establishment was the takeover of the American Enterprise Institute, which had been founded in 1943 by employer-led and free-trade groups for the purpose of opposing federal intervention in the economy. The AEI took part in the rise of the conservative movement in the 1970s by mounting an increasingly powerful ideological opposition to the then-dominant liberalism, to the point that it became the conservative rival of the Brookings Institution. After growing from a handful to more than 100 resident scholars, the AEI in 1986 suffered a budget crisis that reinforced the influence of neoconservatives within the organization. Irving Kristol was the first to join in 1976, and he encouraged other neoconservatives to come for short or long stays, including Democrats from the Coalition for a Democratic Majority, such as Jeane Kirkpatrick, Michael Novak, Penn Kemble, Ben Wattenberg, and Joshua Muravchik. This was one of the places where first- and second-age neoconservatives came to know and understand conservative Republicans. During the movement's third age, the AEI became the neoconservative bastion, around which gravitated most of the important figures in the movement and even some of its institutions (for instance, the *Weekly Standard* and the Project for the New American Century shared a building with the AEI).

The rest of the neoconservative network ranged from Freedom House to the Committee for the Free World, from the Jewish Institute for National Security Affairs to the National Endowment for Democracy, to say nothing of a variety of journals including *Commentary, The Public Interest, The National Interest,* the *New Republic,* and the editorial pages of the *Wall Street Journal.* No summary can possibly cover all the personal relationships, friendships, job recommendations, and even family ties (many of them linked to the Podhoretz and Kristol families). There was, and still is, a definite clannishness to the neoconservative movement. And in a clan in which intellectual pugilism is the fundamental activity, the unwritten but ironclad rule is never to attack a fellow neoconservative.

The 1980s witnessed not a fusion but a greater convergence between first- and second-age neoconservatives. To be sure, differences remained. One sign of this is the fact, noted by Seymour Martin Lipset, that "no neoconservative was assigned to a post affecting economic or welfare policy, such as the Treasury, Commerce, Agriculture, Labor, or Health and Human Services departments. The reason is fairly clear: questions of affirmative action and meritocracy apart, almost all the neoconservatives remained liberals on most domestic policy issues, at least as of the beginning of the Reagan administration."[101] Although the boundary between the first and second ages always remained permeable, as the examples of *Commentary* and Pat Moynihan demonstrate, more and more neoconservatives became "hybrids" as the 1980s proceeded. For instance, Jeane Kirkpatrick remarked that "the single most important change in my views in the last decade has been a much greater appreciation of market economics."[102] Some were prepared to cooperate fully with the conservative right (among them Irving Kristol, Norman Podhoretz, Midge Decter, and Elliott Abrams), while others from both ages of neoconservatism remained social-democratic in orientation (for instance, Daniel Bell, James Woolsey, and Max Kampelman).

As early as 1971, the neoconservatives had been welcomed by the *National Review* with the famous invitation "Come On In, the Water's Fine."[103] But when they grew more influential in the 1980s, the reception from their new allies on the right was much less cordial, as attested by this reaction from conservative historian Stephen Tonsor in 1986:

> It is splendid when the town whore gets religion and joins the church. Now and then she makes a good choir director, but when she begins to tell the minister what he ought to say in his Sunday sermons, matters have been carried too far . . . [Had] Stalin spared Leon Trotsky and not had him murdered in Mexico, he would no doubt have spent his declining days in an office in Hoover Library writing his memoirs and contributing articles of a faintly neoconservative flavor to *Encounter* and *Commentary*.[104]

As the conservative counterestablishment gained power and began to enjoy the fruits of its success, some of its members took a dim view of newly repentant former leftists and Democrats who claimed to offer a more intelligent brand of conservatism and aspired to dictate the country's foreign policy, increase the defense budget, expand the federal government, deepen the deficit, and dominate the intellectual and political world in both New York and Washington.

Various complaints fueled this bitterness. To begin with, there was the increasing neoconservative influence over a number of key institutions in the new establishment, such as the AEI and the Olin, Smith Richardson, and Bradley Foundations—in other words, a competition for money.[105] There were also suspicions that the neoconservatives had not been fully converted. Did they not tolerate the welfare state? Were they not willing to countenance a certain degree of federal intervention? Did they not seek to launch foreign crusades, as Kennedy and Johnson had done? "We are not the world's policeman, nor its political tutor," thundered Pat Buchanan in 1989. "Whence comes this arrogant claim to determine how other nations should govern themselves, or face subversion by NED [the National Endowment for Democracy], the Comintern of the neo-cons?"[106]

In some cases—particularly Buchanan's at the time of the Gulf War—a hint of antisemitism lay behind these attacks. For instance, Russell Kirk revived the old accusation of "dual loyalty" in 1988: in his view, "some eminent Neoconservatives mistook Tel Aviv for the capital of the United States."[107] Midge Decter accused him of antisemitism.[108] The alliance between the neoconservatives and certain elements of the right, most notably the conservative Christian evangelicals—a tactical alliance directed against liberals and forged mainly around the issue of support for Israel but in social terms unnatural and, in a word, bizarre—is in many ways ambivalent. If the biblical prophecy is fulfilled, as Christian Zionists hope, shouldn't the Jews be forced to convert or die? The tensions among the various families of the right (neoconservatives, paleoconservatives, fiscal conservatives, libertarians, Christian rightists, and so on), which William Buckley, the father of modern conservatism and founding editor of the *National Review,* was frequently called upon to arbitrate, would persist and reappear in the third age of neoconservatism.

The Persistence of Centrist Democrats

These difficult relations with traditional conservatives should not obscure the fact that in the 1980s some neoconservatives refused to move to the right and persisted in looking upon the Democratic party as their natural home. The portrait of neoconservatism from Ronald Reagan to Bill Clinton would not be complete if it did not include the Coalition for a Democratic Majority, which had some good years even though it failed to recapture the soul of the party in 1984 and 1988. But something new emerged between 1985 and 1992: a group of centrist Democrats, mainly from southern states, rallied behind a platform that paid more heed to family values than to minorities and favored increased defense spending and wariness of the Soviet Union, a platform that was meant to drive out the leftists on the party's fringes.

Had the CDM finally achieved its goal? No: it was the Democratic Leadership Council (DLC) that succeeded where the CDM had failed. Indeed, one of the DLC's leaders, Bill Clinton, was elected president in 1992. It should therefore come as no surprise that the final years of the CDM were dominated by discussions of a possible merger with the DLC, its younger and more successful sibling. Nor should it come as a surprise that many CDM neoconservatives supported Clinton in 1992.

Success, however, is not a prerequisite of perseverance: that was what Ben Wattenberg, Penn Kemble, and Peter Rosenblatt must have been thinking when they revived the CDM in December 1982, after two years of inactivity. After all, Wattenberg explained, "The Democratic Party is still the majority party in the most powerful nation in the world. It's a very important thing to influence. The prize is enormous—you are talking about what is going to be the intellectual tenor and content of a party that either in the near-term future or the intermediate-term future is going to be in office leading the free world."[109] Kemble wrote that the mission to "return our party to the mainstream" must continue.[110] The CDM was therefore revived in 1983 and reenergized by the advent of a dynamic new executive director, Jay Winik, and by the presidential campaign of 1984.

Once the Coalition's finances were put in order and its debts paid, the board of directors met in Washington on May 18, 1983. The meeting featured a debate on Central America in which the two UN ambassadors among its members, Jeane Kirkpatrick and Pat Moynihan, did not see eye-to-eye (they were growing increasingly apart on the issue).[111] Scoop Jackson was there, as was Congressman Jim Wright of Texas. But one branch of the CDM was missing from this resurrection: the Podhoretz family—Norman, his wife, Midge Decter, and their son-in-law Elliott Abrams. "I was one of those who'd rather switch than fight . . . The balance had shifted after 1972 and had not come back," Abrams explained. "We tried to wrest the Democratic Party back from the left, and we failed," his mother-in-law added.[112]

Then Scoop Jackson died suddenly on September 1, 1983, causing consternation in neoconservative ranks. The CDM decided to organize a symposium in Washington on November 15, both to honor Jackson and to prove that the Scoop Jackson Democrats remained an active wing of the Democratic party. The symposium was a great success and marked the real return of the CDM to the Washington scene. More than fifty journalists attended. Two Democratic primary candidates, Walter Mondale and John Glenn, debated, with each accusing the other of being too dovish (much to the pleasure of the CDM). The speakers' list might have been a page ripped from the 1983 neoconservative directory: Richard Perle, Michael Novak, Martin Peretz, James Woolsey, Edward Koch (the mayor of New York), Evelyn Dubrow (of the International Ladies' Garment Workers' Union), and Ben Wattenberg, among others.[113]

With a boost from the symposium, the CDM was up to speed by the end of 1983 and busy developing new projects dealing with domestic issues and the rules inside the Democratic party.[114] It had to confront four increasingly serious contradictions, however. First, some of the group's most prominent members were now working for the Reagan administration, a circumstance that cast doubts on the party loyalty of the rest. The second contradiction was historical and had to do with the increasing ideological homogenization of the two major American parties. Conservative Democrats (mainly from the South) were vanishing, and at the same time the liberal wing of the Republican party (the "Rockefeller Republicans") was dwindling. Jim Woolsey summed up the increasingly uncomfortable situation of the 1980s and 1990s:

> Those people who have a more organic view of society and a more relaxed attitude about leadership by the federal government on domestic matters and still want a strong defense and foreign policy don't have a natural home in the current American system. They had something of a natural home in the conservative side of the Democratic party, up until relatively recently. But for the bulk of the Congress today, if you're on the Democratic side, you're expected for example to be against ballistic missile defense, and also in favor of a progressive tax system. On the Republican side, you're expected to be in favor of ballistic missile defense but pretty much against a progressive tax system. For people who believe in a progressive tax system and in ballistic missile defense, you go around looking for a home.[115]

The third contradiction had to do with the unions. The AFL-CIO had provided the CDM with essential financial and political support from the beginning. It had also backed neoconservative foreign policy through leaders such as George Meany, Lane Kirkland (cochair of the CPD), and Albert Shanker. But the Reagan years were difficult for labor because of Reagan's very right-wing domestic policies. In August 1981, for example, Reagan dismissed more than 11,000 striking air-traffic controllers. Penn Kemble refused to privilege domestic policy over foreign policy: "To say that you would oppose an administration that was fighting the fight against a totalitarian power that was threatening the very fundamentals of your democratic way of life for the sake of the air controllers' getting a slightly better contract—you have to put things in perspective."[116] But, as one might expect, union leaders did not share this view, not least because the balance of power within the AFL-CIO was shifting: service unions, especially those representing civil service workers, often McGovernite in orientation, were gradually gaining the upper hand over industrial unions in steel and textiles and skilled trades. The industrial unions were the traditionally anticommunist unions of the "vital center."

The fourth and final dilemma for the CDM arose from the fact that Scoop Jackson's demise left the centrist wing of the Democratic party without a leader, an inspiration, and a rallying point. Meanwhile, Pat Moynihan had increasingly distanced himself from the neoconservatives. Elliott Abrams summed up the situation thus: "Senator Jackson is no longer with us, and Senator Moynihan is no longer with us."[117] The change in Moynihan's position was particularly noticeable in two related areas, Central America (on which he opposed the Reagan policy, which in this case was truly neoconservative) and international law, to which he attached more and more importance, while other neoconservatives turned toward unilateralism.[118] The fact that he had to run for reelection in 1982 in New York, a very liberal state, played a role: he moved left during the campaign, but after his election he did not move back to the right. He supported the "nuclear freeze" movement and voted against the MX missile. In 1983 he opposed the invasion of Grenada and protested the mining of Nicaragua's ports.[119] Speaking at New York University's commencement ceremony in 1984, he flung a challenge in the neoconservatives' faces: "The Soviet idea is spent. It commands some influence in the world; and fear. But it summons no loyalty. History is moving away from it at astounding speed. We must be less obsessed with the Soviets. If we must learn to live with nuclear parity, let us keep all the more in mind that we have consolidated an overwhelming economic advantage."[120]

These contradictions did not prevent the CDM from making a valiant effort to persuade the Democratic party to take a firm centrist line on defense issues in the 1984 campaign. It organized an important foreign-policy task force, led by James Woolsey and Max Kampelman (who was nevertheless serving at the time as Reagan's ambassador to the Conference for Security Cooperation in Europe, or CSCE). This remarkably energetic group produced a text titled "Democratic Solidarity."[121] Contributors included Congressmen Les Aspin of Wisconsin and James Scheuer of New York, union leaders Sol Chaikin and Norman Hill, and many others, such as Nathan Glazer, Michael Ledeen, Richard Neuhaus, Michael Novak, Martin Peretz, Arch Puddington, John Roche, Bayard Rustin, and Paul Seabury.

The CDM "platform" for 1984 unsurprisingly emphasized support for democracy ("We contend that the fundamental issue of the contemporary world is the political struggle between the democratic way of life and those who would deny human liberty and political freedom"); support for current policy on Central America and Israel; and the need for a strong America (a firm condemnation of the "nuclear freeze"). Among the concrete measures proposed, a noteworthy idea was the call for an "assembly of democratic nations" ("from Costa Rica to Papua–New Guinea"), which was supposed to reinforce existing defensive ties, encourage democratization in the Communist world, strengthen existing international institutions, and advance the cause of disarmament and peace.[122] This idea, which had first emerged in the late 1970s,[123] had a bright future ahead of it.

Even though Walter Mondale, the winner of the Democratic primaries, had grown up under the wing of Hubert Humphrey in Minnesota and belonged to same circle as Max Kampelman and the Kirkpatricks, quickly garnered the support of the AFL-CIO, and was a defender of Israel, the CDM soon found reason to be disappointed with his nomination. He was simply overwhelmed by the left wing of the party (Mario Cuomo, Jesse Jackson) at the July 1984 San Francisco convention. As a result, CDM members found it hard to disagree when Jeane Kirkpatrick, in her celebrated "Blame America First" speech at the Republican convention in August 1984, attacked the "San Francisco Democrats" for forgetting the confident and optimistic message of Roosevelt, Truman, and Kennedy and for always seeing America's wrongs:

> When our Marines, sent to Lebanon on a multinational peacekeeping mission with the consent of the United States Congress, were murdered in

their sleep, the "blame America first crowd" didn't blame the terrorists who murdered the Marines, they blamed the United States.

But then, they always blame America first.

When the Soviet Union walked out of arms control negotiations, and refused even to discuss the issues, the San Francisco Democrats didn't blame Soviet intransigence. They blamed the United States.

But then, they always blame America first.

When Marxist dictators shoot their way to power in Central America, the San Francisco Democrats don't blame the guerrillas and their Soviet allies, they blame United States policies of 100 years ago.

But then, they always blame America first.[124]

What is more, the CDM failed to influence the Democratic platform, despite the efforts of Ben Wattenberg, Peter Rosenblatt, and Max Kampelman, who championed the "Democratic Solidarity" position with help from Lane Kirkland's assistant Tom Kahn and Charles Krauthammer, a Scoop Jackson Democrat who had worked for the Carter administration, wrote speeches for Mondale for a time, and was just embarking on a second career as a journalist. Clearly, the CDM failed across the board in 1984.

Nevertheless, the group remained undaunted, because most observers interpreted Mondale's loss to Reagan as a call by voters to bring the Democratic party back to the center. Indeed, this was the analysis of the founders of the Democratic Leadership Council in 1985. But the CDM had been harping on this same message since 1972. It accordingly sought to capture the center of the party and succeeded in raising money (mainly from the defense industry). It also created a new task force on party governance led by David Ifshin and a second incarnation of the foreign policy task force under James Woolsey and Congressman Dave McCurdy of Oklahoma. A new CDM newsletter, the *Defense Democrat*, appeared in 1988, in the form of a six-page monthly bulletin.

On April 17, 1985, Les Aspin delivered an important speech to the CDM, of which he was one of the new champions. In it, he put his finger on a fundamental problem that Democrats had faced since the 1970s: the perception by a majority of Americans that the party was too soft and untrustworthy on defense-related issues. As a solution, Aspin put forward several tactical proposals: always offer alternatives when rejecting a weapons program; show greater respect for the military, which defends America; and so on. He also had philosophical suggestions: take the Soviet threat seriously, and not just the threat of nuclear war, as the pacifist movements did. In short, the party should seek to avoid both "Hiroshima"—the risk of nuclear war—and "Auschwitz"—the risk of surrendering to totalitarianism.[125]

Spurred on by Aspin's speech, the CDM developed a program to convince Democrats to adopt a stronger defense policy and take a more hawkish line. The goal was to influence the 1988 Democratic convention,[126] and the main instrument was the Woolsey-McCurdy task force, which included Aspin, Samuel Huntington, Martin Peretz, Charles Robb, Eugene Rostow, and Walter Slocombe, among others. In addition to the now-standard themes of increasing defense spending and promoting democracy, a new importance was attached to Central America, with emphasis on support for the "democratic center." This was also the objective of another small organization created by Penn Kemble in 1985, PRODEMCA (Friends of the Democratic Center in Central America), whose sponsors included Sidney Hook, Elie Wiesel, and Vladimir Bukovsky.

Despite all this effort, the 1988 elections proved as disappointing to CDM neoconservatives as the 1984 elections had been. They briefly entertained hope that Al Gore, a young senator from the South and well versed in defense issues, might be their candidate.[127] But Michael Dukakis prevailed in the primaries, and the CDM's efforts to influence him failed. When Dukakis tried to move back to the center toward the end of the summer, it was too late. He only managed to make himself ridiculous by arranging to be filmed in the hatch of a tank while wearing a helmet that was too big for him—a bitter image to swallow for the "defense Democrats" of the CDM. Once again, the CDM had hoped to move the party to the center, and once again it had failed. In retrospect, the fact that some CDM members (like the Podhoretz family) had lost faith in the Democratic party in 1980 may have seemed justified. Of course, there was always hope that 1992 might be different.

Neoconservatives and "New Democrats"

Before turning to the 1992 presidential campaign and the Clinton phenomenon, let us briefly consider the evolution of the Democratic party in the 1980s and the central role played by the Democratic Leadership Council in rebuilding the party. Although it is clear that the Democratic Leadership Council succeeded where the CDM failed, the literature devoted to the party's reinvention in the years 1985–1992 has had too little to say about the pioneering role and distinctive contribution of the CDM. Because the "New Democrats" eclipsed the "Cold War Democrats,"[128] the CDM is too often seen as a symbol of the 1970s and 1980s and of the defeat of centrists by the party's left wing, leading to the defection of Democrats such as Jeane Kirkpatrick, Norman Podhoretz, and Elliott Abrams. But it was also a precursor of the victorious comeback of 1992.

The 1984 election confirmed not only Reagan's popularity but also Republican gains in the South and Southwest. Even moderate Democrats were defeated by the Republicans, whose ads attacked "San Francisco liberals." For the first time, a majority of southern whites voted Republican. Hence southerners and centrists in the Democratic party could no longer remain indifferent: their challenge was to change the party's image and orientation. This was the task that the Democratic Leadership Council would take on. The DLC was a group of centrist Democrats that came into being on February 28, 1985, but failed to sway the party's choice in 1988: the left-wing groups succeeded in nominating Michael Dukakis, while DLC candidate Al Gore failed in his bid to move the party back toward the center.[129]

From 1988 to 1991 the DLC therefore sought to transform itself, concentrating on creating state chapters and formulating new ideas to be incorporated into an integrated, coherent centrist platform.[130] The group recruited new centrist members and in June 1989 founded the Progressive Policy Institute (PPI), a think tank to develop new ideas. It also launched a magazine, the *New Democrat*. In a short pamphlet titled *The Politics of Evasion: Democrats and the Presidency,* William Galston and Elaine Karmack, two veterans of the Mondale campaign, unburied the hatchet: the two authors attacked the "liberal fundamentalism" of the party's left wing, which they argued had driven traditional voters away.[131] They insisted on the importance of values relative to social and economic issues, in some ways reviving the idea that Ben Wattenberg and Richard Scammon had put forward twenty years earlier in *The Real Majority.* The publication of the Galston-Karmack pamphlet made waves in the party and marked the DLC's decisive turn to the center.

This time the DLC found its champion in Bill Clinton, who proved to be an able candidate and in return received valuable campaign assistance from the DLC's powerful network. Claiming to transcend the liberal/conservative divide, Clinton and the DLC aimed for a "third way" (the term did not actually come into widespread use until the mid-1990s) that would incorporate some of the Reagan reforms, take seriously such middle-class issues as crime, education, and family values rather than focusing exclusively on minority issues, and advocate reform of the federal government without denying that it had an important and positive role to play.[132] With involuntary assistance from Ross Perot (a third-party candidate who captured 19 percent of the vote) and from a bad economy, Bill Clinton and Al Gore managed to defeat George H. W. Bush in the November 1992 presidential election.

In some respects, the DLC looks like a successful makeover of the CDM, even though there were significant differences between the two groups: the DLC was an organization of politicians, not intellectuals; domestic issues predominated; it was not as close to the unions as the CDM; and it was much larger. It was only reasonable to ask whether there could be cooperation between the waning CDM, the weaknesses of whose political model had often been exposed but which had a name and a prestigious though controversial past, and the DLC, whose star was rapidly rising and which seemed to have a shot at changing the game.

From the outset, relations between the two groups were excellent, and contacts began early. For instance, one month after succeeding Richard Gephardt as head of the DLC, on May 6, 1986, Charles Robb addressed the CDM on the occasion of receiving its Henry Jackson Freedom Prize. He stressed the need for a strong defense.[133] Peter Rosenblatt, thanking Robb in a subsequent letter, raised the possibility of a merger.[134] But actual discussion of a merger did not begin until two years later, after Dukakis lost the 1988 election. Rosenblatt wrote to Sam Nunn to discuss the idea of a moderate Democratic think tank modeled on the Heritage Foundation, which was to deal with political issues of all kinds but especially foreign policy and defense issues. "I hope and believe that we at CDM could essentially merge many of our functions with those of the new organization, drawing on the reputation we have achieved within the party."[135]

A think tank was in fact created: this was the Progressive Policy Institute, mentioned above, under the direction of Will Marshall. But the CDM had not been involved, and the Progressive Policy Institute had no real interest in foreign and defense policy. Over the next few months the CDM floundered, unable to decide between a flexible association of some sort with the DLC, the use of CDM resources to form a "defense and international affairs center" within the DLC/PPI, or a full-fledged merger with the DLC. In February and May 1989 there were two meetings between Al From and Will Marshall (representing the DLC and the PPI) and Penn Kemble, Peter Rosenblatt, and Ben Wattenberg (representing the CDM).[136] In the end, however, there was no merger. Peter Rosenblatt explains: "Al From never articulated any opposition to it; he just didn't move on it."[137]

On the DLC side, Will Marshall emphasizes the "negative" reasons for the absence of a merger.[138] The CDM was an example of what didn't work: it was useful mainly as a warning of pitfalls to avoid. Not only the DLC but above all the PPI sought to avoid repeating the CDM's mistakes, including the marginalization that the CDM had suffered within the party. Furthermore, the DLC and PPI saw themselves as less ideological than the Scoop Jackson Democrats and had no ties to the unions. Although they shared the CDM's critique of the party's liberal left wing, they did not want a merger to make them the heirs to years of conflict and accumulated rancor. It was better to make a fresh start. For all these reasons, the DLC, while recognizing a certain kinship and honoring the CDM's patient and useful efforts, did not take the steps that would have been needed to effect a true merger.

As a result, the CDM simply faded away. On February 19, 1991, a truck from the National Archives parked outside the offices of Peter Rosenblatt. It had come to pick up the CDM archives, which were to be transported to the LBJ Presidential Library in Austin, Texas.[139] Symbolically, things had come full circle: the CDM returned to the "vital center," while another organization finished the job of converting the Democratic party.

The Clinton Administration and the Centrist Democrats

On April 20, 1993, Peter Rosenblatt used one of the last sheets of CDM letterhead to answer a query concerning the organization. "CDM has been inactive for some years and we have recently decided to dissolve the organization upon the ground that its major objectives have been achieved with the election of president Clinton."[140] But was Bill Clinton really a "CDM Democrat"? And if the organization no longer existed during the 1992 campaign, did all the pillars of the CDM support him and view him as one of their own?

They at least gave him the benefit of the doubt, recognizing that he was clearly not a McGovernite. After all, CDM neoconservatives did not like George H. W. Bush, who in their view was too inclined to a realpolitik perspective. Richard Schifter, who knew Clinton personally before 1992, even described him as a "Hubert Humphrey Democrat" and tried to bring about a rapprochement in the (vain) hope that such influential figures as Jeane Kirkpatrick and Richard Perle might be won over.[141] Other CDM Democrats were more clearly supportive of Clinton: Schifter's old friend and ally Max Kampelman cosigned a letter of support with James Woolsey. Peter Rosenblatt and Ben Wattenberg came out in favor of Clinton, as did Morris Amitay and David Ifshin, both of whom were closely involved with the work of the CDM. Penn Kemble and Joshua Muravchik went even further, joining the Clinton campaign and defending the candidate against accusations that he was soft on defense and foreign policy. In 1992 they helped draft speeches for Clinton in which the Arkansas governor accused Bush of "coddling dictators from Peking to Baghdad" and came out strongly in support of democracy and human rights, especially in the nascent states that had once been part of the Soviet Union. Beyond the now-defunct CDM, other personalities like Martin Peretz, Aaron Wildavsky, Sam Huntington, and Edward Luttwak (whether neoconservatives or fellow travelers) also came out for Clinton.[142]

Peter Rosenblatt recalls that his friend Tony Lake, who became Clinton's chief foreign policy adviser, courted him early in the campaign and asked for a list of names of potential appointees; but this time the outcome was somewhat better than in 1976.[143] James Woolsey was named director of the Central Intelligence Agency. Penn Kemble was appointed assistant director of the U.S. Information Agency. Richard Schifter obtained a post on the National Security Council. Joshua Muravchik had hoped for a human rights post in the State Department, but a chorus of protests from left-wing Democrats kept him from getting it.[144] Peter Rosenblatt was offered the post of ambassador to the Conference for Security Cooperation in Europe, which he declined on the grounds that it was not sufficiently influential. He also declined several lower-level positions. Les Aspin, an ally of the CDM, was named secretary of defense.

How did CDM neoconservatives ultimately judge Clintonism? Disillusionment came very quickly, particularly in regard to Somalia and above all Bosnia, where Clinton temporized instead of using force against Slobodan Milošević.[145] More generally, the president, having been elected primarily on domestic issues, paid little attention to foreign affairs. Aspin was forced to resign after the failure of the U.S. intervention in Somalia. Woolsey quit his CIA post after two years, frustrated by his lack of access to the president. The first two or three years—until the "resumption of leadership" signified by the 1995 intervention in Bosnia—were certainly difficult. Those who ultimately participated in the Clinton administration are unsurprisingly less negative: "I thought we had influence in the Clinton administration," says Penn Kemble. "It was not like the Carter situation. Our views didn't prevail, certainly not on Bosnia and in the whole Balkan situation; it took far too long. But in the end, they came around to our position."[146]

To be sure, the majority of neoconservatives did not share this view, if only because they had gone over to the Republican party and in so doing markedly altered neoconservatism itself. The year 1995 marked the advent of the third age of the movement.

7

THE THIRD AGE:
NATIONAL GREATNESS CONSERVATIVES

Neoconservatism is dead. Long live neoconservatism! How else to describe what was happening in the mid-1990s? Toward the middle of the decade, Norman Podhoretz, Irving Kristol, and Seymour Martin Lipset—to mention a few of the best-known "fathers" of the movement—wrote epitaphs and eulogies. Neoconservatism "no longer exists as a distinctive phenomenon requiring a special name of its own" (Podhoretz). It had dissolved into the conservative movement after triumphing over both communism and the New Left. It "was a generational phenomenon, and has now been pretty much absorbed into a larger, more comprehensive conservatism" (Kristol). The term "neoconservatism" had "lost its meaning as commentators applied it beyond its original application to strongly anti-communist leftists" (Lipset).[1]

Yet in September 1995, William (Bill) Kristol created a new magazine, the *Weekly Standard,* and barely two years later joined with Robert Kagan and Gary Schmitt to found the Project for the New American Century (PNAC). A new corpus of ideas took shape, and some of those ideas were directly descended from the Cold War and the fertile period 1989–1992—that is, from the second age of neoconservatism. That being the case, why distinguish a third age, starting in 1995? The first reason for the distinction is the marked change in the international context: the Communist empire had disappeared; America's relative power had greatly increased; and new challenges (such as al-Qaeda) had emerged. A second, more important reason is that neoconservatives were now clearly positioned on the right, as members of the Republican family. Their profile was no longer that of former radicals, former liberals, or even former Democrats; most neocons were now born conservatives. Finally, what distinguished third-age neoconservatives was their foreign policy stance. On domestic issues, the new neoconservatism did not differ much from other strains of conservatism.

But then, was it still "neoconservatism"? Robert Kagan and Bill Kristol initially rejected the label: until the late 1990s they preferred to speak of "neo-Reaganism."[2] And how things had changed since the 1960s, when neoconservatism was about domestic issues and was part of the liberal family! Still, the intellectual and political kinship with the second age, that of the Scoop Jackson Democrats, was undeniable, and there was a strong resemblance in terms of organizational forms and influence on public opinion. Hence the label stuck. And neoconservatives did not remain in obscurity for long, thanks to their role in promoting the war in Iraq in 2003. Although America's difficulties in the Middle East have to some extent discredited the movement, it has remained on course and continues to be a force in American politics that cannot be ignored, and will certainly play a prominent role again.

Seeds of Renewal at the End of the Cold War

To understand the third age of neoconservatism, we must take a brief look back at the years 1989–1992 and the reaction of neoconservatives to the fall of the Berlin Wall and the new international situation.[3] The contrast between the "cold geniuses," who until 1991 considered the Soviet Union more dangerous than ever and wanted America to remain on the alert, and the "pragmatics," who were more willing to recognize the changes that were under way, was reinforced by another distinction between the champions of "democratic globalism," who wanted the United States to embark on a mission of democracy promotion, and the advocates of a return to realism and a narrow definition of the national interest.

The latter group, which was clearly in the minority, was led by Irving Kristol, who had never shared the views of the Scoop Jackson Democrats anyway. The heart of the disagreement between the two groups was the idea that, during the Cold War, democracy promotion had been intimately intertwined with the containment of communism. Once communism had disappeared, Kristol argued, democracy promotion was no longer an essential element of American foreign policy. In June 1990 he explained that he no longer even found the "international" pages of the

New York Times interesting, because they were filled with stories re-counting, for example, the details of Charles Taylor's revolt against the government of Liberia:

> What am I supposed to feel and think? If the Soviets (or the Chinese or even the Cubans) were involved, I would know what to think, since we would then be confronting a challenge. But this is a purely internal Libe-rian matter, and while I am saddened by the sufferings of the Liberian peo-ple caught up in this conflict, I see no reason why Liberia today should even be within the purview of American foreign policy—or why the *Times* should be devoting so much space to it. There are many other examples that can be given, but they all add up to one conclusion: With the end of the Cold War, an era of American foreign policy has come to a close. We won that war. "Global containment" of communism did work—far better, indeed, than we anticipated.[4]

In that case, what direction should American foreign policy take?

> The only innovative trend in our foreign-policy thinking at the moment de-rives from a relatively small group, consisting of both liberals and conser-vatives, who believe there is an "American mission" actively to promote democracy all over the world. This is a superficially attractive idea, but it takes only a few moments of thought to realize how empty of substance (and how full of presumption!) it is. In the entire history of the U.S., we have successfully "exported" our democratic institutions to only two na-tions—Japan and Germany, after war and an occupation. We have failed to establish a viable democracy in the Philippines, or in Panama, or anywhere in Central America.[5]

Few other neoconservatives followed Kristol's realist line. Among them were Nathan Glazer and, to a certain extent, Jeane Kirkpatrick. In an issue of *The National Interest* devoted to this debate in the fall of 1990, Glazer declared that "the time for modesty" had arrived, while Kirkpatrick evoked "a normal country in a normal time."[6] To be sure, in her 1979 article "Dictatorships and Double Standards," Kirkpatrick had already attacked "the belief that it is possible to democratize govern-ments, anytime, anywhere, under any circumstances . . . Many of the wisest political scientists of this and previous centuries agree that demo-cratic institutions are especially difficult to establish and maintain—be-cause they make heavy demands on all portions of a population and because they depend on complex social, cultural and economic conditions." But now, without abandoning the defense and encouragement of democracy (which remained, in her words, "enormously desirable"), Kirkpatrick recommended that priority be given to domestic affairs and that the United States should adopt a more discreet international role.[7]

For most other neoconservatives, however, these views looked disturbingly like good old realpolitik, which had led to détente and other distasteful policies. Indeed, the majority of them (including Midge Decter, Eugene Rostow, Carl Gershman, Penn Kemble, James Woolsey, Joshua Muravchik, Michael Novak, Michael Ledeen, Norman Podhoretz, and Elliott Abrams) belonged to a second school of thought, which advocated a more interventionist posture and continued to favor democracy promotion. In their eyes, the contest with the Soviets had been above all ideological, and the defense of democracy had been not just a byproduct of the containment of Communism but its very raison d'être. In the same issue of *The National Interest*, Ben Wattenberg defended a policy of "neo-manifest destinarianism," which meant supporting and encouraging liberal democracy wherever possible, most notably by public diplomacy (the National Endowment for Democracy, propaganda radio, the U.S. Information Agency, foreign aid, and so on). Such was the vocation of the United States as the "first universal nation" (to borrow from the title of a book he wrote on the subject).[8] As for Joshua Muravchik, in 1991 he published a book with a title that could not have made his position more clear: *Exporting Democracy: Fulfilling America's Destiny*. This echoed the title of a book that Gregory Fossedal had published two years earlier: *The Democratic Imperative: Exporting the American Revolution*. Muravchik explained that, in the long run, realism was not realistic and that the only way to create a "favorable environment" for the United States was to encourage the proliferation of democratic regimes, for research had confirmed the intuition that the more democratic the world was, the more peaceful.[9]

In 1996 Michael Ledeen published *Freedom Betrayed: How America Led a Global Democratic Revolution, Won the Cold War, and Walked Away;* and Joshua Muravchik published *The Imperative of American Leadership: A Challenge to Neo-Isolationism*, to fight the rampant isolationism of the 1990s.[10] The idea of these books was simple: America had a special responsibility, a special vocation. It would betray its own universalist values if it did not intervene, especially in the Balkans, to enforce respect for human rights, defend democracy, and shape the world in its own image. This idea of betrayal of American values and complicity with dictatorial regimes was pushed to the limit in the title of a book by David Wurmser (an associate of Richard Perle's) that appeared in 1999: *Tyranny's Ally*. If America had the means to overthrow the tyrant Saddam Hussein and did not do so, then it was an objective ally of tyranny.[11]

Although the center of gravity of the neoconservative movement in the 1990s was closer to democratic globalism than to realism, some neoconservatives did not go as far as Muravchik, Ledeen, and Wurmser. The columnist Charles Krauthammer suggested a middle way: to support democracy everywhere but to spread it actively, that is by military intervention, only where vital American interests were also at stake. In Krauthammer's view, such interests were not at stake in the Balkans in the 1990s, and he therefore differed with the vast majority of neoconservatives, who favored intervention first in Bosnia and then in Kosovo. In 2004 he theorized his version of neoconservatism, which he called "democratic realism" to distinguish it from "democratic globalism." American interventions were to be more selective. It was fine to declare, as President George W. Bush had done, that the United States was prepared to put an end to tyranny everywhere, but America should act on that intention only "where it counts" (for instance, in Afghanistan and Iraq but not in Liberia or Burma).[12]

In the early 1990s other seeds of renewal were planted that would mature only several years later, this time in the strategic realm. While Congress was becoming increasingly interested in the "peace dividend"—the savings that could now be realized in the defense budget—Dick Cheney, who was then secretary of defense, and Paul Wolfowitz, then number three at the Pentagon, worried about the cuts and sought to define a military strategy for the post–Cold War period. Several versions of a new strategy were drafted, only to be overtaken by events (such as the Gulf War and the demise of the Soviet Union).[13] Finally, in March 1992, a draft strategy was leaked to the press.[14]

This "Defense Planning Guidance," which was drafted by Wolfowitz's staff (most notably Scooter Libby and Zalmay Khalilzad, who would later play important roles under George W. Bush) and shaped in part by advice from outsiders such as Richard Perle and Albert Wohlstetter,[15] stated that America should make it its mission to discourage any other power from aspiring to world leadership (or challenging American leadership) by maintaining clear military superiority while taking the interests of other powers into account. This leak unleashed a storm in Washington and allied capitals, and the administration ultimately distanced itself from the text (which it could not actually disavow because it was not even an official document). Subsequent revisions made few concessions, however. Although a more acceptable multilateral terminology was used, the strategy of asserting hegemony remained. In addition, Dick Cheney, just before leaving the Pentagon in January 1993, insisted on publishing another version of the original document with only slight modifications but under a new title, "Defense Strategy for the 1990s: The Regional Defense Strategy."[16]

"Defense Planning Guidance" and Cheney's text laid the groundwork for the neoconservative approach to the post–Cold War era, which continued beyond the great divide of September 11, 2001. The goal was to prevent the emergence of a new rival comparable to the Soviet Union. To that end, the United States sought to prevent any power from dominating any region of the world, which might then be used as a base for a strategy of global domination. "Together with our allies, we must preclude hostile nondemocratic powers from dominating regions critical to our interests and otherwise work to build an international environment conducive to our values," "a peaceful democratic order in which nations are able to pursue their legitimate interests without fear of military domination." For example, "we also must encourage and assist Russia, Ukraine, and the other new states of the former Soviet Union in establishing democratic political systems and free markets so they too can join the democratic 'zone of peace.'"[17]

The United States could not depend solely on collective approaches to international security and would have to maintain the forces necessary to act alone. Furthermore, "history suggests that effective multilateral action is most likely to come about in response to U.S. leadership, not as an alternative to it."[18] In short, whenever the international community was divided, the United States would have to take the lead, and its allies would eventually follow, more often in the form of an ad-hoc coalition than through the United Nations. As for the defense of Europe, prudence was the watchword: the United States should block the emergence of exclusively European security organizations that might compete with NATO. To sustain such a unilateral policy, a robust military was essential, not only to intervene when necessary but also to make the cost of challenging American leadership prohibitive. Other countries must be dissuaded from considering such an idea seriously.[19]

To gain a better understanding of these neoconservative ideas, we must place them in the context of the strategic debate as it unfolded in Washington in the 1990s. Basically, there were four main options for remaking the American military machine.[20] A neo-isolationist strategy would obviously have allowed drastic reductions in the military budget, but most analysts rejected it as unrealistic: a power vacuum would invite chaos and war. The second option, "selective engagement," focused almost exclusively on the great powers (China, Russia, Japan, and the European Union), the only powers capable of altering the international order. Regional conflicts were of interest only if they threatened the global equilibrium, which was not the case in the Balkans, for example. Although this option would require a substantial military budget, expenditures would be smaller than during the Cold War. By contrast, the third option demanded a high level of military spending: this was the strategy of global hegemony, as set forth more or less bluntly in the "Defense Planning Guidance" of 1992. The fourth and final option was collective security, or multilateralism: world order would be maintained by the United Nations (and NATO), so that costs would be shared with other nations, allowing the United States to decrease its defense budget.

Although Bill Clinton seemed to opt for the fourth grand strategy at the beginning of his first term, he later shifted to a mixture of options two and three. George W. Bush, though initially tempted by selective engagement, clearly chose a strategy of global hegemony, and the ideas set forth in "Defense Planning Guidance" would find validation in his administration's official position papers and practice. In the meantime, they were widely heralded and championed by the neoconservatives of the third age.

Profile of Third-Age Neoconservatism

Although the seeds of renewal were planted by 1992, the neoconservative movement remained moribund, as attested by the obituary notices mentioned earlier. Years would pass before a new political dynamic began to emerge at the end of the twentieth century. This took place on the conservative end of the political spectrum, around the *Weekly Standard,* the Project for the New American Century, and the American Enterprise Institute. Soon history seemed to repeat itself at an interval of twenty years.

The PNAC resembled both the Coalition for a Democratic Majority (in that it challenged isolationist tendencies within its own party—this time the G.O.P.) and the Committee on the Present Danger (in that it sought to remobilize America). Many of the people associated with the organization joined the new administration, just as members of the CPD had joined the Reagan administration. Like Reagan, George W. Bush embraced some neoconservative ideas. There was a battle with realists (with Brent Scowcroft and Colin Powell playing the roles of Henry Kissinger and George Shultz) as well as with the CIA, which was accused, as in 1976, of being insufficiently alarmist (the Office of Special Plans was reminiscent of Team B). Neoconservatives found bureaucratic allies to help them carry the day (with Rumsfeld and Cheney in the role of Caspar Weinberger). "Old Europe" (France and Germany) joined Iraq in the role of "villain," which the Europeans had previously played in 1981–1983 in the Siberian pipeline and Euromissile affairs. Finally, in Bush's second term, neoconservatives quit an administration that increasingly embraced the realist line and was prepared to compromise with "evil"—the "empire of evil" under Reagan and the "axis of evil" (Iran, North Korea) under Bush.

Although neoconservatives still did not constitute a party, claimed no elected officials or voters, and remained a group of intellectuals clearly in the minority in Washington, they were more powerful and more effective under George W. Bush than their predecessors had been under Reagan. Reasons for this difference include a more coherent intellectual and political position, remarkable political and media savvy (especially in Bill Kristol), and a greater convergence between their views and those of top officials, largely as result of the course of events. In 2003 Dick Cheney ordered thirty copies of the *Weekly Standard* delivered to the White House every week, and the paper, already influential with the policy elite, also gained influence through the media (especially the Fox News Network).[21] Still, the fact remains that neither the *Weekly Standard* nor the PNAC was on good terms with the Bush campaign team or, later, the Bush administration—an administration that Kristol, Kagan, and their associates did not hesitate to criticize harshly, attacking even their "ally" Donald Rumsfeld, to say nothing of Colin Powell and Condoleezza Rice. James Mann reports that well before September 11, 2001, Rice received Kristol after the *Weekly Standard* vehemently criticized the administration for being "soft on China." She preferred to discuss issues with him directly rather than through the press.[22] In other words, the PNAC, like the CPD under Carter, combined strategies of internal and external influence.

The *Weekly Standard* published its first issue in September 1995 thanks to the efforts of a small group led by Kristol and including David Brooks, Fred Barnes, Christopher Caldwell, John Podhoretz (Norman's son), and Robert Kagan.[23] The weekly clearly belonged to the conservative end of the spectrum, but its tone was modern, liberated, and often humorous, a far cry from the tone of traditionalist conservatism. Kristol obtained the money to start the paper from Rupert Murdoch, the Australian press magnate, and with it he sought to change conservatism's intellectual direction and alter the balance of power within the Republican party.

In the very first issue, Robert Kagan was pleased to note that NATO forces had bombed Serbia, thereby undermining both conventional wisdom (that military intervention is always destined to fail) and the Powell doctrine (which recommended extreme caution in the use of military force): "A timid superpower poses a greater danger to the present world order than ten Serbias."[24] Conservatives, especially in Congress, were furious: most had opposed intervention in Bosnia, in part because it was Bill Clinton's decision and in part because they felt it was not America's responsibility to intervene in the Balkans. The *Weekly Standard* eventually came to represent the quest for "national greatness," a neoconservative line that was opposed by right-wing isolationists, or "paleoconservatives," led by Pat Buchanan (and to some extent by Senator Jesse Helms of North Carolina). They also led the fight against widespread Republican apathy in international affairs. With the end of the Cold War, many Republicans wanted to cut foreign aid and even military spending.[25] For the same reason, neoconservatives soon came into conflict with libertarians in the Republican party (represented by the Cato Institute), who wanted to diminish the role of the state no matter what the price.

How could America be a great country capable of assuming its role in the world arena if the state became weaker and weaker? "How can Americans love their nation if they hate its government?"[26] Foreign policy preferences quietly dictated a "national greatness conservatism" in domestic policy, a conservatism compatible with a robust government if not a strong one. It was to be a conservatism less obsessed with avoiding interventionism and more concerned with the notion of patriotism. After all, as Charles Krauthammer pointed out in the same first issue of the *Weekly Standard,* Republicans like Newt Gingrich were proposing a negative liberty (leave individuals alone and roll back the welfare state) rather than a positive liberty (free adherence to some lofty collective goal), and with such a program they could not go very far.[27] "A conservatism that organizes citizens' resentments rather than informing their hopes will always fall short of fundamental victory," as Brooks and Kristol put it.[28]

In truth, the national-greatness conservatism that Brooks and Kristol sought to define in 1997 was not very elaborated, but insofar as there was such a thing as a third-age neoconservative sensibility with respect to domestic affairs, this was its central theme. The influence of this debate can be seen in the *Weekly Standard*'s support of Senator John McCain of Arizona in the 2000 Republican presidential primaries. McCain had approved of the interventions in Bosnia and Kosovo, whereas neoconservatives regarded George W. Bush (whose relations with Bill Kristol were not good for reasons dating from the period 1989–1992) as a copy of his father, a realist in foreign policy, a prisoner of the hidebound Republican establishment, and a tool of the Christian right. "McCain doesn't say that government is oppressive and just needs to get out of the way. He says he wants to reform government to make us proud. He's proposed campaign finance reform, education reform, Social Security reform, a campaign against lobbyist-driven pork-barrel spending." A former fighter pilot and prisoner of war, McCain did not look upon government as "an evil that needs to be dismantled." Rather, he asserted

> that public service is the noblest calling. As important but less obvious, at least until last week, McCain would redirect a religiously based moral conservatism into a patriotically grounded moral appeal. When McCain talks about remoralizing America, he talks in terms of reinvigorating patriotism. As his February 28 Virginia Beach speech shows nicely, when John McCain starts talking about religious faith, he ends up talking about patriotism.[29]

That was why neoconservatives loved him. And, in the 1990s, had he not chaired the International Republican Institute, the branch of the National Endowment for Democracy that was managed by the Republican party?

This position on domestic politics should not be allowed to obscure the fact that third-age neoconservatives were first and foremost conservative Republicans: the *Weekly Standard*'s primary target was Bill Clinton, even if the paper occasionally supported his foreign policy. One way in which third-age neoconservatives differed from their second-age counterparts was that none of them (except for those who belonged to both—or even all three—ages of the movement) had been a liberal Democrat—much less a Trotskyist. To be sure, Bill Kristol had been a volunteer (at the age of sixteen) in Hubert Humphrey's 1968 campaign as well as in Scoop Jackson's 1972 campaign and later helped Pat Moynihan run for the Senate in 1976. But the last effort was prompted by personal loyalty: he has always voted Republican in presidential elections and has always thought of himself as "antileft." He also served as chief of staff to William Bennett, secretary of education under Reagan, and later to Dan Quayle, vice-president under George H. W. Bush (he was even referred to as "Quayle's brain," the vice-president not being known for his intellectual acumen). His interest in foreign policy developed somewhat later, largely as a result of his discussions with Robert Kagan.

Like Kristol, Kagan was an "heir," the hawkish conservative son of a hawkish conservative professor of ancient Greece and military history (Donald Kagan of Yale) who never displayed any leftist leanings. He held posts in the campaigns of several Republican candidates and in Ronald Reagan's State Department after working briefly at *The Public Interest* (1981). As a prolific author and polemicist, Kagan played a particularly important role in the construction of third-age neoconservatism, including his role as cofounder of the Project for the New American Century in 1997. A year earlier, he had collaborated with Bill Kristol on an important article for *Foreign Affairs*, "Toward a Neo-Reaganite Foreign Policy," a veritable manifesto of renascent neoconservatism, which called upon Republicans to overcome their complacent apathy in foreign policy (symbolized by presidential candidate Bob Dole) and acquiescence in the country's isolationist mood and return to a Reaganite policy of military superiority and moral clarity.[30]

But at a dinner in New York a few months later, in the company of Norman Podhoretz and Midge Decter, Kristol and Kagan lamented the disappointing response to their article, the lack of interest in foreign affairs among Americans, and the climate of neo-isolationism that enveloped even the Republican Congress (Newt Gingrich's "Contract with America" had virtually nothing to say about foreign policy). The CDM and CPD were even mentioned as examples during that dinner: not only did America need to be shaken from its apathy, but the reigning orthodoxy within the party (the Republican party this time) needed to be challenged.[31] One thing led to another, and soon there was agreement on the need to create a new organization to promote a "neo-Reaganite foreign policy."

Kristol and Kagan obtained money from the John Olin Foundation to organize two dinners in Washington. The purpose was to bring together various key figures in order to move the project forward. They offered Gary Schmitt the post of director of the Project for the New American Century, which set up shop in 1997 in an office sublet from the *Weekly Standard* in the building occupied by the AEI. Schmitt, a political scientist specializing in the presidency and intelligence issues, is a typical specimen of a third-age neoconservative. Like many others, he had worked in the Reagan administration and found a job through the neoconservative network (with *The National Interest*), and he had never been a Democrat: the closest he had come was a job with Pat Moynihan on the Senate Intelligence Committee in the early 1980s. But when Moynihan abandoned the Scoop Jackson Democrats and moved toward a more traditional liberal position, most notably in his 1982 reelection campaign, Schmitt resigned his post on grounds of political disagreement and accepted a job at the White House.[32]

The PNAC, being something between a think tank and a "citizens' committee," reminds us of the CPD, but its structure was different—and far more modest. It was organized around a very small core group, consisting essentially of Schmitt, Kristol, and Kagan, who were joined for a time by Tom Donnelly, Mark Lagon, Dan McKivergan, Ellen Bork, and Reuel Gerecht, along with Bruce Jackson and Randy Scheunemann (both as members of the tiny "council"). There was also a large group of people who signed particular texts, whether petitions or, more often, "letters," on Serbia, Taiwan, the military budget, Iraq of course, and many other issues. Signing one of these texts did not make them members of the PNAC, especially since any number of them were Democrats who did not share the neoconservative approach to other issues.[33] The PNAC published a few in-depth studies and monographs in addition to the famous "letters" that helped bring it to public attention. For a brief period it attempted to influence Congress, but legislators were not particularly receptive: the PNAC position on the Balkans went so against the grain of the conservative consensus and so ruffled the feathers of certain congressmen that the group lost funding from one foundation after a member of Congress chose to retaliate.[34]

The PNAC and the *Weekly Standard* were key nodes in the neoconservative network, along with Kenneth Weinstein's Hudson Institute, a think tank. To a certain extent the media also helped spread the word: the Fox News Network, the editorial pages of the *Wall Street*

Journal, the *Washington Times*, the *New York Post*, and of course *Commentary* and the *New Republic*. Certain bastions of traditional conservatism were increasingly identified with neoconservatism: the American Enterprise Institute, of course, but also the venerable *National Review*, which became increasingly hospitable to neoconservative arguments, especially after the arrival of Rich Lowry in 1997.[35] In addition, "culture war neoconservatism" continued to make headway, most notably with the "theocons," the mostly Catholic neoconservatives such as Richard Neuhaus, Michael Novak, and George Weigel, and two ecumenical organizations, the journal *First Things* and the Ethics and Public Policy Center.[36] Finally, it would be tedious to list all the neoconservative-inspired "citizens' committees" that flourished in the 1990s and 2000s, but among the most prominent were the Committee to Expand NATO, the Committee for the Liberation of Iraq, the Project on Transitional Democracies, and a third Committee on the Present Danger, this time focused on the Islamist peril—but not nearly as influential as its predecessors.

The Neoconservative Approach to the World

As with the first two ages of neoconservatives, we can identify a basic set of principles while keeping in mind the diversity of the movement and the way in which it changed over time.

First, one could not be a third-age neoconservative without believing in the need for the United States to play an active role in the world and to assert and defend an American-led world order to ensure peace. "Today," Kagan and Kristol argued,

> the absence of a Soviet empire does not alter the fundamental purposes of American foreign policy. Just as sensible Americans after World War II did not imagine that the United States should await the rise of the next equivalent of Nazi Germany, so American statesmen today ought to recognize that their charge is not to await the arrival of the next great threat. Rather, it is to shape the international environment to prevent such a threat from arising in the first place. To put it another way: The overarching goal of American foreign policy—to preserve and extend an international order that is in accord with both our material interests and our principles—endures. Americans must shape this order, for if we refrain from doing so, we

can be sure that others will shape it in ways that reflect neither our interests nor our values.[37]

As they saw it, the question that everyone was asking after the Cold War—where is the threat?—was not the right one. The real danger was that the United States might, out of laziness or stinginess, turn its back on its responsibility to keep the peace, as Europe (and the United States) had done in the 1930s, with results that were plain to see.

The real danger was that America might allow a unique moment in the history of the world to pass without acting: for the first time a democracy with no intention of conquering and subjugating other countries was the most powerful country in the world. "The appropriate goal of American foreign policy, therefore, is to preserve that hegemony as far into the future as possible. To achieve this goal, the United States needs a neo-Reaganite foreign policy of military supremacy and moral confidence."[38] This article revived the ambition of the "Defense Planning Guidance" to preserve the unipolar moment as the best way of defending and extending the "democratic zone of peace," starting with the countries on Russia's fringe (hence the support for NATO, Ukraine, the small democracies of Eastern Europe, and so on).

This brings us to a second basic principle of third-age neoconservatism and one of the few serious connections with the thought of philosopher Leo Strauss: the importance of political regimes, a point on which neoconservatives and realists disagree. For neoconservatives, a tyranny is not the same thing as a democracy—morally speaking, to be sure, but above all in strategic terms. As Charles Krauthammer observed:

> Democracies are inherently more friendly to the United States, less belligerent to their neighbors, and generally more inclined to peace. Realists are right that to protect your interests you often have to go around the world bashing bad guys over the head. But that technique, no matter how satisfying, has its limits. At some point, you have to implant something, something organic and self-developing. And that something is democracy.[39]

The logic that ties these first two principles together is clear: the more active America's role in enlarging the "democratic zone of peace" and the smaller the number of dictatorial regimes, the greater the security of the United States and the rest of the world. That is why the charge that has been leveled against the neoconservatives, that democracy promotion is merely a fig leaf for imperialism and militarism, misses the mark: it is not so much a moralistic camouflage as an element of their strategic calculus—which happens to be the right thing to do in principle.

Some neoconservatives even see the quest for freedom as a veritable locomotive of history, which causes the world to move in the direction they desire. George W. Bush, like Pat Moynihan before him, invoked the universal "thirst for freedom" and, drawing on Natan Sharansky, insisted on the "transformative power of freedom," even in the Middle East—a theme also taken up by Michael Novak, who refuses to see Islam as an obstacle to democracy, as so many claim.[40] There is finally a domestic aspect to this: a nation's foreign policy is a mirror in which it can see a reflection itself, its health, and its moral condition. A prudent, timid, and cynical (in other words, realist) approach to international affairs is not worthy of America; it neither inspires nor edifies its own citizens.

But what reason is there to believe that other nations would accept the Pax Americana as a Pax Democratica, even if it is pursued with the best intentions? The answer can be found in the third neoconservative principle: benevolent empire. This idea was championed mainly by Robert Kagan, who argued that, compared with past empires, American hegemony was benign and therefore a stroke of good fortune for the rest of the world: "America may be arrogant; Americans may at times be selfish; they may occasionally be ham-handed in their exercise of power. But, *excusez-moi*, compared with whom? Can anyone believe that were France to possess the power the United States now has, the French would be less arrogant, less selfish, and less prone to making mistakes?" To say nothing of Russia or Saudi Arabia. The best indication of the benign character of American hegemony, Kagan continued, was that no one sought seriously to contest it, except perhaps China, whose "military buildup has not exactly been viewed by its neighbors as creating a more harmonious environment."[41] In other words, Americans, by seeking their own security, brought peace and order to the rest of the world—a veritable global public good.

If hegemony, or even "empire" (an ambiguous concept that many neoconservatives reject but others, such as Bill Kristol, accept, and still others, such as Max Boot, insist on),[42] is benevolent, and if America establishes world order for the common good, then its hands should be free. It cannot fulfill its responsibilities with one hand tied behind its back by other powers that benefit gratuitously from the order it establishes. In other words, while collective action is good, America should feel free to act unilaterally: this was the fourth principle of neoconservatism, a principle directly inherited from the 1970s and 1980s. The UN is not only ineffective; it is illegitimate. The only possible setting in which democracy can be exercised is the nation. The General Assembly of the United Nations puts countries such as India and Libya on a footing of equality, which is absurd, while the Security Council grants to a dictatorship and a semidictatorship veto power over what the international community does. What is more, even the Europeans agreed to sidestep the Security Council for the Kosovo operation in 1999. Hence in the case of a military operation, the mission should determine the shape of the coalition (an ad-hoc coalition of the willing) rather than allowing the coalition to determine, and inevitably constrain, the mission, as was the case in the Gulf War. This point had been made in the "Defense Planning Guidance" document as early as 1992.

More generally, as in the second age of neoconservatism, international law is looked upon with disdain, with few exceptions (Eugene Rostow and Pat Moynihan earlier and to a certain extent Joshua Muravchik more recently). The legitimacy to act derives solely from the American people and from the unique responsibility the United States has for maintaining order. As for treaties—concerning nuclear tests, biological weapons, antipersonnel mines, and so on—they constrain America while allowing hostile powers to cheat. Who seriously believes that weakening the United States and strengthening international law is going to protect Taiwan, Israel, or South Korea? Charles Krauthammer mocked naïve Democrats and Europeans who "believe in paper" (treaties) as a means of achieving world order, whereas neoconservatives "believe in power."[43]

To maintain this order, the United States needs massive military resources as well as the political will to use them: this is the fifth basic principle of neoconservatism. This means that the nation must agree to sustained military spending—and neoconservatives have not allowed a year to go by since 1972 without calling for an increase in the defense budget, especially in the 1990s and 2000s, when the rapid growth of the U.S. gross domestic product meant that the Pentagon budget as a percentage of GDP had shrunk to historic lows (around 3 to 4 percent). As for readiness to intervene militarily abroad, that was of course the issue that divided neoconservatives from realists, who preferred to make limited and selective use of force in accordance with the "Powell doctrine," which laid down all sorts of drastic conditions for foreign interventions. Furthermore, with the exception of Afghanistan, neoconservatives consistently supported and Colin Powell consistently opposed foreign military operations (the Gulf War, Somalia, Bosnia, Kosovo, and Iraq), a fact that explains why Robert Kagan attacked the future secretary of state even before the 2000 election and Lawrence Kaplan followed suit after his nomination.[44] Neoconservatives wanted America to get over the Vietnam syndrome (fear of an indecisive military commitment unsupported by the American public and extended in time) and observed that the country's relative (and absolute) military capability had increased significantly, as the Gulf War and especially the victory in Afghanistan had demonstrated. In short, it was time for America to stop being excessively cautious.

The Neoconservative Planisphere

These basic principles can be elaborated by theme and region, leading to further distinctions between the neoconservative vision of the world and the visions of liberals and realists.

For instance, Europe's image among neoconservatives, which had started to deteriorate with détente and the disputes of the early 1980s, continues to decline. Neoconservatives even developed a form of Europhobia at the time of their campaign in favor of war in Iraq.[45] The most important text in this vein is Robert Kagan's "Power and Weakness" (2002), which depicts Europe as a region that has turned its back on history and lives in a Kantian paradise of perpetual peace, in which relations of force have been replaced by voluntary relinquishments of sovereignty.[46] This bubble of peace is certainly a boon for humanity in view of the wars that Europe has unleashed on the world, but a weakened Europe can no longer lay claim to a serious international role or even understand the United States, which remains firmly rooted in history and whose military might is what allows Europe to live in peace, since it ensures order in a dangerous world where it is sometimes necessary to resort to force.

As we have seen, the neoconservatives' uncompromising defense of Israel is a consequence partly of the personal attachment of many neoconservatives to the Jewish state but more broadly of the insistence on defending democracy. As Garry Dorrien has convincingly shown, "Hardline Zionism is a major component of their ideology but not the key to everything else."[47] It nevertheless leads to a distortion of the neoconservative vision of the Middle East, most notably by minimizing the role of the Israel-Palestine conflict, and this heavily influenced their policy recommendations (see below). Similarly, their wariness of and hawkish attitude toward China, which reached somewhat hysterical proportions in the late 1990s, were not directed specifically against the Middle Empire but rather derived from their insistence on maintaining American hegemony and discouraging regional powers deemed to be "threatening." In some respects, the attacks of September 11, 2001, had an unexpected—and beneficial—effect by reducing the alarmist level of concern with China and distracting the attention of neoconservatives and other hawks.

Alarmism and exaggeration of the threat remain distinctive traits of the neoconservatives, in the tradition of NSC-68, Team B, and the CPD. For instance, in June 1998 a Republican congressman from California, Christopher Cox (aided by Scooter Libby), was assigned to review the CIA's estimates of military spending by the People's Republic of China. It will come as no surprise that Cox "discovered" that China was engaged in vast espionage operations within the United States for the purpose of improving its own nuclear weapons programs and that its military expenditures were double the CIA estimates.

A month later, in July 1998, a committee looking into the ballistic missile threat, headed by Donald Rumsfeld and including Paul Wolfowitz and James Woolsey, "discovered" that the threat to America was more serious and more imminent (five years) than the CIA had estimated (ten to fifteen years) and thus justified rapid deployment of an antimissile system.[48] These predictions were partially verified in the case of North Korea but not for the other countries. It is also noteworthy that although neoconservatives continued to advocate antimissile systems, they were less ardent than before because they worried that an antimissile shield might tempt the Republican party into a "fortress America" isolationism.

In addition, "nuclear neoconservatism" (see Chapter 5), promoted mainly by the National Institute for Public Policy (NIPP), an organization founded in 1981 by Colin Gray and Keith Payne and greatly influenced by the thinking of Albert Wohlstetter, recommended that priority be given to the development of "bunker-buster" weapons capable of destroying chemical and biological arms caches, and also that the United States should maintain a substantial nuclear arsenal. These were the conclusions of the report "Rationale and Requirements for Nuclear Forces and Arms Control" (January 2001), which to a great extent became the official nuclear policy of George W. Bush (the "Nuclear Posture Review" of 2002).[49] Among the authors were veterans of the CPD, including Eugene Rostow, William Van Cleave, Fred Iklé, Max Kampelman, Charles Kupperman, and Colin Gray, along with some new people such as Bob Joseph, Steve Hadley, and Steve Cambone, who would play important roles in the Bush administration.

Of all the possible threats to America that might have warranted international activism, there was one that neoconservatives essentially ignored in the 1990s: terrorism. As Jacob Heilbrunn notes, in the week of September 11, 2001, the front page of the *Weekly Standard* was devoted to the cultural impact of the 1970s television series *Gilligan's Island.*[50] Although it is easy in retrospect to point out what was a widely shared blind spot, this failure is nonetheless symptomatic of a vision of the world in which states are the only actors that need to be taken seriously: transnational phenomena and nonstate actors do not count. For instance, in 2000, in a symposium published by *Commentary,* to which many neoconservatives contributed, Charles Krauthammer prepared a list of American national interests in which he emphasized four priorities:

> First, containing, deterring, and, if necessary, disarming rogue states that are acquiring weapons of mass destruction, states that could threaten with unprecedented power not only our allies and our troops abroad, but eventually America itself.
>
> Second, containing a rising China, a country whose position on the globe at the turn of the 21st century is comparable to that of Germany at the turn of the 20th—a large, growing, former have-not, seeking its place in the sun, pushing inexorably against its neighbors.
>
> Third, maintaining vigilance against the possibility of a resurgent, revanchist Russia.
>
> Fourth, maintaining order as the ultimate guarantor of international peace and stability. As the only nation that can project power anywhere in the world decisively and overwhelmingly, our role is to husband our resources to meet supraregional challenges—i.e., those that threaten not just a country or a region but the stability of the international system itself.[51]

The word "terrorism" was mentioned only twice, in passing, in the symposium. Similarly, in an anthology published in the same year, edited by Kagan and Kristol and titled *Present Dangers* in homage to the CPD (and to Podhoretz's 1980 pamphlet), terrorism was not included,[52] nor was it mentioned in any of the PNAC publications.

For neoconservatives, however, there was no threat that could not be handled with a larger military budget, more patriotism, and a few victorious foreign interventions, and they were quick to fit the September 11 attacks into their vision of the world. In their view, the attacks on New York and Washington proved two points of their credo. First, America had not made a sufficient show of its force over the past two decades. If it had demonstrated greater determination in Lebanon (which it quit after the 1983 attack on a Marine barracks there), Iraq (after the expulsion of Saddam Hussein from Kuwait in 1991 and the failed assassination attempt on former president George H. W. Bush in 1993), Somalia (which it left after American soldiers were killed there in 1993), and especially after the attacks of the past decade (on the World Trade Center in 1993, the American military base in Khobar, Saudi Arabia, in 1996, American embassies in Africa in 1998, and the Navy's USS *Cole* in 2000), it would not have projected an image of weakness, which encouraged the terrorists.

More than that, neoconservatives interpreted September 11 in ideological terms. The attacks marked the beginning of "the Fourth World War" (the third being the Cold War): this argument was made first by Eliot Cohen in 2001 and then taken up by James Woolsey and Norman Podhoretz.[53] The conflict was a war, not a police operation, even if that characterization did not please liberals or Europeans. Like the Cold War against communism, this war against "militant Islam" or, indeed, "Islamofascism" was global; it called for both violent and nonviolent responses; it required America to mobilize; it would last for a long time; and it was by nature ideological. The underlying causes of terrorism were not to be sought in underdevelopment, much less in the rancor that the Arab-Muslim world felt toward the United States, but rather in the absence of democracy in the Middle East. Terrorism was above all a by-product of tyrannies in the region, of regimes that foreign policy "realists" had always protected. The neoconservatives quickly returned the debate to the more familiar level of the state: the real problem lay with states that produced and above all supported terrorism—states that Paul Wolfowitz contended should be "ended." And among those states was obviously Iraq, which neoconservatives had already had in their sights for years.

George W. Bush: From Suspicion to Divine Surprise

Before turning to the campaign in favor of intervention in Iraq, we must pause for a moment to consider the administration of George W. Bush—

and the president himself. As in the case of Ronald Reagan, it is worth asking to what extent Bush was a neoconservative president. In framing an answer to this question, the issue that looms largest is of course the Middle East. Without rehashing our earlier discussion of the complex relations between neoconservatism and the war in Iraq, we can point to the many "exogenous" factors that made this intervention possible and have nothing to do with neoconservatism. First, there was the climate of fear and patriotism that dominated public opinion in the wake of the attacks. Second, the attacks profoundly altered the perception of risks on the part of decisionmakers, lowering the threshold of tolerance with respect to proliferation of weapons of mass destruction (WMD) and support for terrorism. Third, there was a feeling that the evil had to be attacked at its root, that treating symptoms was not good enough. Fourth, there was acute awareness of the political, military, and moral cost of containing Saddam Hussein. However, the ideas developed in neoconservative circles provided a coherent pattern weaving these elements together and offering a strategy that was defended by many administration officials and partially adopted by the president himself.

Before September 11 the bond between neoconservatives and the president was by no means secure; as we have seen, neoconservatives had gravitated more toward John McCain in the primaries. Still, in July 1998 the governor of Texas invited Paul Wolfowitz to advise him on foreign policy. Wolfowitz was his second foreign policy adviser, after Condoleezza Rice, whose career had previously been linked to that of Brent Scowcroft, the very realist national security adviser of the first President Bush. When the younger Bush sought to expand his national security team, known as "the Vulcans," Wolfowitz tapped Richard Perle, so that various conservative tendencies were represented, including neoconservatism. Several of the other "Vulcans" (in particular Richard Armitage and Robert Zoellick) had signed many of the PNAC letters.[54]

Despite this entourage, George W. Bush's first presidential campaign inspired little enthusiasm among neoconservatives. Bush attacked Clinton not for his reluctance to assert a robust American-dominated world order but rather for being too quick to use force in foreign interventions, which ended in "nation-building" operations—a subsidiary mission that American forces should never be asked to assume. Condoleezza Rice published an article in *Foreign Affairs* that summed up candidate Bush's program, and realpolitik predominated in every paragraph, with scarcely a mention of human rights or democracy. Thus America ought to mobilize "all available resources" to overthrow Saddam Hussein (who was described as "isolated" and "weakened"), but invasion certainly did not figure in the plan, which did not go beyond advocating support for the opposition. In any case, "rogue states" would not last long, and it was enough to remain patient while deploying an antimissile shield as quickly as possible.[55]

Against this grand strategy of "selective engagement," tepid internationalism, and outspoken humility ("If we are an arrogant nation, they will resent us," Bush explained), Democratic candidate Al Gore, who proclaimed the need for decisive American leadership, almost looked better to neoconservatives.[56] For example, Lawrence Kaplan, writing in the *New Republic,* noted that "George W. Bush flatly admits he won't intervene to stop 'genocide in nations outside our strategic interest.' For all his invocation of Reagan, his 'distinctly American internationalism' amounts to nothing more than a variation of old-world realpolitik and an echo of Gerald Ford."[57] But 2000 was not 1992, and in spite of such objections George Bush received the benefit of the doubt.

Once the new administration took office, neoconservatives sought to win a hearing for their views. At the behest of Elliott Abrams's Ethics and Public Policy Center, some twenty of them circulated an appeal, "Idealism without Illusions," urging President Bush to put democracy, human rights, and religious freedom at the heart of his agenda, for example by redirecting nonhumanitarian aid to the "defense of freedom and the struggle against tyranny." The petition denounced the "genocide" in the Sudan and religious persecution in China (Uighurs, Christians, Falun Gong). "American leadership must never remain indifferent to tyranny, must never be agnostic about the virtues of political and economic freedom, must always be concerned with the fortunes of fragile democracies," the petitioners insisted. Among them were Norman Podhoretz, Midge Decter, Max Kampelman, Ben Wattenberg, James Woolsey, Michael Novak, Richard Neuhaus, and William Bennett, along with newer names such as Paula Dobriansky, Mark Lagon, and Mark Palmer.[58]

If the new administration's appointments were any indication, however, the battle was not yet won. Indeed, the Bush administration perpetuated the factions and contradictions found earlier among Ronald Reagan's staff. The State Department, dominated by realists led by Colin Powell and Richard Armitage, was opposed by the Pentagon and the vice-president's office, where hawks and neoconservatives gathered around Donald Rumsfeld and Dick Cheney. Genuine neoconservatives were included but in lower-ranking positions: Paul Wolfowitz was number two at Defense; Douglas Feith—a veteran of the Reagan administration who was close to Richard Perle and who had been associated with Richard Pipes, Elmo Zumwalt, and Max Kampelman—was number three;[59] Scooter Libby was the vice-president's chief of staff; Elliott Abrams was senior director at the National Security Council. As for Condoleezza Rice, the president's national security adviser, she was considered to be more of a realist and in any case did not much alter the internal balance of power.

In fact neoconservative influence depended largely on Donald Rumsfeld and Dick Cheney—labeled "aggressive nationalists" by Ivo Daalder and James Lindsay[60]—who shared with neoconservatives the conviction that America must show its strength in order to be respected in the world. But were they neoconservatives? Rumsfeld was never a Democrat, but he was a member of the CPD and cochaired the Committee for the Free World with Midge Decter in the 1980s, and he was also a member of the board of Freedom House, so it is clear that he was not impervious to considerations about democracy and ideological battles. But strategic calculations were paramount with him, not the vision of democratic peace under American leadership. The way in which he approached the war in Iraq, with the intent of using it as a model for transforming the American military while deliberately—and fatally—neglecting postinvasion planning, clearly reveals his priorities: to eliminate a potential threat, restore the image of American power, and install a friendly regime in Baghdad—and little did it matter whether that regime was democratic or autocratic. It will come as no surprise that he was a frequent target of the *Weekly Standard*.

Dick Cheney, the other objective ally of the neoconservatives, was never a Democrat either, nor was he known for his interest in ideological issues. After September 11, however, he became the mainstay of neoconservatives, sharing their vision for transforming the Middle East or, at a minimum, striking a blow hard enough to change the status quo in the Arab world. The scholars Bernard Lewis and Fouad Ajami appear to have had a major influence on his understanding of the region, according to Brent Scowcroft, who has said that he no longer recognized his old friend from the Ford and Bush administrations.[61] There is no denying that after September 11 Cheney gradually came to play a key role in defining an extremely pessimistic and exaggerated view of the terrorist threat faced by the United States and the need to do whatever it took, regardless of the cost, to deal with it. On Iraq his view broadly coincided with that of the neoconservatives.

The first few months of the Bush administration were hardly comforting to neoconservatives. After a Chinese fighter plane collided with an American spy plane in April 2001, President Bush agreed to present his excuses to Beijing in the wake of the spy plane's forced landing on Chinese soil. In the *Weekly Standard* Bill Kristol and Robert Kagan expressed their outrage: the incident amounted to "a national humiliation," a veritable "capitulation," an act of appeasement worthy of the 1930s.[62] The policy adopted for dealing with rogue states was hardly reassuring: on Iraq, a continuation of the containment policy with mild changes in sanctions, and a soft line on North Korea, at odds with the initial plan. In the eyes of neoconservatives, it was Colin Powell, now secretary of state, who had ensured that the realist line would prevail. Worst of all was the defense budget, which remained so low that in July 2001 Kristol and Kagan bluntly advised Rumsfeld, now secretary of defense, and Wolfowitz, his number two, to resign so as to issue a wake-up call to America.[63]

In the days that followed the September 11 attacks, the attitude of neoconservatives at first remained quite critical. On September 14 Gary Schmitt issued this blast: "The country's been attacked and the president seemed more concerned with being the FEMA chief than the commander in chief. They can't be telling people things should be normal but there's a war going on."[64] But very quickly they took the measure of the astonishing transformation of George W. Bush—of which they approved. To be sure, the president, a novice in foreign policy, had never offered a glimpse of who he really was. He had appeared to share his father's cynical realism, though at times he had shown signs of more idealistic aspirations. In his major foreign policy speech as a candidate in 1999, he had evoked the "evil" that had survived the demise of the "empire of evil," quoting Sharansky, Havel, Walesa, and Mandela, and had alluded to the glorious progress of democracy in the world: in 1941 there had been a dozen democratic countries, and now there were 120. "The most powerful force in the world is not a weapon or a nation but a truth: that we are spiritual beings, and that freedom is 'the soul's right to breathe.'"[65]

After September 11 this aspect of the president's worldview loomed larger and larger, even before the Iraq war, ultimately making him a true neoconservative, especially in his Second Inaugural Address in January

2005, in which he declared that "it is the policy of the United States to seek and support the growth of democratic movements and institutions in every nation and culture, with the ultimate goal of ending tyranny in our world."[66] It will come as no surprise that neoconservatives cheered this announcement, while realists and many conservatives were dismayed. Indeed, as a whole the "Bush doctrine" was largely inspired by neoconservative ideas in both of its "pillars"—democratic peace and American power.

The Neoconservative Bush Doctrine

Like the Reagan doctrine, the Bush doctrine took some time to find its definitive form and remained somewhat hazy. Charles Krauthammer, the "discoverer" of the Reagan doctrine, may have been a bit hasty in characterizing Bush's as one of "soft unilateralism."[67] Later, after September 11, he saw it as a determination not to distinguish between terrorists and the states that harbored them, and still later as a synonym for preventive war or regime change. But it turned out to be more complex and comprehensive than any of these definitions implied.[68] Essentially, it was based on the idea of using American power to promote democratic peace, especially in the Middle East.

The first pillar of the Bush doctrine was the belief that democratic regimes do not seek war; thus, promoting democracy could potentially bring about universal peace. "Free societies," he said in 2002, "do not intimidate through cruelty and conquest, and open societies do not threaten the world with mass murder."[69] In 2003 he was still more specific: "The world has a clear interest in the spread of democratic values, because stable and free nations do not breed the ideologies of murder."[70] In 2005 he put the point in even more theoretical terms: "The advance of freedom within nations will build the peace among nations."[71]

In other words, if the Middle East became democratic, America's security problems in the region—terrorism and proliferation of weapons of mass destruction—would ultimately disappear. Hence it was essential to "transform" the Middle East, and a regime change in Iraq was a way to get the ball rolling: "A new regime in Iraq would serve as a dramatic and inspiring example of freedom for other nations in the region."[72] Bush's faith in the virtues of democracy was itself based on sincerely universalistic beliefs that the president shared with most other neoconservatives: just as cynics had been mistaken in the past about the possibility of establishing democracy in Germany and Japan, these neoconservatives argued, they were wrong today about the prospects for democracy in the Arab-Muslim world, because the desire for freedom was universal. For that reason there should be no reluctance to call evil evil, as Reagan had done twenty years earlier, or to set an example of moral clarity by refusing to negotiate with a hateful regime (and thus prolong its existence) when there was a possibility of changing it.

This democratic core of the Bush doctrine set the president in opposition not only to realists but also to much of American foreign policy as it had been conducted since the "Quincy pact" of 1945, which sealed the alliance between Franklin Roosevelt and the king of Saudi Arabia: American forces would provide the kingdom with a security guarantee in exchange for regional stability and a supply of oil to the West. Bush therefore repudiated "sixty years of Western nations excusing and accommodating the lack of freedom in the Middle East," for this policy had allowed authoritarian regimes to survive and ultimately given rise to terrorism.[73] True realism, realism for the long term, therefore meant democracy promotion. "Some who call themselves realists question whether the spread of democracy in the Middle East should be any concern of ours. But the realists in this case have lost contact with a fundamental reality: America has always been less secure when freedom is in retreat; America is always more secure when freedom is on the march."[74]

If the main pillar of the Bush doctrine—transforming the Middle East in order to promote a "democratic peace"—concerned the ends of American foreign policy, the second pillar concerned the means, and in the first instance the means of action. America must be able to act alone. To borrow the words of Donald Rumsfeld, which also happen to be a neoconservative mantra, "the mission defines the coalition," rather than the reverse. The famous "coalition of the willing" in Iraq in 2003 was a good example of this mindset. Furthermore, America should reserve the right to act preemptively, because terrorist attacks (unlike troop movements toward borders) cannot be detected before they occur. More generally, the Bush doctrine rested on maintaining American hegemony, an idea already articulated in the "Defense Planning Guidance," whose basic tenets had long since become a part of the neoconservative agenda. The "National Security Strategy" of 2002 asserted: "Our forces will be strong enough to dissuade potential adversaries from pursuing a military build-up in hopes of surpassing, or equaling, the power of the United States."[75]

Clearly, there is a strong family resemblance between the Bush doctrine and neoconservatism. That fact, however, did not prevent the president from drawing upon a range of other sources for his foreign policy, including his evangelical faith and his belief in the importance of standing firmly behind principled decisions once taken—a belief derived, according to some commentators, from the program in which he enrolled to overcome his problems with alcohol in the 1980s. Last but not least, several of the principles advocated by neoconservatives, such as unilateralism and preventive war, were shared by all hawks and were largely a consequence of the situation in which America found itself after September 11.

It is also important to recognize that the Bush doctrine was never really applied to regions other than the Middle East, and in any case it was necessary to make some allowance for existing realities. Hence in the eyes of neoconservatives, although Bush's heart was in the right place, the realists too often succeeded in persuading him to go against his own instincts—for instance, in the decision to turn to the United Nations before the invasion of Iraq, owing to pressure from Colin Powell and Condoleezza Rice. During Bush's second term, moreover, although the president's rhetoric became increasingly idealistic and neoconservative, realities on the ground, such as the eruption of civil war in Iraq, made implementation of the Bush doctrine impossible. Iran and Syria were obvious candidates for regime change, but any plans for such undertakings were put on hold as early as mid-2003, when the situation in Iraq started deteriorating. This shows how closely the Bush doctrine was linked to a very distinctive moment in the evolution of American hegemony, when anything suddenly seemed possible. By the end of Bush's second term, the "freedom agenda" was in retreat, and realists seemed to be making gains everywhere: on Iran, North Korea, the Israel-Palestine conflict, and so on.

In the last analysis, George W. Bush was a more neoconservative president than Ronald Reagan in an international context that was more propitious to neoconservatism, at least after September 11. His presidency will forever be linked to the war in Iraq, which was its centerpiece, and neoconservatives had worked actively since 1997 to bring about some sort of intervention, ultimately winning the president's consent in the wake of the September 11 attacks. Why Iraq? Because intervention there was possible and even desirable in view of the vexed question of its purported weapons of mass destruction, as well as the fact that the country was at the nexus of the authoritarian status quo in the Middle East, an obstacle to the transformation of the region into a zone of democratic peace, which for neoconservatives was the ultimate solution to the problem laid bare by September 11.

The Drums of War

Sources abound on the neoconservative campaign in favor of military intervention in Iraq; here it will suffice to recall the main outlines.[76] As James Mann points out, no important official in the administration of George Bush Sr. had advocated going to Baghdad to topple Saddam Hussein in 1991, not even Paul Wolfowitz, partly because no one imagined that he would be able to remain in power.[77] Over the years, however, neoconservatives had come to see that decision as a mistake and, indeed, had come to see the postwar decision to allow Saddam to use helicopters to put down Kurd and Shi'ite rebellions as a crime (Wolfowitz had opposed it at the time).

As the 1990s wore on, it appeared that Saddam Hussein, who had initially complied with UN Resolution 687 ordering him to disarm, had learned how to evade the scrutiny of UN inspectors. Their departure in 1998 led to several crises and bombings of Iraq, the most important of which came in December 1998 under Bill Clinton. Saddam had also managed to thwart coup attempts by various opposition groups. His defiant stand forced the United States to maintain a substantial military force in the region, mainly to enforce the no-fly zones in the north and south of Iraq. Yet there was little information about the progress that Saddam had made in his efforts to acquire weapons of mass destruction.

In 1997 a number of neoconservatives concluded that this situation was at once dangerous, politically costly, and amoral, both because of Saddam's tyranny and because of his evasion of international sanctions. They advocated a switch from a strategy of containment to one of regime change. On November 12, 1997, David Wurmser wrote in the *Wall Street Journal* that "Iraq Needs a Revolution" (aided by America), and three weeks later Zalmay Khalilzad and Paul Wolfowitz published an article in the *Weekly Standard* titled "Overthrow Him."[78] The common feature of these two articles was their rejection of the strategy of a coup d'état, which had already failed several times and could only lead to a new tyranny, in favor of a strategy of armed support to opposition forces prepared to attack Saddam (perhaps from an enclave in the north) and topple his regime. Their role was to be the same as that assigned to "freedom fighters" under the Reagan doctrine.

The instrument that neoconservatives proposed for this role was the Iraqi National Congress, led by Ahmed Chalabi, a Shi'ite who had left Iraq with his family in the late 1950s and studied in the United States with Albert Wohlstetter. Close to two other Wohlstetter disciples, Paul Wolfowitz and Richard Perle, Chalabi (the founder of a bank in Jordan from which he later allegedly embezzled funds and who was living at the time in London) had created the INC in 1992 in order to bring "free Iraqis" together for the purpose of overthrowing Saddam Hussein. Both the CIA and the State Department regarded him as unreliable, however—a judgment that for neoconservatives came close to counting in his favor. Chalabi was able to expand his network at annual conferences that the American Enterprise Institute (and in particular Richard Perle) organized at Beaver Creek in Colorado with personalities such as ex-president Gerald Ford and experts and politicians such as Rumsfeld, Cheney, John McCain, and Joe Lieberman.[79]

There were also open letters calling for the overthrow of the Iraqi tyrant. For instance, the Committee for Peace and Security in the Gulf (a group organized in 1990 by Richard Perle and Representative Stephen Solarz from New York to support the Gulf War) published one on February 19, 1998, stating that Iraq was "ripe for a vast insurrection" and that "free Iraqis" might regain control of the country little by little with American support.[80] A better-known example is the PNAC letter of January 26, 1998, which was signed by Elliott Abrams, Richard Armitage, John Bolton, Paula Dobriansky, Francis Fukuyama, Donald Rumsfeld, James Woolsey, and Robert Zoellick, among others.[81]

On October 31, 1998, this campaign bore fruit: Congress passed and President Clinton signed the "Iraq Liberation Act," which had been drafted by Randy Scheunemann, then on the staff of Senate Republican leader Trent Lott of Mississippi. As a result regime change in Iraq became the official new policy of the United States. Given the stakes involved, the appropriation for the purpose ($98 million) was modest. It was distributed to several groups, most notably Chalabi's Iraqi National Congress. But the Clinton administration had no intention of doing more, even after the bombing campaign of December 1998. As mentioned earlier, George W. Bush did not make any real commitment on this issue in the 2000 presidential campaign. By the middle of 2001,

Colin Powell was negotiating at the UN for "smart sanctions" against Iraq, and it was taken for granted that nothing would really change.

Nevertheless, the neoconservative campaign must have had some influence, for on September 12, 2001, President Bush ordered Richard Clarke, who was in charge of counterterrorism at the National Security Council, to look into possible links between the attacks of the previous day and Saddam Hussein, even though early signs all pointed clearly to al-Qaeda.[82] In the following weeks the major strategic question was whether to attack Iraq or Afghanistan—or perhaps Afghanistan first, then Iraq. Donald Rumsfeld and Paul Wolfowitz favored the first option, with quiet support from Dick Cheney, but they were opposed by Colin Powell and the military (in the person of the chairman of the Joint Chiefs of Staff, Hugh Shelton), who pointed out that attacking Iraq would make it difficult to build an international coalition, especially since there was no clear link between September 11 and Saddam Hussein.[83]

These were precisely the arguments that neoconservatives did not want to hear. On September 20, 2001, the PNAC published a letter describing the battlefields of the War on Terror. The first priority was to destroy the Bin Laden network in Afghanistan (which would not require an invasion). Immediately after that came the overthrow of Saddam Hussein. "Failure to undertake such an effort will constitute an early and perhaps decisive surrender in the war on international terrorism."[84] In reality, the neoconservatives' worries were misplaced; George W. Bush had already decided to take action against Saddam Hussein if circumstances allowed. As early as November 2001 he ordered Donald Rumsfeld to update invasion plans.[85]

In 2002 and 2003 neoconservatives would intensify their campaign in two directions. With the administration, and most notably at the Pentagon, they began to question CIA estimates on the grounds that the agency denied the link between Saddam and Bin Laden and minimized the threat of the Iraqi dictator's weapons of mass destruction. The first task fell to the tiny Counterterrorism Evaluation Group, established in October 2001 by Douglas Feith (number three at the Pentagon) and headed by David Wurmser and Michael Maloof.[86] In September 2002 the second task was assigned to the Office of Special Plans, a somewhat larger organization put together by Paul Wolfowitz and Douglas Feith and headed by Abram Shulsky and William Luti but ultimately reporting to Scooter Libby in Vice-President Cheney's office.[87]

The information on Iraq that the Office of Special Plans collected was not submitted to intelligence professionals but passed directly to principal decisionmakers in the administration via a parallel channel, which also fed the media outside the government. The attitude was the same as for Team B: when it came to analyzing intelligence, the CIA was criticized for seeing only capabilities and not intentions—in other words, what Saddam would like to do and might be able to achieve.[88] The problem was that the new information collected by the Office of Special Plans came largely from tainted or delusive sources provided by Ahmed Chalabi's Iraqi National Congress, such as the defector known as "Curveball," who gave false information about the Iraqi chemical weapons program. Worse, as revealed by the devastating "Downing Street Memo," a secret British note on planning for the war dated July 2002 and revealed by the press in 2005, "C. reported on his recent talks in Washington. There was a perceptible shift in attitude. Military action was now seen as inevitable. Bush wanted to remove Saddam, through military action, justified by the conjunction of terrorism and WMD. But the intelligence and facts were being fixed around the policy."[89]

The other aspect of the neoconservative campaign was public and political and sought to generate and reinforce public and elite support for the war. This goal was tirelessly pursued by the PNAC and the *Weekly Standard,* as well as the AEI, the third Committee on the Present Danger, and the Foundation for the Defense of Democracies, with assistance from friendly journalists. In November 2002 the Committee for the Liberation of Iraq was organized with Randy Scheunemann as chair and Bruce Jackson, the former vice-president of Lockheed-Martin and former chair of the Committee to Expand NATO, as director. This all-out propaganda campaign spared no adversary of intervention, from Colin Powell to France, and did not refrain from tapping into public fears or exaggerating the threat while minimizing the costs of intervention. For instance, Bill Kristol and Lawrence Kaplan wrote a book in favor of intervention, *The War over Iraq,* in which they advocated a lengthy occupation to establish a democracy (unlike Rumsfeld, who wanted to get out of Iraq as quickly as possible), but they envisioned a force of 75,000 men initially to be reduced to just a few thousand after a year or two, for a cost of $16 billion per year.[90] In early 2009, at the end of Bush's term, the United States had a force of 150,000 soldiers in Iraq at a cost of more than $10 billion per month.

Although the neoconservative campaign suffered some temporary reverses, as when the president decided to take his case for war to the UN, it ultimately attained its goal on March 19, 2003, when Bush ordered American forces to attack Iraq.

Neoconservatives and Neoliberals

The year 2003 is a good one to use for taking stock, not of the heart of the neoconservative movement, which was doing quite well, but of those who might be called "fellow travelers," liberal Democrats and intellectuals who to some extent shared the neoconservative vision of America's role in the world—those who are sometimes called "liberal hawks" or "neoliberals."

We have seen how, between 1972 and 1992, second-age neoconservatives progressively abandoned the Democratic party, especially in the "great migration" of 1980. To be sure, the Coalition for a Democratic Majority continued the struggle for the soul of the party, and the emergence of "New Democrats" under the aegis of the Democratic Leadership Council seemed to show that they had been right about the need to take the party more to the center, although the early years of the Clinton presidency tended to widen the gap between neoconservatives and Democrats, especially on military issues (the defense budget, homosexuals in the military, and so on). But neoconservatives approved of some aspects of Clinton's foreign policy: the interventions in Bosnia (even though it came too late) and Kosovo (even though it was clumsy and hesitant), the increasing insistence on the need for American leadership, the description of America as the "indispensable nation" by Secretary of State Madeleine Albright, the creation of the "community of democracies" in 2000 (in which Penn Kemble played a role). All of these were initiatives that neoconservatives approved more than they could accept the neo-isolationism of the Republicans.

The international context of the 1990s lent itself to a degree of intellectual rapprochement between neoconservatives and liberals with respect to the use of American power, helping to heal the wounds created by the Vietnam War in the 1960s. In the post–Cold War world, force turned out to be useful for stopping massacres, ethnic cleansing, and genocide, and liberals who had opposed Reagan-style militarism and the Gulf War (synonymous with oil and imperialism) found themselves supporting humanitarian intervention in the Balkans against Slobodan Milošević, since this intervention would be moral, fully justified, and conducted in a multilateral framework. This was what Paul Starobin called the new "theology of hawkish liberalism," which saw former doves such as Britain's Prime Minister Tony Blair (who had opposed Reagan's policies) and the liberal Madeleine Albright (who defended the "nuclear freeze") call upon the West to use force to prevent ethnic cleansing.[91]

As a result, while realists declined to intervene in Bosnia ("We don't have a dog in that fight," James Baker explained) and the Republican Congress feigned dovishness to make trouble for Bill Clinton, some liberals, such as Anthony Lewis of the *New York Times,* Michael Walzer of *Dissent,* and freelance journalist and policy analyst David Rieff, who described Bosnia as his generation's Spanish Civil War, along with French and German veterans of the protest movements of 1968, overcame their antimilitarist instincts to call for intervention. This put them on the side of neoconservatives, who for the most part wanted to intervene for moral and strategic reasons (as a show of force and in order to enforce the Pax Americana). The situation made for "strange bedfellows," as Norman Podhoretz put it.[92]

Typical of this convergence was the *New Republic,* which remained liberal in domestic policy and hawkish in foreign policy and soon called for America to intervene in the Balkans (and Rwanda). Led by Leon Wieseltier and Martin Peretz, soon joined by Lawrence Kaplan and Peter Beinart, the magazine attracted a group of second-age neoconservatives who had not joined the Republican party. Among politicians, Senator Bob Kerrey of Nebraska and even more Senator Joe Lieberman of Connecticut seemed to embody this tradition.[93] Lieberman was a liberal hawk, a "New Democrat" who favored intervention in the Balkans as early as 1992 and described himself as a "Harry Truman, JFK, Scoop Jackson, and Bill Clinton Democrat," adding that "I agree more often than not with Democrats on domestic policy. I agree more often than not with Republicans on foreign and defense policy."[94]

In addition to "humanitarian interventions," neoconservatives and some liberals made common cause on the Committee to Expand NATO: Will Marshall of the Progressive Policy Institute, Phil Gordon, Ron Asmus, Greg Craig, and Elaine Shokas, Madeleine Albright's chief of staff, joined Bruce Jackson, Randy Scheunemann, Richard Perle, and Paul Wolfowitz, among others. After September 11, however, these new alliances were put to the test by the interventions in Afghanistan and especially Iraq.

One group of liberals proposed an ideological interpretation of the new international situation, just as the neoconservatives did. The best known of these, Paul Berman (a member of the editorial board of *Dissent* and the author of *Terror and Liberalism,* a book about Islamist and Ba'athist ideologies, which he lumps together and treats as deriving from essentially the same European matrix) and George Packer (who edited a volume titled *The Fight Is for Democracy*), argued that the War on Terror was no different from the Cold War: it was above all a war of ideas that pitted liberal democracies against Islamism, a totalitarian ideology and Middle Eastern version of Nazism and Communism.[95] It was therefore necessary to defend freedom and wage a war of ideas in the Arab-Muslim world.

If some Democrats and liberals decided to support the intervention because of this analysis, others supported it for strategic reasons, because they believed it to be the least bad of the available solutions; one such was Kenneth Pollack of the Brookings Institution, a former National Security Council staffer under Bill Clinton, who wrote the most influential book in favor of intervention.[96] Just before the invasion, moreover, a number of Democrats (Will Marshall, Ivo Daalder, James Steinberg, Ron Asmus, and Martin Indyk), some of whom had previously opposed the war, signed a PNAC letter supporting it and joining neoconservatives in demanding a major American effort and the commitment of substantial resources to ensure a successful occupation and to rebuild ties with allies. Finally, Joe Lieberman came out in favor of war against Saddam Hussein as early as October 2001.

In the period 2002–2004 several Democrats and "neoliberals" proposed a critique of Bush's foreign policy that did not deny the ideological aspect of the War on Terror or democracy promotion, which they deemed appropriate. For instance, Will Marshall's Progressive Policy Institute, which, as we saw earlier, filled the political and ideological void left by the Coalition for a Democratic Majority after June 1989, published two texts, one in 2003 and the other in 2006, which invoked the shades of Roosevelt, Truman, and Kennedy in an effort to stake out a Democratic alternative in foreign policy.[97] The central idea was that although liberal imperialism (the active spread of democracy) was good and strong American leadership was desirable, the Bush administration had undermined these principles by its disastrous execution of the mission, most notably by acting unilaterally and ignoring nonmilitary instruments such as development aid and the war of ideas. This was more or less the thesis of Peter Beinart's book *The Good Fight,* which called upon Democrats to revive the tradition of Truman and the Cold War liberals, from the creation of Americans for Democratic Action to the early 1960s—in other words, the 2006 version of the CDM program.[98]

Indeed, this kinship casts doubt on the usefulness of the label "neoliberalism": isn't it the same thing as neoconservatism? Ron Asmus and Ken Pollack deny that this is the case: for them, neoliberals are distinguished from neoconservatives by a less systematic advocacy of the use of force, greater attention to "nation building," according greater centrality to the Israel-Palestine peace process, and of course a preference for multilateralism.[99] Nevertheless, the convergences are striking, particularly since neoconservatives adopted certain ideas emanating from the neoliberals, such as a major nonmilitary initiative to promote democracy in the Arab world, which began as a suggestion by Asmus and Pollack in 2002 and became the Bush administration's "Greater Middle East" (later rebranded "Broader Middle East and North Africa") initiative in 2004.[100] In fact, neoliberals are essentially second-age neoconservatives. This phenomenon was clearly perceived by Anatol Lieven, who recommended that "the Democratic Party should encourage these figures to take the same route to the Republican Party as their Scoop Jackson predecessors, but much more quickly, and give them a strong push along the way."[101]

Another commentator was equally harsh on "neoliberals" for their role in encouraging and legitimating the neoconservatives' agenda. Writing in 2007, Tony Smith argued that it was the former and not the latter who supplied the intellectual backbone of the Bush doctrine, at least with regard to three of its sources of inspiration.[102] The first of these was democratic peace theory, which was elaborated by liberal political scientists (such as Michael Doyle and Bruce Russett) in the 1980s and 1990s and which held that democracies did not go to war with one another— and this, as we have seen, was the heart of the Bush doctrine in the Middle East. And indeed, neoconservatives from Joshua Muravchik as early as 1991 to the PNAC did take an interest, albeit limited, in the theoretical aspects of "the democratic peace," as did the Bush administration, in an increasingly explicit manner.[103]

The second source of inspiration incorporated studies of "democratic transition," which sought to show that in the end, the transition to democracy was not as complicated as previously believed, as shown by the example of Eastern Europe in the early 1990s. Finally, the third source

was typically liberal: it was the "right," and later the "duty," to intervene, the theory of which was elaborated by Bernard Kouchner and
Mario Bettati in the late 1980s. Traditional Westphalian sovereignty,
they argued, could be challenged in cases of humanitarian emergency,
genocide, ethnic cleansing, war crimes, and so on. This view was
codified by the UN, which in 2005 approved a resolution on the "responsibility to protect." Pushing this logic to the limit, couldn't one argue that Saddam Hussein was a threat to his own people? Shouldn't he,
too, be punished by loss of his sovereignty?

There is no denying that these three intellectual developments played a
role, but probably more in explaining the weakness of liberal opposition
to the intervention in Iraq than in the construction of the Bush doctrine.
In other words, they were not so much causal factors as conditions
of possibility or acceptability. Whereas the Bush doctrine was elaborated in formal exchanges between the president, the neoconservatives
(Bill Kristol for the Second Inaugural Address, with input from George
Weigel),[104] and other conservatives (such as Michael Gerson) who spoke
more in moral or religious terms, the contribution of liberal academics—
and champions of the right of intervention—was indirect and served
mainly to deepen and bolster ideas that had formed the basis of the
neoconservative worldview since the 1970s and, even more, since the
end of the Cold War. To put it another way, although any archeology of
the Bush doctrine must include neoliberals, and although the main ideas
that made the war in Iraq possible and thinkable cannot be understood
without them, the role of neoconservatives was certainly more direct and
decisive.

From Triumph to Doubt

May 2003 was a euphoric moment: for the second time in less than two
years, the United States had overthrown a bloody dictatorship without
major difficulty. There was no question of stopping there, however—on
the contrary. While America's most perfidious allies must be treated as
they deserved ("Punish France, ignore Germany, and forgive Russia,"
as Condoleezza Rice summed up),[105] attention should now be focused
on other "rogue states." Depending on the observer, candidates for regime change included Syria and Iran, of course, but sometimes also
Hezbollah, the Palestinian Authority, or, for the most ambitious, Libya,
North Korea, and Sudan.[106] Pushing the Bush doctrine to the limit, some

neoconservatives did not hesitate to raise the issue of America's deeply ambiguous alliance with Saudi Arabia and the kingdom's role in radicalizing and financing terrorists. But such criticism was going too far, as one neoconservative, Laurent Murawiec, learned the hard way when he was fired by the RAND Corporation in the summer of 2002 for a presentation he made to the Defense Policy Board (a consulting panel employed by the Pentagon and headed at the time by Richard Perle)—a presentation that was highly critical of Saudi Arabia. This episode did not stop *Commentary* and the *Weekly Standard* from publishing articles quite critical of the Saudis, however.[107]

But this moment of euphoria and omnipotence lasted no more than a few months before succumbing to the blunders of the occupation and the intensification of the insurgency, punctuated by murderous attacks. A year to the day after George W. Bush's highly publicized landing on the deck of an aircraft carrier, where he congratulated the American military on its "mission accomplished," the first details of the Abu Ghraib scandal, involving the humiliation and torture of Iraqi prisoners, appeared in the press, while Ted Koppel, on ABC-TV, read one by one the names of the 721 soldiers killed in Iraq.

In that gloomy spring of 2004, the first regrets began to be heard from the neoconservative side. David Brooks acknowledged that the pessimists had been proved right and the optimists in the neoconservative camp proved wrong.[108] Fouad Ajami, an academic who lent weight to neoconservative arguments, was obliged to admit his errors: "We are strangers in Iraq, and we didn't know the place."[109] Somewhat earlier in 2004, Francis Fukuyama, who had silently disapproved of the war, lost patience with the arrogant and unrealistic declarations of neoconservatives, especially Charles Krauthammer in a triumphalist speech at the AEI.[110] He engaged in a polemic with Krauthammer and ultimately broke with neoconservatism, joining the ranks of the "renegades," following in the footsteps of Pat Moynihan and Michael Lind.[111]

Over the next few years, as the situation in Iraq worsened, other neoconservatives such as Kenneth Adelman and Richard Perle absolved themselves of responsibility by insisting that the overthrow of Saddam, which they had indeed advocated, had been poorly executed. Perle had this to say:

> Huge mistakes were made and I want to be very clear on this: they were not made by neoconservatives, who had almost no voice in what happened,

and certainly almost no voice in what happened after the downfall of the regime in Baghdad. I'm getting damn tired of being described as an architect of the war. I was in favor of bringing down Saddam. Nobody said, "Go design the campaign to do that." I had no responsibility for that.[112]

The guilty "architect" was actually Donald Rumsfeld, who from the beginning had shown no interest in what would happen after the invasion, which in any case he wanted to use as a showcase for the modernization of the American military. Rumsfeld, who had long been a target of neoconservative criticism, came under renewed attack from the *Weekly Standard* from 2004 until his resignation in 2006. As for neoliberals, they felt that they had been taken in. From Leon Wieseltier to Peter Beinart, many repudiated their support for the war, and the *New Republic,* which admitted errors in 2004, expressed its "deep regrets" in a 2006 editorial.[113]

In early 2009, Richard Perle went a step further in distancing himself and the neocons from the Iraq war, with a somewhat schizophrenic defense: there was "no such thing as a neoconservative foreign policy," and its influence on the Bush administration had been grossly exaggerated.[114] Trying to explain "why 50 million conspiracy theorists have it wrong," he offered a mix of good and bad arguments. Among the good arguments, he was right to deny that the neocons had ever advocated "imposing democracy by force." He was also right to point out the absence of solid documentation about the influence that neoconservative advisers had exercised over Bush or his non-neoconservative principals—a very complex task. But he also turned the role of ideology into a straw man, arguing that common-sense "risk management," rather than ideological fervor, had inspired the administration policy in the War on Terror. The argument goes only so far: pragmatic decisions are taken on the basis of representations and principles. And they were informed, in part, by the worldview offered by neocons and sometimes shared or partly shared by non-neocon hawks like Dick Cheney and Donald Rumsfeld. Perle's denial of the existence of a neoconservative school of thought in foreign policy is even more unconvincing. He argues that neoconservatism is "essentially a disposition on domestic issues, originating with liberals who had become disenchanted with the efficacy of government"— what we call first-age neoconservatism. In the past, however, far from refusing to recognize the existence of "such a thing as a Neocon attitude in the questions of foreign and defense policy" (second- and third-age neoconservatism, of which he is a prominent representative),[115] Perle had talked about it openly and explicitly, and was never on the record contesting the label when used in the realm of foreign policy about him and others.[116]

On the whole, however, neoconservatives—especially those associated with the PNAC and the *Weekly Standard*—did not try to distance themselves from the Iraq war. The fact that no weapons of mass destruction had been found in Iraq was of little import: not only had all Western countries and all American leaders agreed (to one degree or another) that they existed, but the weapons of mass destruction were surely not the only good reason to overthrow Saddam.[117] The violence in Iraq could be blamed on Rumsfeld's fecklessness, and in any case it was much overblown. Neoconservatives regularly defended the Bush administration against the pessimism and defeatism of journalists and commentators. Although they had to keep a low profile while the United States suffered reverses in the Middle East, they trumpeted moments that seemed to validate the Bush doctrine, such as Bush's reelection in November 2004 against Democrat John Kerry, the successful elections in Afghanistan (October 2004) and especially Iraq (January 2005), and the "cedar revolution" in Lebanon (February 2005), which led to the departure of Syrian forces in April. Although the PNAC shut down its operations in the summer of 2006, it did so mainly because it had achieved its goal, and the American Enterprise Institute, which had taken little interest in foreign policy in the 1990s, was back in the foreign policy game.[118]

Although President Bush's rhetoric became increasingly neoconservative in his second term, in fact he moved more toward realism and to all intents and purposes abandoned the "freedom agenda" that he had previously promoted (with respect to Egypt, for example). This shift was in large part the result of the decline of American power in the wake of the setbacks in Iraq, so that the administration was forced to make concessions on Iran and North Korea, to mention two examples. It was Condoleezza Rice, now secretary of state, who increasingly called the shots, while neoconservatives were eased out: Paul Wolfowitz became head of the World Bank, and Douglas Feith quit the Pentagon in 2005.

Although the time of bold initiatives was over, a small group of neoconservatives continued to hang on, and the president himself was not yet ready to give up on what he considered his most important initiative, the war in Iraq and the effort to transform the Middle East. Evidence for this continuing commitment can be seen in two episodes. The first occurred in the summer of 2006, when Israel launched an offensive against Hezbollah in southern Lebanon, and neoconservatives and their allies (such as Elliott Abrams, David Wurmser, and John Bolton) worked to make sure that Israel would have enough time to complete its operation.[119] Some months later, the president deliberately ignored the Baker-Hamilton report on Iraq, the fruit of the bipartisan Iraq Study Group, which recommended entering into negotiations with Syria and Iran, becoming more involved in the conflict between Israel and Palestine, and ending combat operations in order to train the Iraqi army and ultimately begin a large withdrawal of American troops.

Instead, the president chose to listen to neoconservatives and to follow the strategic recommendations of the AEI's Fred Kagan (the brother of Robert and son of Donald), who, along with retired General Jack Keane and some of the commanders on the ground (David Petraeus and Raymond Odierno), recommended a temporary increase in American troop strength in Iraq in order to restore security and create space for political reconciliation: the "surge" strategy, launched in 2007, had positive effects on the situation in Iraq.[120]

On balance, how can we sum up the influence of neoconservatives and the Bush doctrine on the position of the United States in the world and the international system? One difficulty has to do with the fact that the invasion of Iraq was indeed botched, and neoconservatives can justifiably point out that they constantly insisted on the need for more troops in order to make the occupation "successful." Another is the fact that George W. Bush always insisted that the only judgment that mattered to him was history's, not that of his contemporaries; by 2015 or 2025, people would see him not only as the liberator of Afghanistan and Iraq but also as the leader who decisively pushed the Middle East closer to a democratic transformation.[121]

This argument is specious: no one knows what the world would have looked like in 2008 had there been no intervention in Iraq, and the same is even more true for 2015 or 2025. By contrast, we can sum up the pros and cons of the situation at the end of Bush's term, and the balance at that point did not appear to be positive—except, of course, for the overthrow of the Taliban and Saddam Hussein, two intrinsically valuable accomplishments. From a geopolitical standpoint, America was able to withdraw its troops from Saudi Arabia, but it had to maintain a strong presence in Iraq, while Iran had been substantially strengthened by U.S. difficulties in Iraq and Afghanistan (both old enemies of Tehran). Between 2002 and 2009, resources had been diverted from the war in Afghanistan to the war in Iraq, and this shift had contributed to the deterioration of the Afghan situation, which by the end of Bush's term had become critical. The intervention in Iraq did nothing to advance the War on Terror or the effort to prevent proliferation—on the contrary. The invasion of Iraq became a recruiting tool for al-Qaeda, which also benefited from diminishing pressure on the Afghan front (by the end of 2008 there was no task force in charge of tracking down Bin Laden).[122] Tehran saw its leverage increased, and was able to push ahead on its nuclear program. The image of the United States in the world had seriously deteriorated since the invasion. The "empire" was less than ever seen as "benevolent." It was rather perceived as unpredictable and destabilizing—a part of the problem rather than the solution. The weakening of America had encouraged hostile states—often made more confident by the high price of petroleum—to challenge the world order. More broadly, one can argue that the war in Iraq, far from establishing the supremacy of American leadership, had accelerated the evolution toward a multipolar world.

For America itself, the cost of the war in Iraq until 2008 had been considerable, on the order of $1 trillion (and perhaps as much as $3 trillion in overall economic impact in the long run, according to Joseph Stiglitz).[123] Iraqi victims numbered in the tens of thousands, while more than 4,000 Americans had been killed and 30,000 wounded. Furthermore, although the situation in Iraq was somewhat calmer as a result of the "surge" of 2007 and other factors, there was no assurance that progress would continue. Efforts at democracy promotion in the region, far from being spurred by the invasion, were discredited by association with the war, generating a backlash that has strengthened authoritarian regimes.[124] Politically speaking, setbacks in foreign policy contributed heavily to the decline of the Republican party after 2006, and some have even speculated that Iraq could have the same effect on the Republicans that Vietnam had on the Democrats.

But what went wrong? Where did the neoconservatives of the third age, the neocons, go astray?

The Shortcomings of the Neocon Vision

Neoconservatives have been the victims of so many exaggerations and conspiracy theories that we must begin by repeating the obvious: they were merely one source of inspiration among others for a complex, multifarious policy that was shaped largely by the course of events. In other words, it makes no sense to attribute all the failings of the Bush administration to the neocons. To the extent that they did have a voice, however, and a voice that counted, we can try to pinpoint their errors of judgment.

The most surprising of the neoconservatives' errors has to do with the conditions under which American power is exercised, a subject that has been one of their central concerns. But perhaps it was precisely because neoconservatism stemmed from a patriotic reaction to the denigration of America and because it enjoyed a victory of sorts and therefore validation with the fall of the Berlin Wall that it was condemned to see the world of the twenty-first century through an overconfident and distorting prism. That prism left the neocons unable to see the limits of America's actual capacity to engineer positive change and its room for maneuver in the world. Or perhaps third-age neoconservatism was merely the intellectual expression of the considerable increase in the relative power of the United States, of the illusion, especially after the intoxicating victory in Afghanistan, that America could do anything. In that case, neoconservative hubris was largely the result of a rationalization of America's position in the international system. After all, the argument that the American empire is "benevolent" does have merit, at least until it is invoked as a pretext to exempt the United States from rules of prudence and cooperation, or even to ignore the opinions and interests of the rest of the world.

There was no shortage of arrogance in the neocon approach. Intellectual arrogance to begin with, in spite of the movement's origins: whatever became of the law of unintended consequences? It vanished behind a feeling of omnipotence, which suggested—exaggerating only slightly—that America could change the course of history in the Middle East and usher the Arab world into modernity. And it was replaced by the intellectually problematic claim that the status quo in the region was more dangerous and more costly than change—even violent change—would be. It will come as no surprise that conservatives were driven to apoplexy by the insolence and rashness of the neocons, by their readiness to play the role of social engineers and sorcerer's apprentice. Political arrogance was also in abundant supply. "Lead, and they will follow" was the slogan first of the neoconservatives and then of the Bush administration for dealing with allies. But manly, confident assertion of objectives was not enough to persuade the other members of the international community that those objectives were justified, and there were limits to what America could do alone. Military arrogance was also involved: no army has ever been better prepared than the American armed forces to destroy a conventional enemy, but it struggled with guerrilla warfare and the challenges of reconstruction. It must be said that neocons, to their credit, never minimized the effort that it would take to conduct an imperial policy. But that admission in turn leads to a questioning of the seriousness of policy recommendations that could not be backed up by the American public. Finally, the cliché that a show of force is enough to convince the enemy to give up or at least respect the superior force—a notion that many neoconservatives shared with other hawks—turned out to be quite naïve.

This arrogance was intimately related to one trait of neoconservatism that is part of the "American national style" in general: the underestimation of nationalism as an important political force—meaning both the nationalism of the United States, which blinds Americans, and the nationalism of other countries, manifested, for instance, in the reaction of Iraqis to the invasion of their country.[125] "There was a failure to understand the effect our power would have on other people around the world," admitted David Brooks in 2004. "We were so sure we were using our might for noble purposes, we assumed that sooner or later, everybody else would see that as well."[126] This self-righteousness, and its use to justify exemption from the rules that apply to others, gives rise to paranoid or even just plain nationalist reactions in other countries. And it creates a vicious circle: since the United States does good, it ought not to be bound by the same rules as the rest of the world. The problem, of course, is that the rest of the world doesn't see it that way.

The neocons' vision suffered from another sin: intellectual laziness. The Cold War world was complicated, and the post–Cold War world even more so. When Richard Perle spoke of Albert Wohlstetter, he explained that his teacher, trained in mathematics, was a rigorous thinker: "For Albert, it was just impermissible to assume anything. You had to run down every fact, every proposition. He was a mathematical logician by training."[127] It is hard to avoid the conclusion that Wohlstetter's disciples did not learn the lesson—or did not apply it to Iraq.

For an anecdotal but interesting example of this lack of rigor, consider the support that Paul Wolfowitz, Richard Perle, and James Woolsey offered to Laurie Mylroie, an AEI researcher with an increasing weakness for conspiracy theory.[128] After the 1993 attack on the World Trade Center, Mylroie became convinced that Saddam Hussein had ordered it, along with all the subsequent attacks, including the 1995 Oklahoma City bombing (which was in fact perpetrated by Americans opposed to the federal government), as well as the September 11 attacks and the envelopes containing anthrax that were sent through the mail a few weeks later. There was nothing absurd about the initial suspicion, since Saddam had indeed ordered an attack on Bush Sr. in 1993, but there was no tangible proof of the rest, only some extremely tenuous arguments. Intelligence professionals quickly reached a consensus that there was no tie between Iraq and al-Qaeda. But that conclusion did not stop Mylroie from publishing, in 2000, a book elaborating her fantastic hypotheses, a book on which Wolfowitz and Perle heaped praise.[129] Woolsey agreed, remarking on the back cover that "a thorough, incisive, solitary scholar can be worth far more than battalions of bureaucrats," after which Wolfowitz sent him on a special mission to the United Kingdom in late 2001 to check on one of Mylroie's allegations. Of course, some neoconservatives wanted to believe the story because it supported their political designs and served as anti-Saddam propaganda. But what would "Albert" have said?

He probably would have been equally dissatisfied with the intellectual laziness evident in the analysis of a fundamental aspect of the War on Terror: the nature of the struggle and of the people involved in it. Not only did neoconservatives miss the terrorist threat, which caught them by surprise (*pace* Roberta Wohlstetter), but after September 11 they continued to analyze the threat at the state level, where they were on more familiar ground. For instance, they made it their goal to attack states that harbored terrorists without trying to understand the peculiar logic of al-Qaeda's deterritorialized terrorism. Indeed, many neocons— as well as neoliberals such as Paul Berman—deliberately confused distinct groups: the radical Sunnis of al-Qaeda, the Shi'ites of Iran and Hezbollah, and the "fascists" of the Ba'ath party, who were secular. By combining these distinct groups into a single mortal enemy of the United States, they overlooked ways of fighting "terror" more effectively. Furthermore, the insistence on "moral clarity" did not always encourage the search for various shades of gray, which might have proved useful in the battle against terrorist groups.[130]

This complex of limitations brings us to another fundamental problem of third-age neoconservatism: the lack of regional expertise concerning the Middle East. In the United States, this field of study has suffered immeasurably from disputes stemming from the conflict between Israel and the Palestinians. When Richard Perle argued that the persistent failure of the U.S. approach toward the Middle East "stems from both the curious ideas about American leadership and the abysmal state of expertise that are held by many regional specialists, particularly in our intelligence community,"[131] he was repeating a standard refrain according to which these specialists were prisoners of pro-Arab, anti-Israeli, anti-American, and generally leftist prejudices. In his pamphlet *Ivory Towers on Sand,* Martin Kramer attacked American academic experts (and especially Edward Said, who died in September 2003) for not having understood the way in which the Arab-Muslim world had evolved over the past several decades, specifically with regard to the persistence of authoritarian regimes and the constant rise of Islamism.[132] Subsequently, the right developed its own alternative set of experts, mainly associated with the *Middle East Quarterly,* a journal founded in 1994 by Daniel Pipes, the son of Richard (whose orbit included Michael Rubin, Bernard Lewis, Fouad Ajami, Patrick Clawson, and, of course, Martin Kramer).

In addition to the very small number of neoconservatives familiar with the region, such as Michael Rubin and Reuel Gerecht, and the generally limited knowledge of the "complicated Orient," another factor was that expert advice was politicized, militant, and often focused on Israel. The Jewish state, as we have seen, had been important to neoconservatives as far back as the 1960s. As the Middle East became central to America's geopolitical concerns, unconditional support for Israel became increasingly decisive in their approach to international affairs. Seeing the Middle East through "Israeli lenses" led to a distortion of perspective that caused them to underestimate the importance of the Palestinian quest for nationhood in the region's troubles and to mistake the nature of America's enemies.

In this regard, the polemic in 2002 between columnist Robert Novak (a libertarian conservative who was close to the paleoconservatives, skeptical about the presence of weapons of mass destruction in Iraq, and strongly opposed to intervention) and David Frum is quite revealing. Novak wrote approvingly of Nebraska Senator Chuck Hagel's statement that, contrary to what neoconservatives were arguing, "the road to Jerusalem does not pass through Baghdad," meaning that the fall of Saddam Hussein was not a prerequisite for solving the Palestinian problem. Most importantly, he criticized Condoleezza Rice for saying that Hezbollah, and not al-Qaeda, was "the most dangerous terrorist organization in the world."[133] Although Rice was not necessarily wrong in absolute terms, it was difficult, especially at that moment, not to see al-Qaeda as the most dangerous organization from an American, rather than Israeli, standpoint; and this was why Novak attacked the Bush policy as "Israel-centric." A few months later, David Frum retorted in a violent article charging Novak with "terror denial," defeatism, and lack of patriotism, as well as rampant antisemitism (for blaming 9/11 on America's support for Israel).[134]

Lawrence Kaplan and others were right to point out that neoconservatives supported interventions to defend Muslims in Somalia, Bosnia, and Kosovo; and, once again, Zionism is not the right key to understanding them.[135] Nevertheless, in their intellectual and political approach to the Middle East, the close alliance with Israel often led them to identify the Jewish's state's struggle with that of the United States: the same enemy (Islamic terrorists), the same tactics (preventive war, unilateralism, "show of force"), and the same cause ("they hate us for what we are"). This perspective was not analytically sound. Although it was normal for America to worry about the fate of a close ally, this undue identification with Israel and the tendency to see things through an Israeli prism undoubtedly helped to create an inaccurate picture of the region and led to unrealistic policy recommendations, opening the United States to accusations of hypocrisy and condemning the "transformation of the Middle East" to being nothing but wishful thinking.

One unfortunate episode in that transformation—the January 27, 2006, elections to the Palestinian Council—illustrates one final problem inherent in the neoconservative vision and the Bush doctrine, namely, democratic dogmatism, yet another consequence of intellectual laziness. Democracy was supposed to bring peace and justice, but these elections put Hamas in power and precipitated a protracted crisis with Israel while doing great damage to the United States, which could not recognize these "democratic" results. Not only was democracy not a magic wand, but implanting it was not as simple as some neoconservatives—as well as neoliberals such as Larry Diamond—sometimes described it.[136]

"You hear people mock [the objective of establishing democracy in Iraq] by saying that Iraq isn't ready for Jeffersonian democracy," Wolfowitz says, citing a line that Colin Powell has been known to use. "Well, Japan isn't Jeffersonian democracy, either. I think the more we are committed to influencing the outcome, the more chance there could be that it would be something quite significant for Iraq. And I think if it's significant for Iraq, it's going to cast a very large shadow, starting with Syria and Iran, but across the whole Arab world, I think."[137]

The idealism, the naïveté, of some neoconservatives was partly the result of a simplistic conception of democracy, as revealed by another quote from Wolfowitz: "Export of democracy isn't really a good phrase," he was right to protest in 2004. But then he went on: "We're trying to remove the shackles on democracy."[138] The underlying assumption was that democracy is the default regime, which emerges spontaneously when a tyrant is overthrown. In this case, beyond the democratic dogmatism, we again encounter two problems with the thought of the neocons: their lack of knowledge of Iraq and the region (which led, for instance, to unduly optimistic predictions about the unlikelihood of civil war) and their tendency to minimize the impact of American military action.

In the end, no matter what pinnacle of power America had achieved, there was no escaping the complexity attached to wielding that power. The Lilliputians may have been wrong to want to tie Gulliver down, but those who preached that the giant should be unbound did not adequately anticipate the dilemmas that his uninhibited behavior would raise in a complex world. Perhaps they had too much confidence in him—and in themselves.

The Resilience of Neoconservatism

Ten years after neoconservatism was declared dead even by its "fathers," the assumption was largely shared around 2006 that the movement had been so discredited by the failure of the Iraq war that it would never recover. Yet the fact remains that today evidence of its death is scarce, and there are many reasons to consider it still a potent force in Washington, only waiting for a more favorable political environment in which to exert its influence on American foreign policy again.

It can even be argued that neocons have won the battle against their archenemies, the realists, for the soul of the Republican party, and for dominance in the Washington foreign policy community. Two of the leading candidates for the 2008 presidential nomination, Rudy Giuliani and John McCain, had many neoconservative advisers on their staffs.

Senator McCain, who ultimately won the nomination, relied on Randy Scheunemann to head his foreign policy team, which included Robert Kagan, Max Boot, Gary Schmitt, and James Woolsey. As we have seen, McCain had already been the neoconservatives' first choice in 2000. During the 2008 campaign he took a very hard line on the Iranian nuclear program, recommended the creation of a "league of democracies" (an idea that had surfaced in neoconservative circles in the 1970s), advocated the expulsion of Moscow from the G8, and declared that "we are all Georgians" when Russian forces invaded the little Caucasian country in August 2008.[139]

Beyond presidential politics, basic political attitudes within the Republican party seem to have aligned, if not with the neocons per se, at least with a hawkish and interventionist version of foreign policy, while Democrats and independents seem to have remained firmly in the realist camp. For example, according to a Pew poll in 2009, a majority of Democrats say that decreasing the U.S. military presence overseas (62 percent) and stepping up diplomatic efforts in Muslim countries (57 percent), a combination that can be described as close to the prescriptions of the realists (as expressed in the Baker-Hamilton commission, for example), would have a greater impact than military action in reducing the terrorist threat. Republicans disagree: 62 percent say that increasing the U.S. military presence abroad is the right answer, while only 22 percent think that stepping up diplomatic efforts will change anything—a combination that reflects the view of hawks and neocons.[140]

This result indicates that the effort mounted by the *Weekly Standard* and the PNAC in the 1990s—to steer Republicans away from their isolationism and convert them to interventionism—has succeeded, whether because of their efforts or by virtue of September 11 and the War on Terror. As a powerful symbol of this success, former vice-president Dick Cheney, a close ally of the neocons, is on record as having questioned whether Colin Powell, his former colleague in the Bush administration and a leading realist, was still a Republican, saying he thought Powell "had already left the party."[141]

More importantly still, the real source of power of the neoconservative movement over its three ages, the mostly Washington-based network of like-minded magazines, think tanks, committees, journalists, and intellectuals, is thriving. Neocons are still dominant at the American Enterprise Institute, the Hudson Institute, in *Commentary,* the *Weekly Standard,* and the editorial pages of the *Wall Street Journal.* Their views are present in the editorial pages of the *Washington Post* (where Bill Kristol and Robert Kagan each has a monthly column, and Charles Krauthammer a weekly one), in the *National Review,* the *New Republic,* and many other publications.

The neocons' firepower also draws upon the views of younger men and women, and it is regenerating itself. Members of the nonpartisan Council on Foreign Relations, for example, include not only Elliott Abrams, born in the late 1940s, but also Max Boot, born in the late 1960s, and the adjunct senior fellow Dan Senor, born in the early 1970s. In 2008 Lawrence Kaplan launched a new magazine, *World Affairs,* which is not exclusively neoconservative (its editorial board is ideologically diverse), but which does feature many neocons and neoliberals like Joshua Muravchik, Peter Beinart, Christopher Hitchens, and Reuel Gerecht. Better still, in 2009 Bill Kristol, Robert Kagan, and Dan Senor launched a new organization, the Foreign Policy Initiative, which is strikingly reminiscent of the Project for the New American Century. It is a very small but vocal organization mostly writing open letters to the president signed by neocons and sometimes liberals or neoliberals.[142] Staffed by young operatives (including Jamie Fly, Dan Senor, Rachel Hoff, Daniel Halper, etc.), it is fighting isolationist tendencies on both sides of the spectrum (on Afghanistan, for example), advocating a higher defense budget and a hawkish stance on most issues, and promoting a robust support for democracy and human rights abroad—in other words, the same program articulated by Bill Kristol and Robert Kagan in their 1996 *Foreign Affairs* article, "Toward a Neo-Reaganite Foreign Policy," only expressed differently: "strategic overreach is not the problem and retrenchment is not the solution."[143]

The realist school of foreign policy, which was first challenged by the Scoop Jackson Democrats (the second-age neoconservatives) in the early 1970s, also has its magazines and think tanks, most notably *The National Interest*—ironically created by Irving Kristol in 1985—which is published by the Nixon Center. It has prestigious figureheads like Brent Scowcroft, James Baker, Colin Powell, and Richard Haass, and academic commentators or talented bloggers like Stephen Walt, Andrew Bacevich, and Andrew Sullivan. They might be virtually dominant, in the sense that their views are closer than the neocons' to those of the Obama administration and tend to be more acceptable to mainstream elite opinion. But neocons tend to dominate the debate in the Republican party (all the more easily because President Obama is taking a realist and pragmatist approach to international affairs), as well as on the intellectual scene. In 2008, for example, Robert Kagan's book *The Return of History and the End of Dreams,* which described the emerging international situation as a struggle between the forces of democracy and the enduring forces of autocracies (led by China and Russia), was one of the most influential books in the United States and beyond, six years after his article "Power and Weakness," however misguided, had redefined the debate on transatlantic relations.[144]

Neocons are not only still present on the Washington scene; they are also launching new magazines and organizations and articulating policy recommendations for the future, because they believe that they can rely on a version of history that validates their vision. This phenomenon provides the best indication of the continued resilience of neoconservatism: the existence of a narrative buttressing the neocon view of the world and policy prescriptions. As we have seen, neoconservative historiography was already rich at the end of the Cold War. In the 1930s Churchill had been right and appeasers wrong. In the 1970s the supporters of confrontation and rearmament had been right and the supporters of détente wrong; the fall of South Vietnam could have been avoided if the Democratic Congress had not cut and run, and the phenomena of the boat people and the autogenocide in Cambodia could have been avoided. The "neoconservative Reagan" had been right, and the critics of Star Wars, the "evil empire" rhetoric, and the support for the "freedom fighters" had been wrong, as attested by Reagan's victory in the Cold War.[145]

Other highly debatable "lessons of history" were added to the neocon narrative in the third age.[146] The interventions in Bosnia and Kosovo in the 1990s proved that America remained the indispensable nation and that military force worked. The invasion of Iraq in 2003 was more costly and difficult than first hoped, but it eventually turned the country into a stable democracy. The military surge of 2007, vociferously opposed by liberals and realists, and imposed by a valiant White House, turned the situation around, proving that sending more troops, not retreating, was the right decision. The forced regime change in Iraq led a scared Libya to abandon its WMD program in late 2003. It ushered in a new era of democratic movements in the Middle East, especially in Lebanon, and replaced a deadly status quo by a democratic wave that will ultimately prevail, restoring George W. Bush to his rightful place in history.

Neocons can continue to boast a vibrant intellectual network, a capacity to influence the public debate, a clear vision of America's role in the world—and this vision is grounded in an increasingly large historiography of their own. To influence American foreign policy again, all they need is the alignment of a mobilized and interventionist public opinion and a sympathetic administration, as in 1980–1985 and 2001–2005. Given the cyclical character of American foreign policy, such a moment will probably present itself again in the next decades.

EPILOGUE:
INTERPRETING NEOCONSERVATISM

The question of the future of neoconservatism largely depends on the interpretation one gives of the movement—and on whether one believes in the existence of an "essence" of neoconservatism beyond the historical vagaries of a label whose meaning very quickly outstripped its etymology.

The warning issued at the beginning of this book needs to be repeated here: neoconservatism is such a diverse thing that the term has always been close to meaningless. It will therefore come as no surprise to learn that multiple and contradictory interpretations have been proposed, most of them focusing on whatever aspect of the movement has seemed most important to the interpreter. The more specific and firmly grounded the interpretation (for example, defining neoconservatism as the intellectual expression of a particular sociological profile), the less likely it is, as a matter of logic, to enlighten us about the movement as a whole. Conversely, the more general the interpretation ("neoconservatives are former leftists who turned to the right"), the less it helps us to grasp the specificity and substance of neoconservatism.

Let us begin, then, by eliminating interpretations that I take to be fundamentally erroneous. For instance, a veritable industry has grown up around the role of the philosopher Leo Strauss as the inspiration of neoconservatives.[1] This interpretation does not work. For a small number of neoconservatives, Strauss was a meaningful influence, but not more important than others. For instance, although Paul Wolfowitz took two courses with Strauss himself at the University of Chicago (on Plato and Montesquieu), the courses that really excited him—and did more to shape his view of the world—were Albert Wohlstetter's on strategy. This fact leads us to an unexpected and indirect but ultimately more convincing interpretation of the role of Strauss. In their youth, a number of future neoconservatives of the second and third ages were attracted to study political philosophy with Strauss or his disciples, the Straussians (Allan Bloom at Cornell being the most celebrated). But whether out of personal inclination or a desire to gain knowledge of political realities or because they encountered a charismatic teacher (such as Albert Wohlstetter at Chicago, Sam Huntington at Harvard, and Myron Rush at Cornell) or perhaps simply to get academic credits from a different discipline, many also took classes in security studies and ended up making their careers in that field.[2]

Even more compelling is the fact that Strauss always insisted on remaining aloof from the politics of his time (he witnessed the collapse of the Weimar Republic in Germany before emigrating to the United States) and almost never made statements about the issues of the day. He was a complex thinker who insisted on the importance of studying premodern philosophers, and there are in his work at most a few points that one might mention as having influenced some neoconservatives: his insistence on distinguishing among political regimes (and in particular on calling tyranny by its name), his critique of historicism and relativism, his wariness of liberal internationalism, and his emphasis on the importance of patriotism. On the other hand, nothing was more foreign to his thinking than the idea of global promotion of democracy by the United States.

Furthermore, although some neoconservatives did do doctoral theses in political philosophy with Straussians—Bill Kristol, for example, worked on the *Federalist Papers* at Harvard under Harvey Mansfield— most believe that although Strauss is "compatible and consonant" with neoconservatism, "he is not necessary," in Kristol's words, to understand it, much less to understand its approach to foreign policy.[3] As for Robert Kagan, arguably the most influential neocon intellectual, he is even more blunt on the subject: "I just want to make clear that I am not a Straussian. Not that there's anything wrong with that. Some of my closest friends are Straussians, and I have long admired the work of Allan Bloom, Harry Jaffa, Harvey Mansfield, and Thomas Pangle—though not, I must say, Leo Strauss himself, since I have never understood a word the political philosopher wrote. I mean not a single word."[4]

Kagan explains that his views were shaped by those of his father, a historian like him, who argued endlessly with his Cornell colleague Allan Bloom on Strauss's interpretation of Plato's *Republic*. Kagan father and son deem Straussians to be fundamentally wrong because they are ahistorical, believing that "the great thinkers [are] engaged in a dialogue with one another across time. This [makes] them slight the historical circumstances in which great thinkers did their thinking."[5]

A second unconvincing interpretation holds that neoconservatism is "in essence" a Jewish movement. This is based on the observation that a majority of neoconservatives are Jews. There are several problems with this analysis. As we have seen, many of the most prominent neoconservatives are not Jewish, and the overwhelming majority of American Jews are not neoconservatives. Jews are disproportionately represented in almost all left and liberal political movements in the United States, as well as among intellectuals. These are well-established facts of political life in America since the turn of the twentieth century. In fact, only the white-supremacist extreme right (Kevin McDonald in *Occidental Quarterly*, for example) pushes this ethnic logic to its conclusion by considering neoconservatism as one possible expression of Jewishness.[6] Certain paleoconservatives associated with Pat Buchanan use similar reasoning in a more implicit and less forthright way so as to protect themselves against charges of antisemitism. Analogous conspiracy theories can also be found on the extreme left (among followers of Lyndon LaRouche, for example).[7]

Other commentators are more subtle, and free of any possible anti-semitic motives, in identifying the underground links between Jews and the neoconservative movement. To begin with, Jews were overrepresented in the ranks of the extreme left in the 1930s and 1940s, for many had brought their ideology with them from Europe. And quite a few socialist and Trotskyist intellectuals later moved to the right for reasons we explored earlier, so they logically made up a large portion of deradicalized intellectuals. A second line of argument notes the anti-Zionist (and in some cases antisemitic) turn taken by some leftist liberals and radicals in the 1960s. Among traditional Cold War liberals, Jews reacted against this more strongly than non-Jews, and in the process moved to the right. A third factor was the recognition of the fragility of all democracies and therefore the importance of American military power after the shock of the Six-Day War in 1967. The United States was the only power in the world capable of protecting Israel and other free nations, and this perception led some Jews to adopt a generally hawkish stance in foreign policy.

One additional factor has also been proposed: the possible impact in the 1960s of the growing awareness of the Holocaust and of new interpretations, most notably Hannah Arendt's, of the history of the Jews of Europe and Russia in the nineteenth and twentieth centuries. History showed that traditional elites had protected the Jews against populist movements, the "masses," and nationalist and other passions, at least until those elites were delegitimized by the political and social upheavals of their time.[8] From this it followed that the best way for Jews to protect themselves was to work to strengthen the foundations of the established order and to beware of revolutionaries. In other words, they should forge alliances with conservatives.

More recently, Jacob Heilbrunn has argued that the particular mentality of American Jews in the twentieth century and their reaction to the Holocaust provide the main explanation for neoconservatism, which he takes to be "a Jewish phenomenon."[9] As he sees it, the lesson of the Shoah—"Never again!"—led American Jews to support American power as the ultimate rampart against totalitarianism in all its forms (fascism, Nazism, communism, Islamism), for in the end, whatever form it may take, totalitarianism always turns against the Jews. The problem with this interpretation is that it fails to explain why the vast majority of American Jews, far from embracing neoconservatism, have remained liberals; nor does it explain why non-Jews became neoconservatives. Furthermore, the Holocaust had enormous influence on the worldviews of any number of American leaders, both Jewish and non-Jewish (including Richard Holbrooke, Madeleine Albright, and Scoop Jackson), yet not all of them became neoconservatives. Conversely, when Paul Wolfowitz returned from a trip to Warsaw, during which he had passed through the Umschlagplatz, where members of his father's family had probably been held on their way to the gas chambers of Treblinka, he was asked whether the Shoah occupied a central place in his vision of the world: his answer was no.[10] It is of course true that many third-age neoconservatives (such as Richard Perle, David Wurmser, Douglas Feith, and Elliott Abrams) were close to Israel's Likud party, but their hard Zionist positions, which were not shared by all neoconservatives, cannot by themselves explain the neoconservative worldview.

Heilbrunn is on more solid ground, however, when he develops the sociological part of his interpretation, which meshes with that of any number of other commentators to yield a far more convincing though still incomplete explanation. Who, after all, are the neoconservatives? Not simply men of the left who evolved toward the right as they grew older or who, in Irving Kristol's famous phrase, were "mugged by reality." Their sociological profile is richer and more specific. Sidney Blumenthal, who focused primarily on first-age neoconservatism, points to a threefold alienation: personal, professional, and political.[11]

The individuals in question were mostly second-generation Jewish immigrants caught between two cultures, torn between their American identities and their Jewish roots in Eastern Europe, which they wanted to put behind them by adopting a compensatory patriotic "Americanism." They were also among the first American Jews to attain the upper reaches of the academic world, because quotas limiting the presence of Jews in Ivy League universities (Norman Podhoretz entered Columbia in 1946 under a Jewish quota of 17 percent)[12] were gradually eliminated over the 1950s and 1960s. Just as they conquered these new realms and achieved the rank of professor in the great WASP universities, the student revolt turned their campuses upside down. The students—most of whom came from the middle and upper classes and had not lived through the Depression—repudiated their teachers and proposed radical critiques of the world of knowledge that these Jews, many of them from poor families in Brooklyn, had idealized and worked so hard to conquer. Nathan Glazer attests to this portrait: "We could not assuage student disorder by reminding students that they were the most fortunate of generations in the most idyllic of places (which they, of course, already knew). The student revolt spread from Berkeley to Columbia, where Dan Bell taught, and to many other college campuses. It was a disorder that made no sense to those of us who had come from harder circumstances."[13]

Finally, there was political alienation: in the mid-1960s, just when they thought they had secured a place in the administration of generous and progressive liberalism in the tradition of the New Deal, Truman, and Kennedy, they were displaced by the forces of the "New Politics." Radicals and minorities (blacks, women, Latinos) captured the Democratic party and subverted its meritocratic principles—for instance, by insisting on proportional representation for minorities. In other words, neoconservatism was first and foremost an attempt by certain Jewish intellectuals to rationalize their threefold alienation. It was a vague, essentially defensive doctrine elaborated in opposition to an even more generous and progressive view of what liberalism meant: following a classic pattern of political sociology, the last to be admitted to society's elite ranks attempted to shut the door behind them.

This interpretation accounts for an important aspect of neoconservatism, but only in the early years of its history. Michael Lind offers a variation on this sociological theme that allows us to go a little further.[14] Lind, a former neoconservative who quit the movement when it took a pro-Likud turn and allied itself with Zionist Christian fundamentalists in the 1990s, argues that neoconservatism was largely the fruit of a reaction against the northeastern WASP establishment by those whom it excluded: not only New York Jews but also certain Catholics (such as Pat Moynihan, Michael Novak, Richard Neuhaus, and William Bennett) and certain New Deal liberals from the South and Southwest (such as Jeane Kirkpatrick, James Woolsey, Penn Kemble, and Lind himself).[15] Indeed, one finds virtually no neoconservatives from the Protestant establishment of the Northeast. Taking this observation as his starting point, Lind describes a reaction of these social minorities against the establishment and the creation of a counterestablishment, which would ultimately bring them to power in the 1980s.

Given that neoconservatism is an intellectual and political phenomenon, however, should we not look for intellectual and political rather than sociological and identity-related causes? In this respect, possible interpretations depend on the position one takes on two fundamental questions.

The first of these questions centers upon the following question: Was neoconservatism a pure reaction, a repudiation, or was it a positive innovation, the creation of a new school of thought? Both interpretations are plausible. Neoconservatism was clearly a reaction to certain American political phenomena: the student protest, the counterculture, the New Left, the failures of the war on poverty, the violent and sectarian excesses of the black movement, the policy of détente with the Soviet Union, and, more generally, the evolution—or, rather, evolutions—of liberalism, which carried the Democratic party in their wake. Neoconservatism was born of a rejection of those evolutions and fed on their persistence, as well as their novel manifestations in the 1970s and 1980s, and it took up new issues only to counter innovations on the liberal side. To put it in more political terms, neoconservatism might be described as the intellectual manifestation of the "silent majority," the sophisticated version of white middle-class America's reaction to the upheavals of the 1960s. This basically negative interpretation poses a problem, however:

the phenomena against which neoconservatism was reacting steadily declined in importance on the American—and obviously on the international—scene in the 1980s and 1990s, yet it survived them.

Did it, then, have a dynamic of its own? In the second interpretation, neoconservatism did indeed begin as an opponent of liberalism gone awry, but it subsequently acquired a momentum of its own and developed into an innovative school of thought with its own philosophical and political antecedents. It offered an original and purely American vision of the world and a distinctive approach to social and political realities, a compound of skepticism and moralism. In foreign policy, it represented a combination of the Wilsonian and Jacksonian traditions that survived the demise of the Communist enemy that had once defined it.[16] Clearly, these two interpretations can ultimately be combined: neoconservatism arose in reaction to the failures of liberalism, became stronger each time liberals overreached, and developed a set of ideas that transcended its oppositional and reactionary reflexes. Although it never became a full-fledged political doctrine in its own right, it was more than a rejection of liberalism.

The second fundamental question is the following: Does neoconservatism belong to the history of liberalism or to the history of conservatism? In one sense, it can be interpreted as one of the possible ways in which liberalism could have evolved, a strain of liberalism that lost the battle for the label "liberal." The "vital center" liberalism of the 1940s and 1950s was not left-wing in orientation and was in some respects socially cautious if not downright conservative; it coexisted, moreover, with the left wing of the party, which wanted to accelerate the process of reform. In the 1960s the left wing eventually prevailed, taking the very definition of liberalism with it. But those who remained faithful to the "vital center," to the mixture of anticommunism abroad and traditional social progress at home, could rightfully claim to have descended from the anticommunist, antifascist New Deal liberalism of the 1930s, even though some of them felt obliged to become Republicans, at least in regard to foreign policy.

Conversely, Irving Kristol saw neoconservatism solely as an integral component of the conservative renaissance in the United States. As usual with Kristol, this interpretation seems somewhat idiosyncratic and self-serving. Nevertheless, he convinced many scholars that American conservatism, which William Buckley "invented" in 1955 with the *National Review*, underwent a second birth when Jewish intellectuals finally took an interest in it, raising its intellectual level above the mediocre and broadening what was originally a very narrow provincial outlook (before undergoing a third "birth" with the arrival of the Christian right).[17] In place of the original conservative ideology of free markets and unbridled capitalism, which was utopian and not very popular, neoconservatism provided the veritable ideological infrastructure of conservatism and enabled it to prevail intellectually. It also allowed Republicans to replace Democrats as the "party of ideas."

Kristol's interpretation is the history of the winner: there is no doubt that neoconservatism today looks more like a branch of conservatism than a branch of liberalism, at any rate on domestic issues. On foreign affairs, however, things look different: the neoconservatives' Wilsonianism, their moralism, their penchant for upsetting the status quo, and their defense, for foreign policy reasons, of a strong state with a powerful military—all these are traits that neoconservatives share more with liberals than with conservatives. After all, as a philosophy, the default position of conservatism in foreign policy tends to be isolationist (as the Republican party was until the 1940s), or, when isolationism is no longer tenable, it tends to be realist and prudent, not to say cynical, rather than interventionist.

Which leads us to another interpretation of neoconservatism, based solely on its foreign policy aspects, and thus concerned with the second and above all the third ages of the movement. One can see neoconservatism as an avatar of American messianism, as the expression of an underlying nationalism that has been present since the country was born, a reincarnation of Wilsonianism in a new, more martial form. Owing to American exceptionalism ("a city on a hill"), the United States has swung from protection to projection, from isolationism (synonymous with preserving the American model) to imperialism (synonymous with extending the model around the world). See in this light, neoconservatism is above all a sign of the resurgence of this nationalist—but also universalist—faith, on the model of French Jacobin nationalism, an offshoot of the French Revolution of 1789, which was mixed with a universalist credo.

This explanation points us toward the most persuasive overall interpretation of the various facets and ages of the movement: neoconservatism is fundamentally a manifestation of patriotism or even nationalism. First-age neoconservatism was in essence a reaction against the perceived drift of liberalism in the 1960s, against the challenge that

America's children had thrown down to their society and its system, and against the systematic denigration of America that accompanied the protests of the New Left. Similarly, the second age was above all a repudiation of the defeatism that followed the Vietnam War and the attacks on America's moral character that went with it. It sought to replenish the nation's energy, to defend the country, and to reaffirm its values—values that were incompatible with accommodation with the enemy (Kissinger's détente) but fully consonant with human rights and freedom, the values of all humanity. Finally, the third age expanded America's defense of its interests and of democracy to include its active promotion, in a more malleable international context that saw America dominant as never before. It exalted national greatness and made what George W. Bush called the "transformative power of freedom" one of the guiding principles of U.S. foreign policy, while looking to foreign crusades to strengthen citizen virtues at home.

Seeing neoconservatism as a form of nationalism only strengthens the likelihood that it will remain an intellectual political force of some importance on the American scene and that it will someday make its influence felt once more, even though its fortunes now seem on the decline. Although it will always remain a minority school of thought, it resonates with certain deep currents in the American psyche, has a simple and powerful message, and is borne by a historical vision that justifies it in the eyes of those who want to believe. In short, neoconservatism has a future.

APPENDIX

NOTES

INDEX

APPENDIX

THE THREE AGES OF NEOCONSERVATISM

People mentioned in this table do not necessarily consider themselves neoconservatives.

Age and general agenda	Positioning, heroes, and adversaries	Center of gravity, key words, and campaigns
First age (1965–1990s) **"The Neoconservatives"**	A branch of liberalism, a faction still located on the left	Domestic policy
Reaction to leftward evolution of American liberalism, to counterculture, to 1960s protests, and to failures of social engineering	*Heroes:* Alexis de Tocqueville Lionel Trilling Sidney Hook	*Key words:* "Law of unintended consequences" "New class" "Adversary culture" "Deradicalization"
	Adversaries: Students for a Democratic Society Tom Hayden Free Speech Movement Irving Howe Michael Harrington *Ramparts* *New York Review of Books* *Dissent* Black Panthers	*Campaigns:* Against New Left Against counterculture Against feminism Against ecology
Second Age (1972–1992) **Scoop Jackson Democrats**	Centrist family of Democratic party, then shift to Reagan	Foreign policy (and a dose of domestic policy)
Reaction to George McGovern and the "New Politics"; attempt to move Democratic party back to center Opposition to détente and isolationism Failure to take party back and migration to Reagan right in 1980	*Heroes:* Winston Churchill Harry Truman John F. Kennedy Lyndon Johnson Reinhold Niebuhr Max Shachtman Scoop Jackson Albert Wohlstetter Pat Moynihan	*Key words:* "Culture of appeasement" "Finlandization" "Nuclear War" "Vietnam Syndrome" "Human rights" "Silent majority" "Quotas" "Primaries" "Economic growth"

Sociological type and principal figures	Main publications, organizations, think tanks, public institutions	Presidential support
Intellectuals and academics, often past radicals (New York) Irving Kristol Nathan Glazer** Daniel Bell Pat Moynihan** Seymour M. Lipset James Q. Wilson Norman Podhoretz** *** Midge Decter** *** Aaron Wildavsky Edward Banfield John Bunzel Paul Seabury** Lewis Feuer	*The Public Interest* *Commentary*	1968: Hubert Humphrey 1972: Scoop Jackson and Hubert Humphrey in primaries, then divided between McGovern and Nixon (mostly Nixon)
Political activists of the Democratic party and hawks (Washington, D.C.) Jeane Kirkpatrick*** Max Kampelman Eugene Rostow Ben Wattenberg*** James Woolsey*** Peter Rosenblatt Penn Kemble Michael Novak*** Bayard Rustin John Roche Joshua Muravchik*** Paul Wolfowitz***	*Commentary* *New Republic* (to some extent) *Wall Street Journal* (editorial pages) *The National Interest* (to some extent) Coalition for a Democratic Majority Committee on the Present Danger Jewish Institute for National Security Affairs	1976: Scoop Jackson in primaries, then Carter 1980: Reagan 1984: Reagan 1988: G. H. W. Bush 1992: Divided Clinton/ G. H. W. Bush

Age and general agenda	Positioning, heroes, and adversaries	Center of gravity, key words, and campaigns
	Ronald Reagan AFL-CIO Soviet dissidents Solidarity movement in Poland Contras in Nicaragua *Adversaries:* Americans for Democratic Action George McGovern George Kennan *Foreign Policy* Paul Warnke Tony Lake Jesse Jackson Henry Kissinger	*Campaigns:* Against détente Against isolationism Against Helsinki Against SALT II For intervention in Central America
Third Age: "The Neocons" (1995–) A distinct voice within conservatism, essentially on foreign policy Hegemonism and democratic globalism; an inherited neoconservatism, no longer a conversion	A subset of the Republican right, still at war with liberals but now especially against realists *Heroes:* Theodore Roosevelt Winston Churchill Ronald Reagan Rupert Murdoch Joe Lieberman Tony Blair Bernard Lewis Natan Sharansky *Adversaries:* Pat Buchanan Brent Scowcroft Colin Powell Saddam Hussein Yasser Arafat	Foreign policy *Key words:* "National greatness" "Benevolent Empire" "Unipolarity" "Chinese threat" "World War IV" "Islamofascism" "Regime change" "Democratization" "Transformation of the Middle East" *Campaigns:* For intervention in Balkans, Afghanistan, Iraq, Iran Against the UN

Note: ** indicates belonging to second age, *** to third age.

Sociological type and principal figures	Main publications, organizations, think tanks, public institutions	Presidential support
Richard Perle*** Elliott Abrams*** Martin Peretz*** Linda Chavez Carl Gershman*** Richard Pipes Walter Laqueur*** Michael Ledeen*** Elmo Zumwalt Charles Krauthammer*** William Bennett*** Frank Gaffney*** Francis Fukuyama	Friends of the Democratic Center in Central America Committee for the Free World American Enterprise Institute Freedom House National Endowment for Democracy Institute on Religion and Democracy	
Conservatives who were born conservatives (Washington, D.C.) William Kristol Robert Kagan David Brooks Gary Schmitt Tom Donnelly David Frum Lawrence Kaplan Max Boot Abram Shulsky Randy Scheunemann Doug Feith John Podhoretz Daniel Pipes Reuel Gerecht I. Lewis Libby Mark Lagon Bruce Jackson Clifford May Frederick Kagan David Wurmser Hillel Fradkin Danielle Pletka George Weigel Dan Senor Charles Fairbanks	*Weekly Standard* *Commentary* *New Republic* (to some extent) *Wall Street Journal* (editorial pages) Project for the New American Century American Enterprise Institute Hudson Institute Ethics and Public Policy Center Center for Security Policy Committee on the Present Danger (third incarnation) Committee to Expand NATO Committee for the Liberation of Iraq Project on Transitional Democracies Foundation for Defense of Democracies Foreign Policy Initiative	1996: Bob Dole 2000: John McCain in primaries, then G. W. Bush 2004: G. W. Bush 2008: John McCain

NOTES

Introduction

1. George W. Bush, speech to the American Enterprise Institute, Hilton Hotel, Washington, D.C., February 26, 2003, available at http://georgewbush -whitehouse.archives.gov/news.

2. On the importance of democratic peace theory in the Bush doctrine, see Tony Smith, *A Pact with the Devil: Washington's Bid for World Supremacy and the Betrayal of the American Promise* (New York: Routledge, 2007).

3. Norman Podhoretz, "Neoconservatism—A Eulogy," *Commentary*, March 1996; Irving Kristol, "The Neoconservative Persuasion," *Weekly Standard*, August 25, 2003.

4. See, for example, Podhoretz, "Neoconservatism—A Eulogy"; Irving Kristol, *Neoconservatism: The Autobiography of an Idea* (New York: Free Press, 1995), p. xi; Seymour Martin Lipset, *American Exceptionalism: A Double-Edged Sword* (New York: W. W. Norton, 1996), p. 200; James Nuechterlein, "The End of Neoconservatism," *First Things* 63 (May 1996): 14–15; Mark Gerson, *The Neoconservative Vision: From the Cold War to the Culture Wars* (Lanham, Md.: Madison Books, 1996), p. 27.

5. Gary J. Dorrien, *The Neoconservative Mind: Politics, Culture, and Ideology* (Philadelphia: Temple University Press, 1993).

6. Gerson, *The Neoconservative Vision.*

7. Jacob Heilbrunn, *They Knew They Were Right: The Rise of the Neocons* (New York: Doubleday, 2008).

8. Irving Kristol, "Tongue-Tied in Washington," *Wall Street Journal*, April 15, 1991.

9. John Ehrman, *The Rise of Neoconservatism: Intellectuals and Foreign Affairs, 1945–1994* (New Haven: Yale University Press, 1995).

10. Quoted in Fred Siegel, "Liberalism," in *The Reader's Companion to American History*, ed. Eric Foner and John Garraty (Boston: Houghton Mifflin, 1991), p. 654.

11. Arthur Schlesinger Jr., *The Vital Center: The Politics of Freedom* (1949; reprint, New Brunswick, N.J.: Transaction, 1997). John Ehrman, *The Rise of Neoconservatism,* chap. 1, rightly insists on the importance of "vital center liberalism."

12. Pierre Hassner, "L'empire de la force ou la force de l'empire?," *Cahier de Chaillot* no. 54 (September 2002): 44.

13. Kenneth Pollack, *The Threatening Storm: The Case for Invading Iraq* (New York: Random House, 2002).

14. Alain Frachon and Daniel Vernet, *L'Amérique messianique: Les guerres des néo-conservateurs* (Paris: Seuil, 2004).

15. Ivo Daalder and James Lindsay, *America Unbound: The Bush Revolution in Foreign Policy* (Washington, D.C.: Brookings Institution Press, 2003).

16. Paul Wolfowitz, interview by Sam Tanenhaus for *Vanity Fair,* May 9, 2003.

17. For a neoconservative insider account of the debates and the reasoning that followed the attacks, see Douglas Feith, *War and Decision: Inside the Pentagon at the Dawn of the War on Terrorism* (New York: HarperCollins, 2008).

18. George W. Bush, State of the Union address, January 29, 2002, available at http://georgewbush-whitehouse.archives.gov/news.

19. George W. Bush, speech to National Endowment for Democracy, November 6, 2003, available at http://georgewbush-whitehouse.archives.gov/news.

20. Smith, *A Pact with the Devil.*

21. Alexis de Tocqueville, *Democracy in America,* trans. Arthur Goldhammer (New York: Library of America, 2004), bk. II, pt. 2, chap. 5, pp. 598–599.

1. Incubation

1. This account of CCNY in the 1930s draws heavily on the documentary film of New York intellectual life in the period by Joseph Dorman and on the book derived from the film, *Arguing the World: The New York Intellectuals in Their Own Words* (Chicago: University of Chicago Press, 2000), p. 222.

2. Bell quoted in Dorman, *Arguing the World,* pp. 33 and 44.

3. Glazer quoted in ibid., p. 46. The *Partisan Review* became increasingly restive under American Communist party tutelage and broke with it in 1936.

4. Irving Kristol, "Memoirs of a Trotskyist," in *Reflections of a Neoconservative: Looking Back, Looking Ahead* (New York: Basic Books, 1983), p. 12.

5. Julius and Ethel Rosenberg were found guilty of spying for the Soviet Union and executed in 1953.

6. Kristol quoted in Dorman, *Arguing the World,* p. vii.

7. See chap. 2 of Gary J. Dorrien, *The Neoconservative Mind: Politics, Culture, and Ideology* (Philadelphia: Temple University Press, 1993), pp. 19–67.

8. This passage draws on ibid.

9. Sidney Hook, *Towards the Understanding of Karl Marx* (1933; reprint, New York: Prometheus Books, 2003).

10. "Manifesto of the Committee for Cultural Freedom," reproduced in Sidney Hook, *Out of Step: An Unquiet Life in the Twentieth Century* (New York: Carroll and Graf, 1987); cf. Alan M. Wald, *The New York Intellectuals: The Rise and Decline of the Anti-Stalinist Left from the 1930s to the 1980s* (Chapel Hill: University of North Carolina Press, 1987), pp. 91–97.

11. Mark Gerson, *The Neoconservative Vision: From the Cold War to the Culture Wars* (Lanham, Md.: Madison Books, 1996), pp. 34–35.

12. At West Point on June 1, 2002, George W. Bush said: "Yet moral clarity was essential to our victory in the Cold War"; available at http://georgewbush-whitehouse.archives.gov/news. See also William Bennett, *Why We Fight: Moral Clarity and the War on Terrorism* (Washington, D.C.: Regnery, 2003).

13. Dorrien, *The Neoconservative Mind*, pp. 63 ff.

14. George F. Kennan, "The Sources of Soviet Conduct," *Foreign Affairs*, Summer 1947. In the late 1970s the neoconservatives of the Committee on the Present Danger would attack Kennan's analysis on this very subject. Where they saw a Soviet will to conquer and rule, Kennan saw a prudent and basically defensive strategy (see Chapter 5).

15. Dorrien, *The Neoconservative Mind*, p. 48.

16. George W. Bush, "Address to a Joint Session of Congress and the American People," September 20, 2001, available at http://georgewbush-whitehouse.archives.gov/news.

17. I continue to rely essentially on Dorrien, *The Neoconservative Mind*, chap. 2.

18. John Ehrman, *The Rise of Neoconservatism: Intellectuals and Foreign Affairs, 1945–1994* (New Haven: Yale University Press, 1995), p. 15; Arthur Schlesinger Jr., *The Vital Center: The Politics of Freedom* (1949; reprint, New Brunswick, N.J.: Transaction, 1997).

19. Everything on the UDA and ADA is from Steven M. Gillon, *Politics and Vision: The ADA and American Liberalism, 1947–1985* (New York: Oxford University Press, 1987).

20. The founding manifesto of the ADA is reproduced on the companion website to the book, www.neoconservatism.vaisse.net, "Manifesto of the Americans for Democratic Action (1947)."

21. Reinhold Niebuhr, *The Children of Light and the Children of Darkness: A Vindication of Democracy and a Critique of Its Traditional Defense* (New York: Scribner's, 1944).

22. On Niebuhr and the reception and distortion of his thought by liberals and neoconservatives, see Paul Elie, "A Man for All Reasons," *Atlantic*

Monthly, November 2007, available at http://www.theatlantic.com/doc/200711
/reinhold-niebuhr (accessed July 20, 2008).

23. Schlesinger, *The Vital Center,* preface to the 1998 ed.

24. Ibid.

25. Ibid.

26. On the history of anticommunism in the United States, see esp. Richard
Gid Powers, *Not without Honor: The History of American Anticommunism*
(New York: Free Press, 1995); on McCarthyism, see Marie-France Toinet, *La
chasse aux sorcières: 1947–1957* (Brussels: Complexe, 1984).

27. This account of the Congress for Cultural Freedom relies on Peter
Steinfels, *The Neoconservatives: The Men Who Are Changing America's Politics*
(New York: Simon and Schuster, 1979), pp. 29 ff.; Dorrien, *The Neoconserva-
tive Mind,* pp. 50 ff.; Gerson, *The Neoconservative Vision,* pp. 49 ff. The most
important book on the subject is Pierre Grémion, *Intelligence de l'anticom-
munisme: Le Congrès pour la liberté de la culture à Paris, 1950–1975* (Paris:
Fayard, 1995); see also Peter Coleman, *The Liberal Conspiracy: The Congress
for Cultural Freedom and the Struggle for the Mind of Postwar Europe* (New
York: Free Press, 1989); and Raymond Aron, *Le spectateur engagé* (Paris:
Librairie Générale, 2005) and *Mémoires* (Paris: Julliard, 1983).

28. Sidney Hook, *Heresy—Yes, Conspiracy—No!* (New York: John Day,
1953).

29. Schlesinger, *The Vital Center,* chap. 9.

30. Irving Kristol, "'Civil Liberties' 1952: A Study in Confusion," *Commentary,* March 1952, p. 229.

31. Arthur Schlesinger, "Letters from Readers: Liberty and the Liberal,"
Commentary, July 1952.

32. See esp. Antoine Coppolani, "La résistible évolution du libéralisme
américain: Du consensus libéral au mouvement néoconservateur," in *La démo-
cratie aux États-Unis et en Europe, 1918–1989,* ed. Hélène Fréchet (Paris: Edi-
tions du Temps, 1999).

33. Louis Hartz, *The Liberal Tradition in America* (New York: Harcourt
Brace, 1955).

34. Daniel Boorstin, *The Genius of American Politics* (Chicago: University of
Chicago Press, 1953).

35. Coppolani, "La résistible évolution du libéralisme américain"; Richard
Hofstadter, *The American Political Tradition and the Men Who Made It* (New
York: Knopf, 1948) and *The Age of Reform* (New York: Vintage Books, 1955).

36. Daniel Bell, *The End of Ideology: On the Exhaustion of Political Ideas in
the Fifties* (New York: Free Press, 1960).

37. Arthur Schlesinger, "Liberalism in America: A Note for Europeans," in
The Politics of Hope (Boston: Houghton Mifflin, 1963), p. 71, quoted in Coppolani, "La résistible évolution du libéralisme américain."

38. Godfrey Hodgson, *America in Our Time* (New York: Doubleday, 1976), pp. 73, 89–90, quoted in Steinfels, *The Neoconservatives*, p. 274.

39. Dorman, *Arguing the World*, pp. 54–55.

40. Nicolaus Mills and Michael Walzer, *50 Years of "Dissent"* (New Haven: Yale University Press, 2004).

41. Gillon, *Politics and Vision*, chap. 4.

42. Ibid., chap. 5; see also John Kenneth Galbraith, *The Affluent Society* (Boston: Houghton Mifflin, 1958).

43. Russell Kirk, *The Conservative Mind, from Burke to Santayana* (Chicago: Regnery, 1953).

44. William F. Buckley Jr., *God and Man at Yale: The Superstitions of Academic Freedom* (Chicago: Regnery, 1951).

45. Irving Kristol, "American Conservatism, 1945–1955," *Public Interest* 121 (Fall 1995): 82.

46. Pierre Melandri, *Reagan: Une biographie totale* (Paris: Laffont, 1988).

47. The manifesto is reproduced in Mitchell Cohen and Dennis Hale, eds., *The New Student Left: An Anthology* (Boston: Beacon Press, 1966), p. 220.

48. In 1946 the pediatrician Benjamin Spock published *The Common Sense Book of Baby and Child Care*, which became a best-seller. Among other things, it recommended treating children more as persons. Spock was later politically active against the war in Vietnam, nuclear weapons, for legalization of drugs, etc.

49. Jeane J. Kirkpatrick, *On the Celebration of Hubert Humphrey* (Washington, D.C.: Wilson Center, 1980), p. 22; originally delivered as a speech at the Wilson Center in October 1980.

50. E. J. Dionne, *Why Americans Hate Politics* (New York: Simon and Schuster, 1992).

51. The account of events in Berkeley is inspired by André Kaspi, *États-Unis 68: L'année des contestations* (Paris: Complexe, 1988), pp. 78–83; and Antoine Coppolani, *Gouverner la Californie: L'expérience du "Libéralisme responsable," 1958–1966*, 2 vols. (Doctoral thesis, University of Paris III Sorbonne Nouvelle, 1998).

52. Mario Savio, "An End to History," *Humanity*, no. 2 (December 1964), reprinted in Michael Miller and Susan Gilmore, eds., *Revolution at Berkeley* (New York: Dial Press, 1965).

53. Nathan Glazer, "What Happened at Berkeley," in Miller and Gilmore, *Revolution at Berkeley*, pp. 161–162.

54. Seymour Martin Lipset and Paul Seabury, "The Lesson of Berkeley," *The Reporter*, January 28, 1965; reprinted and extended in *The Berkeley Student Revolt: Facts and Interpretations*, ed. Seymour Martin Lipset and Sheldon Wolin (Garden City, N.Y.: Doubleday, 1965), p. 349 (thanks to Antoine Coppolani for calling my attention to this quote).

55. Sol Stern, "A Deeper Disenchantment," *Liberation*, February 1965, reprinted in Miller and Gilmore, *Revolution at Berkeley*, pp. 227–238; quotation on p. 227.

56. James Petras and Michael Shute, "Berkeley '65," *Partisan Review*, Spring 1965, reprinted in Miller and Gilmore, *Revolution at Berkeley*, p. 209.

57. Gillon, *Politics and Vision*, chaps. 6–9.

58. Ibid., chap. 8.

59. Jacob Heilbrunn, *They Knew They Were Right: The Rise of the Neocons* (New York: Doubleday, 2008), p. 109.

60. Kirkpatrick, *On the Celebration of Hubert Humphrey*, p. 23.

2. The First Age

1. Daniel Bell, *The End of Ideology: On the Exhaustion of Political Ideas in the Fifties* (New York: Free Press, 1960).

2. Daniel Bell, *The Coming of the Post-Industrial Society: A Venture in Social Forecasting* (New York: Basic Books, 1973).

3. Kristol quoted in Gary J. Dorrien, *The Neoconservative Mind: Politics, Culture, and Ideology* (Philadelphia: Temple University Press, 1993), p. 71.

4. Irving Kristol, *Reflections of a Neoconservative: Looking Back, Looking Ahead* (New York: Basic Books, 1983), pp. 4 ff.

5. Irving Kristol, "Forty Good Years," *Public Interest*, Spring 2005. The editorial in the first issue is reproduced on the companion website to the book, www.neoconservatism.vaisse.net, "*The Public Interest*: First Table of Contents and Editorial (1965)."

6. Michael Harrington, *The Other America: Poverty in the United States* (New York: Macmillan, 1962).

7. Daniel Bell and Irving Kristol, "What Is the Public Interest?," *Public Interest*, Fall 1965.

8. Daniel Patrick Moynihan, "The Professionalization of Reform," *Public Interest*, Fall 1965.

9. Irving Kristol, "New Right, New Left," *Public Interest*, Summer 1966.

10. Kristol, "Forty Good Years," p. 5.

11. Nathan Glazer, "Neoconservative from the Start," *Public Interest*, Spring 2005, p. 13.

12. Nathan Glazer, "Housing Problems and Housing Policies," *Public Interest*, Spring 1967.

13. Daniel Patrick Moynihan, "A Crisis of Confidence?," *Public Interest*, Spring 1967; Aaron Wildavsky, "The Political Economy of Efficiency," *Public Interest*, Summer 1967.

14. James Q. Wilson, "The Bureaucracy Problem," *Public Interest*, Winter 1967.

15. John Bunzel, "Black Studies at San Francisco State," *Public Interest*, Fall 1968.

16. Mark Gerson, *The Neoconservative Vision: From the Cold War to the Culture Wars* (Lanham, Md.: Madison Books, 1996), pp. 96 ff.

17. James Coleman, "Equal Schools or Equal Students?," *Public Interest*, Summer 1966.

18. Gerson, *The Neoconservative Vision*, p. 97; Nathan Glazer, "The Limits of Social Policy," *Commentary*, September 1971; see also Glazer, *The Limits of Social Policy* (Cambridge, Mass.: Harvard University Press, 1988).

19. Aaron Wildavsky, "Government and the People," *Commentary*, August 1973.

20. Daniel Patrick Moynihan, *The Politics of a Guaranteed Income: The Nixon Administration and the Family Assistance Plan* (New York: Vintage Books, 1973), p. 52.

21. Daniel Bell, "The Cultural Contradictions of Capitalism," and Robert Heilbronner, "On the Limited 'Relevance' of Economics," *Public Interest*, Fall 1970; Irving Kristol, *On the Democratic Idea in America* (New York: Harper and Row, 1972).

22. On Moynihan, see esp. Godfrey Hodgson, *The Gentleman from New York: Daniel Patrick Moynihan, A Biography* (Boston: Houghton Mifflin, 2000); and Robert Katzmann, *Daniel Patrick Moynihan: The Intellectual in Public Life* (Baltimore: Johns Hopkins University Press, 2004).

23. Peter Steinfels, *The Neoconservatives: The Men Who Are Changing America's Politics* (New York: Simon and Schuster, 1979), p. 108.

24. Nathan Glazer and Daniel P. Moynihan, *Beyond the Melting Pot: The Negroes, Puerto Ricans, Jews, Italians and Irish of New York City* (Cambridge, Mass.: MIT Press and Harvard University Press, 1963).

25. For an overview, see Daniel Patrick Moynihan, *Maximum Feasible Misunderstanding: Community Action in the War on Poverty* (New York: Free Press, 1969).

26. This text was published as "The Politics of Stability," *New Leader*, October 9, 1967, and reproduced in Patrick Moynihan, *Coping: Essays on the Practice of Government* (New York: Vintage Books, 1973), pp. 185–194.

27. Moynihan, *Maximum Feasible Misunderstanding*, p. xxix.

28. This analysis draws on Steinfels, *The Neoconservatives*, p. 258.

29. Of course many neoconservatives were not Jewish; among the non-Jews were Scoop Jackson, Jeane Kirkpatrick, Elmo Zumwalt, Penn Kemble, Peter Berger, George Weigel, James Q. Wilson, Michael Novak, Richard John Neuhaus, William Bennett, James Woolsey, Patrick Glynn, James Nuechterlein, Zalmay Khalilzad, Michael Lind, Francis Fukuyama, and Pat Moynihan. The last three in this list would eventually quit the movement.

30. Glazer, "Neoconservative from the Start," p. 17.

31. On this point, see esp. David Wyman, *The Abandonment of the Jews: America and the Holocaust, 1941–1945* (New York: Pantheon, 1984); and Françoise Ouzan, *Ces Juifs dont l'Amérique ne voulait pas (1945–1950)* (Brussels: Complexe, 1995).

32. Pauline Peretz, *Le combat pour les Juifs soviétiques: Washington—Moscou—Jérusalem 1953–1989* (Paris: Armand Colin, 2006).

33. Judith Apter Klinghoffer, *Vietnam, Jews, and the Middle East: Unintended Consequences* (New York: St. Martin's Press, 1999).

34. Nathan Glazer, "The Jewish Role in Student Activism," *Fortune,* January 1969; Arthur Liebman, *Jews and the Left* (New York: John Wiley and Sons, 1979), p. 541.

35. Antoine Coppolani, "The Jewish Radical: Étudiants américains contestataires face aux guerres du Vietnam et du Kippour," *Histoire et Défense* 1, no. 35 (1997): 79–95.

36. Klinghoffer, *Vietnam, Jews, and the Middle East,* p. 155.

37. Ibid., p. 171.

38. See Peretz, *Le combat pour les Juifs soviétiques,* chap. 4.

39. Quoted in Yossi Shain, *Marketing the American Creed Abroad: Diasporas in the United States and Their Homelands* (Cambridge: Cambridge University Press, 1999), p. 141.

40. Norman Podhoretz, *Breaking Ranks: A Political Memoir* (New York: Harper and Row, 1979), p. 335.

41. Nathan Glazer, "Blacks, Jews and the Intellectuals," *Commentary,* July 1969.

42. Klinghoffer, *Vietnam, Jews, and the Middle East,* p. 163.

43. The original petition is reproduced on the companion website to the book, www.neoconservatism.vaisse.net, "'To Uphold Our Own Honor . . .': Petition in Favour of Israel Published by Americans for Democracy in the Middle East (7 June 1967)."

44. The original petition is reproduced at www.neoconservatism.vaisse.net, "'The Moral Responsibility in the Middle East': Petition in Favour of Israel Published by Americans for Democracy in the Middle East (4 June 1967)."

45. Klinghoffer, *Vietnam, Jews, and the Middle East,* p. 171.

46. On this point, see esp. Murray Friedman, *What Went Wrong?: The Creation and Collapse of the Black-Jewish Alliance* (New York: Free Press, 1995); and Jonathan Kaufman, *Broken Alliance: The Turbulent Times between Blacks and Jews in America* (New York: Scribner's, 1988).

47. Shain, *Marketing the American Creed Abroad,* p. 133.

48. Irving Kristol, "Why Jews Turn Conservative," *Wall Street Journal,* September 14, 1972, p. 18.

49. Kristol, "Forty Good Years."

50. On Podhoretz, see esp. Norman Podhoretz, *Making It* (New York: Random House, 1967), and above all *Breaking Ranks.* On his writings, see Norman

Podhoretz and Thomas Jeffers, eds., *The Norman Podhoretz Reader: A Selection of His Writings from the 1950s through the 1990s* (New York: Free Press, 2004); see also Dorrien, *The Neoconservative Mind*, chap. 4; and Gerson, *The Neoconservative Vision*, chap. 3.

51. Podhoretz, *Breaking Ranks*, p. 10.

52. Sidney Blumenthal, *The Rise of the Counter-Establishment: From Conservative Ideology to Political Power* (New York: Harper and Row, 1988), pp. 133 ff.

53. Dorrien, *The Neoconservative Mind*, pp. 148 ff.

54. Podhoretz, *Breaking Ranks*, pp. 111 ff.

55. Staughton Lynd, "How the Cold War Began," *Commentary*, November 1960.

56. Paul Goodman, *Growing Up Absurd: Problems of Youth in the Organized System* (New York: Random House, 1960).

57. Dorrien, *The Neoconservative Mind*, pp. 147 ff.

58. Norman Podhoretz, "The Know-Nothing Bohemians," *Partisan Review*, Spring 1958; analyzed by Gerson, *The Neoconservative Vision*, pp. 76 ff.

59. Podhoretz, *Breaking Ranks*, p. 197.

60. For an account of the war between the intellectual magazines, see Merle Miller, "Why Norman and Jason Aren't Talking," *New York Times Magazine*, March 26, 1972, pp. 104 ff.

61. Podhoretz, *Breaking Ranks*, pp. 206 ff.; John Schaar and Sheldon Wolin, "Berkeley and the Fate of the Multiversity," *New York Review of Books*, March 11, 1965. In the end, Glazer's article did appear in Podhoretz's magazine: Nathan Glazer, "What Happened at Berkeley," *Commentary*, February 1965.

62. Tom Wolfe, *Radical Chic & Mau-Mauing the Flak Catchers* (New York: Farrar Straus Giroux, 1970).

63. Norman Podhoretz, "Is It Good for the Jews?," *Commentary*, February 1972; and Podhoretz, *Breaking Ranks*, p. 334.

64. Norman Podhoretz, "A Certain Anxiety," *Commentary*, August 1971.

65. Podhoretz, *Breaking Ranks*, p. 302.

66. Walter Laqueur, "Revolutionism and the Jews," *Commentary*, February 1971.

67. Louis Harap, "'Commentary' Moves to the Right," *Jewish Currents*, December 1971.

68. Glazer, "What Happened at Berkeley"; Bayard Rustin, "'Black Power' and Coalition Politics," *Commentary*, September 1966; Diana Trilling, "On the Steps of the Law Library: Liberalism and the Revolution of the Young," *Commentary*, November 1968; Tom Kahn, "Why the Poor People's Campaign Failed," *Commentary*, September 1968.

69. Noam Chomsky, "Vietnam, the Cold War and Other Matters," *Commentary*, October 1969; Dorrien, *The Neoconservative Mind*, pp. 162–163.

70. Dorothy Rabinowitz, "The Radicalized Professor: A Portrait," *Commen-*

tary, July 1970; Rabinowitz, "The Activist Cleric," *Commentary*, September 1970; Midge Decter, "The Liberated Woman," *Commentary*, October 1970, quoted in Dorrien, *The Neoconservative Mind*, p. 353.

71. Steinfels, *The Neoconservatives*, p. 48.

72. See esp. Wildavsky, "Government and the People."

73. Michael Harrington and Ronald Radosh, "Ronald Radosh and Michael Harrington: An Exchange," *Partisan Review* 55, no. 1 (1989).

74. Seymour Martin Lipset, "Jews Are Still Liberals and Proud of It," *Washington Post (Outlook)*, December 30, 1984. See also Lipset, "Neoconservatism: Myth and Reality," *Society*, July–August 1988, pp. 29–37.

75. The young Shachtmanites had actually succeeded in renaming the party before the defection of Harrington and his allies.

76. Michael Harrington, "The Welfare State and Its Neoconservative Critics," *Dissent*, Autumn 1973, pp. 435–454. The critical page of this article is reproduced on the companion website to the book, www.neoconservatism .vaisse.net, "Dissent and the Attack on 'Neoconservatives' (1973)." Note that "neoconservative" in this original use was not hyphenated. That is one reason why I have adopted this spelling. The other is that neoconservatism was not merely a "new conservatism" but a distinctive movement. It deserves an appellation of its own to distinguish it from the "new conservatism" of the post-1955 *National Review*.

77. Ibid., p. 454. This prediction may remind us of columnist George Will's summary of the accomplishments of first-age neoconservatism: "Without *The Public Interest*, No Newt Gingrich"; quoted in Gerson, *The Neoconservative Vision*, p. 349.

78. Gerson, *The Neoconservative Vision*, p. 26; Jacob Heilbrunn, *They Knew They Were Right: The Rise of the Neocons* (New York: Doubleday, 2008), p. 21.

79. Norman Podhoretz, "Neoconservatism: A Eulogy," *Commentary*, March 1996.

80. Robert Bartley, "Irving Kristol and Friends," *Wall Street Journal*, May 3, 1972, p. 20. Irving Kristol himself said in 2005 (Kristol, "Forty Good Years") that it was after he turned Republican in 1972 that Michael Harrington and *Dissent* coined the term "neoconservative," an observation that seems somewhat egocentric, since Harrington makes no mention of this in his 1973 article, which focuses on Nathan Glazer, Daniel Bell, and Pat Moynihan. For uses of "new conservatives," see, for example, Robert Lekachman, "Toward a Reordered Economy," *Dissent*, Autumn 1972, p. 579, which uses the expression "new conservatives of the social sciences"; and Joseph Epstein, "The New Conservatives: Intellectuals in Retreat," *Dissent*, Spring 1973.

81. Bartley, "Irving Kristol and Friends."

82. Ibid.

83. Robert Bartley, "A Most Improbable 'Conservative,'" *Wall Street Journal*, November 19, 1970, p. 18.

84. Editorial, "Come On In, the Water's Fine," *National Review*, March 1971.

85. Bartley, "A Most Improbable 'Conservative.'"

86. Lipset, "Jews Are Still Liberals."

87. Irving Kristol, "What Is a Neo-Conservative?," *Newsweek*, January 19, 1976, p. 17.

88. Kristol, *Reflections of a Neoconservative*, p. 76.

89. Podhoretz, *Breaking Ranks*, p. 16.

90. Here I am following chap. 3 of Steinfels, *The Neoconservatives*, in particular his five "positions"; as well as Gerson, *The Neoconservative Vision*.

91. This was the theme of the Trilateral Commission report on the "governability of democracies." Samuel Huntington, "The Democratic Distemper," in "The American Commonwealth, 1976–," special issue of *Public Interest*, Fall 1975.

92. See Irving Kristol, "On Conservatism and Capitalism," *Wall Street Journal*, September 11, 1975.

93. David T. Bazelon, *Power in America: The Politics of the New Class* (New York: New American Library, 1967); see also his article "The New Class," *Commentary*, August 1966.

94. See Nathan Glazer, "Nixon, the Great Society, and the Future of Social Policy: A Symposium," *Commentary*, May 1973; and the special section edited by Eli Ginzberg and Robert Solow in *Public Interest*, Winter 1974, esp. pp. 8 and 212.

95. Harrington, "The Welfare State and Its Neoconservative Critics."

96. Steinfels, *The Neoconservatives*, pp. 189 ff.

97. For Kristol's definition of intellectuals, see Irving Kristol, "Intellectuals and Foreign Policy," *Foreign Affairs*, July 1967, pp. 395–399; reprinted in Kristol, *Neoconservatism: The Autobiography of an Idea* (New York: Free Press, 1995), pp. 75–91. For pejorative descriptions of intellectuals, see, e.g., Rabinowitz, "The Radicalized Professor."

98. Kristol, *On the Democratic Idea in America*, p. 35.

99. James Q. Wilson, "Liberalism versus Liberal Education," *Commentary*, June 1972; quoted in Gerson, *The Neoconservative Vision*, p. 103.

100. Edward Banfield, *The Unheavenly City* (Boston: Little, Brown, 1970).

3. The Second Age

1. James Q. Wilson, *The Amateur Democrat: Club Politics in Three Cities* (Chicago: Chicago University Press, 1962).

2. Ibid., pp. 131 and 195; quoted in A. James Reichley, *The Life of the*

Parties: A History of American Political Parties (New York: Free Press, 1992), p. 344.

3. Penn Kemble, "The Democrats after 1968," *Commentary,* January 1969, pp. 35–41.

4. Penn Kemble and Joshua Muravchik, "The New Politics and the Democrats," *Commentary,* December 1972, pp. 78–84.

5. Michael Malbin, "Democratic Delegate Rules Influencing Candidates' Strategies," *National Journal,* December 6, 1975, pp. 1664–72.

6. Kevin Phillips, *The Emerging Republican Majority* (New York: Arlington House, 1969).

7. A "critical realignment" is a durable coalescence of voting blocs that ensures a party's domination for decades. Critical realignments are said to have occurred in the United States in 1896 and 1932. The idea of a critical realignment is explored in Paul Kleppner et al., *The Evolution of American Electoral Systems* (Westport, Conn.: Greenwood Press, 1981).

8. Richard M. Scammon and Ben J. Wattenberg, *The Real Majority,* rev. ed. (New York: Primus/Donald I. Fine, 1992), pp. ii–iii.

9. "Announcing: Democrats for Nixon," *New York Times,* August 16, 1972, p. C43. The original ad is reproduced on the companion website to the book, www.neoconservatism.vaisse.net, "Democrats for Nixon (1972)."

10. Interview with Ben Wattenberg, June 6, 2001.

11. Interview with Richard Schifter, September 28, 2004.

12. A chronological table of CDM officials is offered on the companion website to the book, www.neoconservatism.vaisse.net, "Chronological Table of the CDM, 1972–1992."

13. Ben Wattenberg, *This USA: An Unexpected Family Portrait of 194,067,296 Americans Drawn from the Census* (Garden City, N.Y.: Doubleday, 1965). See Wattenberg's memoir, *Fighting Words: A Tale of How Liberals Created Neo-Conservatism* (New York: Thomas Dunne Books, 2008).

14. Interview with Ben Wattenberg, June 6, 2001.

15. Interview with Penn Kemble, June 11, 2003.

16. Interview with Max Kampelman, July 2, 2001; and Max M. Kampelman, *Entering New Worlds: The Memoirs of a Private Man in Public Life* (New York: HarperCollins, 1991).

17. See Jeane Kirkpatrick, "An American Girlhood," *Weekly Standard,* February 5, 2007.

18. Midge Decter, *The New Chastity and Other Arguments against Women's Liberation* (New York: Coward, 1972).

19. Evron Kirkpatrick to Ben Wattenberg, September 27, 1972, and Nelson Polsby to Ben Wattenberg, September 27, 1972, "Draft CDM Founding Statement," Personal Papers of Peter R. Rosenblatt, box 17, Lyndon Baines Johnson Presidential Library, Austin, Texas (hereafter Rosenblatt Collection).

20. Memo, Penn Kemble to Ben Wattenberg and Richard Schifter, November 8, 1972, "Board of Directors—Minutes," box 7, Rosenblatt Collection.

21. "Come Home, Democrats," *New York Times* and *Washington Post,* December 7, 1972. The original manifesto is reproduced on the companion website to the book, www.neoconservatism.vaisse.net, "Come Home, Democrats (1972)."

22. A list of the signatories to the manifesto is offered on the companion website to the book, www.neoconservatism.vaisse.net, "Analysis of Signatories of the 'Come Home, Democrats' Manifesto (1972)."

23. Interview with Joshua Muravchik, July 18, 2001.

24. Interview with Penn Kemble, June 11, 2003.

25. On Shanker, see Richard Kahlenberg, *Tough Liberal: Albert Shanker and the Battles over Schools, Unions, Race, and Democracy* (New York: Columbia University Press, 2007).

26. Interview with Peter Rosenblatt, June 9, 2003.

27. Richard Schifter to Max Kampelman, Peter Rosenblatt, Ben Wattenberg, and Penn Kemble, January 8, 1975, "CDM (1972–1973)," box 63, Rosenblatt Collection.

28. Minutes of meeting, October 22, 1975, "CDM—Ex. Ctte Minutes," box 62, ibid.

29. Abzug quoted by Ben Wattenberg, *Fighting Words,* p. 136.

30. Minutes of Board of Directors meeting, November 22–23, 1974, "Board of Directors—Minutes," box 7, Rosenblatt Collection.

31. For Wattenberg's estimate, see Joseph Gerri, "Democratic Coalition Rejects New Left," *Minneapolis Tribune,* February 1973; Financial Report, December 1, 1972–October 31, 1973, and November 1, 1973–November 30, 1974, "Board of Directors—Minutes," box 7, Rosenblatt Collection.

32. Interview with Joshua Muravchik, July 18, 2001.

33. Press release, April 26, 1973, "Media Press Conferences + Releases," box 36, Rosenblatt Collection.

34. *CDM Notes,* December 1973.

35. Memo, Penn Kemble to Ben Wattenberg, n.d., "CDM—Task Force on the Charter commission—Notes etc.," box 44, Rosenblatt Collection.

36. Memo, Penn Kemble to Max Kampelman, Peter Rosenblatt, Ben Wattenberg, and Richard Schifter, January 10, 1975, "CDM (1976–1981 missing) 1975 & 1982," box 63, ibid.

37. *CDM Notes,* May 1975.

38. Malbin, "Democratic Delegate Rules Influencing Candidates' Strategies."

39. Minutes of meeting, September 18, 1975, "Executive Committee," box 56, Rosenblatt Collection.

40. "Come Home, Democrats" (see companion website for the original).

41. Robert Semple, "McGovern's Position on Foreign Policy: A Broad Pattern Seems to Be Emerging," *New York Times,* September 13, 1972.

42. Norman Podhoretz, "The Present Danger," *Commentary,* March 1980, p. 31; reprinted in Podhoretz, *The Present Danger* (New York: Simon and Schuster, 1980), p. 31.

43. Jeane Kirkpatrick, "Why We Don't Become Republicans," *Common Sense* 2 (Fall 1979): 27–35.

44. This table draws on distinctions set forth by John Ehrman, *Neoconservatism: Intellectuals and Foreign Affairs, 1945–1994* (New Haven: Yale University Press, 1995); and in my master's thesis, *"Foreign Policy, 1970–1995: La puissance américaine en question,"* directed by Pierre Melandri (University of Paris–X Nanterre, 1995).

45. Zbigniew Brzezinski, *Between Two Ages: America's Role in the Technetronic Era* (New York: Viking, 1970); interview with Zbigniew Brzezinski, July 23, 2001.

46. Walt Rostow, *The Stages of Economic Growth: A Non-Communist Manifesto* (Cambridge: Cambridge University Press, 1960).

47. Quoted in *CDM Notes,* December 1973; and Minutes, November 3, 1973 (inaccurately dated 1974), "Board of Directors—Minutes," box 7, Rosenblatt Collection.

48. "Eugene V. Rostow to Head New Democratic Foreign Policy Task Force—CDM Group Questions Optimism about Detente," press release, February 8, 1974, "Media Press Conf + Releases," box 36, ibid.

49. A list of the members of the task force is offered on the companion website to the book, www.neoconservatism.vaisse.net, "Members of Gene Rostow's Task Force (1974–76)."

50. *The Quest for Détente* (also titled *CDM Task Force Report on Détente*), report of the foreign policy task force chaired by Eugene Rostow (Washington, D.C.: Coalition for a Democratic Majority, July 31, 1974).

51. Raymond L. Garthoff, *Detente and Confrontation: American-Soviet Relations from Nixon to Reagan* (Washington, D.C.: Brookings Institution Press, 1994).

52. Ibid., p. 2.

53. "Draft Resolution on Detente for *Coalition for a Democratic Majority,*" n.d., "Board of Directors—Minutes," box 7, Rosenblatt Collection.

54. See the summary in Bernard Gwertzman, "Democrats Score Nixon on Detente," *New York Times,* August 1, 1974.

55. Interview with Penn Kemble, June 11, 2003.

56. Henry Kissinger to Eugene Rostow, Coalition for a Democratic Majority, August 19, 1974, "Miscellaneous Correspondence," box 52, Rosenblatt Collection.

57. Eugene Rostow to Henry Kissinger, September 4, 1974, ibid.

58. Proposed agenda, CDM Board of Directors, November 22–23, 1974, "Board of Directors—Minutes," box 7, Rosenblatt Collection; Minutes of Board of Directors meeting, November 22 and 23, 1974, "Board of Directors—Minutes," ibid.; *CDM Notes,* January–February 1975.

59. Penn Kemble to Peter Rosenblatt, May 9, 1975, "CDM (1976–1981 missing) 1975 & 1982," box 63, Rosenblatt Collection.

60. Text reproduced in *Congressional Record,* May 6, 1975, H3721-326.

61. Minutes of Executive Committee meeting, April 16, 1975, "Minutes," box 56, Rosenblatt Collection.

62. "For an Adequate Defense," *Wall Street Journal,* May 12, 1975.

63. Typed notes for a speech, February 8, 1976, "New York Board Meeting Feb 7 & 8 General," box 38, Rosenblatt Collection.

64. "Detente Is Not a Bad Word, Mr. President!," fundraising advertisement, "Detente Ad, April 5, 1976," ibid.

65. Proposed agenda, CDM discussion, September 15, 1977, "Sept. 15th Meeting," box 23, ibid. The United States did in fact withdraw from the International Labour Organization from 1977 to 1980 (with the support of the AFL-CIO under George Meany and Lane Kirkland) to protest the undue influence of the Soviet Union and the proliferation of resolutions condemning Israel, which had nothing to do with labor issues.

66. Interview with Joshua Muravchik, July 18, 2001.

67. Interview with Richard Schifter, September 28, 2004.

68. Interview with Ben Wattenberg, June 6, 2001.

69. Interviews with Charls Walker, July 16, 2003, and Richard Schifter, September 28, 2004.

70. The two Elmo Zumwalts, father and son, wrote a book about this poignant story: *My Father, My Son* (New York: Macmillan, 1986).

71. See http://www.chinfo.navy.mil/navpalib/news/news_stories/zumwalt.html (accessed December 2004), http://www.history.navy.mil/faqs/faq93–1.htm (accessed June 2008), and http://history.navy.mil/photos/pers-us/uspers-xz/e-zumwt.htm (accessed June 2008).

72. Richard Goldstein, "Elmo R. Zumwalt Jr., Admiral Who Modernized the Navy, Is Dead at 79," *New York Times,* January 3, 2000.

73. Interview with Richard Schifter, September 28, 2004.

74. Elmo R. Zumwalt Jr., *On Watch: A Memoir* (New York: Quadrangle, 1976).

75. Ben Wattenberg and James O'Hara to Ernest Lefevre, January 22, 1975, "B9 Zumwalt Capitol Hill Seminar," box 38, Rosenblatt Collection.

76. Interview with Richard Schifter, September 28, 2004.

77. Text of eulogy delivered at the funeral of Elmo Zumwalt, January 7, 2000 (text supplied by its author, Richard Schifter).

78. Interviews with Penn Kemble, June 11, 2003, and Peter Rosenblatt, June 9, 2003.

79. Memo, Schifter to Kampelman, Rosenblatt, Wattenberg, and Kemble, January 8, 1975, "CDM (1972–1973)," box 63, Rosenblatt Collection.

4. Divergence

1. Much of the biographical information presented here is drawn from Robert G. Kaufman, *Henry M. Jackson: A Life in Politics* (Seattle: University of Washington Press, 2000).

2. Founded in 1905 as the Intercollegiate Socialist Society, the League for Industrial Democracy (renamed in 1921) always remained anticommunist. The Students for a Democratic Society emerged from its "youth organization" in 1960.

3. Quoted by Ben Wattenberg, *Fighting Words: A Tale of How Liberals Created Neo-Conservatism* (New York: Thomas Dunne Books, 2008), p. 101.

4. Kaufman, *Henry M. Jackson*, p. 36.

5. Pauline Peretz, *Le combat pour les Juifs soviétiques: Washington—Moscou—Jérusalem 1953–1989* (Paris: Armand Colin, 2006), pp. 12–13.

6. See the interview of Richard Perle by Ben Wattenberg on PBS, November 14, 2002, "Richard Perle: The Making of a Neoconservative," transcript available at www.pbs.org/thinktank/transcript1017.html (accessed July 10, 2008).

7. See Samuel Pisar, *Coexistence and Commerce: Guidelines for Transactions between East and West* (New York: McGraw-Hill, 1970).

8. Raymond Garthoff, *Détente and Confrontation: American-Soviet Relations from Nixon to Reagan* (Washington, D.C.: Brookings Institution Press, 1994).

9. See Peretz, *Le combat pour les Juifs soviétiques,* chap. 5, esp. pp. 246–249; and Garthoff, *Détente and Confrontation,* pp. 508 ff.

10. See app. 3 in Peretz, *Le combat pour les Juifs soviétiques.*

11. Albert Wohlstetter, "The Delicate Balance of Terror," *Foreign Affairs,* January 1959, available at http://www.rand.org/publications/classics/wohlstetter/P1472/P1472.html (accessed July 10, 2008).

12. Alain Frachon and Daniel Vernet, *L'Amérique messianique: Les guerres des néo-conservateurs* (Paris: Seuil, 2004), pp. 98 ff.

13. Fred Kaplan, "Interview with Paul Nitze," p. 5 (no folder), box 366, Committee on the Present Danger Collection, Hoover Institution Archives, Stanford, Calif.

14. Paul Wolfowitz, "Defending the 'Ancient Dream of Freedom,'" speech delivered at the award ceremony for the "Scoop" Jackson Prize, Jewish Institute for National Security Affairs, November 21, 2002, available at http://www.jinsa.org/articles/articles.html/function/view/categoryid/1366/documentid/1839/history/3,2359,2166,1366,1839 (accessed July 10, 2008).

15. Strobe Talbott, *The Master of the Game: Paul Nitze and the Nuclear Peace* (New York: Knopf, 1988), p. 116.

16. Interview of Richard Perle by Ben Wattenberg on PBS, 2002.

17. Chris Suellentrop, "Richard Perle: Washington's Faceful Bureaucrat," *Slate,* August 23, 2002.

18. See, for example, Robert Kaiser, "Behind-Scenes Power over Arms Policy," *Washington Post,* June 24, 1977.

19. On Wolfowitz, the best reference is James Mann, *Rise of the Vulcans: The History of Bush's War Cabinet* (New York: Viking, 2004).

20. This influence is visible in the Carter doctrine and in the rapid-reaction forces established to intervene in the Gulf, which would later become Central Command (CENTCOM).

21. Interview with James Woolsey, July 19, 2001.

22. Kaufman, *Henry M. Jackson,* chap. 13.

23. See esp. Norman Podhoretz, "Vietnam and Collective Guilt," *Commentary,* March 1973; Podhoretz, "Making the World Safe for Communism," ibid., April 1976; Podhoretz, "The Present Danger," ibid., March 1980. See also Podhoretz, "The Culture of Appeasement," *Harper's,* October 1977.

24. Daniel P. Moynihan, "Was Woodrow Wilson Right?," *Commentary,* May 1974; and Moynihan, "The United States in Opposition," ibid., March 1975.

25. Kaufman, *Henry M. Jackson,* pp. 65 ff.

26. Jacob Heilbrunn, "The Moynihan Enigma," *American Prospect* 8 (July–August 1997).

27. John Ehrman, *Neoconservatism: Intellectuals and Foreign Affairs, 1945–1994* (New Haven: Yale University Press, 1995), p. 85.

28. Typed notes for a speech, February 8, 1976, "New York Board Meeting Feb 7 & 8 General," box 38, Personal Papers of Peter R. Rosenblatt, Lyndon Baines Johnson Presidential Library, Austin, Texas (hereafter Rosenblatt Collection).

29. "CDM 1976 campaign and Convention program," n.d., "CDM Future," box 40, Rosenblatt Collection.

30. Interview with Peter Rosenblatt, June 9, 2003.

31. E. J. Dionne, *Why Americans Hate Politics* (New York: Simon and Schuster, 1992), p. 126.

32. Interview with Ben Wattenberg, June 6, 2001. The full text of the 1976 platform is available at the website of the American Presidency Project, http://www.presidency.ucsb.edu/platforms.php. See the chapter "International Relations" (accessed July 10, 2008).

33. *Political Observer,* July 1976.

34. Stephen Rosenfeld, "Secretary of State Scoop Jackson?," *Washington Post,* June 18, 1976.

35. Interview with Penn Kemble, June 11, 2003.

36. Draft of *Political Observer,* Summer 1977, "*Newsletter*—Summer 77," box 32, Rosenblatt Collection.

37. Seymour Martin Lipset to Ben Wattenberg, Penn Kemble, and Peter Rosenblatt, August 19, 1976, "CDM Future," box 40, ibid.

38. Penn Kemble to CDM Members, July 8, 1976, "CDM (1976–1981 missing) 1975 & 1982," box 63, ibid.

39. Minutes of meeting, July 9, 1976, "CDM—Ex. Cttee Minutes," box 62, ibid.

40. A list of the names recommended by CDM to the Carter administration is offered on the companion website to the book, www.neoconservatism.vaisse .net, "List of CDM Recommendations for Carter Nominations (1976)."

41. Interview with Peter Rosenblatt, June 9, 2003.

42. Interview with Zbigniew Brzezinski, July 23, 2001.

43. A list of the names recommended by CDM for ambassadorial appointments in the Carter administration is offered on the companion website to the book, www.neoconservatism.vaisse.net, "List of CDM Recommendations to Jimmy Carter for Ambassadorial Appointments (1977)."

44. Interview with James Woolsey, July 19, 2001.

45. Interview with Max Kampelman, July 2, 2001; and Max M. Kampelman, *Entering New Worlds: The Memoirs of a Private Man in Public Life* (New York: HarperCollins, 1991).

46. Quoted in Morton Kondracke, "The Neoconservative Dilemma," *New Republic,* August 2, 1980.

47. Paul Seabury to Pat Moynihan, February 10, 1977, "CDM Future," box 40, Rosenblatt Collection.

48. Carl Gershman, "The Rise and Fall of the New Foreign-Policy Establishment," *Commentary,* July 1980, pp. 13–24.

49. Paul Warnke, "Apes on a Treadmill," *Foreign Policy* 18 (Spring 1975).

50. A chronological table of CDM officials is offered on the companion website to the book, www.neoconservatism.vaisse.net, "Table of CDM (1972–1992)."

51. Jack Germond and Jules Witcover, "Jackson, Moynihan Revive Coalition," *Washington Star,* May 29, 1977.

52. See Dionne, *Why Americans Hate Politics.*

53. Press release, "Hang Tough, Mr. President," May 14, 1977, "Open Letter to Carter," box 49, Rosenblatt Collection.

54. See, for example, "Democratic Group Backs Carter on Human Rights," *New York Times,* May 15, 1977; and Murrey Marder, "Carter, Hill Experts on SALT Meet Today," *Washington Post,* May 18, 1977. Valerio Giannini to CDM, May 24, 1977, "Open Letter to Carter," box 49, Rosenblatt Collection.

55. James Earl Carter, Speech on Human Rights and Foreign Policy, Notre Dame University, May 23, 1977, available at http://usinfo.org/docs/democracy/ 55.htm.

56. Press release, November 3, 1977, "Middle East Statement," box 21, Rosenblatt Collection.

57. News release, "CDM Warns against Cancelling Neutron Weapons," April 7, 1978, "Neutron Bomb," box 32, ibid.

58. Hodding Carter to Ben Wattenberg, May 30, 1978; Carl Wack to Joshua Muravchik, May 8, 1978; Stuart Eizenstat to Joshua Muravchik, May 11, 1978; and Patricia Derian to Joshua Muravchik, April 26, 1978, "Indochinese refugees—Letter to the president," all in box 20, ibid.

59. News release, "Democrats Blast Saudi Arms Sale; Call It 'Act of Retreat,'" May 7, 1978, "News Release," box 23, ibid.

60. "Coalition for Democratic Majority Joins Criticism of Foreign Policy," *Washington Post,* May 6, 1978; "Dmeocrats [*sic*] See Peril in Planes for Saudis," *New York Times,* May 7, 1978.

61. "Unilateral Restraint: The Experiment That Failed," letter and text, Joshua Muravchik to CDM Board Members, June 16, 1978, "6/22/78 Board Meeting," box 32, Rosenblatt Collection; and press release, June 25, 1978, "June 22—Panel + Board Meeting," box 7, ibid.

62. Interview with Jim Woolsey, July 19, 2001.

63. Interview with Max Kampelman, July 2, 2001.

64. This is the view of Peter Rosenblatt, interviewed on June 9, 2003.

65. Ehrman, *Neoconservatism;* and Jay Winik, *On the Brink: The Dramatic, Behind-the-Scenes Saga of the Reagan Era and the Men and Women Who Won the Cold War* (New York: Simon and Schuster, 1996). Winik's book is marred by numerous inaccuracies and should be treated with caution.

66. Interview with Jeane Kirkpatrick, July 2, 2001.

67. Interview with Max Kampelman, July 2, 2001.

68. Interview with Jeane Kirkpatrick, July 2, 2001.

69. Mann, *Rise of the Vulcans,* p. 130.

70. Interview with Penn Kemble, June 11, 2003.

71. Harry Truman, "Address of the President of the United States delivered before a joint session of the Senate and the House of Representatives, recommending assistance to Greece and Turkey," available at http://trumanlibrary .org.

72. John F. Kennedy, Inaugural Address, January 20, 1961, available at http://www.jfklibrary.org.

73. Robert Kagan, "Neocon Nation: Neoconservatism, c. 1776," *World Affairs,* Spring 2008; and Kagan, *Dangerous Nation: America's Place in the World, from Its Earliest Days to the Dawn of the Twentieth Century* (New York: Knopf, 2006).

74. On this episode, see George Shultz, *Turmoil and Triumph: My Years as Secretary of State* (New York: Scribner's, 1993).

75. Mann, *Rise of the Vulcans,* pp. 131–137.

76. Daniel P. Moynihan, "The Politics of Human Rights," *Commentary*, August 1977.

77. Moynihan, "Was Woodrow Wilson Right?," p. 30.

78. George F. Kennan, *The Cloud of Danger: Current Realities of American Foreign Policy* (Boston: Little, Brown, 1977).

79. Moynihan, "The Politics of Human Rights," p. 26.

80. See, for example, Podhoretz, "Making the World Safe for Communism."

81. Nathan Glazer, "American Values and American Foreign Policy," *Commentary*, July 1976, p. 37.

82. Jeane Kirkpatrick, "Dictatorships and Double Standards," *Commentary*, November 1979, pp. 34–45.

83. Mann, *Rise of the Vulcans*, pp. 91–93.

84. Kirkpatrick, "Dictatorships and Double Standards," p. 45.

85. Michael Ledeen, "How to Support the Democratic Revolution," *Commentary*, March 1985, p. 43.

86. Ben Wattenberg, Draft Preface, n.d., "Bar-Ilan Persian Gulf," box 47, Rosenblatt Collection; speech by George W. Bush to the National Endowment for Democracy, November 6, 2003, available at http://georgewbush_whitehouse.archives.gov/news.

87. CDM to Jimmy Carter, n.d., "White House MTG," box 59, Rosenblatt Collection.

88. See Paula Dobriansky, "Advancing Democracy," *National Interest*, Fall 2004.

89. Liz Sidoti, "McCain Favors a 'League of Democracies,'" *Washington Post*, April 30, 2008.

90. Press release, April 17, 1979, "Press Release Rhodesian Elections," box 19, Rosenblatt Collection.

91. Peter Berger, "Are Human Rights Universal?," *Commentary*, September 1977.

92. Moynihan, "The Politics of Human Rights," p. 23. See Walter Laqueur, "The Issue of Human Rights," *Commentary*, May 1977.

93. Laqueur, "The Issue of Human Rights," p. 32.

94. Podhoretz, "Making the World Safe for Communism"; Kaufman, *Henry M. Jackson*, p. 293; editorial, *Wall Street Journal*, July 23, 1975, p. 14.

95. Draft issue of *Political Observer*, March 1978, "Draft of *Newsletter*," box 32, Rosenblatt Collection.

96. A list of events and the original invitation for a CDM "Human Rights dinner" are reproduced on the companion website to the book, www.neoconservatism.vaisse.net, "Dinners and Ceremonies Organized by the CDM in Support of Communist Dissidents (1975–1980)."

97. Draft issue of *Political Observer*, March 1978.

98. Natan Sharansky with Ron Dermer, *The Case for Democracy: The Power of Freedom to Overcome Tyranny and Terror* (New York: Public Affairs, 2004).

99. On union support, see the 1975 pamphlet *Toward an Adequate Defense,* reproduced in *Congressional Record,* May 6, 1975, H3721-326.

100. Interview with Richard Schifter, September 28, 2004; Douglas Feith, *War and Decision: Inside the Pentagon at the Dawn of the War on Terrorism* (New York: HarperCollins, 2008), p. 29.

101. Kaufman, *Henry M. Jackson,* p. 132.

102. "Draft Resolution on Detente for *Coalition for a Democratic Majority,*" n.d., "Board of Directors—Minutes," box 7, Rosenblatt Collection.

103. Moynihan, "The United States in Opposition."

104. Richard Perle, "Thank God for the Death of the UN," *The Guardian,* March 21, 2003.

5. Nuclear Alarm

1. Roberta Wohlstetter, *Pearl Harbor: Warning and Decision* (Stanford: Stanford University Press, 1962).

2. There is no biography of Albert Wohlstetter. There are, however, two collections of essays in honor of the Wohlstetters: Andrew M. Marshall, J. J. Martin, and Henry Rowen, eds., *On Not Confusing Ourselves: Essays on National Security Strategy in Honor of Albert and Roberta Wohlstetter* (Boulder: Westview Press, 1991); and Robert Zarate and Henry Sokolski, eds., *Nuclear Heuristics: Selected Writings of Albert and Roberta Wohlstetter* (Carlisle, Pa.: Strategic Studies Institute, 2009), available at http://www.strategicstudiesinstitute.army.mil/pubs/display.cfm?PubID=893. The RAND Corporation has also made a number of their texts available at the following site: http://www.rand.org/publications/classics/wohlstetter/ (accessed June 4, 2009).

3. James Digby and J. J. Martin, "On Not Confusing Ourselves," in Marshall, Martin, and Rowen, *On Not Confusing Ourselves,* pp. 3–16.

4. Interview with Pierre Hassner, December 4, 2003.

5. Albert Wohlstetter, "The Delicate Balance of Terror," *Foreign Affairs,* January 1959, pp. 211–234; available at http://www.rand.org/publications/classics/wohlstetter/P1472/P1472.html (accessed July 20, 2008).

6. Ibid., p. 218.

7. Introductory remarks by the Honorable Paul H. Nitze, May 1, 1978 (5 pp.), box 334, Committee on the Present Danger Collection, Hoover Institution Archives, Stanford, Calif. (hereafter CPD Collection).

8. Paul Nitze, "Deterring Our Deterrent," *Foreign Policy,* Winter 1976–77.

9. Wohlstetter, "The Delicate Balance of Terror," p. 227.

10. Samuel F. Wells, "Sounding the Tocsin: NSC-68 and the Soviet Threat," *International Security* 4 (Fall 1979): 116–158.

11. Transcript, press conference, November 11, 1976, "PRESENT DANGER: INITIAL PRESS CONFERENCE 11 November 1976," box 288, CPD Collection.

12. Anne Hessing Cahn, *Killing Detente: The Right Attacks the CIA* (University Park: Pennsylvania State University Press, 1998), pp. 11 ff.

13. *"Intelligence Community Experiment in Competitive Analysis—Soviet Low Altitude Air Defense: An Alternative View. Report of Team 'B,'"* December 1976 (declassified document) (cited hereafter as *Soviet Strategic Objectives*).

14. Cahn, *Killing Detente,* p. 146.

15. Ibid., p. 158.

16. *Soviet Strategic Objectives,* p. 5. The executive summary of the original Team B report is reproduced on the companion website to the book, www .neoconservatism.vaisse.net, "Soviet Strategic Objectives: An Alternative View. Report of Team B (1976)."

17. *Soviet Strategic Objectives,* pp. 3–4.

18. Ibid., pp. 2–3.

19. Ibid., p. 2.

20. Donald P. Steury, "How the CIA Missed Stalin's Bomb Dissecting Soviet Analysis, 1946–50," *Studies in Intelligence* 49, no. 1 (April 15, 2007), available at http://www.cia.gov/library/center-for-the-study-of-intelligence/csi-publications/csi-studies/studies/vol49no1/html_files/stalins_bomb_3.html.

21. See esp. Raymond Garthoff, "Estimating Soviet Military Intentions and Capabilities," in *Watching the Bear: Essays on CIA's Analysis of the Soviet Union,* ed. Gerald K. Haines and Robert E. Leggett (Langley, Va.: Center for the Study of Intelligence, Central Intelligence Agency, 2003).

22. Central Intelligence Agency, *Allocation of Resources in the Soviet Union and China—1983* (Washington, D.C.: Government Printing Office, 1983), p. 306. See also Robert M. Gates, *From the Shadows: The Ultimate Insider's Story of Five Presidents and How They Won the Cold War,* 2d ed. (New York: Simon and Schuster, 1996); and James Risen, "CIA Counters Critics of Its Cold War Work," *New York Times,* November 25, 1999.

23. See James Noren, "CIA's Analysis of the Soviet Economy," in Haines and Leggett, *Watching the Bear.*

24. Ibid.; see Directorate of Intelligence, CIA, "Soviet Defense Spending: Recent Trends and Future Prospects. An Intelligence Assessment," July 1983; and Raymond Garthoff, *The Great Transition: American-Soviet Relations and the End of the Cold War* (Washington, D.C.: Brookings Institution Press, 1994), p. 41; as well as Garthoff, "The 'Spending Gap,'" *Bulletin of the Atomic Scientists,* May 1984, pp. 5–6.

25. Garthoff, "Estimating Soviet Military Intentions and Capabilities," p. 101.

26. David Binder, "New CIA Estimate Finds Soviets Seek Superiority in Arms," *New York Times,* December 26, 1976.

27. Max Kampelman, preface to Charles Tyroler II, ed., *Alerting America: The Papers of the Committee on the Present Danger* (Washington, D.C.: Pergamon-Brassey's, 1984), p. xv.

28. On the first CPD, see Wells, "Sounding the Tocsin."

29. On this point, see my article "Les néoconservateurs américains et l'Europe: Sous le signe de Munich," *Relations internationales* 120 (Winter 2004): 447–462.

30. Edna Rostow, untitled text (5 pp.), ed. Eugene Rostow, August 1989, last folder, box 365, CPD Collection.

31. Paul H. Nitze with Ann M. Smith and Steven L. Rearden, *From Hiroshima to Glasnost: At the Center of Decision—A Memoir* (New York: Grove Weidenfeld, 1989), pp. 353–354.

32. Ibid., p. 5.

33. Ibid., pp. 42–43.

34. Strobe Talbott, *The Master of the Game: Paul Nitze and the Nuclear Peace* (New York: Knopf, 1988), pp. 40 ff. Nicholas Thompson, Nitze's grandson, suggests instead that the meeting took place in the summer of 1943; Nicholas Thompson, "Worthy Opponents," *Boston Globe,* April 3, 2005.

35. X, "The Sources of Soviet Conduct," *Foreign Affairs,* July 1947, pp. 566–582, available at http://www.foreignaffairs.org/19470701faessay25403/x/the-sources-of-soviet-conduct.html (accessed July 20, 2008).

36. Ibid., p. 575.

37. On NSC-68, see Ernest May, *American Cold War Strategy: Interpreting NSC 68* (Boston: Bedford/St. Martin's, 1993); and Wells, "Sounding the Tocsin," p. 130.

38. This was how Acheson put it in his memoir, *Present at the Creation: My Years in the State Department,* rev. ed. (New York: W. W. Norton, 1987), p. 272.

39. Wells, "Sounding the Tocsin," p. 141.

40. Nitze, *From Hiroshima to Glasnost,* p. 181.

41. On this point, see Pierre Melandri, "L'administration Nixon et la négociation SALT I," *Relations internationales* 69 (Spring 1992).

42. Interview with Charls Walker, July 16, 2003.

43. Eugene Rostow, "For an Adequate Defense," *Wall Street Journal,* May 12, 1975.

44. Richard Allen to Eugene Rostow, May 12, 1975, and Allen to Charls Walker, May 13, 1975, "CPD—Houston Solicitation Sept. 1977," box 447, CPD Collection.

45. Interview with Richard Allen, July 17, 2003.

46. Documents on the CPD's budget and sources of funding are offered on the companion website to the book, www.neoconservatism.vaisse.net, "Budget and Sources of Funding of the CPD (1976–1992)."

47. For a chronological table of CPD officials, as well as a complete list of all CPD directors, see the companion website to the book, www.neoconservatism.vaisse.net, "Chronological Table of the CPD (1976–1992)" and "A Complete List of CPD Directors (1976–1992)."

48. Max Kampelman to Jeane Kirkpatrick, November 19, 1976, "[Max M. Kampelman]," box 291, CPD Collection.

49. Interview with Richard Allen, July 17, 2003.

50. Contrary to what is stated in Kampelman, preface to Tyroler, *Alerting America*, p. xviii.; cf. transcript, press conference, November 11, 1976, "PRESENT DANGER: INITIAL PRESS CONFERENCE 11 November 1976," box 288, CPD Collection.

51. Eugene Rostow, draft memorandum, December 1, 1975, "CPD Exective Comm. Minutes," box 334, CPD Collection. Some CPD documents are included in Tyroler, *Alerting America*. A complete chronological list of CDP publications is offered on the companion website to the book, www.neoconservatism .vaisse.net, "The Publications of the CPD (1976–1992)."

52. Memo, Eugene Rostow to Members of Planning Group, Committee on Foreign and Defense Policy, April 28, 1976, "folder #1: Common Sense and the Common Danger," box 275, CPD Collection.

53. "Report on Media Reaction to Initial Press Conference, November 11, 1976," December 9, 1976, "COMM. ON PRESENT DANGER Meeting—Dec. 15, 1976," box 447, ibid. The report is available on the companion website to the book, http://neoconservatism.vaisse.net/doku.php?id=how_the_committee _on_the_present_danger_will_operate.

54. CPD, "How the Committee on the Present Danger Will Operate—What It Will Do and What It Will Not Do," September 8, 1976.

55. Transcript, press conference, November 11, 1976, "PRESENT DANGER: INITIAL PRESS CONFERENCE 11 November 1976."

56. "Report on Media Reaction to Initial Press Conference, November 11, 1976."

57. "On US Dealings with the Soviet Union," *New York Times*, January 11, 1977.

58. CPD, "The Nation's Editors Speak Up on 'The Present Danger,' with a Section on Soviet Reaction."

59. Eugene Rostow to Board of Directors, March 30, 1977, "PRESENT DANGER: SALT PRESS CONFERENCE 6 July 1977," box 288, CPD Collection.

60. Reagan quoted in Talbott, *Master of the Game*, p. 4.

61. Reagan quoted in George Wilson, "A Build-up in U.S. Forces; Reagan Advisers Urge Military Build-up," *Washington Post*, June 16, 1980. Murrey Marder, "US as 2d Best Is Fairy Tale, Kissinger Says," *Washington Post*, April 12, 1976.

62. This argument was proposed by Joe Fowler at the CPD's annual news conference in 1987, and everyone seemed in agreement, according to the minutes. See Select 1987 Annual Meeting Remarks, 7 pp., "11th Annual Meeting, 5–6 November 1987," box 221, CPD Collection.

63. Eugene Rostow, booklet of transcripts of 1978 Annual Meeting, Rostow, cassette 2, p. 5, box 164, ibid.

64. John Roche, "Moscow and the 'Window of Opportunity': A Cautionary Brief," n.d., "John P. Roche," box 365, ibid.

65. Ron Suskind, *The One Percent Doctrine: Deep Inside America's Pursuit of Its Enemies since 9/11* (New York: Simon and Schuster, 2006).

66. Richard Pipes, *Survival Is Not Enough: Soviet Realities and America's Future* (New York: Simon and Schuster, 1984). The title, whether deliberately or not, seems to be a direct response to the title of a chapter in Raymond Aron's *Paix et guerre entre les nations:* "To survive is to conquer."

67. Eugene Rostow to Members of the Board of Directors, June 2, 1977, "Memos to Board—1976–1981," box 337, CPD Collection.

68. Talbott, *Master of the Game,* p. 149.

69. Minutes of meeting, January 26, 1977, "CPD Executive Comm. Minutes," box 334, CPD Collection.

70. Eugene Rostow to Cyrus Vance, April 7, 1977, "CPD Eugene V. Rostow 1977," box 109, ibid.

71. Eugene Rostow to Cyrus Vance, July 16, 1977, and Rostow to Charles ` Tyroler, July 25, 1977, ibid.

72. Minutes of meeting, August 3, 1977, "CPD Executive Comm. Minutes," box 334, ibid.

73. Eugene Rostow to the Board of Directors and to the Executive Committee, August 10, 1977, "CPD: *SALT*—White House Conference 8/4/77," box 288; Rostow to the Board of Directors, August 23, 1977, "Memos to Board—1976–1981," box 337; and E. V. R., Memorandum for the files, n.d., and handwritten letter, Rostow to Charles Tyroler, "Friday" (probably August 5, 1977), "CPD: *SALT*—White House Conference 8/4/77," box 288, CPD Collection.

74. "Talking Points for Opening Statement by E. V. Rostow," August 4, 1977, "CPD: *SALT*—White House Conference 8/4/77," box 288, ibid.

75. (No title) talking points for Paul Nitze, August 4, 1977, ibid.

76. Cf. Fred Kaplan, "Interview with Paul Nitze," p. 7 (no folder), box 366, ibid.

77. E. V. R., Memorandum for the files, n.d., "CPD: *SALT*—White House Conference 8/4/77," box 288, ibid.

78. Rowland Evans and Robert Novak, "A Touchy Carter: Shades of Former Presidents?," *Washington Post,* August 13, 1977; see also Godfrey Sperling, "Pressuring Carter on Arms," *Christian Science Monitor,* August 22, 1977.

79. Interview with Zbigniew Brzezinski, July 23, 2001, and excerpt from his diary, which he was kind enough to share.

80. Eugene Rostow to the Board of Directors, August 23, 1977.

81. Eugene Rostow to President Carter, September 8, 1977, "CPD Eugene V. Rostow 1977," box 109, CPD Collection.

82. Ibid.

83. Eugene Rostow to Charles Tyroler, September 8, 1977, ibid.

84. Carter administration directives are available on the website of the Federation of American Scientists, at http://www.fas.org/irp/offdocs/nsdd/index.html. PD-18 can be found at http://www.fas.org/irp/offdocs/pd/pd18.pdf (accessed July 20, 2008).

85. This was PRM-10 (Presidential Review Memorandum), available at the website of the Federation of American Scientists, http://www.fas.org/irp/offdocs/prm/prm10.pdf (accessed July 20, 2008).

86. Interview with Samuel Huntington, June 19, 2004.

87. Ibid.

88. Handwritten notes, no author, "9/16/77 with Dr. Huntington," "CPD Executive Comm. Minutes," box 334, CPD Collection.

89. Eugene Rostow to President Carter, September 19, 1977, "CPD Eugene V. Rostow 1977," box 109, ibid.

90. Zbigniew Brzezinski to Eugene Rostow, October 11, 1977, "Executive Committee Calls—Agenda 1976–1977," box 266, ibid.

91. Minutes, November 11, 1977, "First Annual Meeting," box 164, ibid.

92. On the SALT II negotiations, the primary reference is Strobe Talbott, *Endgame: The Inside Story of SALT II* (New York: Harper and Row, 1980). See also Raymond L. Garthoff, *Detente and Confrontation: American-Soviet Relations from Nixon to Reagan* (Washington, D.C.: Brookings Institution Press, 1994). Finally, see Pierre Melandri, *Une incertaine alliance: Les États-Unis et l'Europe, 1973–1983* (Paris: Publications de la Sorbonne, 1988).

93. (No title) talking points for Paul Nitze, August 4, 1977.

94. Brian J. Auten, *Carter's Conversion: The Hardening of American Defense Policy* (Columbia: University of Missouri Press, 2008).

95. Transcript, Eugene Rostow to CPD Board of Directors, November 11, 1977, pp. 66–67 (no folder), box 166, CPD Collection.

96. This is revealed in a document cited by Auten, *Carter's Conversion*, chap. 5: NSC Memorandum from Brzezinski to President Carter, Subject: NSC Weekly Report, no. 36, November 11, 1977, p. 2, Declassified Documents Reference Service, Document No. CK3100099284.

97. The primary reference on the SALT II ratification debate is Dan Caldwell, *The Dynamics of Domestic Policy and Arms Control: The SALT II Treaty Ratification Debate* (Columbia: University of South Carolina Press, 1991). See also Auten, *Carter's Conversion*.

98. This is the judgment of Garthoff, *Detente and Confrontation*, pp. 906–907.

99. Robert G. Kaiser, "Culver Challenges Jackson, Blasts Leaks on SALT," *Washington Post*, November 8, 1977.

100. "Notes on discussion with Landon Butler 13 June 1978" and memorandum of conversation, July 11, 1978 (no folder), box 273, CPD Collection.

101. "Notes on discussion with Landon Butler 13 June 1978."

102. Memorandum of conversation, July 11, 1978.

103. Ibid.

104. Talbott, *Endgame,* p. 174.

105. Minutes of meeting, June 20, 1979, "CPD Executive Comm. Minutes," box 334, CPD Collection.

106. Rostow remarks, "8–9 November 1979 Third Annual Meeting," box 163, ibid.

107. Ibid.

108. See, for example, Caldwell, *Dynamics of Domestic Policy and Arms Control,* p. 60.

109. See, for example, Eugene Rostow to Scoop Jackson, September 27, 1979 (no folder), box 109, CPD Collection.

110. Kenneth H. Bacon, "Nitze, Long a Backer of Arms Curbs, Now Is a Key Critic of SALT," *Wall Street Journal,* June 29, 1979.

111. See, for example, Garthoff, *Detente and Confrontation,* p. 906; Caldwell, *Dynamics of Domestic Policy and Arms Control,* p. 71.

112. On the Carter administration's campaign, the reference is still Caldwell, *Dynamics of Domestic Policy and Arms Control,* p. 63.

113. Zbigniew Brzezinski, *Power and Principle: Memoirs of the National Security Adviser, 1977–1981* (New York: Farrar Straus and Giroux, 1983), p. 189.

114. Gates, *From the Shadows,* pp. 155 ff.

115. Garthoff, *Detente and Confrontation,* p. 908.

6. Migration to Power

1. Memo, Richard V. Allen to George H. W. Bush, February 24, 1992, "Richard V. Allen Executive Committee," box 385, Committee on the Present Danger Collection, Hoover Institution Archives, Stanford, Calif. (hereafter CPD Collection).

2. Interview with Richard Allen, July 17, 2003.

3. Eugene Rostow to Scoop Jackson, April 21 and June 12, 1980 (no folder), box 207, CPD Collection.

4. Eugene Rostow to Edward Kennedy, April 25 and May 7, 1980, ibid.

5. Max M. Kampelman, *Entering New Worlds: The Memoirs of a Private Man in Public Life* (New York: HarperCollins, 1991), p. 253.

6. "Reagan for president," press release, April 20, 1980, "Richard V. Allen 1979–1984 Executive Committee," box 337, CPD Collection.

7. Statement before the Republican Platform Committee by Nitze and Pipes, "Platforms—Democratic, Republican," box 17, ibid.

8. Press release, Reagan-Bush Campaign Committee, July 29, 1980, "Present Danger: Reagan, Ronald," box 168, ibid.

9. See, for example, "Rostow, Nitze Rap Carter on SALT II, Back Reagan," *Washington Star,* October 25, 1980.

10. Norman Podhoretz, *The Present Danger: Do We Have the Will to Reverse the Decline of American Power?* (New York: Simon and Schuster, 1980), p. 36.

11. Memo, Penn Kemble to CDM friends, n.d., "Testimony—Platform Cttee June 80," box 18, Personal Papers of Peter R. Rosenblatt, Lyndon Baines Johnson Presidential Library, Austin, Texas (hereafter Rosenblatt Collection); "A Platform for the 1980's," n.d., "Platform & it-com," box 16, Rosenblatt Collection.

12. Jeane Kirkpatrick, "Why We Don't Become Republicans," *Common Sense* 2 (Fall 1979): 32.

13. Ibid., p. 33.

14. Anecdote recounted by Jay Winik, *On the Brink: The Dramatic, Behind-the-Scenes Saga of the Reagan Era and the Men and Women Who Won the Cold War* (New York: Simon and Schuster, 1996), p. 94.

15. Abrams quoted in Mark Gerson, *The Neoconservative Vision: From the Cold War to the Culture Wars* (Lanham, Md.: Madison Books, 1996), p. 187; Symposium, "Liberalism and the Jews," *Commentary,* January 1980, with contributions by Elliott Abrams, p. 17, and Gertrude Himmelfarb, p. 44.

16. Kirkpatrick, "Why We Don't Become Republicans," p. 34.

17. Interview with Jeane Kirkpatrick, July 2, 2001.

18. Interview with Penn Kemble, June 11, 2003.

19. A list of members of the Coalition for a Democratic Majority who switched to Reagan is offered on the companion website to the book, www.neoconservatism.vaisse.net, "CDM Members Joining Reagan in 1980."

20. Norman Podhoretz, "The Neo-conservative Anguish over Reagan's Foreign Policy," *New York Times Magazine,* May 2, 1982, p. 30.

21. On Reagan as founding member, see Charles Tyroler II, ed., *Alerting America: The Papers of the Committee on the Present Danger* (Washington, D.C.: Pergamon-Brassey's, 1984), p. 341. On Reagan as a member of the executive committee, see Jerry W. Sanders, *Peddlers of Crisis: The Committee on the Present Danger and the Politics of Containment* (Boston: South End Press, 1983), pp. 217 and 282.

22. Eugene Rostow to Ronald Reagan, March 31, 1977, "Present Danger: Reagan, Ronald," box 168, CPD Collection.

23. Interview with Richard Allen, July 17, 2003.

24. Draft letter, Ronald Reagan to Noble Foundation, n.d. (end of 1979), "CPD Foundations: Noble," box 382, CPD Collection.

25. Examples of op-ed pieces and speeches by CPD members, including Ronald Reagan, are offered on the companion website to the book, www.neoconservatism.vaisse.net, "CPD's Reach in the Media, Including

through Ronald Reagan's Columns." Reagan's radio commentary, including the "Rostow Speeches," can be found in *Reagan in His Own Hand: The Writings of Ronald Reagan That Reveal His Revolutionary Vision for America* (New York: Free Press, 2001). These texts document Reagan's extensive intellectual activity.

26. Ronald Reagan to Eugene Rostow, November 6, 1978, "Present Danger: Reagan, Ronald," box 168, CPD Collection.

27. A chronological table of CPD officials and a complete list of all CPD directors are offered on the companion website to the book, www .neoconservatism.vaisse.net, "Chronological Table of the CPD (1976–1992)" and "A Complete List of CPD Directors (1976–1992)."

28. A copy of this letter is offered on the companion website to the book, www.neoconservatism.vaisse.net, "Ronald Reagan, Newly Elected President, Writes to His Former CPD Colleagues (7 November 1980)." Source: "MEMOS TO BOARD—1976–1981," box 337, CPD Collection.

29. A list of the main CPD members receiving nominations in the Reagan administration is offered on the companion website to the book, www .neoconservatism.vaisse.net, "Executive Functions of CPD Members in the Reagan Administration." See also David Shribman, "Group Goes from Exile to Influence," *New York Times,* November 22, 1981.

30. See Winik, *On the Brink.*

31. See, for example, Richard Pipes, "Misinterpreting the Cold War: The Hard-Liners Had It Right," *Foreign Affairs,* January–February 1995, pp. 154–161.

32. Christopher Layne, "The Overreaching Reagan Doctrine," *Wall Street Journal,* April 15, 1987.

33. See Pierre Melandri, *Reagan: Une biographie totale* (Paris: Laffont, 1988).

34. NSDD-32, pp. 1–2. This was the thirty-second document issued by Reagan's National Security Council. The administration's declassified NSDDs are available at the website of the Federation of American Scientists, http://www.fas .org/irp/offdocs/nsdd/index.html.

35. On destabilization operations, see Peter Schweizer, *Victory: The Reagan Administration's Secret Strategy That Hastened the Collapse of the Soviet Union* (New York: Atlantic Monthly Press, 1994); Robert M. Gates, *From the Shadows: The Ultimate Insider's Story of Five Presidents and How They Won the Cold War,* 2d ed. (New York: Simon and Schuster, 1996).

36. Jeane Kirkpatrick, "Dictatorships and Double Standards," *Commentary,* November 1979.

37. The text of Reagan's June 8, 1982, speech is available at the website of the Reagan Library, http://www.presidentreagan.info/speeches/crusade.cfm (accessed July 22, 2008).

38. Edna Rostow, untitled text (5 pp.), ed. Eugene Rostow, August 1989, last

folder, box 365, CPD Collection; and Strobe Talbott, *Deadly Gambits: The Reagan Administration and the Stalemate in Nuclear Arms Control*, 2d rev. ed. (New York: Vintage Books, 1985), p. 54.

39. See, for example, Eugene Rostow to Richard Allen, April 20, 1981 (no folder), box 206, CPD Collection.

40. Talbott, *The Master of the Game: Paul Nitze and the Nuclear Peace* (New York: Knopf, 1988), p. 178.

41. Talbott, *Deadly Gambits*, p. 142.

42. Ibid., p. 168.

43. Talbott, *Master of the Game*, p. 13.

44. Quoted in Talbott, *Deadly Gambits*, p. 18.

45. On Reagan and SDI, see Frances FitzGerald, *Way Out There in the Blue: Reagan, Star Wars, and the End of the Cold War* (New York: Simon and Schuster, 2000).

46. See Kampelman, *Entering New Worlds*, chaps. 15–17.

47. Talbott, *Master of the Game*, pp. 383 ff.

48. Robert Tucker, "The Middle East: Carterism without Carter," *Commentary*, September 1981.

49. Podhoretz, "Neo-conservative Anguish over Reagan's Foreign Policy."

50. Ibid., p. 30.

51. Sidney Blumenthal, *The Rise of the Counter-Establishment: From Conservative Ideology to Political Power* (New York: Harper and Row, 1988), p. 147.

52. Norman Podhoretz, "Appeasement by Any Other Name," *Commentary*, July 1983.

53. Norman Podhoretz, "The Reagan Road to Détente," *Foreign Affairs: America and the World 1984*, vol. 63, no. 3 (1984), pp. 447–464.

54. "Interview with Television Network Broadcasters," December 4, 1987, available at http://www.reagan.utexas.edu/archives/speeches/1987/120387d .htm (accessed July 22, 2008).

55. See James Mann, *The Rebellion of Ronald Reagan: A History of the End of the Cold War* (New York: Viking, 2009).

56. Podhoretz, "Appeasement by Any Other Name"; Edward Luttwak, "Why We Need More 'Waste, Fraud and Mismanagement' in the Pentagon," *Commentary*, February 1982; Walter Laqueur, "What We Know about the Soviet Union," ibid., February 1983; and Laqueur, "Glasnost and Its Limits," ibid., July 1988.

57. Patrick Glynn, "Why an American Build-Up Is Morally Necessary," *Commentary*, February 1984; Angelo Codevilla, "Is There Still a Soviet Threat?," ibid., November 1988.

58. See John Ehrman, *Neoconservatism: Intellectuals and Foreign Affairs, 1945–1994* (New Haven: Yale University Press, 1995), pp. 175 ff.

59. Jean-François Revel, *How Democracies Perish* (Garden City, N.Y.: Doubleday, 1984); and Revel, "Is Communism Reversible?," *Commentary,* January 1989.

60. See Ehrman, *Neoconservatism,* p. 178.

61. Francis Fukuyama, "The End of History?," *National Interest,* Summer 1989.

62. Cf. Eugene Rostow to Members of the Board, July 2, 1981, "Fundraising Letters 1981," box 463, CPD Collection.

63. CPD, *Countering the Soviet Threat—US Defense Strategy in the 1980s,* pamphlet, May 9, 1980, reprinted in Tyroler, *Alerting America,* pp. 178–183.

64. William Van Cleave to Charles Tyroler, February 13, 1982, "CPD Quick Fix Pamphlet," box 491; and letter and memo, Leonard Sullivan to Charls Walker, March 2, 1982, "Legislative File: 'Is the Reagan Defense Program Adeq.,'" box 87, CPD Collection.

65. CPD, *Is the Reagan Defense Program Adequate?,* pamphlet, March 17, 1982, reprinted in Tyroler, *Alerting America,* pp. 184–201.

66. Michael Getler, "Panel Says Ex-Member Reagan Fails to Bolster Defense," *Washington Post,* March 18, 1982.

67. Ronald Reagan to Charls Walker, July 12, 1982, reprinted in Tyroler, *Alerting America,* pp. 331–333.

68. See, e.g., handwritten note, Charls Walker to Charles Tyroler, January 17, 1983 (no folder), box 206, CPD Collection.

69. CPD, *Can America Catch Up?: The US–Soviet Military Balance,* pamphlet, November 30, 1984.

70. "Progress on Balance Sheet," July 10, 1984, box 493, CPD Collection.

71. Richard Perle to Charls E. Walker, July 27, 1984 (no folder), box 353, ibid.

72. Talbott, *Master of the Game,* p. 373.

73. Martin Amis, "Nuclear City: The Megadeath Intellectuals," in *Visiting Mrs. Nabokov and Other Excursions* (New York: Vintage Books, 1995), pp. 25–26.

74. CPD, *Soviet Defense Expenditures,* pamphlet, May 16, 1989.

75. Eugene Rostow to CPD Executive Committee, n.d. (April/May 1989), "EXEC 1–9–90," box 220, CPD Collection.

76. Various annotated Rostow drafts, untitled folder, ibid.

77. Eugene Rostow to members of the Executive Committee, April 23, 1990, untitled folder, ibid.

78. Douglas Dillon to Charles Tyroler, September 23, 1988, "C. Douglas Dillon," box 282, CPD Collection.

79. Elmo Zumwalt to Charles Tyroler, November 15, 1990, "Elmo Zumwalt," box 182, ibid.

80. Documents on the CPD's budget and sources of funding are offered on

the companion website to the book, www.neoconservatism.vaisse.net, "Budget and Sources of Funding of the CPD (1976–1992)."

81. Press release, "Committee Issues Analysis of US-Soviet Military Balance," n.d., "MIL BAL 91," box 219, CPD Collection. The box contains several copies of this pamphlet, which shows that it was published.

82. Podhoretz quoted in Francis Clines, "Neo-Conservatives Taunt 'Evil' in Soviet Habitat," *New York Times,* June 21, 1989.

83. Gaffney quoted by John Judis, "The Conservative Crackup," *American Prospect,* September 1990, p. 35.

84. Kristol quoted in E. J. Dionne, "Cold Warrior Meltdown," *Washington Post,* December 19, 1990; see also Irving Kristol, "Defining Our National Interest," *National Interest,* Fall 1990, p. 16.

85. Irving Kristol, "Taking Glasnost Seriously," *Wall Street Journal,* December 8, 1987.

86. Irving Kristol, "The Soviets' Albatross States," *Wall Street Journal,* July 22, 1988.

87. See Blumenthal, *Rise of the Counter-Establishment.*

88. James Q. Wilson and George L. Kelling, "Broken Windows: The Police and Neighborhood Safety," *Atlantic Monthly,* March 1982.

89. Christopher Jencks, "Is the Public School Obsolete?," *Public Interest* 2 (Winter 1966): 18–27.

90. Edward Rothstein, "Mission Accomplished, a Journal Folds," *New York Times,* May 9, 2005.

91. Arthur Laffer and Robert Mundell, "The Mundell-Laffer Hypothesis: A New View of the World Economy," *Public Interest,* Spring 1975.

92. Kristol obtained an AEI grant for Jude Wanniski to write *The Way the World Works* (New York: Basic Books, 1978).

93. Irving Kristol, *Two Cheers for Capitalism* (New York: Basic Books, 1978).

94. Gerson, *The Neoconservative Vision,* p. 239.

95. Irving Kristol, "Forty Good Years," *Public Interest,* Spring 2005.

96. Michael Novak, *The Spirit of Democratic Capitalism* (New York: Simon and Schuster, 1982). On Novak, see the excellent chap. 5 in Gary J. Dorrien, *The Neoconservative Mind: Politics, Culture, and Ideology* (Philadelphia: Temple University Press, 1993).

97. National Conference of Catholic Bishops, *The Challenge of Peace: God's Promise and Our Response* (Washington, D.C.: Office of Publishing and Promotion Services, United States Catholic Conference, 1983). A good summary of this text is available at http://www.americancatholic.org/Newsletters/CU/ac0883.asp.

98. Richard Neuhaus, *Doing Well and Doing Good: The Challenge to the Christian Capitalist* (New York: Doubleday, 1992).

99. Damon Linker, *The Theocons: Secular America under Siege* (New York: Doubleday, 2006).

100. Quoted in Gerson, *The Neoconservative Vision,* p. 349.

101. Seymour Martin Lipset, *American Exceptionalism: A Double-Edged Sword* (New York: W. W. Norton, 1996), p. 197.

102. Quoted in Adam Meyerson, "Welfare State Conservatism: Jeane Kirkpatrick Speaks about Her Domestic Policy Views," *Policy Review,* Spring 1988, p. 5.

103. Editorial, "Come On In, the Water's Fine," *National Review,* March 1971.

104. Stephen Tonsor, "Why I Too Am Not a Neoconservative," *National Review* 38 (June 20, 1986): 55, quoted in Gerson, *The Neoconservative Vision,* p. 314.

105. Gerson, *The Neoconservative Vision,* pp. 312 ff.; and Judis, "The Conservative Crackup."

106. Buchanan quoted in Judis, "The Conservative Crackup," p. 33.

107. Russell Kirk, "The Neoconservatives: An Endangered Species," *Heritage Lectures,* no. 178 (1988), available at http://www.heritage.org/Research/PoliticalPhilosophy/HL178.cfm (accessed July 20, 2008).

108. Judis, "The Conservative Crackup," p. 33.

109. Quoted in Gideon G. Rose, "The Radical Democrats at CDM," *Yale Political Monthly,* December 1983.

110. Memo, Penn Kemble to CDM Directors, n.d., "CDM—Current Matters," box 66, Rosenblatt Collection.

111. Peter Rosenblatt to CDM Board Members, May 10, 1983, ibid.

112. Quoted in David Shribman, "Democrats of 'Mainstream' Regroup to Try Again," *New York Times,* May 23, 1983.

113. The original invitation and program for this conference are reproduced on the companion website to the book, www.neoconservatism.vaisse.net, "The CDM Symposium in Honor of Scoop Jackson (15 November 1983)."

114. Executive Committee Meeting, December 5, 1983, "Exe. Ctte Meeting, Dec. 5, 1983," box 7, Rosenblatt Collection.

115. Interview with James Woolsey, July 19, 2001.

116. Interview with Penn Kemble, June 11, 2003.

117. Abrams quoted in Fred Barnes, "The Death of the Jackson Wing," *American Spectator,* March 1984, pp. 26–27.

118. See Daniel Patrick Moynihan, *On The Law of Nations* (Cambridge, Mass.: Harvard University Press, 1990).

119. See Jane Perlez, "After Much in Common, a Split on Central America," *New York Times,* June 30, 1983.

120. Moynihan quoted in Ehrman, *Neoconservatism,* p. 167.

121. CDM, "Democratic Solidarity: Proposals for the 1984 Democratic Party

Platform on Foreign Policy and National Defense," "CDM—Current Matters," box 66, Rosenblatt Collection.

122. Ibid., p. 2.

123. See page 141 of this volume.

124. Jeane Kirkpatrick, speech to the Republican Convention, Dallas, August 20, 1984, available at http://www.cnn.com/ALLPOLITICS/1996/conventions/san.diego/facts/GOP.speeches/past/84.kirkpatrick.shtml.

125. Speech text for delivery to CDM, "A Democratic Defense Policy: Defense without Nonsense," untitled folder, box 58, Rosenblatt Collection.

126. "A Program to Strengthen Support for Defense in the Democratic Party," n.d., untitled folder, ibid.

127. Peter Rosenblatt to Ben Wattenberg, Penn Kemble, and James Woolsey, October 8, 1987, "General (cont')," box 64, ibid.

128. John F. Hale, "The Making of the New Democrats," *Political Science Quarterly* 110 (Summer 1995): 207–232; and Kenneth Baer, *Reinventing Democrats: The Politics of Liberalism from Reagan to Clinton* (Lawrence: University Press of Kansas, 2000).

129. Hale, "The Making of the New Democrats," p. 214.

130. Baer, *Reinventing Democrats,* p. 120.

131. William Galston and Elaine Karmack, *The Politics of Evasion: Democrats and the Presidency* (Washington, D.C.: Progressive Policy Institute, 1989).

132. Hale, "The Making of the New Democrats," p. 225.

133. "Remarks of Gov. Charles Robb, Chairman, DLC, *The Coalition for a Democratic Majority,*" Washington, D.C., May 6, 1986 (no folder), box 7, Rosenblatt Collection.

134. Peter Rosenblatt to Charles Robb, May 13, 1986, large green folder, box 66, ibid.

135. Peter Rosenblatt to Sam Nunn, October 11, 1988, "DLC," ibid.

136. Fax, Penn Kemble to Peter Rosenblatt, n.d. (May 1989), "General," box 64, ibid.

137. Interview with Peter Rosenblatt, June 9, 2003.

138. Interview with Will Marshall, January 28, 2004.

139. Fax, Peter Rosenblatt to Ben Wattenberg and Penn Kemble, February 19, 1991, "General," box 64, Rosenblatt Collection. The CDM was not legally dissolved until 1992, shortly before the election of Bill Clinton.

140. Peter Rosenblatt to Stuart Goodwin, April 20, 1993, ibid.

141. Interview with Richard Schifter, September 28, 2004; Schifter quoted in Winik, *On the Brink*, p. 601.

142. Fred Barnes, "They're Back! Neocons for Clinton," *New Republic* 207 (August 3, 1992): 12–14.

143. Interview with Peter Rosenblatt, June 9, 2003.

144. Interview with Penn Kemble, June 11, 2003.

145. See Joshua Muravchik, "Lament of a Clinton Supporter," *Commentary*, August 1993.

146. Interview with Penn Kemble, June 11, 2003.

7. The Third Age

1. See Norman Podhoretz, "Neoconservatism: A Eulogy," *Commentary*, March 1996, available at http://www.aei.org/publications/pubID.18103/pub_detail.asp; Irving Kristol, *Neoconservatism: The Autobiography of an Idea* (New York: Free Press, 1995), p. xi; Seymour Martin Lipset, *American Exceptionalism: A Double-Edged Sword* (New York: W. W. Norton, 1996), p. 200.

2. Interview with William Kristol, July 24, 2003; and Robert Kagan and William Kristol, "Toward a Neo-Reaganite Foreign Policy," *Foreign Affairs*, July–August 1996.

3. The best source for following debates on foreign policy doctrine in the 1990s and for the evolution of neoconservatives is Gary Dorrien, *Imperial Designs: Neoconservatism and the New Pax Americana* (New York: Routledge, 2004).

4. Irving Kristol, "In Search of Our National Interest," *Wall Street Journal*, June 7, 1990.

5. Ibid.

6. *National Interest*, Fall 1990, special section on "America's Purpose Now," contributions by Nathan Glazer, "A Time for Modesty," and Jeane Kirkpatrick, "A Normal Country in a Normal Time."

7. Jeane Kirkpatrick, "Dictatorships and Double Standards," *Commentary*, November 1979, p. 37; "enormously desirable": Kirkpatrick, "A Normal Country in a Normal Time," p. 42.

8. Ben Wattenberg, "Neo-Manifest Destinarianism," *National Interest*, Fall 1990; Wattenberg, *The First Universal Nation: Leading Indicators and Ideas about the Surge of America in the 1990s* (New York: Free Press, 1991).

9. Joshua Muravchik, *Exporting Democracy: Fulfilling America's Destiny* (Washington, D.C.: AEI Press, 1991), esp. p. 8; Gregory Fossedal, *The Democratic Imperative: Exporting the American Revolution* (New York: Basic Books, 1989).

10. Joshua Muravchik, *The Imperative of American Leadership: A Challenge to Neo-Isolationism* (Washington, D.C.: AEI Press, 1996); Michael Ledeen, *Freedom Betrayed: How America Led a Global Democratic Revolution, Won the Cold War, and Walked Away* (Washington, D.C.: AEI Press, 1996).

11. David Wurmser, *Tyranny's Ally: America's Failure to Defeat Saddam Hussein* (Washington, D.C.: AEI Press, 1999).

12. Charles Krauthammer, "Democratic Realism: An American Foreign Pol-

icy for a Unipolar World," Irving Kristol Lecture for 2004, February 12, 2004, available at http://www.aei.org/publications/pubID.19912,filter.all/pub _detail.asp.

13. See James Mann, *Rise of the Vulcans: The History of Bush's War Cabinet* (New York: Viking, 2004).

14. Patrick Tyler, "U.S. Strategy Plan Calls for Insuring No Rivals Develop: A One-Superpower World," *New York Times,* March 8, 1992.

15. Mann, *Rise of the Vulcans,* p. 210.

16. Secretary of Defense Dick Cheney, "Defense Strategy for the 1990s: The Regional Defense Strategy," January 1993, available at http://www .informationclearinghouse.info/pdf/naarpr_Defense.pdf. See also Tony Smith, *A Pact with the Devil: Washington's Bid for World Supremacy and the Betrayal of the American Promise* (New York: Routledge, 2007), p. 7.

17. Cheney, "Defense Strategy for the 1990s," pp. 2, 4, and 6.

18. Ibid., p. 6.

19. Cheney, "Defense Strategy for the 1990s."

20. The four options are drawn from Barry Posen and Andrew Ross, "Competing Visions for U.S. Grand Strategy," *International Security,* Winter 1996–97.

21. David Carr, "White House Listens When Weekly Speaks," *New York Times,* March 11, 2003.

22. Mann, *Rise of the Vulcans,* p. 316.

23. Interview with William Kristol, July 24, 2003.

24. Robert Kagan, "Mission Possible," *Weekly Standard,* September 18, 1995, p. 22.

25. Interview with William Kristol, July 24, 2003.

26. David Brooks and William Kristol, "What Ails the Right," *Wall Street Journal,* September 15, 1997.

27. Charles Krauthammer, "A Critique of Pure Newt," *Weekly Standard,* September 18, 1995.

28. Brooks and Kristol, "What Ails the Right."

29. David Brooks and William Kristol, "The Politics of Creative Destruction," *Weekly Standard,* March 13, 2000.

30. Kagan and Kristol, "Toward a Neo-Reaganite Foreign Policy."

31. Interview with William Kristol, July 24, 2003.

32. Interview with Gary Schmitt, August 1, 2008.

33. The left-wing website "Right Web" lists the signers of the principal PNAC texts at http://www.publiceye.org/pnac_chart/pnac.html.

34. Interview with Gary Schmitt, August 1, 2008.

35. Dorrien, *Imperial Designs,* p. 196; Jacob Heilbrunn, *They Knew They Were Right: The Rise of the Neocons* (New York: Doubleday, 2008), p. 214.

36. Damon Linker, *The Theocons: Secular America under Siege* (New York: Doubleday, 2006).

37. Robert Kagan and William Kristol, "Burden of Power Is Having to Wield It," *Washington Post,* March 19, 2000; quoted in Heilbrunn, *They Knew They Were Right,* p. 221.

38. Kagan and Kristol, "Toward a Neo-Reaganite Foreign Policy," p. 23.

39. Krauthammer, "Democratic Realism," p. 15.

40. Natan Sharansky with Ron Dermer, *The Case for Democracy: The Power of Freedom to Overcome Tyranny and Terror* (New York: Public Affairs, 2004); Michael Novak, *Universal Hunger for Liberty: Why the Clash of Civilizations Is Not Inevitable* (New York: Basic Books, 2004).

41. Robert Kagan, "The Benevolent Empire," *Foreign Policy,* Summer 1998, p. 30.

42. See, for example, Max Boot, "The Case for American Empire: The Most Realistic Response to Terrorism Is for America to Embrace Its Imperial Role," *Weekly Standard,* October 15, 2001.

43. Charles Krauthammer, "The Clinton Paper Chase," *Washington Post,* October 25, 2002.

44. Robert Kagan, "The Problem with Powell," *Washington Post,* July 23, 2000; Lawrence Kaplan, "Colin Powell," *Prospect* (U.K.), February 2001.

45. On this point, see my article "Les néoconservateurs américains et l'Europe: Sous le signe de Munich," *Relations internationales,* no. 120 (Winter 2004).

46. Robert Kagan, "Power and Weakness," *Policy Review,* June–July 2002.

47. Dorrien, *Imperial Designs,* p. 207.

48. "Report of the Commission to Assess the Ballistic Missile Threat to the United States," available at http://www.fas.org/irp/threat/missile/rumsfeld/toc.htm (accessed August 3, 2008).

49. National Institute for Public Policy, "Rationale and Requirements for U.S. Nuclear Forces and Arms Control—Executive Report," January 2001, available at http://www.nipp.org/adobe/volume%201%20complete.pdf (accessed August 2, 2008). The 2002 "Nuclear Posture Review" is still classified, but leaked excerpts can be found at http://www.globalsecurity.org/wmd/policy/dod/npr.htm.

50. Heilbrunn, *They Knew They Were Right,* p. 235.

51. "American Power—for What? A Symposium" (Elliott Abrams, William F. Buckley Jr., Eliot A. Cohen, Francis Fukuyama, Frank Gaffney, Owen Harries, Jacob Heilbrunn, Robert Kagan, Zalmay Khalilzad, Jeane Kirkpatrick, Charles Krauthammer, William Kristol, Michael Ledeen, Edward Luttwak, Walter McDougall, Joshua Muravchik, Joseph Nye, David Rieff, Peter Rodman, Robert Tucker, Paul Wolfowitz), *Commentary,* January 2000.

52. Robert Kagan and William Kristol, *Present Dangers: Crisis and Opportunity in American Foreign and Defense Policy* (New York: Encounter, 2000).

53. Eliot Cohen, "World War IV: Let's Call the Conflict What It Is," *Wall Street Journal,* November 20, 2001; James Woolsey, "World War

IV," *FrontPage Magazine*, November 22, 2002; Norman Podhoretz, *World War IV: The Long Struggle against Islamofascism* (New York, Doubleday, 2007).

54. Mann, *Rise of the Vulcans*, p. 249.

55. Condoleezza Rice, "Promoting the National Interest," *Foreign Affairs*, January–February 2000.

56. Mann, *Rise of the Vulcans*, p. 257.

57. Lawrence Kaplan, "Trading Places: How the Democrats Became Hawks," *New Republic*, October 23, 2000, p. 28.

58. Steven Mufson, "Bush Urged to Champion Human Rights," *Washington Post*, January 26, 2001.

59. See Heilbrunn, *They Knew They Were Right*, p. 257.

60. Ivo Daalder and James Lindsay, *America Unbound: The Bush Revolution in Foreign Policy* (Washington, D.C.: Brookings Institution Press, 2003).

61. Jeffrey Goldberg, "Breaking Ranks: What Turned Brent Scowcroft against the Bush Administration?," *New Yorker*, October 31, 2005.

62. Robert Kagan and William Kristol, "A National Humiliation," *Weekly Standard*, April 16, 2001.

63. Robert Kagan and William Kristol, "No Defense," *Weekly Standard*, July 23, 2001.

64. Quoted in Dana Milbank, "Crisis Brings Shift in Presidential Style," *Washington Post*, September 14, 2001.

65. George W. Bush, "A Distinctly American Internationalism," speech in Simi Valley, Calif., November 19, 1999, available at http://georgewbush _whitehouse.archives.gov. All speeches by George W. Bush cited later in this chapter are available at the same Web address.

66. George W. Bush, Second Inaugural Address, January 20, 2005.

67. Charles Krauthammer, "The Bush Doctrine," *Washington Post*, May 4, 2001.

68. On this point see Smith, *A Pact with the Devil*, chap. 1; Podhoretz, *World War IV*, chap. 3; see also "Defending and Advancing Freedom: A Symposium," *Commentary*, November 2005.

69. George W. Bush, speech at the United Nations, September 12, 2002.

70. George W. Bush, speech at American Enterprise Institute, February 26, 2003.

71. George W. Bush, speech in Brussels, February 21, 2005.

72. George W. Bush, speech at AEI, February 26, 2003.

73. George W. Bush, speech to National Endowment for Democracy, November 6, 2003.

74. George W. Bush, "President Bush Speaks at Air Force Academy Graduation," June 2, 2004.

75. National Security Council, "The National Security Strategy," September

2002, p. 30, available at http://georgewbush_whitehouse.archives.gov/nsc/nss/2002/index.html.

76. See esp. Mann, *Rise of the Vulcans;* Dorrien, *Imperial Designs;* Heilbrunn, *They Knew They Were Right;* and George Packer, *The Assassins' Gate: America in Iraq* (London: Faber and Faber, 2006).

77. Mann, *Rise of the Vulcans,* p. 189.

78. David Wurmser, "Iraq Needs a Revolution," *Wall Street Journal,* November 12, 1997; Zalmay Khalilzad and Paul Wolfowitz, "Overthrow Him," *Weekly Standard,* December 1, 1997.

79. Elizabeth Drew, "The Neocons in Power," *New York Review of Books,* June 12, 2003.

80. Committee for Peace and Security in the Gulf, "Open Letter to the President," February 19, 1998, available at http://www.iraqwatch.org/perspectives/rumsfeld-openletter.htm.

81. PNAC, "Letter to President Clinton," January 26, 1998, available at http://www.newamericancentury.org/iraqclintonletter.htm.

82. Richard Clarke, *Against All Enemies: Inside America's War on Terror* (New York: Free Press, 2004).

83. Bob Woodward, *Bush at War* (New York: Simon and Schuster, 2002).

84. PNAC, "Letter to President Bush on the War on Terrorism," September 20, 2001, available at http://newamericancentury.org.bushletter.htm; see also Tom Donnelly and Gary Schmitt, "What Our Enemies Want; and What Our Goals Should Be," *Weekly Standard,* September 24, 2001.

85. Woodward, *Bush at War.*

86. See James Risen, "How Pair's Finding on Terror Led to Clash on Shaping Intelligence," *New York Times,* April 28, 2004. In his book, Douglas Feith contends that the Counterterrorism Evaluation Group's only task was to compile, not create, intelligence. See Feith, *War and Decision: Inside the Pentagon at the Dawn of the War on Terrorism* (New York: Harper, 2008), pp. 116–118.

87. See Seymour Hersh, "Selective Intelligence: Donald Rumsfeld Has His Own Special Sources. Are They Reliable?," *New Yorker,* May 12, 2003. See also Patrick W. Lang, "Drinking the Kool-Aid," *Middle East Policy,* Summer 2004, available at http://www.mepc.org/journal_vol11/0406_lang.asp (accessed July 28, 2008). In his book, Douglas Feith counters that the Office of Special Plans was simply a standard intelligence office focusing on Iraq and a consumer, not a producer, of intelligence. See Feith, *War and Decision,* p. 294. After an investigation of the two offices, the Inspector General of the Department of Defense concluded in 2007 that "While such actions were not illegal or unauthorized, the actions were, in our opinion, inappropriate given that the products did not clearly show the variance with the consensus of the Intelligence Community and were, in some cases, shown as intelligence products. This condition occurred because [The Office of the Under Secretary of Defense for Policy (OUSD[P]),

headed by Feith] expanded its role and mission from formulating Defense Policy to analyzing and disseminating alternative intelligence. As a result, the OUSD(P) did not provide 'the most accurate analysis of intelligence' to senior decision makers." See Department of Defense Inspector General, February 9, 2007, "Report on Review of the Pre-Iraqi War Activities of the Office of the Under Secretary of Defense for Policy" (Report No. 07-INTEL-04), available at http://www.fas.org/irp/agency/dod/ig020907-decl.pdf (accessed on December 8, 2009).

88. See Dorrien, *Imperial Designs*, p. 186.

89. "The Secret Downing Street Memo," *Sunday Times*, May 1, 2005, available at http://www.timesonline.co.uk/tol/news/politics/election2005/article387390.ece.

90. William Kristol and Lawrence Kaplan, *The War over Iraq: Saddams's Tyranny and America's Mission* (New York: Encounter Books, 2003), pp. 97–98.

91. Paul Starobin, "The Liberal Hawk Soars," *National Journal*, May 15, 1999. See also Adam Wolfson, "Humanitarian Hawks? Why Kosovo but Not Kuwait," *Policy Review* 98 (December 1999–January 2000).

92. Norman Podhoretz, "Strange Bedfellows: A Guide to the New Foreign-Policy Debates," *Commentary*, December 1999.

93. Lawrence Kaplan, "Trading Places," *New Republic*, October 23, 2000.

94. Senator Joe Lieberman on *FOX News Sunday*, January 29, 2007, transcript available at http://www.foxnews.com/story/0,2933,247844,00.html.

95. Paul Berman, *Terror and Liberalism* (New York: W. W. Norton, 2003); George Packer, ed., *The Fight Is for Democracy: Winning the War of Ideas in America and the World* (New York: Harper, 2003).

96. Ken Pollack, *The Threatening Storm: The Case for Invading Iraq* (New York: Random House, 2002).

97. Progressive Policy Institute, "Progressive Internationalism: A Democratic National Security Strategy," October 30, 2003, available at http://www.ppionline.org/ppi_ci.cfm?contentid=252144&subsecid=900020&knlgAreaID=450004; and Will Marshall, *With All Our Might: A Progressive Strategy for Defeating Jihadism and Defending Liberty* (Lanham: Rowman and Littlefield, 2006).

98. Peter Beinart, *The Good Fight: Why Liberals—and Only Liberals—Can Win the War on Terror and Make America Great Again* (New York: HarperCollins, 2006).

99. Ron Asmus and Ken Pollack, "The Neoliberal Take on the Middle East," *Washington Post*, July 22, 2003.

100. Ron Asmus and Ken Pollack, "The New Transatlantic Project," *Policy Review* 115 (October–November 2002).

101. Anatol Lieven, "Liberal Hawk Down," *The Nation*, October 25, 2004.

102. Smith, *A Pact with the Devil*, pp.12–14.

103. Cf. Muravchik, *Exporting Democracy*, p. 8; interview with Gary Schmitt, August 1, 2008; Condoleezza Rice, "The Promise of Democratic Peace—Why Promoting Freedom Is the Only Realistic Path to Security," *Washington Post*, December 11, 2005.

104. Linker, *The Theocons*, p. 140.

105. Quoted in Jim Hoagland, "Three Miscreants," *Washington Post*, April 13, 2003.

106. On these lists, see Dorrien, *Imperial Designs*, p. 243.

107. See Thomas Ricks, "Briefing Depicted Saudis as Enemies: Ultimatum Urged to Pentagon Board," *Washington Post*, August 6, 2002.

108. David Brooks, "For Iraqis to Win, the U.S. Must Lose," *New York Times*, May 11, 2004.

109. Fouad Ajami, "Iraq May Survive, but the Dream Is Dead," *New York Times*, May 26, 2004.

110. Krauthammer, "Democratic Realism."

111. See Michael Lind, "A Tragedy of Errors," *The Nation*, February 5, 2004; Francis Fukuyama, *America at the Crossroads: Democracy, Power, and the Neoconservative Legacy* (New Haven: Yale University Press, 2006).

112. Richard Perle quoted in David Rose, "Neo Culpa," *Vanity Fair*, January 2007.

113. Editorial, "Were We Wrong?," *New Republic*, June 28, 2004; editorial, "Obligations," ibid., December 4, 2006.

114. Richard Perle makes the case for exaggeration in his article "Ambushed on the Potomac," *National Interest*, no. 99 (January–February 2009), and argues that neoconservative foreign policy does not exist in an on-the-record discussion about the article held at the Nixon Center (which publishes *The National Interest*) on February 19, 2009, aired by C-SPAN and available at http:// www.c-spanarchives.org/library/index.php?main_page=product_video_info &products_id=284162–1. See also Dana Milbank, "Prince of Darkness Denies Own Existence," *Washington Post*, February 20, 2009.

115. Richard Perle, interview with Justine Rosenthal, editor of *The National Interest*, February 19, 2009, available at http://www.youtube.com/watch?v= UCSgOnNeL14.

116. See, for example, the interview by Ben Wattenberg on PBS, November 14, 2002, "Richard Perle: The Making of a Neoconservative," transcript available at www.pbs.org/thinktank/transcript1017.html; and Perle's quote in Michelle Goldberg's article, "Is This the Neocon Century?," *Salon.com*, December 17, 2003: "Not only is the neoconservative movement not over, it's just beginning."

117. See Robert Kagan and William Kristol, "The Right War for the Right Reasons," *Weekly Standard*, February 23, 2004.

118. Interview with Gary Schmitt, August 1, 2008.

119. Heilbrunn, *They Knew They Were Right*, p. 273.

120. See Fred Kagan, ed., "Choosing Victory: A Plan for Success in Iraq—Interim Report," available at http://www.realclearpolitics.com/RCP_PDF/ChoosingVictory.pdf.

121. See, for example, Dan Eggen, "Citing History, Bush Suggests His Policies Will One Day Be Vindicated," *Washington Post,* June 9, 2008.

122. Interview with Bruce Riedel, April 13, 2009.

123. See Joseph Stiglitz and Linda Bilmes, *The Three Trillion Dollar War: The True Cost of the Iraq Conflict* (New York: W. W. Norton, 2008).

124. See Thomas Carothers, "The Backlash against Democracy Promotion," *Foreign Affairs,* March–April 2006.

125. See Stanley Hoffmann, *Gulliver's Troubles, or the Setting of American Foreign Policy* (New York: McGraw-Hill, 1968), chap. 5.

126. Brooks, "For Iraqis to Win, the U.S. Must Lose."

127. Interview with Richard Perle by Ben Wattenberg on PBS, November 14, 2002.

128. Peter Bergen, "Armchair Provocateur: Laurie Mylroie: The Neocons' Favorite Conspiracy Theorist," *Washington Monthly,* December 2003.

129. Laurie Mylroie, *Study of Revenge: Saddam Hussein's Unfinished War against America* (Washington, D.C.: AEI Press, 2000); and Mylroie, *The War against America: Saddam Hussein and the World Trade Center Attacks: A Study of Revenge,* rev. ed. (New York: Regan Books, 2001).

130. See William Bennett, *Why We Fight: Moral Clarity and the War on Terrorism* (New York: Doubleday, 2002).

131. Richard Perle, introduction to Wurmser, *Tyranny's Ally,* p. xii.

132. Martin Kramer, *Ivory Towers on Sand: The Failure of Middle Eastern Studies in America* (Washington, D.C.: Washington Institute for Near East Policy, 2001).

133. Robert Novak, "Sharon's War," *Washington Post,* December 26, 2002.

134. David Frum, "Unpatriotic Conservatives," *National Review,* April 7, 2003.

135. Lawrence Kaplan, "Toxic Talk on War," *Washington Post,* February 18, 2003.

136. On this point, see Smith, *A Pact with the Devil,* chap. 5.

137. Bill Keller, "The Sunshine Warrior," *New York Times,* September 22, 2002.

138. Radek Sikorski, "Interview with Paul Wolfowitz," *Prospect* (U.K.), December 1, 2004.

139. John McCain, "We Are All Georgians," *Wall Street Journal,* August 14, 2008, p. A13.

140. Pew Research Center for the People and the Press, "Obama Faces Familiar Divisions over Anti-Terror Policies," February 18, 2009, available at http://people-press.org/report/493/obama-anti-terror-policies.

141. Janie Lorber, "Cheney's Model Republican: More Limbaugh, Less Powell," *New York Times,* May 10, 2009.

142. See, for example, Foreign Policy Initiative, "Open Letter to President Obama on Democracy and Human Rights in Russia," July 1, 2009, available at http://www.foreignpolicyi.org/letter_obama.html (accessed July 10, 2009).

143. See the FPI mission statement at http://www.foreignpolicyi.org/about (accessed July 10, 2009).

144. Robert Kagan, *The Return of History and the End of Dreams* (New York: Knopf, 2008); and Kagan, "Power and Weakness."

145. For a rebuttal of neoconservative historiography, see Christopher J. Fettweis, "Dangerous Revisionism: On the Founders, 'Neocons' and the Importance of History," *Orbis* 53 (Summer 2009): 507–523; and David Hoogland Noon, "Cold War Revival: Neoconservatives and Historical Memory in the War on Terror," *American Studies* 48 (Fall 2007): 75–99.

146. See, for example, the debate in *The National Interest* of September 2008 between Stephen Walt, "The Shattered Kristol Ball," and Joshua Muravchik, "The Future Is Neocon."

Epilogue

1. See in particular Ann Norton, *Leo Strauss and the Politics of American Empire* (New Haven: Yale University Press, 2004).

2. Interpretation suggested by Gary Schmitt, interview, August 1, 2008.

3. Interview with Bill Kristol, July 24, 2003.

4. Robert Kagan, "I Am Not a Straussian. At Least, I Don't Think I Am," *Weekly Standard,* February 6, 2006, p. 16.

5. Ibid., p. 17.

6. Kevin McDonald, "Understanding Jewish Influence III: Neoconservatism as a Jewish Movement," *Occidental Quarterly* 4 (Summer 2004).

7. Lyndon Larouche et al., "Children of Satan—The 'Ignoble Liars' behind Bush's 'No–Exit' War," campaign brochure, 2004.

8. Isidore Silver, "What Flows from Neoconservatism," *The Nation,* July 9, 1977, pp. 49–50.

9. Jacob Heilbrunn, *They Knew They Were Right: The Rise of the Neocons* (New York: Doubleday, 2008).

10. Radek Sikorski, "Interview with Paul Wolfowitz," *Prospect* (U.K.), December 1, 2004.

11. Sidney Blumenthal, *The Rise of the Counter-Establishment: From Conservative Ideology to Political Power* (New York: Harper and Row, 1988), p. 165.

12. Norman Podhoretz, *Breaking Ranks* (New York: Harper and Row, 1979), p. 10.

13. Nathan Glazer, "Neoconservative from the Start," *Public Interest,* Spring 2005, p. 13.

14. Michael Lind, "A Tragedy of Errors," *The Nation,* February 23, 2004; interview with Michael Lind, November 22, 2004.

15. See Michael Lind, *Up from Conservatism: Why the Right Is Wrong for America* (New York: Free Press, 1996), p. 13.

16. On the terminology of Wilsonian and Jacksonian traditions, see Walter Russel Mead, *Special Providence: American Foreign Policy and How It Changed the World* (New York: Knopf, 2001).

17. Irving Kristol, "American Conservatism 1945–1995," *Public Interest,* Fall 1995.

ACKNOWLEDGMENTS

When I started research in early 2001, originally on the Scoop Jackson Democrats, I had no idea what neoconservatism was all about, and I certainly didn't suspect that so many people would help me find out—fellow historians, archivists, neoconservatives, ex-neoconservatives and non-neoconservatives, journalists, and experts in intellectual history. Let me take this space to express my gratitude to them.

On the intellectual and academic side, Professor Pierre Melandri, my thesis adviser, guided me with patience and great erudition, and his continuing advice since 2005 has been precious. Passionate but always friendly discussions with Tony Smith on liberal internationalism, with Stanley Hoffmann on U.S. foreign policy, and with Patrice Higonnet on American nationalism forced me to sharpen my arguments. Pierre Hassner, another great friend, was both a direct witness whom I could interview for some episodes mentioned in the book, such as those relating to Albert Wohlstetter, and a source of deep knowledge and critical reflection. My father, a historian as well, took time away from his own work to follow this research closely, teach me a few useful strategies, and encourage me at the right moments. Sam Wells and Jean-Damien Po provided useful comments on earlier versions of the argument. At various points, Denis Lacorne, Anatol Lieven, Michael Lind, James Mann, David Yost, and Nick Ziegler, among others, shared ideas and useful suggestions with me.

I have also benefited from discussions and exchanges with specialists on specific issues, many of them good friends as well as great scholars. Antoine Coppolani, now a professor at the University of Montpellier, pointed me to the importance of the Berkeley events to understand early neoconservatism, and to useful sources on the subject, and we discussed at length the role of Daniel Patrick Moynihan. Aaron Lobel, while at Brookings, gave me access to the declassified papers of the Team B episode that Ann Cahn had obtained through the Freedom of Information Act, and helped me familiarize myself with the complex issue of Central Intelligence Agency "Soviet estimates," his area of expertise. I also had useful exchanges with Brian Auten on the domestic sources of Carter's defense policy, and with Pauline Peretz on the campaign promoting free emigration for Soviet Jews. Among those who have already written very useful books on neoconservatism upon which I drew, I want here to express particular gratitude to Gary Dorrien and John Ehrman.

I also received help from first-rate archivists and librarians. These include John Wilson at the Lyndon B. Johnson Presidential Library in Austin, Texas, where the papers of the Coalition for a Democratic Majority are deposited; and Carol Leadenham at the Hoover Institution on the Stanford campus, home of the 492 boxes of archives from the Committee on the Present Danger. Both Eugene Rostow and William Van Cleave granted me access to this collection; I especially thank Bill Van Cleave for the confidence that prompted him to write the crucial letter. At the Brookings Institution, throughout the decade, Sarah Chilton has been of great help: no reference is too incomplete, too obscure, or too remote for her to find.

Over the past decade I have been employed by two institutions that provided a congenial and fertile work environment for this research. At the Center on the United States and France of the Brookings Institution, which became the Center on the United States and Europe in 2004, Phil Gordon was a close friend and a fantastic boss, encouraging this research on top of my other projects on transatlantic relations. Brookings is not only a great place to work; it is also a place where talents and strong personalities abound; and I was the happy beneficiary of extremely useful discussions on neoconservatism with wonderful colleagues like E. J. Dionne, Bill Galston, and Peter Rodman before his untimely death in 2008, and with dear friends such as Jeremy Shapiro. At the French Policy Planning Staff (Centre d'Analyse et de Prévision), where I was an adviser from 2003 to 2007, successive directors Gilles Andréani and Pierre Lévy, as well as deputy director Philippe Errera, were extremely supportive of my work.

Other institutions provided useful support. While doing research in Austin, I was welcomed by Frank Gavin and by the LBJ Foundation, which awarded me a grant to work in the archives. At Stanford, Scott Sagan and the Center for International Security and Cooperation were similarly welcoming, offering an office for the duration of my work in the Hoover Institution archives. I am grateful to both.

The thirty or so witnesses—neoconservatives or not—who kindly agreed to be interviewed for this research project are mentioned in the various chapters, and I want to express my gratitude to all of them. In particular I want to thank Gary Schmitt, William Kristol, Zbigniew Brzezinski, and Joshua Muravchik for their willingness to share their personal stories and for their patience in answering my questions, in some cases over several years. I would also like to mention the interviewees who have died in the past decade, each of whom brought me a lot in personal testimony or insights: Sam Huntington, Penn Kemble, Jeane Kirkpatrick, and Eugene Rostow.

While I would not presume to compare myself to Alexis de Tocqueville, we still share a common nationality and a common translator: Arthur Goldhammer, who offered American readers the best—and award-winning—English version of Tocqueville's *Democracy in America,* among other renowned French works. I am flattered that Art agreed to do this translation, and he did a superb job, missing no nuance, offering great prose, even suggesting changes and updates here and there. This was complemented by the swift work done by Kathleen McDermott at Harvard University Press, who guided this book through the demanding publishing process there, and by the subtle and gentle editing of Ann Hawthorne, who accommodated my elliptical French style.

Last but by no means least, my wife, Marie, has not only endured these many years of research with immense grace and patient support, but has also actively contributed to the outcome by astute fine-tuning of the manuscript. I dedicate this book to her, as an expression of my gratitude and deep love.

INDEX

ABM (anti-ballistic missile) treaty, 9, 102, 154, 175, 194

Abortion, 85, 113

Abrams, Elliott, 9, 13, 48, 207; breakfast meeting with Carter, 134; Bush (G. W.) administration and, 241, 242; CDM and, 91, 130; Council on Foreign Relations and, 268; defeat of Communism and, 188; defection from Democratic party, 215; democracy promotion and, 223; Iran-Contra scandal and, 190; Iraq and, 248; on Jews and Republican party, 184; Likud party and, 274; Moynihan's Senate campaign and, 127; Reagan and, 187; in Republican party, 11, 180; Scoop Jackson and, 121, 125; on struggle over Democratic party, 209; third age of neoconservatism and, 278

Abu Ghraib scandal, 256

Abzug, Bella, 93

Acheson, Dean, 101, 119, 153, 161

Adams, John Quincy, 139

Adelman, Kenneth, 193, 194, 256

"Adversary culture," 7, 77, 284

Affirmative action, 7, 76

Afghanistan, 62, 249, 258, 259, 286

Afghanistan, Soviet invasion of, 133, 134, 168, 179, 183; "freedom fighters" against Soviets, 190–191; Soviet withdrawal, 200

Afghanistan, U.S.-led war in, 13, 15, 224, 236, 249; deteriorioration in Bush's second term, 260; initial American victory, 261; isolationism and, 268; neoliberals and, 253

AFL-CIO, 9, 19, 27, 72, 286; balance of power within, 211; CDM and, 91, 93, 94, 104, 106, 210; defense of democracy and, 138; foreign policy and, 136, 210–211; Meany as head of, 122; NED and, 192; Scoop Jackson and, 114; Soviet dissidents and, 144; on Vietnam War, 97. *See also* Unions

Africa, 106

Agent Orange, 107

Ajami, Fouad, 15, 242, 256, 264

Albright, Madeleine, 141, 251, 252, 274

Alekseeva, Lyudmila, 144

Alien and Sedition Act (1798), 32

Allen, Richard, 163, 189, 192; Bush (G. H. W.) and, 181; Reagan and, 182, 185, 187; SALT talks and, 166

Alsop, Stewart, 28

"Amateur politicians," 82, 83

America First Committee, 157

American Center for International Labor Solidarity, 192

American Civil Liberties Union, 71

American Committee on U.S.-Soviet Relations, 116–117, 165

American Enterprise Institute (AEI), 1, 5, 11, 130, 149, 185; arms control talks and, 200; Chalabi and, 248;